M000288295

SPIRITUAL BREAD

by

Mundelein Christian Writers Group

INTRODUCTION

The Christian Writers Group has existed since 2001. We became friends and share our joys and concerns beyond the narrow limitations of our writing, sometimes praying in the meeting for a member or friend. We come from many different churches and doctrines, but we were joined by our love and belief in salvation through Jesus Christ. Some of these devotionals may reflect ideas not necessarily followed by United Church of Christ, but since we are the Mundelein Community Church accepting all wherever they come from and wherever they are on their faith journey, we did not limit or edit the devotionals to a single doctrinal view.

In the beginning, we met on the first and third Tuesdays of the month in a public space. Our purpose was to hone our skills as writers and become published authors who exemplify the craft of writing; the only type of writing not included was journaling. We shared publishing opportunities, information about agents, publishers, self-publishing and contests. All genres were welcome and our members were not limited to Christian writing. While we started with fiction writers, many excellent non-fiction writers joined the group.

Around 2010, the rules for our meeting place changed. We were informed if we wished to continue using the facility twice a month, we had three choices;

- remove any and all reference to religion and eliminate group prayer
- take our chances on the availability of facilities and just "show up"
- reduce our meetings to once a month.

The choices were unacceptable. We were Christians and we would not deny our faith or eliminate prayer. Some of our members were driving an hour or more to get to the meeting, so taking our chances on having space was not a good option. To truly hone our craft and meet deadlines the minimum number of meetings was two a month.

At that point I approached Pastor Alex Molozaiy with our dilemma. As is usual for this generous congregation and pastor, we were offered the use of a room at the church once a month. It made a huge difference for us and we were very grateful.

Many of our members started their publishing careers writing devotionals under the guidance of this group and we came up with the idea of combining them and writing a devotional book for Mundelein Community Church as a thank you. We decided to write a devotional for every day of the year and additional devotionals for days that do not have a firm calendar date such as Easter and Thanksgiving. We added some holidays which are not typically celebrated in a Christian church such as Rosh Hashanah and Yom Kipper. It was a huge challenge which took years to accomplish, much longer than we were expecting.

We hope you find this book useful in your walk with God. It is presented to you with loving thoughts and prayers for each person who picks it up. While the authors retain the rights of their work, Mundelein Community Church is given permission to reprint anything in this book in whatever way best serves the spiritual needs of this congregation.

Unless otherwise noted, all scripture references are from the New International Version.

ABOUT THE AUTHORS

Joanna McGee Bradford lives in the northwest suburbs and is a member of Willow Creek Community Church. After declaring she would never write inspiration or romance, her first published work, "The Day I Received the Death Threat," was published by *Today's Christian Woman Magazine*. Her Christian romance novel, "The Father's Voice" was released by Moody Publishers. In 2015, her poem, "The Caretaker," was a winner in the Utmost Christian Poetry Contest and her article, "Is Your Teen Ready to Drive?" was published by *Thriving Family Magazine*. In addition to working as a corporate Claims Manager and pursuing her love of Christian writing, Joanna also speaks to women's groups. She is now working non-fiction book project.

Megan Ciaburri lives in Roanoke, TX and works as a high school English teacher and coach. She is an aspiring author with several literary works in progress. She attends services at St. Ann Catholic Church, and enjoys reading, crafting and volleyball.

Beth Dumey resides in the Chicago suburbs and calls Willow Creek Community Church home. As a career communicator, she has written for many well-known brands for global companies and marketing agencies. With more than 30 published articles, Beth's writing has appeared in a variety of print and online publications. She delights in the opportunity to learn, express creativity and engage in deep conversation.

Sherri Gallagher lives and works in Mundelein, IL as a consultant and serves the community with her search and rescue dogs. She is a member of Mundelein Community Protestant Church and loves the opportunity to do the scripture reading. She has written three middle grade readers "Trust Your Dog", "Go Find" and "Dangerous Turn Ahead" and four romantic suspense novels "Sophie's Search", "Sliver of Love", "Pine Cone Motel", and "Labrador Tea" which will soon be available on Amazon.

Cathy Harvey is a newly published writer who lives in Lindenhurst, IL. She has been married over 40 years, has 5 grandchildren and 3 children, all of whom served in the military during the 9/11 event: Marines, Army, and Navy. She recently retired from Shepherds College in Union Grove, Wisconsin, a school for young adults with intellectual and developmental disabilities. She has written for the women's column in *VOICE* magazine, and her real-life story of forgiveness was chosen by Loyola Press to be included in "Sharing the Wisdom of Time" by Pope

Francis (2018). She is working on her first book and attends the Village Church of Gurnee, IL.

Judy Knox of Libertyville, IL is a retired high school teacher who now teaches believers how to get more out of their relationship with God. She was a member of Epicenter Church in Gurnee before moving to Arizona. Her devotionals included in this book have been compiled into a separate book called *Dewdrops of Grace*. Her second book, *A Widow's Might: The Secret of Finding Strength in God*, combines her story of discovering new strength in God amid the loss of her husband with practical, scriptural lessons and insights for enriching one's Christian walk. Both books are available on Amazon.com. In addition to writing, Judy enjoys traveling, Bible study, and playing the cello.

Maureen Lang writes stories that celebrate a mix of faith, history and romance. She is the author of more than a dozen Christian novels and seven novellas, with several titles recognized by various awards. Maureen and her husband have three adult children, including their son with Fragile X Syndrome. Visit her at www.maureenlang.com, or follow her on Facebook, GoodReads, or BookBub.

Kristen Long lives in Dry Ridge, KY with her husband Dale. They have a grown son and a daughter serving in the Marine Corps. She works as a receptionist at a senior assisted living facility and spends her days there taking care of her "Silver Saints". They are members of the Pleasant View Baptist Church, working with teens and young adults and driving the transport bus. Kristen and her husband are group leaders in NKY Addictions Program held at their church. She has written a short story which is published in an anthology called "Falling In Love With You" and many short stories for Pre-K/ Kindergarten curriculums.

Since coming to faith in Christ at the tail end of the Jesus Movement, **Michelle Van Loon's** heritage, spiritual hunger and storyteller's sensibilities have shaped her faith journey and informed her writing. She is a regular contributor to Christianity Today's popular Her.meneutics blog, and is the author of *If Only: Letting Go Of Regret* (Beacon Hill Press). She has pieces in four recent devotional projects and has authored two books on the parables of Jesus. She's been a church communications director, served on staff at Trinity International University, and currently serves as a consultant for a handful of small faith-based non-profits. She's currently enrolled part-time at Northern Seminary. She's married to Bill and is mother to three and grandmother to two. Her writing focuses on issues of the church and spiritual formation. She blogs at http://www.patheos.com/blogs/pilgrimsroadtrip.

Born on a 100-degree day in Chicago, Illinois, **Myra Biernat Wells** (1954-2019) learned the wonder of words early on, making storytelling an integral part of her life. Her first book, *Rivers in the Dry Wasteland*, was released in August 2016 with another book, *When Darkness Falls, Joy Rises* to be released soon. Myra admitted to being an unconcerned housekeeper, a marginal cook and a plant killer, but shared her life with her husband, Richard, and her German Shepherd, Lily, the most fun she's ever had! She escaped the frigid winters of Chicagoland and moved to Orange County, California, where she was a member of Saddleback Church.

JANUARY 1 - NEW YEAR'S DAY

The New You
BY SHERRI GALLAGHER

1 Peter 1:22-24

"He committed no sin, and no deceit was found in his mouth." When they hurled their insults at him, he did not retaliate; when he suffered, he made no threats. Instead, he entrusted himself to him who judges justly. He himself bore our sins in his body on the tree, so that we might die to sins and live for righteousness; by his wounds you have been healed.

Life is indeed difficult, partly because of the real difficulties we must overcome in order to survive, and partly because of our innate desire to always do better, to overcome new challenges, to self-actualize. Happiness is experienced largely in striving toward a goal, not in having attained things, because our nature is always to want to go on to the next endeavor. **Albert Ellis**, *The Art & Science of Rational Eating*

What are your New Year's resolutions? Wikipedia says 88% of New Year's resolutions will fail. Part of the reason for failure is the goal is too nebulous and there is no plan to achieve it. Nine out of ten are resolutions are health related - lose weight, eat less junk food. By the end of January, 80% of these resolutions will have fizzled into oblivion.

Before throwing out the whole idea of self-improvement, take a step back. Yes, we should make resolutions to improve our health and earthly life, but first we need to make a resolution to improve our relationship with God. In 1 Corinthians 9 Paul tells us "Do you not know that in a race all the runners run, but only one gets the prize? Run in such a way as to get the prize. Everyone who competes in the games goes into strict training. They do it to get a crown that will not last; but we do it to get a crown that will last forever. Therefore I do not run like a man running aimlessly; I do not fight like a man beating the air."

Paul's advice makes sense whether our goal is to lose ten pounds or become closer to Christ. Write down your resolutions, figure out how to fit them into your busy day, and then do it. If you slip up, don't beat yourself up. Start over and endeavor to win the prize.

Action:

Make a resolution to study the word of God daily and practice it for twenty-one days in a row.

Prayer:
Lord, give us the strength to accomplish our resolutions that draw us closer to You. Amen.

JANUARY 2

Christ's Table
BY SHERRI GALLAGHER

1 Corinthians 11:23-26

For I received from the Lord what I also handed on to you, that the Lord Jesus on the night when he was betrayed took a loaf of bread, and when he had given thanks, he broke it and said, "This is my body that is for you. Do this in remembrance of me." In the same way he took the cup also, after supper, saying, "This cup is the new covenant in my blood. Do this as you drink it, in remembrance of me." For as often as you eat this bread and drink this cup, you proclaim the Lord's death until he comes.

As a teenager I went to church with a friend. As we climbed the narrow spiraling staircase up to the balcony where the teens and latecomers sat my friend whispered in my ear. "When they serve communion, you can't go down. I'll come back as fast as I can but only members of our church are welcome at Christ's table."

Years later, that experience placed a question in my mind as I searched for a church home. I would see communion served and wonder if I would offend someone for partaking - or not. I am a sinner like everyone else and I needed Christ's sacrifice. Was I welcome at His table in this church or not?

I will always remember the first time I heard the pastor invite everyone to Holy Communion telling us "this is the Lord's Table, all are welcome". Openness and loving acceptance by the congregation was a given. The understanding that only God could judge what was in our hearts was a powerful and persuasive answer to my selection of a spiritual home. Every time I hear, "All is ready come and eat" I am reminded of why this church is so special to me and give thanks to God for leading me here.

Action:
Watch for visitor to our church and go out of your way to make them feel welcome.
Prayer:
Lord, help us to understand that Your love and sacrifice was for everyone willing to accept You into their heart and not for a special few. In Jesus' name. Amen.

JANUARY 3

A Lamp Unto My Feet
BY CATHY HARVEY

Psalm 119:105

Your word is a lamp for my feet, a light on my path.

The path you are on is leading to your destiny; therefore, walk thoughtfully.
Anonymous

It was a Saturday in January, and I decided to go for an early morning walk hoping to see some beautiful deer that often wandered the woods behind our apartment complex. It had snowed a little, but the driveway that curved around the back of the apartments and next to the wooded area was cleared, though still wet with melted puddles in the low spots. The morning was cool and quite foggy, but I was bundled up and warm. I liked the fog. It made the morning seem even more quiet than usual with its added mysterious veil. It was still dark, but the streetlamps along the back driveway glowed with a thick white misty halo softly lighting the driveway. It was difficult to see very far ahead, except that the lamps were dotting the way with small circles of light. I noticed that the light from one streetlamp was not strong enough to meet the glow of light from the next one, and there was a patch of darkness in between each lamp post. I looked for deer but had to cautiously watch my own steps also.

It was soothing to walk without haste. I felt calm in the quietness as I meandered unhurried, meditating on verses, talking to God, and sorting out thoughts about family concerns. A security vehicle drove slowly by and the driver encouraged me to be careful, so I turned and started back the same way I had come. Just before reaching our apartment I looked back at the path I had trod. The view was still hazy, but the light from the streetlamps clearly marked the way including the curves in the road.

As if the Lord were speaking directly to me, I heard Him whisper Psalm 119:105, "My Word is a lamp unto thy feet, and a light unto your path." He said it several times as I stood very still looking back at the path. "My Word is a lamp for your feet to light your path." I pondered that for several minutes.

In the fog I saw a very clear object lesson about walking the Christian life. It is very much like going from one dark unknown to another with God revealing just enough to handle the next move forward. When I look back at the path I have walked with Him so far, I can see it was lit each step of the way: one decision at a time, one job at a time, and one move at a time. It was exciting and a little mysterious and foggy too, yet the path was marked, so I could see with the help of

His Word the direction to take. "In Thee, O LORD, do I put my trust: let me never be put to confusion" (Psalm 71:1, KJV).

Action:

Consider your station at this moment or season of your life. Where do you see God leading your next step? Write it down and pray about it.

Prayer:

Heavenly Father, I know where I have been and where I am now. Help me to pause and consider the next step You might be asking me to take to accomplish Your kingdom will in my life. Give me the courage to take one step at a time. Amen.

JANUARY 4

A Living Letter
BY MYRA WELLS BIERNAT

2 Corinthians 3:2-3

You yourselves are our letter; written on our hearts, known and read by everybody...written not with ink, but with the Spirit of the living God; not on tablets of stone, but on tablets of human hearts.

I love writing letters. One year, I made a New Year's resolution that I would write one letter every day. My passion around corresponding with others was so strong, that was the only resolution I have ever kept.

Paul described Christians as living letters. We are read by everyone, but not because of ink and paper. The Spirit of God writes on our human hearts.

Throughout our lives, God sends many love letters our way. If you are like me, there were some that brought great joy, but there were several I suspect you wanted to mark *Return to Sender*. The words seemed harsh and unsympathetic and I wondered if they were really from God. I knew, though, by the return address He had sent them to me, mostly because I needed to grow.

People have sent me letters that I have kept many years. They were so uplifting and encouraging there was no way I could toss something so inspirational. I take them out and read them over and over again because they are such treasures. And when God sends me one of those, I'm filled with a holy joy, an almost unspeakable divine ecstasy.

You are a letter to the world, just as I am one. God has written His message on our hearts and mailed us out to the world. People read His message in our actions. They read His letters in our words.

What do people read in your letters? Will they be welcomed like a soldier so happy to have a letter from home or will they be viewed as junk mail? Are they dreaded like an overdue bill or will people see your letter as one written with exquisite love – wooing them to Christ? What will your letter say today?

Action:

What was the best letter you received? Did you keep it? Since you are a living letter, how do you want your letter to read? Today, send an encouraging letter to someone.

Prayer:

Father, I want to represent You well today. Help me use my words to bring joy. I want to be a living love letter to those I encounter every day. In Jesus' name. Amen.

JANUARY 5

The Upgrade
BY SHERRI GALLAGHER

James 1:19-20

My dear brothers, take note of this: Everyone should be quick to listen, slow to speak and slow to become angry, for man's anger does not bring about the righteous life that God desires.

One that is slow to anger is better than the mighty, and one whose temper is controlled than the one who captures a city. **Proverbs 16:32**

We made our vacation plans four months before we were to depart. It had taken a couple of days to figure out the points systems of the various hotels, but we had worked things out to get a free hotel for the entire stay. Three days before our departure we got an e-mail telling us our hotel would be an additional three hundred dollars per day. Calling customer service was an exercise in frustration. "So sorry," said the bored voice, "you can cancel your reservation if you want." I asked to speak to a supervisor.

After reviewing all the records, the supervisor said she would take care of things, and there would only be a fifty dollar per day additional charge. When we arrived, the desk clerk told us there had been a change and we would not be getting the room we reserved. Frustrated, we decided to see the room we had been given before making a fuss. The bell hop led us down hallways and opened the door on a luxury suite instead of an economy room. It seems the supervisor had used her prerogative to upgrade us because we had held our tempers in a difficult situation.

Action:

The next time you are trying to resolve a problem treat the person helping you with respect and firmly present the facts.

Help me to control my temper and tongue and treat others as I would like to be treated. Amen.

JANUARY 6

New Identity
BY TONJA BRICE

Galatians 3:26-27

So in Christ Jesus you are all children of God through faith, for all of you who were baptized into Christ have clothed yourselves with Christ.

I remember the day very clearly. I was sitting in my new apartment when I happened to look down at some framed photographs propped up against the bookcase. The one in front was a photo of my grandfather, Lloyd, and my grandmother, Kathleen. I had seen the photo many times before as well as plenty of other photos of my grandmother, but on this day I suddenly realized that I looked like her. The revelation was astounding to me. You see, Kathleen had passed away from cancer when my mother was six, so I never had the opportunity to meet her. Lloyd's second wife, Laverne, is who I would know as my grandmother. And while I grew up knowing that Kathleen was my mother's biological mom, the family didn't talk much about it.

I've thought about this moment periodically over the years (it's been more than ten at this point), and I've come to realize I have an identity in my family, one I never considered before. While I realized I had a family with whom I could identify based on biology, I also came to realize that I had an adopted family that cared for and loved me as their own. Laverne's brothers and sisters, nieces and nephews, all accepted me and considered me family merely based on her marriage to Lloyd. How incredible is that?

What is even more amazing is that you, my friend, are adopted. Adopted into the Kingdom of God with full rights and privileges as a first-born son. What does this mean? It means that you have an inheritance that far surpasses anything you can image, and it means that no matter where you go in life, you will always have God's family nearby to help and support you. Why? Because that's what family does.

What do you see when you look at the people beside you at church? Do you see your family? Do you invite them into your home and give them a meal? Do you clothe them when you see their tattered clothes? Do you inquire about their spiritual health? Or are they just people you "happen" to go to church with? If you don't see them as family, why not?

Action:

The next time you are at church, look closely at the people who sit near you in the pew. But don't just look, observe. Do you see someone who needs a smile or a friendly face? Do you see someone who has a need that you can fulfill? If so, do it, whatever it is, simply because they are your family.

Prayer:

Dear Father, I pray that as time goes on, I can learn to love all your children as family. Help me to see the needs of my brothers and sisters and help me to desire to fill their needs out of love for You. In Jesus' name. Amen.

JANUARY 7

Friends
BY MYRA BIERNAT WELLS

Proverbs 27:17

As iron sharpens iron, so one person sharpens another.

I have been fortunate in my life to have friends to meet with regularly, not just to enjoy a cup of tea or a sumptuous lunch, but to speak into each other's lives. Throughout the years, we've learned to trust each other, but more importantly, we've come to challenge each other to become better versions of ourselves.

We are better together. We speak to each other honestly and with courage and try to always turn the other's heart towards God and His purposes. As wonderful as it is to have a friend like that, there is also an uncomfortable vulnerability that goes along with it. I feel uncommonly exposed because my friend can drill deeply into areas I don't always want to talk about. But when I open up, I find it is healthy to bring light to these areas. We all need deep friendships like this.

It is essential that there are people in our lives who will love us right where we are but are not content to leave us there. They help us get to a place of higher living, refined character with a greater love for God. We need friends who will hold us accountable to God's standards…friends to sharpen us. The Bible points this out in Proverbs 27:17, *Iron sharpens iron, so one person sharpens another.* Friends like these lovingly call us to a higher standard - making us wiser and better.

Today, take time to consider your friendships. Do you have friends who sharpen you and challenge God's purposes in your life? Who is making you wiser and better? Is there someone in your life who asks tough questions, shares godly truths and most importantly, confronts you when you need confronting? If you do, thank God. And continue to meet with your friend on a regular basis, granting permission to speak into your life and asking to do the same in their life.

If instead, you find yourself in a wide pool of shallow friends, pray about it. Pray God would bring meaningful friendships into your life and that He will teach you what it is like to be a good, godly friend.

Action:
What friends came to mind as you read this? Send them an encouraging text, email or letter to bless them for their guidance in your life.

Prayer:
Dear God, thank you for friendships. Help me to grow in my ability to pour into the lives of others. Continue to give me strength to be open to godly constructive feedback. Give me the capacity to love others like You love them. In Jesus' name. Amen.

JANUARY 8

Silence Is Wisdom
BY SHERRI GALLAGHER

Proverbs 9:7-12

Not merely an absence of noise, Real Silence begins when a reasonable being withdraws from the noise in order to find peace and order in his inner sanctuary.
Peter Minard

I served on a jury for a malpractice case. A child had drunk an industrial cleaning solution. Permanent damage had resulted, and the emergency room doctors were being sued.

The rest of the jury decided to award a large amount to the child. Their reasoning was; doctors were rich and deserved to pay, the insurance company could afford it, the doctors must have messed up or the child would be healed.

First, I presented the evidence we saw. Then, I presented that an alkaloid burns on contact and there is no saving the tissue. No one wanted to listen. I was yelled at. The foreman asked the judge to remove me from the jury. When I recognized nothing I said would change minds, I remained silent except to vote no award.

Finally, the judge notified us a settlement had been reached. The doctors and attorneys wanted to meet with us. They shared how little of the settlement would have come from insurance and the injury was permanent the moment the child drank the solution. The rest of the jurors were stunned.

Sometimes, when people don't want to hear, the best policy is to remain silent and strong. God is with us in wisdom.

Action:
Remain firm when you know you are taking the correct path.

Prayer:
Lord, be with all emergency room workers in all they face. Amen.

JANUARY 9

A Heart Whisper
BY MYRA BIERNAT WELLS

Isaiah 43:1

Do not fear for I have redeemed you, I have summoned you by name; you are mine.

As I was enjoying a short winter vacation, a respite from Illinois' bitter cold, one of my favorite uncles lay dying. Since he and his wife had no children, after her death, my cousin Briget and I gave him special attention. When he took ill, Briget pretty much took up residence in the hospital. When I returned, I took over and sent her home for some uninterrupted sleep in her own bed.

Before leaving for the hospital, I packed a small bag. I made sure I took my Bible. My uncle was unresponsive at this point, but that evening, I read many passages to him. I wanted his room to be filled with the inescapable presence of God. I whispered God's promises into my uncle's ear. "Be strong and courageous. For the Lord your God goes with you. He will never leave or forsake you" (Deuteronomy 31:6). "Those who know your name, trust in you, for you, Lord, have never forsaken those who seek you" (Psalm 9:10). "I have engraved you on the palms of my hands" (Isaiah 49:16). "Take heart! I have overcome the world" (John 16:33).

At one point, I closed my Bible and started telling my uncle of the great party there would be in heaven when he arrived. It was around that time that a nurse came in to take my uncle's vital signs. As she did that, he slipped from this world to the next. Peacefully, very peacefully.

As I started to cry, a whisper filled the room. After all the whispering I had done in that room, I heard the Voice of Peace speak His presence into my pain. He knew I now needed a word of encouragement. Not an audible word – just a heart whisper. He was right by my side. I knew it as I remembered, "The Lord is close to the brokenhearted and saves those who are crushed in spirit" (Psalm 34:18).

Action:
Read Isaiah 43:1-5. Write down the promises of God identified in this passage.

Prayer:
Dear Lord, thank You for reminding me that You are always with me. Please help me to know deeper levels of peace today in light of Your constant presence. Amen.

JANUARY 10

Two Edges of a Sword
BY JUDY KNOX

Ephesians 6:10-18

For the word of God is living and active. Sharper than any double-edged sword, it penetrates even to dividing soul and spirit, joints and marrow; it judges the thoughts and attitudes of the heart. **Hebrews 4:12**

Here comes the warrior, dressed for battle in his protective armor: helmet, shield, breastplate, loin covering and special footwear. His offensive weapon is a sword. As Christian soldiers we are outfitted in the spiritual armor God provides, and we go into battle with a two-edged sword, which the Bible tells us is "the sword of the Spirit, the Word of God." I remember our pastor stepping up into the pulpit, holding his Bible in the air, and asking, "How many of you have your swords with you today?" Bibles were raised all over the sanctuary to proudly show we had brought them.

The image of a double-edged sword reminds us that the Bible is not just a book we read and quote from, but that we can use the truth found between its covers to do battle with the enemy – a formidable weapon indeed.

Have you ever wondered what the two edges represent? The New Testament was originally written in Greek, and the Greek language contains two words that are translated as *word* in English: *Logos*, which means "scripture" or "written word," and *rhema*, which means "spoken word."

Scholars love to separate and analyze these terms, but the *Logos* and *rhema* are not two separate entities. They are two parts, or two aspects, of God's whole Word. The earliest Christians had only the Old Testament in writing and had to rely mainly on the spoken Word to teach them about what Jesus had said and done, and what their lives were to be like as believers. Today we are blessed to have the written Word in its entirety.

If we have the complete written Word, then why do we still need the spoken Word? The written Word contains the truths we need in order to understand who God is and how He wants us to conduct ourselves. The spoken Word is the Holy Spirit, who Jesus said would teach us and lead us into all truth, bringing to our remembrance what God has spoken to us in His written Word (John 14:26). The Holy Spirit makes the written Word come to life in our hearts. Without the inspiration of the *rhema* Word, the Bible would be just another book. Despite the scholars' debate, the question is not which is more important, but are we opening our hearts to both?

While Bible study is important, we all probably know someone whose thinking is intent on knowing the Word, studying, memorizing, and analyzing it, yet that person's life does not show evidence of having spent time with God and basking in His love. We don't see the fruit of the Spirit coming forth. Another person may claim to be hearing from God, and having amazing spiritual experiences, but his life does not line up with the basic principles set forth in the written Word. I once heard a preacher explain it this way: "Word alone makes you dry up, Spirit alone makes you blow up, Spirit and Word working together help you grow up."

Warriors in Paul's day maintained their weapons by carefully sharpening both edges of the blade so the sword would balance perfectly. Shouldn't we do the same?

Action:
When you read the Bible, ask the Holy Spirit to reveal how what you are reading applies to you today.

Prayer:
Lord, I want to live in balance between the Spirit and the Word. Please speak to me as I read Your word, teaching, leading, and bringing things to my remembrance. Amen.

JANUARY 11

See Me
BY SHERRI GALLAGHER

Matthew 6:1-6

The charity that hastens to proclaim its good deeds, ceases to be charity, and is only pride and ostentation. **William Hutton**

Hollywood stars set some interesting examples. When it comes to charity, most of it is done with a press release and notification to a phalanx of paparazzi. I wonder how much would be done if the press wasn't there.

One Saturday I watched one of the many home improvement shows on television. Former President Jimmy Carter was at a Habitat for Humanity build. A bevy of reporters surrounded him asking him to pose. He turned to them and said, "I suppose you have a job to do and I understand that, but do you know how much work we could get done if you just put those cameras down and picked up some tools for a day? The world can live with a few less pictures of me and a lot more helping hands." He wasn't looking for recognition or accolades; he truly wanted to help.

How much credit are we looking for when we make a donation? Do we need a brick or plaque with our name on it or is treasure in heaven enough? Putting items in the Treats for our Troops bin or giving to the Shepherds Fund are some of the ways we can give without recognition. Maybe if enough of us set the example Hollywood will get the hint.

Action:

Perform an anonymous act of charity.

Prayer:

Lord, help me to give without recognition. Amen.

JANUARY 12

Advice from a Carpenter
BY MYRA BIERNAT WELLS

Mark 6:3

Isn't this the carpenter?

Today's fathers love to teach their sons. The lessons range from how to throw a ball, repair a car, to which quarterback in the NFL is the best. But we rarely think about what lessons Joseph might have taught Jesus.

While living Nazareth, Joseph and Jesus possibly plied their trade in nearby towns as well. Sepphoris, a Galilean town, was completely restored by Herod Antipas during the years Joseph worked as a carpenter. Perhaps Joseph and the young Jesus made the hour's walk to work on the city's reconstruction. While tools and techniques have greatly changed since Biblical times, here are three rules, still applicable today, which Joseph most likely taught his son.

Measure twice – cut once: Wood was scarce in ancient Israel and most carpenters couldn't afford to make mistakes. They proceeded with caution, anticipating the consequences of all they did. Even today, thinking ahead prevents trouble. Measuring our spending against income helps not to exceed it. We should take steps to protect our physical health. Our spiritual growth needs time and work to increase it. Just like timber in Israel, our resources are limited. We should work diligently to use them wisely.

Use the right tools for the job: You wouldn't try to cut down a tree with a hammer. Every carpenter has a special tool for each task. The same is with us. Don't use anger instead of understanding. Don't be indifferent when encouragement is needed. Jesus gave people hope. He wasn't embarrassed to show love and compassion. He mastered using the right tool for the job and as His apprentices, we should do the same.

Take care of your tools and they will take care of you: Using his tools, Joseph provided for his family. God gave us valuable tools: prayer, meditation, fasting, worship, but our most priceless is the Bible. God cares for us when we use its truths, then live them out.

Action:

In the body of Christ, we are all carpenters assigned a task. We can mentor apprentices, teaching them skills to live out their faith. Reach out to a Christian family member or friend and discuss ways you can encourage and help each other live a more devoted godly life.

Prayer:

God, thank You for giving us tools and resources. Impress upon my heart that I am always on the job for You. Lead my heart, hands, head and feet so that I reflect You to all who might watch me today. In Jesus' name. Amen.

JANUARY 13

The KEY Character in the Story
BY BETH DUMEY

Psalm 109:21

But you, Sovereign LORD, help me for your name's sake;
out of the goodness of your love, deliver me.

It is hard for me to believe that life—my life, anyway—is turning out the way it is supposed to. I often tell my friends that when I meet Jesus in heaven, I'm going to ask how it was really supposed to all happen. I want to see the movie without the editorial changes and the alternate ending. The script of my life feels like an adapted screenplay, with the original lost somewhere in translation.

This is not to say I am not responsible for my own choices or that I have a bucketful of regrets. Actually, neither is true. More to the point is that although I understand God's sovereignty theologically, I find it much more difficult to grasp practically. What about the plot twist in my late twenties that stalled my life for two years? Or that long transition just a few years back? Often the events themselves don't make sense, maybe not for years and sometimes not ever.

While I take comfort that God remains sovereign over all these events, it often feels like I am living in a sub-plot with the main story going on without me. Of course, when we're in the middle of the story, we usually don't know what is coming next. Joseph didn't, when he was in Potiphar's house; David didn't, when he was fleeing Saul; Paul didn't, when he was in jail.

When the twists and turns of your life have you muddled, stand firm in God's sovereignty. Even if it feels like your role is ever-changing, remember the key character in your story never does.

Action:

Think of some transitional times in your life. Reflect on how God was sovereign through them.

Prayer:

Lord, You are the author and keeper of my life story. Help me to trust You in leading me through it each day. Amen.

JANUARY 14

Peace
BY SHERRI GALLAGHER

Colossians 3:15-17

Peace is not a relationship of nations. It is a condition of mind brought about by a serenity of soul. Peace is not merely the absence of war. It is also a state of mind. Lasting peace can come only to peaceful people. **Jawaharlal Nehru**

Church services provide a give and a take, recognizing we live in the world but need God to thrive. They start with worldly things, announcements and greetings, move to sharing our concerns for one another, and then the feeding of us with words to guide and lead us in a Christian life. Finally, the benediction sends us back out into the world having found and absorbed into our souls the peace that only God can give. As the service goes on, we each, in our own time and way, breathe a sigh and relax lowering our guard and drawing strength to face another week.

One benediction made this clear to me. "May the Lord bless you and keep you. May He make His face to shine upon you. May He lift His countenance upon you and give you peace. Peace which the world cannot give, peace without which the world cannot live, the love, the joy and the peace of Jesus Christ." Hearing the pastor speak these words from the back of the church always gave me hope and the feeling that I could make it through one more week until I could return to services and feed on God's Word again.

Action:

When you arrive at church, take a few moments to relax and open your heart and mind to the words of peace offered just for you.

Prayer:

Peace be with you until we meet again. Amen.

JANUARY 15
MARTIN LUTHER KING, JR. DAY

I Have a Dream
BY SHERRI GALLAGHER

Romans 14:7-12

I have a dream that one day this nation will rise up and live out the true meaning of its creed: 'We hold these truths to be self-evident: that all men are created equal.'
Dr. Martin Luther King, Jr.

I was eight years old in the summer of 1963, but I still remember that long, hot summer. I remember seeing the grainy, black and white news footage of Dr. King standing on the steps of the Lincoln Memorial and presenting his "I Have a Dream" speech. Even to a little girl his words seemed important, although the strongest memory was of the song *We Shall Overcome*. I also remember the news that he had been shot that April day in 1968. It just didn't make any sense to me.

Several decades later, my three-year-old son asked me a question that spiraled me back to that unjust time. I had been telling him stories of a great-great-grandfather that had been a Union drummer boy in the Civil War when he asked, "Who are African-Americans?" His pre-school class was racially diverse. Deep in my heart, I knew that how I answered that question would impact his interaction with those children. Inspiration struck. I answered, "It doesn't matter; the Union won so we are all the same." We had overcome. We had made great strides.

I decided to read Dr. King's "I Have a Dream" speech before writing this devotional. It was powerful and many parts stand out. "I have a dream that my four children will one day live in a nation where they will not be judged by the color of their skin but by the content of their character." Isn't that how we are told God will judge us? "I have a dream that one day on the red hills of Georgia the sons of former slaves and the sons of former slave-owners will be able to sit down together at a table of brotherhood." Isn't that our hope and expectation at the communion table? Do you think Dr. King would be pleased with our progress? Is there more to do?

Action:
Read one of Dr. Martin Luther King, Jr.'s speeches.
Prayer:
God in heaven, help us to reach the day when all of God's children, black men and white men, Jews and Gentiles, Protestant and Catholics, will be able to join hands

and sing the words, "Free at last! Free at last! Thank God Almighty, we are free at last!"* Amen.
* This is a paraphrase of the closing paragraph to the "I Have a Dream" speech.

JANUARY 16

Left Holding the Pain
BY MYRA BIERNAT WELLS

Psalm 56:8

You keep track of all my sorrows. You have collected all my tears in your bottle. You have recorded each one in your book.

The struggles of my life created empathy - I could relate to pain, being abandoned, having people not love me. **Oprah Winfrey**

One of my guilty pleasures is watching a reality show about brides. Normally funny, recently I viewed two episodes that brought me to tears.

In both, two young brides faced heart-wrenching decisions. One's fiancé was recently diagnosed with ALS (Lou Gehrig's Disease) while the other was just one day out of the hospital recovering from a random act of violence that left her paralyzed from the waist down. Both planned to go ahead with their weddings and when they cried on television, I cried right along with them.

I cried, I kept telling myself, because I felt their pain. But stripped down to its smallest part, I had no idea the kind of torment they were facing. I've never been in those situations, though I have felt the pain of knowing life isn't going to work out the way I planned it to be.

I thought about how many times I've walked beside a friend in the throes of terrible grief and all I yearned for was to make them *feel* better.

How different that is from God! He uses pain to *make* us better; stronger in character, joyful in our dependence on Him, mature in our faith. Psalm 56:8 states that God collects every tear we shed in His bottle. Our pain grieves Him so much He records our tears, every one of them. He does not take pain and our resulting tears lightly.

When pain strikes, in the loneliness, the craziness and the heartache, God is there to hold our hands. He understands your pain because He experienced pain Himself. He sees the hard work you do in the midst of anguish. He values your growth.

God, in His goodness and love, never leaves us holding the pain.

JANUARY 17

The Fourth Cup
BY KRISTEN LONG

Proverbs 27:17

As iron sharpeneth iron; so a man sharpeneth the countenance of his friend.
(KJV)

I love it when my phone rings and my friend says let's meet for coffee. We sit in a comfy restaurant booth with steaming cups of really good coffee, with cream. We chat. We laugh. We share.

Sometimes it takes until the fourth cup for a friend to build up enough strength, courage, and trust, to share what was truly on her heart—the real reason she called me for coffee.

These chats with our trusted companions are never surface conversations like, "Hello! How Is your yellow tabby cat?" No! They are what we have been carrying around in our hearts. "My child...", "I feel...", "I don't understand...", "I've been diagnosed...".

At one time or another, everyone wrestles with certain thoughts and letting friends in is part of the growth process. What do we hope to take away with us from these chats? Are we looking for an accomplice in our anger and bitterness? Are we conspiring in a gossip session to tear someone down? Or did we reach out because we want to make positive, spiritual changes in our thoughts and actions?

Action:
There are steps we can take if change is what we desire, besides ingesting great quantities of caffeine. Confiding in someone about our struggles is an important start, but it is only a start. If we are longing for growth, the friends that we choose to share with must hold us accountable.

We should:
- have a plan of action in place by the time that we part company.
- look up scripture on the subject and meditate on it.

- help to find a professional, if needed, or be an encouragement to get pastoral counsel.
- set a time to call or meet for an update.
- Pray! Pray! Pray! Commit the situation to prayer for a specific amount of time. This is the most important step. We can talk to everyone around us, but if we don't talk to the Lord first and most often, we will not grow.

Prayer:

Lord, please help us to cultivate and feed our friendships in a God-honoring way and take the steps that will strengthen the bond with these friends and with You. Amen.

JANUARY 18

Morning Light
BY SHERRI GALLAGHER

Matthew 5:14-16

You are the light of the world. A city on a hill cannot be hidden. Neither do people light a lamp and put it under a bowl. Instead they put it on its stand, and it gives light to everyone in the house. In the same way, let your light shine before men, that they may see your good deeds and praise your Father in heaven.

Again Jesus spoke to them, saying, "I am the light of the world. Whoever follows me will never walk in darkness but will have the light of life." **John 8:12**

As a child, I was frightened of the bats that hunted mosquitoes in the darkness near our cabin. My Dad said he loved bats; they gave him hope. This didn't make any sense to me, so he explained. He was a soldier in World War II stationed in the Pacific. Standing guard duty in the darkness worried him because he was night-blind. He said he always loved the sound of the fruit bats returning since it meant daylight would follow close behind and he could see again.

The Light of the World is the same. He comes to us with soft whispers in the darkness. Slowly, as we follow His words, we walk into the Light where our vision improves, and we are safe. The difference is His light never ceases to shine.

Maybe that is why reading devotionals in the early morning quiet, as the sun climbs over the horizon, makes the day go better. Starting the day with His words removes the darkness.

Action:

Watch a sunrise.

JANUARY 19

Whom Shall We Fear?
BY MYRA BIERNAT WELLS

Exodus 3:1-21

There is no living that is not afraid when it faces danger. The true courage is in facing danger when you are afraid. **L. Frank Baum**, *The Wizard of Oz*

A thought struck me the other day as I was reading about Moses. He approaches some shrubbery aflame. God speaks, tells him to take off his shoes. "Holy ground," God says.

So, Moses stands before a glimpse of the glory of God. Right there. In bare feet. In the desert sand. God's telling Moses that he'll stand before pharaoh and Moses quakes. "I can't stand before pharaoh," he says. "What if he doesn't believe You sent me?"

What struck me was the "standing before" phraseology. Here was Moses **STANDING BEFORE GOD** and yet he worried about standing before a mere man.

What are your fears today? Whom do you fear? Who or what in your life is bigger than God, or, better put, who or what in your life have you magnified over God because of your own fears and insecurities?

Fast forward history from Moses to today. Those who follow Jesus don't stand before God; in an amazingly wonderful paradox, the very presence of God, through the work of the Holy Spirit, **LIVES INSIDE US**. Whom shall we fear?

Action:
Look to God for your strength. He will give you courage in the face of whatever it is you fear.

Prayer:
"From my distress I called upon the LORD; the LORD answered me and set me in a large place. The LORD is for me; I will not fear; what can man do to me? The LORD is for me among those who help me; therefore, I will look with satisfaction on those who hate me. It is better to take refuge in the LORD than to trust in man. It is better to take refuge in the LORD than to trust in princes." (Psalm 118:5-9 NASB). Amen.

JANUARY 20

Glorious
BY BETH DUMEY

Psalm 24:5

They will receive a blessing from the LORD.

Above us, the Chateau Frontenac stood majestically overlooking the plaza. Stately and elegant, the castle-like hotel presided over the Quebec City skyline. A few feet away a young dark-haired woman floated the lyrics of Ave Maria on the crisp morning air. A gentle breeze blew across from the St. Lawrence River. This morning, Sunday morning, I had a church service in my heart as I experienced the joy of an unexpected trip to a land I had longed to explore.

The worship part of the service was courtesy of the unidentified songstress, whose vibrant pitch rivaled the church bells resounding in the distance. I could have been standing inside a church building with my arms raised, singing as full as my lungs would allow. Instead, my worship was silent, yet just as mighty.

The sermon was equally wordless, as a swell of gratitude rose in me, a reminder of the blessings God is generous to provide even if they are different than we ask or plan. It is the surprise blessings that are often the most delicious, like a chocolate candy with a soft cream center that delights us with a burst of flavor.

Psalm 24:5 reminds us that blessings are extended from the Lord to those who are faithful to Him. The service in my heart that Sunday morning concluded with a walk down cobblestone streets, flanked by Quebecois and scented with the buttery aroma of fresh-baked pastries.

Action:
Consider how God has unexpectedly blessed you recently.

Prayer:
Father, help me to never take for granted Your generosity or lose my sense of wonder in it. Amen.

JANUARY 21

Moonlight Sonata
BY SHERRI GALLAGHER

Genesis 1:14-19

Every day you may make progress. Every step may be fruitful. Yet there will stretch out before you ever-lengthening, ever-ascending, ever-improving path. You know you will never get to the end of the journey. But this, so far from discouraging, only adds to the joy and glory of the climb. **Sir Winston Churchill**

     I run at five in the morning. It is the only way to get a run in before work. It means running in darkness most of the year. I have gotten to love running in a full moon. The road becomes a bright bluish-white path; the trees and bushes are shrouded in black indistinguishable shadows. It is easy to know where to run and brush is not inviting or distracting. The only sound is my own breathing and my shoes hitting the pavement. In daylight the landscape all around the road is clearly distinguishable and provides a great distraction from the path I should be taking. If I spend too much time looking at my surroundings, I trip and fall.

     Sometimes I wish I could follow God's path in moonlight instead of the full light of day. The day-to-day activities: cooking, cleaning, working, exercising all distract me from finding the time to study God's word and the path He has laid out. It gets lost in the commotion.

Action:

Take a walk either in the morning just before sunrise or in the evening as the sun is setting and recite the Lord's Prayer stopping at each sentence to think about what it means in your life.

Prayer:

Guide me in the paths of Your way and lead me away from the distractions and temptations of everyday life. Amen.

JANUARY 22

Shaken and Stirred
BY MYRA BIERNAT WELLS

Luke 17:33

Whoever tries to keep their life will lose it, and whoever loses their life will preserve it.

Faith is taking the first step even when you don't see the whole staircase.
Martin Luther King, Jr.

Life is tough. However, I really think God shakes and stirs us to think outside of our lives and to see the Kingdom of God as bigger than ourselves. I feel this because there have been times in my life when God has shaken me or stirred me out of my comfort zone. It's difficult for all of us when we're in a new situation and need to trust Him fully. When God interrupts my life, I picture Him standing across a bar from me and I'm a needy patron. (Not that I drink, I don't; but everyone knows from the movies that you can tell your bartender, or hairstylist, anything.)

"I'm just not feeling it, God. I'm unsettled."

He smiles. "That's because you've micromanaged your life in such a way that you can always be in control of it."

"Ouch," I say. My insides quake. "Right now, it feels like my whole life is falling apart. I'm in such pain, God. It feels like it will never end. I am so scared." I hang my head.

"Don't hang your head," He says. "You're on a journey. There is a time for everything. You were in a season of healing–a very necessary season. But I'm pushing you out of that season."

"Well, if You could just be so kind as to tell me exactly what this upcoming season will entail, I would really appreciate it."

"I've walked with you through troubles in the past. And you grew. And you still love Me. All good things, right?"

"Yes, I have to admit, God, some of my most profound internal growth came from the devastating times of my life. But I'm freaking scared of stepping out again. You and I both know how clay footed I am. How prone to sin. How small. How needy."

"Yes, but you forget the paradox of my strength made perfect in weakness."

"You know I love You," I say, swallowing again. "You know that, right?"

"Yes, I do. So, I'm asking you to trust Me. Just for the next step."

"Sure, what's that step again?"

God laughs. "Just trust Me. I'll show you in due time. In the meantime, don't beat yourself up over not being enough. No one ever is. Your sufficiency has always been in Me, not in what you accomplish. You are wildly loved by Me simply because I created you. You're my child. The more you realize and rest in that, the more settled and peaceful you will be. All I ask is that you simply take My hand."

Let's all reach across the bar, grab His sacred hand and know we'll never be the same.

Action:
Reach out in faith today and perform a radical act of service.

Prayer:
God, You are the God who knows and loves us. Sometimes we don't listen to Your voice or understand Your leadings. Despite our shortcomings, we know that You know our deepest needs, and You love us more than we love ourselves. Teach us to hear Your counsel. Amen.

JANUARY 23

When Your Ship Comes In
BY BETH DUMEY

Colossians 2:2

My goal is that they may be encouraged in love, so that they may have the full riches of complete understanding, in order that they may know the mystery of God, namely, Christ.

I've often heard, and even repeated, the idiom, "When my ship comes in…" without truly understanding the meaning of it. Of course, the connotation is a special, rather large and life-changing blessing. It is often used in fantasy talk about what plans may transpire when the realities of toil are no longer a constraint. It offers freedom and release from the mundane, daily struggle.

Yet, it is only when I disembarked from a large cruise ship and visited small coastal towns that I realized the practical reality of this phrase. For those retailers relying on the influx of visitors to patronize their stores and cafés, their ship quite literally does come in. As one sundry shop clerk, surveying the line in front of her, said to a caller, "I can't talk right now. A ship came in." Of course, the ship in question was extra traffic for the store and increased sales for the day. It was much less about fantasy and much more about everyday providence.

When we know Christ, our ship has come in! In everyday practical ways, He is leading us, informing us, guiding us. We may or may not be able to fulfill our fantasy plans. More importantly, we are no longer waiting, as the richness of His presence is the most valuable gift. As Colossians 2:2 tells us, knowing Christ is our "full riches."

Action:
Do you secretly plot your fantasy plans for a better life? Have you held these plans up to God and laid them at His feet? Consider doing that now.

Prayer:
Lord, my help comes from You. I want to always see You as the sole resource that is my provider, my leader, my all in all. Amen.

JANUARY 24

Who Loves Ya?
BY SHERRI GALLAGHER

Acts 10:1-48

Then Peter began to speak to them: "I truly understand that God shows no partiality, but in every nation anyone who fears Him and does what is right is acceptable to Him."
Acts 10:34-35 (NRSV)

My husband, Jim, grew up in a church that believed it had an exclusive claim to God. As a young man he asked, "Would a good man who had followed God's laws, prayed and was considerate of others but not a member of their church, be allowed into heaven?" The unequivocal answer was "No." Jim had a hard time with that and eventually, left, much to his mother's sorrow.

In Jonah chapter three, Nineveh a great city of unbelievers, repented, turning away from evil ways and God spared them. Jonah becomes angry with God (chapter 4). Jonah believed he and his people were true believers and God should not have shared His love with "unbelievers." God points out the people and cattle of Ninevah were all His creation and He loved them along with Jonah.

In Acts chapter 10 the way is opened for believers of all nations to be children of God. God repeatedly tells us He loves everyone and wants them to follow in His ways.

Action:
Go find someone you would reject and hold a Bible study with them.

Prayer:
Please help me to love those who are different and outcasts. Amen.

JANUARY 25

Just In Case
BY MYRA BIERNAT WELLS

Revelation 21:5

He who is seated on the throne said, "I am making everything new!" Then He said, "Write this down, for these words are trustworthy and true."

Exiting my interior garage door, I stumbled over an old umbrella lying on the steps. It had been sitting there for a while, discarded in a sense but not quite thrown away. Although its metal spindles were broken and it hardly opened to its full capacity, I kept it "just in case." Just in case the other umbrellas I had magically disappeared. Just in case a calamity hit that might require the use of a broken umbrella. Just in case.

I realized I often have difficulty letting broken things go that have long out-lived their relevance: umbrellas, school textbooks, even past-due relationships. Only recently have I truly believed that if I let some old, malfunctioning parts of my life go, God will make something new. Like dying leaves on a branch, He will prune them and replace them with shiny new leaves or even off-shoots of whole new branches. Perhaps a scarcity mentality has kept me hanging on when releasing would be so much more freeing. Perhaps it is even a fear of: What if that branch is empty for a good, long while?

Revelation 21:5 reminds us that God, in His time, makes everything new. It is this promise that keeps me going when the monotony and routines and even losses threaten to plunge me into despair. Because our Creator sprouts new life, I can release what I am holding on to so I can embrace what He has for me next.

Action:
What do you have a hard time letting go of? Something material? Relational? Perhaps a habit? Acknowledge this and reflect on why you can't let it go.

Prayer:
Father, help me to recognize the "new" You are creating all around me—both externally and internally. Amen.

JANUARY 26

Maintaining Focus
BY BETH DUMEY

Matthew 14:29

Then Peter got down out of the boat, walked on the water and came toward Jesus. But when he saw the wind, he was afraid and, beginning to sink, cried out, "Lord, save me!"

Following the advice of my chiropractor, I eased up on my running program and added elliptical training to my workout. As one not blessed with natural coordination, the moving arm grips along with the rotating platforms for my feet was a bit too much for my body to process at once. When I really got my arms going, my legs moved slower and when I gained momentum with the rotating platforms, my arms weakened. After an hour I was thoroughly exhausted and had only reached half the strength of my regular workout.

As I willed myself to get in sync and find a rhythm, I did okay for a few moments. Inevitably, I would glance down at my feet or reconfigure my stance and lose the momentum I had gained. I was struggling a bit with my body, but I was mostly discouraged by my lack of mental focus. If I just kept going and didn't try to think through what I was doing, I maintained a natural stride. Too much attention to my technique threw me off my game.

When Christ summoned Peter to walk toward him in Matthew 14:29, Peter was able to accomplish the impossible by walking on water. But scripture tells us when he saw the wind, he became afraid. Like most of us, Peter lost his focus and instead saw how easy it would be for him to sink. He took his eyes off his savior and began to fall.

I'm often tempted to be so distracted by my environment or other people's influence or by the difficulty of the task that I, too, take my eyes off the Savior.

Action:

Consider the areas in your life that most often cause you to look away—even momentarily—from Christ. Do you note any patterns?

Prayer:

Lord, help me to stay focused on You as You guide me forward. Amen.

JANUARY 27

A Million Inches
BY SHERRI GALLAGHER

2 Corinthians 9:6-8

Remember this: Whoever sows sparingly will also reap sparingly, and whoever sows generously will also reap generously. Each of you should give what you have decided in your heart to give, not reluctantly or under compulsion, for God loves a cheerful giver. And God is able to bless you abundantly, so that in all things at all times, having all that you need, you will abound in every good work.

I discussed a magazine article with my sister. If a person grew out their hair so an eight-inch ponytail could be cut off, the hair could be donated to make wigs for cancer patients. The challenge is to get a million inches of hair donated. I really wanted to donate, but hair with more than five percent grey or permanently color treated could not be used.

My sister is the beauty maven in the family, and I wanted to find out if I had the dye removed, would it be possible to donate my hair? After some comments only sisters can laugh at, she said no, I couldn't donate. Recognizing my disappointment, she told me not to worry. Her daughter had already made two donations and was in the process of growing her hair for a third, she had all three of us "covered." Here was a pretty, young girl cheerfully and repeatedly giving up her long chestnut hair to help others. Truly God must love her as she gives not with reluctance or compulsion but with a cheerful heart. She had found a way to give to others even when she had no money.

Action:
Participate in a charitable activity and give your time or something other than money.

Prayer:
God, please continue to bless the gentle and generous souls that give from their hearts and use their gifts to comfort those in need. Amen.

JANUARY 28

Power Failure
BY MYRA BIERNAT WELLS

Nehemiah 8:10

Do not grieve, for the joy of the Lord is your strength.

Those pesky blinking clocks are just one of the reasons I hate power outages. We're so dependent on electricity; it's tough to live without it. Food spoils and tempers flare from the boredom. Candlelight is charming for only so long.

Sooner or later, all of us will experience a power failure in life. It may be due to a problem in your marriage. Maybe you'll have to watch someone die slowly from cancer. A job loss may trigger powerlessness.

It is difficult to watch a bad situation unfold and not be able to do something about it. We want to change our circumstances, to figure out what is wrong and solve the problem. But that's not always possible. What do you do when you have no power and all you can do is stand on the sidelines and watch?

The key to surviving one of life's power failures is to surrender the situation to God. The amount of God's power in our lives is proportional to how much we surrender to Him. God can't fill a heart that's full of pride or arrogance.

Surrender is scary. In every other endeavor in life, surrender is a bad thing. But in our relationship with God, it is absolutely essential. And we don't often realize it until we are faced with a situation we are powerless to change. This might explain why surrender is so difficult for us. We'd rather endure unnecessary misery than give in to God.

It takes spiritual maturity built over a number of years in order to live in submission to God. However, He provides many instances that illustrate His faithfulness to us. And as we mature, we realize God can be trusted, not in just the small things but in life's worst tragedies as well. The practice of obedience becomes a proven commodity for us.

Our Christian faith doesn't guarantee a happy ending every time. But we have God's promise to pour His power into our lives – but only to the degree we let Him in. And with God in us, we will survive every power failure we'll ever have to face.

Action:

Make a list of the times in your life when you experienced God's faithfulness. Ponder how you can use that list to surrender your life more fully to God.

Prayer:
Dear Jesus, thank You for Your faithfulness. Help me to live life fully surrendered to You so that when a power failure strikes, I run into Your arms. Amen.

JANUARY 29

Following Mr. Slowie
BY JUDY KNOX

James 1:2-4

My brethren, count it all joy when you fall into various trials, knowing that the testing of your faith produces patience. But let patience have its perfect work, that you may be perfect and complete, lacking nothing. (NKJV)

You will keep him in perfect peace whose mind is stayed on You because he trusts in You.
Isaiah 26:3 (NKJV)

It was a dark and stormy night. Well, not really stormy, but it was very dark and raining steadily. My class that was supposed to end at 4:00 had run very late, and I was finally heading back from Kenosha, Wisconsin, toward my home in Libertyville, Illinois, longing for my comfy chair and warm slippers.

After stopping at my usual gas station to fill the tank, I turned onto the highway where after just a couple of miles at forty-five mph the speed limit would change to fifty-five mph and I would be able to proceed quickly toward the interstate. However, just before I got to the spot where the speed limit changed, I discovered that I was following Mr. Slowie, crawling along at thirty-eight mph. Oh well, I thought, when the speed limit changes to fifty-five, he'll speed up. And he did, all the way up to forty-two mph! I decided not to try to pass him in the no-passing zone on the wet, narrow country highway in the dark. Having made that choice, I now had another choice to make: I could grumble and bristle with annoyance, or I could praise the Lord, thanking Him that when I am walking with Him, I am always in the right place at the right time. I chose option two, cranked up the volume on the praise music CD, and sang along.

Although we never did go faster than forty-two, and Mr. Slowie did not turn off until right before the Interstate, the trip seemed to go incredibly fast. I was enjoying the presence of the Lord, not having to worry much about watching the road because the driver ahead of me was leading the way around all the curves. Finally, he turned off and I went on to the Interstate and drove the few quick miles to my exit. I was really moving along until I was almost at the intersection closest to my home where there was construction going on. I had expected to encounter some traffic, but no one seemed to be moving. I was still in the singing and praising mode, so I just relaxed and waited for traffic to get going.

Eventually we crept forward. When I rounded the curve where you could see the intersection and the stoplights, I also saw the reason for the slow progress: emergency vehicle lights, lots of them. In fact, there had actually been two accidents near that intersection, and it had taken some time to clear the road because everything was hemmed in due to the construction. I realized Mr. Slowie had not only led the way through the dark, but he had kept me from being at the intersection when the accidents took place.

If I had not been following him, would I have been involved too? I'll never know. However, I would definitely have had to sit for half an hour, unable to see what was going on or to turn around, until traffic moved again. Had I chosen to be annoyed at the slow driver, instead of enjoying time with the Lord, I would have arrived at home in a bad mood, unable to enjoy the rest of the evening.

Sometimes things just don't go the way we expect. When these trials come, we have a choice: walk in the Spirit or walk after the flesh. Our decision won't affect God's love for us, but it will certainly affect the outcome of the situation. We can count every trial as joy when we view it as another opportunity to walk in the Spirit.

Action:
The next time you come upon an annoying or frustrating situation, choose to "count it all joy." Praise and thank the Lord for His goodness instead of complaining about the trial.

Prayer:
Father, I thank You that when I keep my heart and mind focused on You, I can walk in the Spirit where there is life and peace. Help me to view the next trial as an opportunity to see Your hand at work in my life. Amen.

JANUARY 30

The Tentmaker
BY SHERRI GALLAGHER

Genesis 3:17-19

To Adam he said, "Because you listened to your wife and ate fruit from the tree about which I commanded you, 'You must not eat from it,' cursed is the ground because of you; through painful toil you will eat food from it all the days of your life. It will produce thorns and thistles for you, and you will eat the plants of the field. By the sweat of your brow you will eat your food until you return to the ground, since from it you were taken; for dust you are and to dust you will return."

Life grants nothing to us mortals without hard work. **Horace**

At a writers group meeting a member despaired over his economic situation. He owned a janitorial service, but his expenses exceeded his income. I offered to introduce him to several business owners I knew that would most certainly hire his company. He turned down my offer. He believed he was called to write a new version of *Pilgrim's Progress* and he expected God to see to his needs. If he took on more clients, he wouldn't have as much time to write.

One of the professional authors gave him candid advice on the economics of writing books. She gently reminded him Paul worked as a tentmaker while preaching and building the church. The discussion made me think of the times I had turned away from honest hard work. God doesn't promise that life will be easy or fun. He does promise he will take care of us, but that care may be a job we don't enjoy yet gives us the ability to support our family, church and ministry.

Action:

Provide the best work product you are able to give your employer, even if you don't like your job.

Prayer:

God, give those in difficult positions the strength to carry on. Amen.

JANUARY 31

Making God Smile
BY MYRA BIERNAT WELLS

1 Peter 1:6-7

In all this you greatly rejoice, though now for a little while you may have had to suffer grief in all kinds of trials. These have come so that the proven genuineness of your faith—of greater worth than gold, which perishes even though refined by fire—may result in praise, glory and honor when Jesus Christ is revealed.

Character is what you are in the dark. **D.L. Moody**

During a PGA-qualifying tournament, golfer J.P Hayes unknowingly used a ball unapproved by the United States Golf Association. No official had seen the mistake, in fact no one knew – except for Hayes. He could have said nothing and kept playing. But when he realized the error, he quickly made the situation known to officials who promptly disqualified him. When asked about his tournament-ending decision, he answered, "Everyone out here would have done the same thing."

Would we? Have you ever promised one thing and done another? Borrowed a neighbor's tool or book and never returned it? Taken home a pen or a pad of paper from work for personal use? If we don't show our character in the small stuff, we'll never do it when hundreds of thousands of dollars are on the line.

One popular definition for integrity is what you do when no one is watching. Character counts. Integrity matters to God. It's difficult to do the moral thing with life's important decisions when making the right decision on the small things is difficult or impossible.

In this world, God isn't as much concerned about your comfort as He is about your character. He wants us to be like Him. That's why He uses life's challenges to cement His authenticity in us, to have our identities so deeply rooted in Him that when challenged, we remember our calling and to Whom we belong.

Living a life of integrity means integrating all you believe, do, think and say. They must all be consistent. The best way to find that consistency is to continually ask yourself, "Will my choice make God smile?" In other words, the choices we make should be pleasing to God – acceptable as worship. Is there a constant prayer in your heart before you act? Do the decisions you make line up with God's commands? If they do, He will be honored, and you will experience a new contentment in your life.

Action:
Memorize Psalm 51:10 MEV, "Create in me a pure heart, O God, and renew a right spirit within me." Make that a consistent prayer – even when faced with tough decisions.

Prayer:
Dear Jesus, You are all that matters to me. Even though I make mistakes, say and do the wrong things, I ask Your forgiveness. Let the small decisions I make every day build my faith so when faced with tough trials, I know exactly who to turn to – You! Amen.

FEBRUARY 1

Tools or Saviors?
BY MICHELLE VAN LOON

Luke 10:3-4

Go! I am sending you out like lambs among wolves. Do not take a purse or bag or sandals; and do not greet anyone on the road.

A true disciple of Christ travels light, right?

We've probably heard messages about how Jesus sent 72 of his first disciples out in His name with instructions that included traveling with only the clothes on their backs (Luke 10:1-17). Paul's impassioned description of what his life as a follower of Christ would underscore the fact that following Christ may be filled with challenge and difficulty, not comfort (2 Cor. 11).

Not long ago, I found myself wondering how a passage from Luke 22 fits with those descriptions. Jesus spoke these words in the hours before His arrest, immediately after He told Peter that Peter would deny Him three times before the rooster crowed the next morning:

> Then Jesus asked them, "When I sent you without purse, bag or sandals, did you lack anything?"
>
> "Nothing," they answered.
>
> He said to them, "But now if you have a purse, take it, and also a bag; and if you don't have a sword, sell your cloak and buy one. It is written: 'And he was numbered with the transgressors'; and I tell you that this must be fulfilled in me. Yes, what is written about me is reaching its fulfillment."
>
> The disciples said, "See, Lord, here are two swords."
>
> "That's enough!" he replied. (Luke 22:35-38)

This doesn't mean that we are to amass a mountain of stuff, particularly considering the whole fabric of Jesus' teaching and ministry. There is wisdom and freedom for each one of us as we submit our lifestyle to the Holy Spirit's unmasking probe and then respond to what He may be telling us about our motives and His purposes for our possessions.

Jesus' words belong in our discussions about discipleship. They do not obliterate the clear words Jesus spoke about the cost of following Him. There is most certainly a time to shed possessions and travel light.

But there is also a time for us to prepare for what He may be calling us to do next. We will be able to hear His direction most clearly as we acknowledge that possessions are meant to be His tools, not our personal saviors.

Action:
Consider whether you are in a season of life where you need to travel light or whether God might be calling you to prepare strategically for a specific task or ministry.

Prayer:
Heavenly Father, help me to understand how to best prepare to serve You faithfully and trust You fully as I step into what You are calling me to do. Thank You for sending Your beloved Son to save me and Your Holy Spirit to guide me. Amen.

FEBRUARY 2
GROUND HOG DAY

Seeing Shadows
BY SHERRI GALLAGHER

Ecclesiastes 3:1-11

There is a time for everything, and a season for every activity under the heavens: a time to be born and a time to die, a time to plant and a time to uproot, a time to kill and a time to heal, a time to tear down and a time to build, a time to weep and a time to laugh, a *time to mourn and a time to dance....A time to be silent and a time to speak, a time to love and a time to hate, a time for war and a time for peace.... He has made everything beautiful in its time.*

The aging process has you firmly in its grasp if you never get the urge to throw a snowball. **Doug Larson**

I must admit I never could keep the whole Punxsutawney Phil thing straight. The claim that if he saw his shadow, we had 6 more weeks of winter didn't make sense. He would only see his shadow on a sunny day so that would mean a thaw, not more snow, right? So how did the whole thing get started? Wikipedia claims Ground Hog Day has its roots in Celtic superstition. If hibernating animals cast a shadow on Feb 2, the winter would last for 6 more weeks. Otherwise, spring would come early. Early farmers had to know when to plant. Plant too early and a frost would kill the young plants. Plant too late and rain might ruin the harvest. It was critical to look for every sign possible or starvation would be the result.

For everything there is a season. Understanding that season is difficult for humans whether it is farming or just living life. Ecclesiastes 3:1 tells us there is a time for every matter under heaven. It is right and it is good. In our lifetime we will laugh and we will cry. The laughter will be all the sweeter for having experienced the tears. There is a time to speak out, when we see injustice or cruelty, and a time to be silent and be the good friend who is there and just listens. When life seems too cruel to bear, sometimes we just need to remember there is a season and this too will pass away.

Action:
Look out at the snow and the frozen gardens, think about the bulbs at work deep beneath the surface and the color they will provide in just a few short weeks.

Prayer:
Lord, thank You for the seasons of joy and for being there to comfort us in seasons of sorrow. Amen.

FEBRUARY 3

A Call to My Father
BY MYRA BIERNAT WELLS

James 1:2-3

Consider it pure joy, my brothers and sisters, whenever you face trials of many kinds, because you know that the testing of your faith produces perseverance.

As the rain pelts my car, I sit in the parking lot fingering my cell phone. Inside, the waterworks are flowing just as violently. Hysterically I cry, feeling fortunate no one can see me. My entire body shakes, still I cradle the phone tightly. I want so much to call my father, to ask him what he would do in this situation, to hear his voice reassuring me that all would be right eventually, most importantly, to bathe myself in his love.

Reclining in my car's seat with the wind howling through the trees, I realize this isn't the first time I've wanted the comfort of my father's arms. No matter your age, there are always times you just want to talk with your daddy because he's the only one who will understand. But I can't call him.

When I was a teenager, my father left for work, came back a few moments later feeling ill and was dead within ten minutes. I was the only one home and emotionally ill-equipped to handle all that happened that day. Could I have helped him more? If I had called the paramedics sooner, would he still be alive?

After my dad's passing and when dealing with life's squalls, the words I've never wanted to hear is "consider it pure joy..." I want comfort, love, understanding – for the pain to go away. Joy seems so far away in the trenches of heartbreak.

I don't know why this world contains such grief and anguish, except it does leave us longing for heaven. Little could console me after my father's death or during other trials in my life. And, hard as I try, I doubt I'm not much comfort during a friend's loss.

But there is Someone who is the Great Comforter. God loves me fiercely. He will never leave me - a Father whose love is true, pure and never-ending. And during those times when nothing can comfort us, He wraps us in His love and reminds us that this world is not all there is. He has not left us as orphans.

Action:
Memorize Deuteronomy 31:8, "It is the Lord that goes before you. He will be with you; He will not leave you or forsake you. Do not fear or be dismayed." Make that a consistent reminder of God's presence – even when faced with life's crushing troubles.

Prayer:
Dear Jesus, when I face with tough trials, I know exactly who to turn to – You! Let me feel Your peace during the storm. Wrap me in Your Arms; show Me Your Love. Amen.

FEBRUARY 4

Talk to the Trees
BY SHERRI GALLAGHER

Hebrews 10:24-25

And let us consider how we may spur one another on toward love and good deeds, not giving up meeting together, as some are in the habit of doing, but encouraging one another—and all the more as you see the Day approaching.

When a man takes one step toward God, God takes more steps toward that man than there are sands in the world of time.
David Benton, *The Work of the Chariot*

The first line in an article in *USA Today* caught my attention. "One in five people find their spiritual energy in trees and mountains." The article went on to explain how most people do not attend any one congregation or denomination, opting for the freedom to mix and match beliefs.

Many of us have experienced situations at church that "turn us off" - the people we judge as hypocritical, the sermon that offends our political beliefs, or hits too close to home, the feeling that attending services has become a "chore" and an obligation. It's so much easier to take a Sunday morning and sip hot chocolate and relax instead of rushing to get out the door.

When I am out in the woods, I feel God so close, like He is giving me a gift of joy. When I was younger and church was forbidden by my parents, time alone in the forest gave me spiritual strength.

However, God has an even better plan. In Matthew 18:19-20 we are told, "For where two or three come together in my name, there am I with them." Feeling the strength, energy and love that flow around us at services buoys us up and carries us through the following week better than a walk in the forest or a couch potato session.

Action:
The next time you think it would be "easier" to skip going to services, recall a time it gave you joy.

Prayer:
Lord, give us the strength to take that step toward You. Amen.

FEBRUARY 5

Head Games
BY SHERRI GALLAGHER

1 Peter 2:12-17

The true measure of a man is how he treats you when others are not looking.
Alessandra Torre

I read a magazine article written by a young man. He talked about waiting to reply to a text so the young woman would worry and wonder, becoming totally focused on him. His theory was supported by a study on rats. If they got a reward every time they pressed a lever, they did not press the lever as often as a rat that couldn't be guaranteed of a reward and would anxiously hit the lever more often. The young man was using this method, equating delaying texting back to delaying the reward for the rat. All I thought was he deserved to marry the rat because a smart girl would walk away from a game player like him.

Jesus would never play head-games like this. We can be certain of God's love. Whether we are right or wrong, smart or not, God does not withhold His love and He does not expect us to withhold our love from each other. In 1 Peter 2:17 we are told, "show proper respect to everyone" whether they are someone begging on the street, in a position of power, or the person which makes your heart beat faster. If you love someone, you don't want them worried or upset. You want to protect them and smooth the path before their feet. You have respect for their feelings.

Action:
Text or send a card with a positive message to someone you love for no reason other than you love them.

Prayer:
Heavenly Father, guide me to show people that I respect them and will treat them with dignity and love. Amen.

FEBRUARY 6

My Voice
BY MYRA BIERNAT WELLS

John 10:27

My sheep listen to my voice; I know them and they follow me.

Surrounded by dogs, he stood desperately trying to locate mine so I could take her home. This amazing dog sitter harbors the dogs in his house rather than in kennels, also giving them free run of his considerable backyard. He is in high demand and takes only about ten canines at a time. As the pack of dogs swirled around his feet vying for attention, in desperation, he called me over to help.

I merely said one word, "Lily." Immediately my black German Shepherd jerked her head up, removed herself from the pack, jumped over the gate delineating the "dog" side of the house from the "people" side, climbed over the owner's living room couch to sit motionless at my side. It was graceful, majestic and sweet all at the same time. No obstacles were going to prevent her from joining me.

It set my mind to wonder: I was created to pursue God; I was created to know God – to be satisfied in Him and Him alone, to worship Him and Him alone. But even as a believer, do I leave my pack and run to God the way Lily ran to me? Am I so content with the swirling demands of my schedule, my relationships, my activities I'd fail to hear my Master's voice? Would I leave everything behind to run to the true source of my satisfaction and hope?

One tiny word and Lily ran to me without hesitation or regret. John 10:27 says, "My sheep listen to my voice; I know them and they follow me."

God turned a beautiful display of loyalty into a valuable lesson. Lily left the cluster of the other dogs because she heard my voice. She recognized me as her Master, knew she belonged to me and longed to be by my side. Like her, I must turn away from anything that muddles my faith and place my trust in Jesus Christ. Just as Lily separated herself, we are called to set ourselves apart and the only way we can live that kind of life is by spending time at His side.

Today, may you feel the incomparable peace of your Master's voice.

Action:
Who or what are you trusting in today? Are you ready to show your loyalty to God by running to Him; by finding contentment just being by His side? Spend some time today in thought and prayer carrying the answers to these questions honestly to God.

FEBRUARY 7

Intercepted
BY BETH DUMEY

Galatians 5:7-8

You were running a good race. Who cut in on you and kept you from obeying the truth? That kind of persuasion does not come from the one who calls you.

My day can be humming along just fine—until an aggressive driver wedges himself into my lane. Or, an e-mail from a colleague at work precipitates dark clouds. Or, an unexpected run-in with a frenemy—yes, even a church frenemy—sets my mind reeling.

Internally I ask: "Why, God, did You let this person hijack my peace of mind this day?" But of course, God didn't necessarily send him or her across my path. Maybe He did, if there was a purpose to the interaction. Or, maybe the messy sinfulness of life just intruded. What's more important is my response. How easily can I process this interception and then release it? Occasionally, I can be a bit obsessive and let my mood dampen an entire day. At times, nothing can break the spell short of a good night's sleep.

But as Paul indicates in Galatians 5:7-8, how I let others influence me—for better or worse—is up to my own discernment. Often, particularly when other Christians are involved, I tend to yield too much influence, even drowning out God's own voice or maybe not discerning it above the others. Instead, I need to seek God's wisdom and lay these "interceptions" at His feet. Perhaps my obedience to God in prayer can transform my darkened emotions and reclaim my sense of peace.

Action:
Think about an interception that you experienced this week. How did you respond? Identify how you can recognize an interception and take it immediately to God.

Prayer:
Lord, I pray that my greatest influence is You and that Your voice is stronger than any other around me. Amen.

FEBRUARY 8

It's the Thought
BY SHERRI GALLAGHER

Luke 6:37-42

The spirit in which a thing is given determines that in which the debt is acknowledged; it's the intention, not the face value of the gift, that's weighed.
Seneca

My mother called, "I sent you a package. You should be getting it soon; I wanted you to know I was thinking of you and Valentine's Day."

The box arrived and I opened it with trepidation. Mom hasn't quite gotten the knack of gift giving. At the ripe old age of eighty, I don't expect her to change. Inside was a package of Halloween candy, a box of Thanksgiving cookies, and a cookie jar without a top. Nope, Mom hadn't changed.

I had two choices; be disappointed and superior as I judged her offerings or accept Mom had been thinking of me.

I disposed of the items and carefully formulated my thank you call. The words didn't sound sincere, so I stopped and looked through my Bible. There it was in Luke. That big old log stuck in my eye. Mom had sent warm thoughts from her heart. At fifty plus, I could count on Mom to care about my feelings. That was the real gift to treasure. The words of thanks came easily from my heart. I picked up the telephone to call her. I also said a prayer of thanks that I still had a mom to call.

Action:
Call someone who thinks of you often and tell them, "Thank you."

Prayer:
Thank You, Father, for all the people who care. Amen.

FEBRUARY 9

While I Was Gone
BY MYRA BIERNAT WELLS

I Thessalonians 5:16-18

Rejoice always, pray continually, give thanks in all circumstances;
for this is God's will for you in Christ Jesus.

I sighed as I opened my front door, returning from a vacation that was more a marathon than recreation. There was no rhythm to my time away, just rush, rush, rush. Ran from one activity to the next trying to see it all, do it all, visit as many people as possible.

My holiday brought back early childhood memories of family car trips. At evening's end we searched the "vacancy" signs in front of motels. We were greatly disappointed when we found a decent one, but the "no vacancy" sign out front was lit.

That memory came wafting back because while I was gone, my soul felt empty. I had hung out a "no vacancy" sign. For nine days, activities pervaded every waking moment with little time spent in sacred communion with God. While I did pray every night before sleeping, that isn't really enough, is it? We need more to deeply fellowship with our Creator.

Ironically, while I wasn't seeking God, I was overcome with joy because I strongly felt Him close by. That's because He lives in us, so His love permeates all we do. He was right beside me all the while. All I needed to do was acknowledge His presence.1 Thessalonians 5:17 says simply, "pray without ceasing." Imagining that meant being down on my knees with my hands folded together, I never thought unceasing prayer was possible. How does God expect us to pray every moment of every day? That question haunted me until I experienced these overbooked days when the truth slammed into me. Our lives should be one giant prayer to God.

I'm not saying to forget about those private extended times alone with God. We most certainly need those. But by acknowledging God's presence in every aspect of our lives, we will experience His sacred love in everything we do.

Those nine vacant days were a wake-up call. My time away taught me I want my life to be more Him, less me...to spend my days acknowledging Him.

Action:
Today, as you do your errands, go to work, clean your house, cook your dinner... invite God along. Talk to Him. Acknowledge His presence.

Prayer:
Dear Lord, forgive me for compartmentalizing my faith. I want all my life, all of it, to be an act of worship. One wholly holy life. In Jesus' name. Amen.

FEBRUARY 10

New Sight
BY BETH DUMEY

Acts 9:18

Immediately, something like scales fell from Saul's eyes, and he could see again.

I was wearing my treasured plaid blazer with suede patches flanking both elbows and one shoulder. Although it was nearly 20 years old, the jacket remained a classic. I bought it on sale, so excited to find such quality at a discount price.

I wore it off and on over the years. It was only this time, after a few unguarded glances, that I realized what others saw. The jacket was missing a suede patch on one shoulder. In my enthusiasm over the cut, the grey fibers, the creamy suede, I missed a key detail. It was irregular. In 20 years, I never saw it the way others did.

I wonder how many other details I've missed due to an idealized view. In Acts 9:18, Paul's (Saul's) sight is permanently altered. "Something like scales fell from Saul's eyes." With his conversion, his vision is renewed. No doubt he saw the Pharisees, the intellectual but hard-hearted, with clarity he was missing before. He may have wondered, as I did with my jacket, why he missed something so obvious.

Similarly, whenever I go through a season of spiritual growth, I later realize I can see much better. A new awareness or insight becomes clearer. Sometimes I begin to understand a perplexing comment made years earlier. Other times, I simply feel a peace about a lingering situation that would have staggered me previously. My internal lens refocuses, and I can see the reality—and all its glorious flaws—before me.

Action:
How is your spiritual sight? What might you be missing that is right before you?

Prayer:
Father, help me see as You see, with clarity, insight, and Christ-infused vision. Amen.

FEBRUARY 11

The Coffee Card
BY SHERRI GALLAGHER

Matthew 6:19-21

Do not store up for yourselves treasures on earth, where moths and vermin destroy, and where thieves break in and steal. But store up for yourselves treasures in heaven, where moths and vermin do not destroy, and where thieves do not break in and steal.
For where your treasure is, there your heart will be also.

And so my fellow Americans: ask not what your country can do for you – ask what you can do for your country. My fellow citizens of the world: ask not what America can do for you, but what together we can do for the freedom of man.
John F. Kennedy

I love Caribou Coffee. My biggest treat is to buy a cup with cinnamon syrup, or at Christmas time an eggnog latte. My family knows I often walk around without enough money in my pocket to buy that cup of joe. It's my way of preventing unnecessary spending and holding to a budget. At Christmas they give me a gift card to Caribou that I treasure.

Last Christmas, Caribou ran a special. If a customer bought a pound of coffee and donated it to the troops, Caribou would match it and ship it overseas. I didn't have the cash, but I did have my gift card, so I bought a pound and well wiped out my chance of having coffee for the rest of the year.

My son saw me do it and he wanted to know why. When I think of those young men and women doing without so much to protect me and my freedom, giving up a cup of coffee is a small price to send them a thank you. That card could easily be lost or misplaced, but the warmth from knowing I gave a cold soldier a hot cup of coffee can never be taken away.

Action:
What small treat can you send to our troops?
Prayer:
God, take care of soldiers everywhere. Amen.

FEBRUARY 12
LINCOLN'S BIRTHDAY

The Strength of Weakness
BY BETH DUMEY

2 Corinthians 12:9

My grace is sufficient for you for my strength is made perfect in weakness.

Imagine losing your mother at the age of nine, experiencing the death of a loved one in your mid-twenties, acquiring debt from a failed retail enterprise, losing several elections despite obvious leadership skills, having your proposal of marriage declined, and later working through another broken engagement before finally marrying.

Add to this a bout of depression. The death of a son. And several more lost elections.

Most of us can project how a life like this is going to end. Yet most of us would be wrong. Despite a jagged trail of obstacles, setbacks, and seemingly endless failures, Abraham Lincoln was elected the 16th President of the United States. He led the country through a civil war that marked the end of slavery. His legacy, and reputed character, has influenced generations.

His ultimate success is even more stunning because of his resiliency. He didn't hide his weaknesses; he rose above them. He continued moving forward. He became a better man, not a bitter man. All the while, God was whittling his character into a person capable of representing a nation divided and bringing it back together again.

When I study the life of Abraham Lincoln, I am humbled. My life, in contrast, seems severely uneventful. I don't believe I could respond with the tenaciousness and fortitude that Lincoln did if I encountered the same series of hardships. Even lesser tragedies have staggered me. Of course, just as in Lincoln's life, God is not done with me yet.

Regardless of what has happened in your life, remember Abraham Lincoln. The best was always yet to come.

Action:
Several Biblical figures—Joseph, David, Paul—just to name a few had to develop a character of resiliency. Study their lives and how God used them despite (perhaps because of) their weaknesses.

Prayer:
Father, instill in us Your godly strength to persevere through life's trials and triumphs. Amen.

FEBRUARY 13

Super Bowl Sunday: Whose side are you on?
BY MYRA BIERNAT WELLS

1 Corinthians 15:26, 54

The last enemy to be destroyed is death.
When the perishable has been clothed with the imperishable, and the mortal with immortality, then the saying that is written will come true: "Death has been swallowed up in victory."

Football is a lot like life – it requires perseverance, self-denial, hard work, dedication and a respect for authority. **Vince Lombardi**

The excitement of the big game is in the air. This time of year, people start sporting their favorite team's jersey, there's heightened chatter in the news about the most appropriate match up and the grocery store's supply of chips and dip, chicken wings and hot dogs vanishes quickly.

The taste of imminent victory is contagious. Why? We were created for victory! The greatest victory on this earth was played out in the resurrection, when Christ escaped the power of death, of Satan, once and for all.

As Super Bowl Sunday approaches, its smell of victory echoes what we have been created for: to stand beside Christ victorious over sin and death because of His sacrifice on the cross.

Football fans love a victory so much that even when all appears lost, they will never give up hope, praying for a miracle often until the very end. Just like a team losing by three touchdowns, when we look back on Jesus' final moments, all appeared lost. Christ was dying on a cross, many of his fans deserting Him. They gave up hope, never expecting a miracle.

But that's precisely what happened: Jesus was raised up and, in that moment, He defeated our final enemy: *The last enemy to be destroyed is death...death is swallowed up in victory.* 1 Corinthians 15:26, 54 (EVS)

The choice to be winners or losers, victorious or defeated, is ours. Every choice we make, every thought we think and word we say score points for God or not. Let us live our lives on this earth in such a way that Christ's victory is flourishing in us. Our reward won't be the Lombardi Trophy, but something infinitely more precious – a smile on our Savior's face.

Action:
Read Galatians 5 and take score of which team has been winning lately. Come up with a game plan that will help you defeat your sin nature more effectively.
Prayer:
Father God, I am flat-out amazed You loved me enough to send Your Son to die for me on the cross. Help me to live my life victoriously by never letting go of You. In Jesus' name. Amen.

FEBRUARY 14
ST. VALENTINE'S DAY

Love, Love, Love
BY SHERRI GALLAGHER

1 John 4:7-21

To love and be loved is to feel the sun from both sides.
David Viscott, *How to Live with Another Person*

According to Wikipedia, the story of a Pope named Valentine who healed his jailer's daughter of blindness, sent her the first valentine, and secretly married young couples against an emperor's decree is a myth. St. Valentine's Day is strictly a commercial holiday.

That is depressing at first, until you turn it around. People enjoy having a day to tell a special someone "I love you" so much that they made up Valentine's Day. Commercial cards were first developed for tongue tied suitors, but they made saying "I love you" so easy that it turned into a burgeoning industry. Did you know teachers receive the most valentines of anyone?

In Pakistan and Saudi Arabia, it is illegal to give Valentines cards, teddy bears, or anything red on February 14th because it is considered a Christian holiday. This has given rise to a huge black market of red roses. Even when it is illegal, people want to show that they love, and having a special day on the calendar is a great reminder.

Romans 4 tells us God is love and those who abide in love abide in God, and God abides in them. So, take time to tell your family you love and appreciate them. Tell hardworking teachers they are appreciated with a valentine from your child and one from you. Whether you buy a card or make it from fabric scraps, the person receiving it is going to get a smile and feel the warmth of love because of you.

Action:

Tuck a valentine someplace unexpected, like a briefcase or lunch box, for someone you love.

Prayer:

Thank You for a day made specifically to say, "I love you." Amen.

FEBRUARY 15

Every Parent's Nightmare - The Shooting at NIU
BY SHERRI GALLAGHER

1 Thessalonians 5:1-11

We do our children no favor by keeping them near, coddling them, or showing them off to visitors. Not that a nursemaid does not sometimes spoil them. But the greatest favor we can do our children is to give visible example of love and esteem to our spouse. As they grow up, they may then look forward to maturity so they too can find such love.
Eucharista Ward, *Match For Mary Bennet*

"Mom, I'm okay. There was a shooting on campus. Can you get hold of Dad? I need to find my friends." My son is a student at NIU. He got himself to safety and then thought of others; his parents and his friends.

In the face of danger, he stayed calm, cool, and collected, or as Paul said, "awake and sober." He moved to safety so others didn't have to be in danger to rescue him. He warned others, protecting them from danger. He comforted the frightened and stunned. He stayed on campus until late that night, helping those struggling to cope.

Paul talks about Christians not being of darkness but children of light. That means stepping outside of ourselves and serving others, especially when we'd like to crawl under the covers and hide. Our place is shining His light in moments of darkness so other may find the light, too.

Action:

Lord, help me reach out even when I am afraid.

Prayer:

Be with us as we shine Your light in the dark and dangerous world. Amen.

FEBRUARY 16

Too Late - The Shooting at NIU
BY SHERRI GALLAGHER

1 Thessalonians 5:1-11

Try as hard as we may for perfection, the net result of our labors is an amazing variety of imperfectness. We are surprised at our own versatility in being able to fail in so many different ways. **Samuel McChord Crothers**

On February 14, 2008 a man opened fire on an innocent group of students at Northern Illinois University. Eight officers arrived within two minutes of the first shot being fired but five innocent lives had already ended. The stress for those officers was extreme because they knew it could happen again and there was nothing more they could do to prevent it. Their concern for the students is tangible, they take their responsibilities seriously. As the parent of a student at NIU there is a level of fear every Valentine's Day that someone will repeat this vile act. Life must go on and we go through our day-to-day activities even as we remember the past. Paul gives us strength through his words in 1Thessalonians 5. He tells us to put on the breastplate of faith and love and the helmet of salvation and directs us to encourage one another.

The one thing I did take away from that awful day was the realization I must make time to tell my family members "I love you." I think about those who might have to pick up and complete the projects I could leave undone and try to make each item my best work ever.

Action:
Do each project with the focus of making it your best work, whether it is doing dishes or learning a new skill.

Prayer:
Lord, give me the strength to always do my best. Amen.

FEBRUARY 17

Walk in the Other Man's Shoes - The Shooting at NIU
BY SHERRI GALLAGHER

Psalm 123:3

Have mercy on us, LORD, have mercy on us, for we have endured no end of contempt.

I have always found that mercy bears richer fruits than strict justice.
Abraham Lincoln

In the days following the shooting at NIU the internet news ran pictures of the shooter's father and his house. My son took one look and asked, "How could they do that to him? He lost his son, too."

The man was in tears in the pictures, but he was looked upon with contempt by the people around him. The public greedily looking for pictures of the "monster's" family. His son had murdered; therefore, the father had no right to grieve. If we are to recover, then we must look at this man and recognize he was also a victim.

The words of this psalm could have been his. Did we offer him hatred or love to heal him and us? Contempt is self-serving. It destroys us and those around us.

Action:
Who have I judged as beneath my notice? Take the time to buy a sandwich for a homeless person.

Prayer:
God, for the sake of my own well-being help me to never feel contempt for others. Amen.

FEBRUARY 18

Facebook - The Shooting at NIU
BY SHERRI GALLAGHER

Psalm 123:4

We have endured no end of ridicule from the arrogant, of contempt from the proud.

Any fool can criticize, condemn, and complain - and most fools do.
Christopher Hampton

Generally, "Face-book" is not a place to find Christian actions, but very little was normal the third week in February 2008. A group of people had decided the shooting at NIU was the deserved wrath of God and were going to the final memorial service to promote that opinion. The students responded in one of the most Christian grassroots efforts I have seen. They had no contact with the protesters; they simply held white tarps in front of the signs to protect those attending the memorial service from the contempt of the proud.

These children set the example we can all follow. They exemplified the light and the hope Christ gave us. They had been touched by a great trial, and yet they responded with love and consideration for others.

Action:
The next time someone scowls at you, smile, and offer a friendly nod.

Prayer:
God, Thank You for people showing us the way of peace and love. Amen.

FEBRUARY 19

Forward Together Forward - The Shooting at NIU
BY SHERRI GALLAGHER

Judges 4:1-7

First it is necessary to stand on your own two feet. But the minute a man finds himself in that position, the next thing he should do is reach out his arms.
Kristin Hunter, *O* magazine

My son walked out the door, returning to NIU. Classes would start the following day. The message was "forward together forward," NIU called out to the surrounding communities, for help. The goal was to have a counselor in every class.

She sent and summoned Barak son of Abinoam from Kedesh in Naphtali and said to him, 'The Lord the God of Israel commands you, Go take position at Mount Tabor, bringing ten thousand from the tribe of Naphtali and the tribe of Zebulun,' Judges 4:6. Deborah called Israel to war. The tribes of Zebulun and Naphtali responded. Just as Barak answered Deborah many answered NIU. They came to serve willingly and without question. Many were stepping out of their normal roles. One normally counseled cancer patients, another came with her therapy dog. They could have turned away. They could have found an excuse. The passages around this one tells us many failed to answer Deborah, but just as God's strength was with Barak, it was also with the counselors at NIU. They came and served.

Action:
What have you done today to serve your community?
Prayer:
Lord, please give a hug to all those willing to serve others. Amen.

FEBRUARY 20

Romance
BY MYRA BIERNAT WELLS

Philemon 1:7

Your love has given me great joy and encouragement, because you, brother, have refreshed the hearts of the Lord's people.

My husband felt his days of romance ended at "I do." He felt that somehow coming home every night after work was enough. "I said I loved you at the altar and it is still in effect until I tell you otherwise." For some reason, he subscribed to the notion he no longer needed to stir up feelings of romance, of clinging to, of pursuing his wife the way he did when we dated.

How different his attitude is from God's. God gets it. He spends His days writing love letters to us. The big question is: do we see them? Do we notice the times God leans over the edge of heaven and sends down a bit of romance to interrupt our routine?

Oh, how often I miss them! He sent one to me the other day, but I didn't understand the sentimentality until about a week later.

My car has sensors in the tires to let the driver know if they are properly inflated. Mine weren't. Before leaving for church, I tried, with no success, to use the car's portable fancy air compressor that plugged into the 12V auxiliary jack. In the church parking lot after service, I attempted once again to turn off the warning message by putting more air in one of the tires. As I stood there, the little compressor chugging away, an Australian man came up to me asking if I needed help. He even offered to change my tire for me.

It was only days later I realized God knew a precious child of His was in desperate need of assistance, so He orchestrated events so a kind soul *from halfway around the world* crossed my path at just the right moment. And I'm left wondering if that thoughtful gentleman even realized he was God's love note to me.

If we live with expectancy that God will make His presence known in our lives, we begin to see Him and His love throughout our days. Signs of His presence can brighten even the darkest moments when you open your eyes to them. All we need to do is be receptive and attentive. Hearing God's voice and sensing His presence is not difficult, but how much we gain from it. Paying attention to His love gives us countless opportunities to rejoice in Him, to feel His love pursing us.

Action:
Today, pay attention to the ways God is romancing you. Don't miss His love notes.

Prayer:
Jesus, thank You for never giving up on me. Thank You for continuing to pursue my heart, even when I miss You romancing me time and again. Help me pay closer attention. Amen.

FEBRUARY 21

Unmistakable Calls
BY BETH DUMEY

Isaiah 45:2

I will go before thee and make the crooked places straight.

One of the teaching pastors at my church left recently to plant a new church in Tennessee. In his final weeks, he spoke about receiving an unmistakable call from God to move to another city and establish a matrix of Christian communities. The central hub will be the church he envisioned. He spoke with enthusiasm and confidence.

How exciting! I thought. If I visit that city, I will definitely stop in, was my next thought. Do only pastors get this clear, direct, succinct affirmation from God about their next steps? I thought finally, feeling more than a little left out.

I have received what I believe is guidance from the Lord. I felt nudged to attend my current church. I felt God showing me an open door when I bought my home. A recent vacation seemed to drop from His hands to mine. Still, it seems when it comes to really big things, I am left trying to find my way in the dark. Despite much prayer, I have not received a prompting or affirmation toward a job or a major life decision. Sometimes these decisions are made by default, as competing options disappear. Perhaps this *is* the hand of God. Maybe my guidance is woven into scripture, awaiting my discovery. Still, it would be awesome to hear that "unmistakable call," whatever that is.

Often, I must remind myself that God speaks to each of us uniquely. Perhaps such direct marching orders would overwhelm me. Perhaps God knows that as a sensitive soul, a gentle beckoning is better for me. Isaiah 45:2 tells us, "I will go before thee and make the crooked places straight." When I am tempted to envy others' clear directions from the Lord, I need to keep in mind that maybe the guidance I really need is in scripture: His promise to lead the way—wherever I go—and make my path straight.

Action:

Think of how you receive guidance from the Lord. Consider how you have responded to this guidance.

Prayer:

Lord, help me to hear You, whether through a roar or a whisper. Help me to understand how You are directing my paths. Amen.

FEBRUARY 22
WASHINGTON'S BIRTHDAY

I Cannot Tell a Lie
BY SHERRI GALLAGHER

Ephesians 4:15

Instead, speaking the truth in love, we will grow to become in every respect the mature body of him who is the head, that is, Christ.

False words are not only evil in themselves, but they infect the soul with evil.
Plato

The legend goes that when George Washington was a boy, he chopped down a cherry tree. When his father asked who had wielded the axe to this food source, George claimed he could not tell a lie, he had done it. As far as anyone can tell, this is a made-up story. The initial version was first reported by biographer

Parson Weems, who interviewed people who knew Washington as a child. That story was widely reprinted in McGuffey Readers - a schoolbook. Adults wanted children to learn a moral lesson from great men in history. By the 1890's historians insisted on scientific research methods for validation and without evidence Weem's report was dubbed fiction.

More and more I seem to be running into people who value lying as a skill. Some people say they need to lie to get ahead in their career. If they were honest and said they hadn't ever done that kind of work before, they would never be given the task leading to a promotion. But wouldn't their chances have been just as good talking about a project with similar goals or requirements? If they do get the assignment and find they don't have the skill set to accomplish it, won't that destroy their career? Others say they lie to save someone's feelings. When a wife asks a husband if her rear-end looks big in a specific dress, he lies to spare her feelings. He could just say something to the effect that he thinks she looks beautiful no matter what she is wearing. It is the truth.

Our directive from God is clear, "you shall not bear false witness." There is no exception. Let us as Christians accept this and present the truth. That does not mean we have to be cruel in our comments. We can look with love for the answer that is the truth, and that does not cut the heart of those who hear our words.

Action:

Watch for the times you would tell a lie and find a way to effect the same result with the truth.

Prayer:

God, help me to guard my tongue against spewing evil and lies. Guide me in finding the truth that adds value and not hurt. Amen.

FEBRUARY 23

The Apology
BY SHERRI GALLAGHER

Matthew 5:43-48

Always forgive your enemies; nothing annoys them so much. **Oscar Wilde**

I thought fiction was the only place the adversary came to learn the error of their ways and apologize to those they have hurt. When a couple spread lies and took eight years of my work, my anger would well up and interfere with my prayers for them. I knew they expected a baby and I offered daily prayers for all to go well and for God to help me to forgive them.

Three years later I received an e-mail from the woman. My hand hovered over the delete key. Gathering my courage, I opened it to read, "I am writing to say I am sorry and that I handled things badly with you. I hope you can find it in your heart to forgive me and if we bump into each other to say hello." Maybe fiction does follow life.

Offering prayers for someone who has hurt you is hard. The pain returns, repeatedly, and you must ask for help in forgiving them over and over again, but it is worth it. I never expected these people to care about the pain they caused. I could have let bitterness eat at me. Instead I prayed for them and was able to recognize when God opened wonderful new avenues for me. I was the richer for the experience.

Action:

Who has hurt you? Pray for them and for the ability to forgive.

Prayer:

Thank You for the strength to forgive those we consider enemies. Amen.

FEBRUARY 24

Guest Book
BY MYRA BIERNAT WELLS

Philippians 4:4

Rejoice in the Lord, always. I will say it again, Rejoice!

In the shadow of Rocky Mountain National Park, my husband and I have found a very special bed and breakfast. Nestled in the majestic Rockies, we enjoy its luxury so much we return year after year. It is a unique place of solitude and rest, requiring you to unplug and unwind: no phones, no television, no radio.

One of my favorite evening activities is to snuggle close to the fireplace and read the entries written in the guest books. Most are variations around the same them: "Love the room. Treasured the breathtaking views. Saw deer come down from the mountains and roam through the ground's wooded areas. Enjoyed being lulled to sleep by the song of the river."

In 1 Chronicles 29:15, we learn we are foreigners and strangers in this land. We are simply visitors here on earth. So, the words we speak are essentially the entries we write in the guestbook of life.

Ouch! Some of the words I've used were crabby, uncaring, downright vile. Are my hard-hearted attitudes all people see in me? I hope not.

Philippians 4:4 tells us to rejoice always. What entries am I writing with my attitudes, actions and words for the world to see?

As I think about the words I write in my guestbook, I want people to know how much I savored each day. I want them to know I thanked God with joy for my husband, my life, for the blessings showering my path. My desire is for them to see, even during the darkest moments, that I prefer the route God has me on over another one. I want them to see the hope that comes from Jesus Christ.

Most of all, I want people to know I so enjoyed my time here walking with the Lord that I wanted to share it with anyone and everyone. What about you?

Action:

What would you *like* to be leaving in your guestbook of life? Write it down. Now, live this day as if you were a walking, talking letter from God to everyone you encounter.

Prayer:

Father, shape me so I will be a love letter to the world. Help my life be a thank you message to You. Let me write words that are an invitation to celebrate the life I have in You. In Jesus' name. Amen.

FEBRUARY 25

Seek the Giver, Not the Gifts
BY JUDY KNOX

John 6:26-33

Seek ye first the kingdom of God and His righteousness, and all of these things shall be added unto you. **Matthew 6:33**

"What sign can you perform then that we may see it and believe you?" the people asked. Just the day before, with only five loaves of bread and two fish Jesus had fed 5,000 men plus women and children, and there were twelve baskets full of leftovers. These were the same people who had been there and had seen that miracle. They had made the effort to follow him to the other side of the sea. Now they were asking Him for a sign.

Just in case He didn't get what they had in mind, they reminded him (hint, hint) that Moses gave their fathers manna to eat in the desert! Actually, as Jesus pointed out, they even got that wrong. It was God, not Moses, who had provided the manna. These people were not truly looking for a sign to prove the spiritual reality of who Jesus was. They were hoping for another free meal! Jesus told them that He was the true bread come down from heaven, but they were only able to understand bread in the physical sense and could not perceive the truth of what He was telling them.

Although we may be amazed at their short-sightedness, before being too critical of these people we need to examine our own hearts. When we go before God, are we seeking provision for our daily needs, or a relationship with the God who provides all our needs? Are we looking for healing, or quality time with the

God who heals all our diseases? Are we trying to find peace in our lives, or do we desire to know the Prince of Peace?

Because God is so good and blesses His children so abundantly, it is easy to let our prayer life slip into a grocery list of wants and wishes instead of letting it be an opportunity to enjoy the presence of God. The Creator of the universe is inviting us to enjoy intimate fellowship with Him, and we are focusing our attention on what we want Him to do for us. Just like the people in Jesus' day, we get caught up in following after the gifts instead of the Giver. And yet He who does not look upon the outward appearance but looks upon our heart assures us that when we seek His Kingdom and His righteousness, all our other needs will be added.

Action:
Spend some time praising and thanking God without asking Him for anything.

Prayer:
Lord, help me to know You better, and to focus on You instead of on the things I want You to do for me. Amen.

FEBRUARY 26

Smile
BY SHERRI GALLAGHER

Matthew 6:22-23, 1 Corinthians 4:11-16

I have witnessed the softening of the hardest of hearts by a simple smile.
Goldie Hawn

I was having "one of those days." My computer had frozen up, my car steered itself into the ditch whenever I went over 45, the house needed a roof, two of the three dogs were sick, we had a freezing rain falling and I was coming down with a cold. To top it off, I was missing a key ingredient for the dinner I'd already started to cook.

I headed for the store, grumbling and annoyed at the blaring horns of those behind my slow-moving vehicle. As I walked in, a stranger smiled at me and I smiled back. I felt a little better and shared my smile with a tired mom trying to navigate the aisles with a cranky toddler. I watched her tense muscles relax and a smile light her face. By the time I got home, all the little problems I faced seemed manageable.

Smile at people, especially someone who looks upset, even if you don't feel like smiling.
Prayer:
God, give me the strength to joyfully handle my day to day problems. Amen.

FEBRUARY 27

The Power of Prayer
BY MYRA BIERNAT WELLS

Psalm 5:3

*In the morning, O LORD, you hear my voice; in the morning,
I lay my requests before you and wait in expectation.*

How often have you prayed for something, but in the back of your mind you doubted God would answer? You desired an answer from God, but thought, "He's too busy." Or "He doesn't care!" Even the disciple Peter had friends with the same issue.

In Biblical times, King Herod murdered many Christians and put even more in prison. James, the brother of John, was put to death and Peter was thrown into prison awaiting trial. His friends gathered to pray for Peter's release. While they were still praying, they heard a knock at the door.

Rhoda, a servant girl, approached the door and asked, "Who is it?" To which Peter, now freed, answered, "It's Peter." Recognizing Peter's voice, Rhoda was so excited God had answered their prayers she failed to open the door, leaving Peter standing outside while she ran to tell the group who was there! Her excitement was met with their utter disbelief. Could it be even though they prayed for Peter's release, they hadn't really expected God's answer?

Sometimes we pray about a situation and miss God's glory standing outside the door because of our unbelief and low expectations! We make our God too small. We fail to take into account all the miracles in the Bible. And we often discount the times God has intervened on our behalf in the past. When we do that, our prayer life becomes stale instead of expectant.

Sometimes I fear we lower our spiritual expectations to match the experiences of people we know, rather than hold onto the promises in the Bible. We look around and see what occurs with other believers and that's where we set the bar. We lead mediocre lives, forfeiting the abundant life Jesus came to give us. By covering our prayers with belief, our lives can be off the scale of excitement as we live God's great adventure for us.

Action:

When you pray to God today, expect God to answer. Use your quiet time with God to raise your expectations in order to experience the vibrant, full life Jesus came to give.

Prayer:

Dear Lord, forgive me for praying and not expecting You to answer. I lay my prayer requests before You today specifically for _____ _____. (Fill this spot with your request.) I wait in eager expectation for how You will use my prayer to draw me closer to You. Amen.

FEBRUARY 28

Images
BY BETH DUMEY

Genesis 1:27

So God created man in his own image, in the image of God he created them; male and female he created them.

I have never been photogenic. Images of me range from cringe-worthy to tolerable. Every several years, after dozens of pictures are captured, I may come across one that I am pleased to have. Whatever it is that transfers from flesh to photo, I lack. Perhaps scientists will discover a DNA strand for photogenic capabilities, and I can be their experimental test subject.

Photos matter less though than actual images. In Genesis 1:27, scripture tells us we are created in the image of God. An image is a reproduction or imitation, and this concerns me more than any photograph. If I am, in fact, a reproduction of God, I wonder how this comes across to those I interact with daily. Do they walk away thinking they have just viewed a snapshot of His holiness, His grace, His kindness? Are they drawn toward and embracing of the image they see before them? More often than not, I don't think so.

It is a staggering responsibility to represent our God in the flesh, and scripture tells us we do. Yet, so often this "image" is marred, fuzzy, out-of-focus. I seldom think of this image-bearing as I am shouting at the driver in the next lane who drifts too close or when I am straining to talk about myself when I should be listening to my friend. Almost daily, I cringe at the image others are seeing. Yet, I straighten my posture, take a deep breath, and assure myself that He who is working in me (Philippians 1:6) is enhancing this image (airbrushing my rough spots!) every moment.

FEBRUARY 29 - LEAP YEAR

What Can You Do in a Day?
BY SHERRI GALLAGHER

Genesis 1

A single day is enough to make us a little larger. **Paul Klee**

2 Peter 3:8 tells us a day is as a thousand years, and a thousand years is as a day unto the Lord. Read the entire first chapter of Genesis and think about what the Lord accomplished in six days. So, what can we accomplish in a day? We can't create day and night, but we could plant a garden. We can't create dry land out of the watery depths, but we can visit a shut-in.

It is not exactly every four years we get an extra day. According to the Gregorian Calendar, if the year is evenly divisible by four but not divisible by 100, unless it is divisible by 400, then it is a leap year. That is because it takes the earth 365.242199 days to circle the sun. Our normal year is 365 days leaving an itsy-bitsy bit under one-quarter of a day in our flight around the sun unaccounted for. If we didn't add a day about every four years, we would be off almost a month in as little as 100 years. Eventually, if we didn't have leap day, we would be celebrating the 4th of July in the middle of winter and Christmas in the summer.

Think about it, we have a whole extra day this year. So, what will you do with this treasure? Take a break and take your children or grandchildren to Shedd Aquarium? How about the observatory? Make it a spa day for yourself? Get a start on that novel you always wanted to write? How about spending the day doing a Bible study?

Action:
Look up Bible passages with the word "day" in them and reflect on how they are the same and how they are different.
Prayer:
Lord, thank You for the gift of this extra day. Guide my studies as I use part of it to know You better. Amen.

MARCH 1

Access Denied
BY JUDY KNOX

Psalm 139:1-6, 23-24

Behold, I stand at the door and knock. If anyone hears My voice and opens the door, I will come in to him and dine with him, and he with Me. **Revelation 3:20**

After struggling for months with my lumbering dinosaur of a computer, I finally realized it was time to order a new one. When it arrived, I was delighted with the quick and easy set-up, faster speed, improved graphics, and all the new software.

Of course, as time went on, I downloaded more programs, tweaked the settings, and added features. I didn't notice at first that my Internet connection was becoming a little sluggish or that my word processing program was taking longer and longer to open. Eventually, though, it became obvious that something wasn't working right.

I called the manufacturer's help line for assistance. The technician said that some of my software programs were conflicting with one another, which could be fixed very easily. He would be happy to help me. All I had to do was give him permission to access my computer remotely from half-way around the planet and all would soon be well.

I found the prospect of letting an unseen, far-off stranger mess around in my computer too frightening to contemplate, so I declined his offer of help and continued to put up with the less-than-perfect performance. However, the time came when I knew the procedure could no longer be put off, so I called once again and submitted to the process. I was fascinated as I watched the little arrow moving around on my screen, clicking on various icons and navigating mysterious menu screens. Soon the computer was acting like its old (new) self. Afterwards, I wondered why I had been so reluctant to accept the help that had been there for me all along.

Sometimes when I find myself out of sorts, I try to make adjustments. I tweak and fiddle with my conflicting thoughts and emotions until my performance becomes sluggish just like a computer whose programs are conflicting with one another. The solution of course is to submit to the Master Technician, the one who created me. If I will allow Him access to my heart, He will come in and fix whatever needs fixing and make the needed adjustments. He really wants to help me, but just like the computer technician He can only do the work if I give Him access. He will not come barging in.

MARCH 2

What Did He Write?
BY SHERRI GALLAGHER

John 8:6
But Jesus bent down and started to write on the ground with His finger.

Friends, Romans countrymen, lend me your ears; I come to bury Caesar, not to praise him. The evil that men do live after them; the good is oft interred with their bones...
William Shakespeare, *Julius Caesar*

So, what did Jesus write?

The Pharisees were all puffed up, they were ready to catch Jesus and trumpet His failure to all around. If He called to stone her, they would point to His words about forgiveness. If Jesus let her go, they would tell everyone He violated God's laws. Much like Brutus' funeral speech in Julius Caesar, they were so sure that they were right and could take Jesus down with their impassioned speech. This time they had Him. Much like Antony, Jesus didn't engage the Pharisees directly. As a matter of fact, it sounds like He pretty much ignored them and bent to write in the dirt. But did He ignore them?

Did He write the names of the Pharisees and their sins? Some people point to Jeremiah 17:13 "Those who depart from Me shall be written in the earth, because they have forsaken the Lord, the fountain of living waters," and propose this is how Jesus fulfilled Jeremiah's prophecy.

Did He write one of the two new commandments, "love your neighbor as yourself"? Mark 12:31

Did He write a single word, not just to the woman but for all who were present, "forgiven"?

We don't know what He wrote. What we do know is He didn't argue eloquently, He didn't argue at all. He asked a simple question directing each person there to look first to their own shortcomings before pointing fingers at others.
Action:
Ready to argue? Take a deep breath and decide if that is what Jesus would do.

MARCH 3

Lektor of My Bodyguard
BY SHERRI GALLAGHER

1 Peter 2:23-25

When they hurled their insults at him, he did not retaliate; when he suffered, he made no threats. Instead, he entrusted himself to him who judges justly. "He himself bore our sins" in his body on the cross, so that we might die to sins and live for righteousness; "by his wounds you have been healed." For "you were like sheep going astray," but now you have returned to the Shepherd and Overseer of your souls.

But I say to you, Do not resist an evildoer. But if anyone strikes you on the right cheek, turn the other also. **Matthew 5:39**

Lektor is a large German Shepherd. He's ninety-eight pounds of solid muscle and has inch long razor-sharp teeth. Were someone to attack me, he would rush to my defense without me giving a single command.

When I was new to sport tracking, an expert took my dog's leash to "show me how it was done." Lektor went to work as best he knew how. When he made a mistake this "expert" started kicking my dog as hard as he could. Lektor could have seriously injured this man. Instead he offered a "sit" and then a "down" and then came to the "heel" position at my side while I directed the man to stop and return my dog.

When someone says or acts in a manner that hurts me, I try and follow the direction set out in 1 Peter 2:23 and accept the hurt and trust God to make it right, just as my dog accepted the hurt and trusted me to correct the situation.

Action:
The next time someone hurts your feelings, resist the urge to "bite back." Walk away.

Prayer:
Lord, give me the strength to follow in a path that does not feel natural but is right. Amen.

MARCH 4

Enough, Already!
BY MYRA BIERNAT WELLS

Jeremiah 1:5

Before I made you in your mother's womb, I knew you, before you were born, I set you apart.

Today was picture day and I hate having my picture taken. I don't like the reflection in the mirror. Plus, this was no ordinary picture; it was about to be flashed up on the Internet for millions to see. I didn't want my image to cause thousands of computer screens all over the world to crack. All I remember that morning was crying out, "I'm not pretty enough!"

Do you ever tell yourself you're not enough – not smart enough, not talented enough, not rich enough, not fit enough? Join the club! One of the enemy's favorite weapons is to keep us in bondage to feelings of inferiority, insecurity and inadequacy. But in God's eyes, we are enough. We've been equipped by Him and empowered by the Holy Spirit to do everything God calls us to do!

We are so valuable to Him He sent His only Son to restore our brokenness. Why then are we so quick to pull out the tape measure and gauge ourselves not in how God feels about us, but against other's opinions of us? Why do we sit in silent defeat by these unfair comparisons which further shatter our self-confidence?

Those in Christ's early lineage certainly could have felt this way. Think they were all stellar individuals? Well, think again! Jacob was a liar. Moses was a stutterer. Gideon was a coward, David, an adulterer. Rahab was a prostitute while Esther was an orphan. And yet God used each one of them to impact His kingdom. Taking in how God worked in their lives, I often wonder why I don't allow God to set me free from my "not good enough" pity party.

The truth is we are God's unique creations and He loves us just as we are. He uses us when we are obedient to Him. He gives us power to conquer our doubt when we rely on Him. When God looks at you, He sees Jesus. And Jesus is always good enough.

Action:
Do you believe that God loves you unconditionally? Read Psalm 139. Record its truths and how that changes your perspective. Once you gathered its wisdom, write Psalm 139 in your own words.

Prayer:

Heavenly Father, I know I am deeply loved, completely forgiven and fully pleasing to You. Help me overcome my insecurities. Let me see Your love as all I need and no longer measure myself against others. With you, I am more than enough. Amen.

MARCH 5

Blessings
BY MYRA BIERNAT WELLS

Hebrews 11:6

And without faith it is impossible to please God, because anyone who comes to him must believe that he exists and that he rewards those who earnestly seek him.

When we lose one blessing, another is often most unexpectedly given in its place.
C.S. Lewis

Will Rogers sought advice from his friend, Eddie Cantor. Will wanted to make some important changes in his act but was worried about the danger of such changes, explaining he wasn't sure if they would work. Eddie Cantor's response was, "Why not go out on a limb? That's where the fruit is!" The same is true of faith.

Faith is the ability to trust what we cannot see. Faith is willing to take risks, embrace the unseen and step away from what appears safe. As long we stay preoccupied with our fear, our faith is impotent. We can mentally agree we serve a powerful God who loves us and has a great plan for our life, but that belief is worthless until it settles in our hearts and changes the way we live.

Authentic faith naturally produces action but can be hindered unless we abandon ourselves entirely to it. Sometimes I am quick to believe the lie that God is angry with me and as a result, will not bless my life or meet my needs. The truth is God is willing and waiting to pour out His favor and blessings on a life of faith. Hebrews tells us faith always honors God and God always honors faith. "Without faith no one can please God. Anyone who comes to God must believe that he is real and that he rewards those who truly want to find him." (Hebrews 11:6, NCV).

But faith also means anything that makes us cry out to God can be counted as a blessing. Why? When we are desperate and in pain, we have no answers, with darkness closing in, we cry out to God and He comes! Not because we have earned His presence or His mercy, but because we cried out with a tiny seed of faith, as His children, knowing He is not only able but that He will joyfully comfort us.

Read Psalm 86:15, "But you, Lord, are a compassionate and gracious God, slow to anger, abounding in love and faithfulness." Make a list of the words in this verse that describe God. What do these words tell you about God's willingness to bless your life? What is the first step of faith you need to take today? Are you willing to take it right now?

Prayer:
Father, I come to You today with a faith that seems so small. I want to believe You, Lord. I want to walk by faith, knowing that You will keep every promise You have ever made. Help my unbelief, Lord. In Jesus' name. Amen.

MARCH 6

Grammy
BY SHERRI GALLAGHER

Acts 9: 36-43

The charity that hastens to proclaim its good deeds, ceases to be charity, and is only pride and ostentation. **William Hutton**

Whenever I was too sick to go to school I would go to Grammy's house. She always had fun games I could play in bed and she made homemade alphabet soup and sat with me for hours helping to spell words in spoonfuls of broth. Grammy always had baskets of food to take to church members that needed assistance or just a little something to brighten their day.

Grammy developed dementia and by the time my teen years rolled around confusion filled her days. As I helped to take care of her, I remembered all those she had helped and wondered where they had gone. No one dropped by with a basket of goodies or a friendly ear to listen to her rambling stories.

I was angry at first, but thanks to her state of mind, Grammy didn't notice she was abandoned. Now I understand Grammy was like Dorcas. She didn't need thanks; she had the joy of helping others without the need for acknowledgement.

Action:
Take the time to visit someone who hasn't been to church in a while.

Prayer:
Thank You, Lord, for those who love and help for the joy of helping. Amen.

MARCH 7

Bracketology
BY MYRA BIERNAT WELLS

Matthew 16:26

What good will it be for a man if he gains the whole world, yet forfeits his soul?

According to Yahoo! Sports Facts, fans spend on average 75 minutes filling out their brackets – nearly twice as long as a regulation college basketball game. Ordinarily, men spend nearly 30 minutes more on their bracket selections than women. To show loyalty to their teams, 1 in 7 fans have called in sick to watch March Madness at home. Of those who didn't call in sick, 7% get in trouble for watching the NCAA tournament at work. Even the President gets into the act as his brackets are even posted on the White House's webpage.

While toiling over one's brackets might win you the office pool, we daily face even bigger decisions. Remaining loyal to God requires thousands of daily choices: "Do I stay faithful to God or do I do this thing – knowing it is outside His will for me? Does living the Golden Rule make me godly, or one of the world's biggest suckers?"

As Christians, we run against the world's standards. Maybe our bracket will require us to switch jobs so we can spend more time with our family. Our bracket could mean walking away from a dating relationship because she isn't a Christian. Or a bracket could require overcoming your hurt to reach out to the one who wounded you in an effort towards reconciliation. Perhaps winning your bracket involves giving money and resources to those who have none.

Pastor Charles Stanley often quotes the front porch advice he heard from his father, George Washington Stanley, "Obey God and leave all the consequences to Him." When facing the brackets of my life, I want to score a three-pointer by using the strength God gives me and show folks that I will not waver from His truth.

Just as it isn't easy to pick the NCAA college basketball champion, it isn't always easy to muster the courage of trusting in God despite difficult decisions. But if you do, God will give you the power to succeed. He will reward your integrity and your loyalty to Him.

And someday, you'll stand before Him and hear those precious words, "Well done, good and faithful servant."

Action:
Think about the places in your life where God is asking you to do something difficult. Praise Him in advance for giving you the courage to stay faithful to Him.

MARCH 8

Furrowed Brow
BY BETH DUMEY

Isaiah 11:3

And he will delight in the fear of the Lord.

Is he looking at me? On the wall in my office, a calendar displaying a picture of a Pug staring intently greets me each day. Dark eyes, a sad gaze, and a perpetually furrowed brow and forehead make me feel a bit sorry for him. Is he sad? Worried? Lonely? That vertical line of wrinkles on his forehead is the clincher, a visible sign of apprehension.

I can relate. My go-to emotion is anxiety. When things are going well, I question: how long can this last? When they take a nosedive, I question: will it be like this forever? When an unexpected gift comes my way, well, let's just say I'm waiting for the backlash.

Of course, there's a reality to this cycle. Good times don't last forever. Struggles will eventually follow abundance. It is the consequence of life after Eden. Yet, I would like to think some untainted, cortisol-free moments—let's even say days—of bliss are possible.

That's why Isaiah 11:3 intrigues me, as it connects delight with fear. Is it possible to be delighted by fear? The fear indicated in the passage is the fear of the Lord. This is not a troubling apprehension or a trembling uneasiness. Rather this "fear" signals a depth of respect for the power and sovereignty of our Lord. This fear is recognition of His awesomeness, His care, and His wisdom in directing our lives. Perhaps if both Pug and I can loosen our grip on worldly fears and grab on to Godly fear, our foreheads would be much smoother.

Action:
Think about how often you feel anxious. What is the source of your anxiety? How can you minimize it?

Prayer:
Lord, though none of us live anxiety-free lives, help us put our concerns in Your hands and see them from Your perspective. Help us remember that our only true "fear" is awe of You. Amen.

MARCH 9

Good Intentions
BY SHERRI GALLAGHER

John 8:31-32

To the Jews who had believed him, Jesus said, 'If you hold to my teaching, you are really my disciples. Then you will know the truth, and the truth will set you free.'

A false witness will not go unpunished, and a liar will be destroyed. **Proverbs 19:9**

Mary lounged in my kitchen chair and sipped a cup of steaming coffee.

"It happened again," she said. "Andrew was supposed to go play with Jimmy but was so engrossed in his Legos he didn't want to go. I called Jimmy's mother and lied about Andrew being sick. Two hours later, Andrew was crushed that he couldn't go to Jimmy's house and play. What am I going to do?" she asked. "I never know how to handle these situations."

My friend spoke a lie to protect two children from disappointment, but both ended up unhappy. She could have built her child's character by insisting he keep his word. Instead she taught him deceit is acceptable. Will lying come easier to him when questioned about drugs or smoking?

There was a reason for "You shall not bear false witness." It hurts both the speaker and the receiver. God asks us for the truth in our dealings with Him and each other. This lie let down the children and frustrated the mother.

Action:
The next time you are going to tell a "white lie," find a truthful answer that is positive or keep silent.

Prayer:
Lord, help us to speak the truth in kind and loving words when it seems easier to lie. Amen.

MARCH 10

How Not to Pray
BY MYRA BIERNAT WELLS

Psalm 119: 57-58

You are my portion, LORD; I have promised to obey your words. I have sought your face with all my heart; be gracious to me according to your promise.

"Come on, God. I'm drowning here. Please help me out of this situation. I really need a miracle from you." This was absurd. No matter how devout the words sounded, my prayer was still more of a demand – like God was a celestial genie who was supposed to satisfy my every want. Instead of leaning into God, anxious to hear the whispered will of my Lord, I got out the list of my desires, my demands, my will.

When we approach God with our shopping cart filled only with our desires, we miss what matters most: the pursuit of God and all the blessings found only in Him. We blur the line between *our* plans and His path for us. So often our requests drown out what the Spirit whispers to us. Instead of letting that conversation grow longer, we crowd out the reality that any pain we feel in this life is miniscule compared with the glory we will share with God.

Our prayers should prioritize God above all else. David, the psalmist, called out to God in the midst of his trouble, but also recognized that God was enough. *"I cry to you, O Lord;" I say, "You are my refuge, my portion in the land of the living."* (Psalm 142:5).

In these unpredictable times, in the moments when the pain of life overcomes my hope, God is the only place I should go. I should run to Him and bury myself in His strength and protection. But too often my prayers only recognize my problems and not the reasons why I run to God in the first place – His love, His wisdom, His sovereignty.

When my prayers become only what I want, I get too caught up in God's presents – and forget entirely about living in His presence. Because the only place I can find not only refuge from my circumstances, but contentment in the midst of them, is in the center of my surrender to His will.

To deepen your relationship with God, set aside your list of wants and go to God with a heart of worship and adoration. Get lost in His presence. Remember His mercy. Relish the grace He has shown to you. Love Him; seek Him. But above all else choose His will.

Action:
Read, then ponder this passage: "As the deer pants for streams of water, so my soul pants for you, O God. My soul thirsts for God, for the living God" (Psalm 42:1-2). Then spend some time in prayer asking the Lord to increase your thirst for Him.

Prayer:
Dear God, please forgive me when all I do is come to You with my wishes, my desires. Let me seek Your heart first because You are all I need. Thank You for helping me surrender my needs to Your will. Amen.

MARCH 11

What Prayer Can Do
BY BETH DUMEY

Proverbs 19:21

Many are the plans in a man's heart, but it is the Lord's purpose that prevails.

I imagined strolling through Powell's Bookstore on my way to the Armory. Once there, I would engage in spiritually compelling conversation with new friends. The conference I desired to go to was intended to help us explore new facets of our "story." All I had to do was save for the registration fee, arrange a flight to Portland, and pray about the opportunity.

As I prayed, I received no affirmation. The early deadline neared, and I waited until the end of the month to decide. I prayed that if I was meant to go, I would cross paths with at least one other person going. Because I attend a large church, this was not a stretch of faith. The conference leader spoke at an event only a few months earlier and drew thousands of eager listeners. Still, no one stepped forward.

I unpacked my disappointment and focused on what else God might do with that weekend. Soon, I was invited to another retreat, in neighboring Door County, Wisconsin. Scanning the brochure, I imagined a restful ride through the country. Upon arrival, I would journal alongside Lake Michigan as multi-hued leaves dropped from branches high above me. This time, I prayed that God would provide a ride and a friend to join me for the journey. I felt a surge of energy as I prayed, as if, yes, this was the one.

I received my answer on the day of the registration deadline. A ride was available and a friend opted to go. Despite an over-packed car and a few missed turns, we arrived in the evening as the fragrance of wood-burning fireplaces misted like incense through the camp. We gathered for storytelling and, even after a few hours, I knew I was exactly where I was supposed to be.

By Sunday, fully filled, bonded with others in our group, and rejoicing in the eloquence of the majestic cedar trees, I was grateful that God knew what I needed more than I did. Instead of airport lines and retail allure, I rested in the purity of nature, the bounty of community, and the untethered serenity of His presence.

Action:

Think about how tightly you hold on to your plans. Is there any area that God is asking you to release?

Prayer:

Lord, I know Your plans are greater than my own. Help me to yield to all that You have for me. Amen.

MARCH 12

Neighbors
BY SHERRI GALLAGHER

1 Thessalonians 5:1-11

In youth we learn; in age we understand. **Marie Ebner von Eschenbach**

We bought a house for our son on a quiet street with elderly neighbors. They were very concerned to find out college boys would be living next door. They expected late night, loud, drunken parties.

What they got were three quiet young men that voluntarily shoveled walks, returned garbage cans from the curb, and were always available for heavy lifting. There was the occasional football game in the backyard and grilling was a way of life, but the neighbors were thrilled to have them next door.

One neighbor even got out his snow blower and cleared all the driveways, saving the boys from the distraction of clearing snow during Finals Week.

1 Thessalonians 5:6 is about being alert to the return of Christ, but it is also a good reminder about the needs of others. Avoid being in a self-centered pleasure-seeking state. Instead, look for Christ's return and occupy yourself with how you can serve those around you.

Action:

Offer to help an elderly neighbor.

Prayer:

Lord, watch over the elderly and the young and open my eyes to their needs. Amen.

MARCH 13

God Sees You
BY MYRA BIERNAT WELLS

Genesis 16:13

"You are the God who sees me," for she said, "I have now seen the One who sees me."

People, even those closest to us, will let us down. They disappoint us. And so does God. Often, we expect God to fill all our wants and desires the way we think He should. When our wishes aren't met, we guard our hearts against future disappointments by lowering our expectations and trust. Make no mistake about it, though. God see us. God understands. He doesn't separate Himself from us.

Hagar was a servant owned by Abraham and Sarah. When God promised Abraham an heir, Sarah was well beyond child-bearing years, so Abraham slept with Hagar and soon an heir was conceived. That wasn't God's promise and Sarah became pregnant. A jealous Sarah banished Hagar and her son from their home. In the desert, out of hope and preparing to die, Hagar experienced God. We too can know the God who sees us.

In Jesus, we have a High Priest who understands everything we are going through. Whether that be a financial crisis, stern words from a boss or the death of a loved one. Hebrews 4:15 tells us: *We have a chief priest who is able to sympathize with our weaknesses. He was tempted in every way that we are, but he didn't sin.* The word sympathize comes from two Greek words, *smy* and *pathos*, meaning to suffer with. We are never alone in our suffering. Like Hagar, who experienced God firsthand in the midst of her exile in the desert, we can find God's glory in our darkness moment if we only keep our eyes open.

The God who wrote the story of your life doesn't just sit back and watch it play out. No, He is right beside you every step of the way. Jesus is the only one who adds warmth, victory and perseverance to our lives. Any low-lying storm hanging over us is banished by the light of His love for us. The God who created the birds in the sky and all that lives in the deep is with you every moment of the day.

We are always loved. We are always seen. God cares about our dreams, longing and every inch of our hearts because He *cares* about us. We can laugh in the face of hopelessness because we are held tightly in the arms of God.

Action:

Have you ever felt like God didn't care about you? Do you realize many people in the Bible felt the same way? Read Hebrews 13:5 – *I will never leave you; never will I forsake you.* Spend a few moments today contemplating the meaning of the word never.

Prayer:

Dear Father, I praise You that You are the God who sees me. You know everything I am going through, everything I've gone through and all the challenges in the future. Thank You for watching over me and always doing what is in my best interest. I love You, Lord. Amen.

MARCH 14

Pi Day
BY SHERRI GALLAGHER

1 Corinthians 13:12

For now, we see only a reflection as in a mirror; then we shall see face to face. Now I know in part; then I shall know fully, even as I am fully known.

How great is God - beyond understanding! The number of his years is past finding out.
Job 36:26

A friend posted on Facebook that she didn't understand all the hoopla about Pi Day, but then she was a word person not a math person. She would enjoy a piece of pie and skip the whole math nonsense.

What is Pi? It is the relationship of a circle to its diameter and no matter the size of the circle, Pi remains the same. Without Pi we would not have pie, or wheels, or tires, or arches or anything that uses a circle. Of course, we didn't even know about Pi when we found these objects so useful. We just accepted them and used them, and over time and with study our knowledge of them grew. But here is the thing, we still don't know Pi. It has been calculated out to 67,000 digits with no repeat pattern and no end in sight.

Our understanding of God is something like our understanding of Pi. We know He exists. We know following His words adds value to our lives. We accept His love and His sacrifice without really thinking about its impact on our lives. The more we study His word and act with love, faith, hope and charity the more we learn and understand, but there is always so much more to learn. Just like Pi, God is just there, and the amazing thing is there is always more to learn.

How cool is that?

Action:

Every time today you touch something that has a circle, like a steering wheel or a pan, think of how God has touched your life in a positive way.

Prayer:

Loving God who is with us always, thank You for the wonders of this world You have given to us. Amen.

MARCH 15

Friday Mornings
BY SHERRI GALLAGHER

Psalm 51:10-12

Create in me a pure heart, O God, and renew a steadfast spirit within me. Do not cast me from your presence or take your Holy Spirit from me. Restore to me the joy of your salvation and grant me a willing spirit, to sustain me.

Take rest; a field that has rested gives a bountiful crop. **Ovid**

I love Friday mornings. The dogs wake me when the sun has just turned the sky a pearl gray and my family still slumbers peacefully. I feed my canines and walk through my clean, silent house enjoying the fresh smells and neat organization. I brew a cup of tea and sit at my desk full of hope and new ideas. There isn't anything pressing and for just a few minutes I can focus on God without a distraction. I have time to ask him to do to me what I've done to my home. Clean, organize, focus and lead me in the steps to joy and salvation.

As the days of the week progress the house will get less organized and a lot dustier. There will be more distractions for me, things that must be done immediately to keep everything running smoothly and caring for others, things that draw me away from focusing on God and looking to Him for the guidance to sustain me. By Thursday I'll need to stop and scrub and polish and clean and then Friday will be there, and I will have time to ask God to cleanse and guide me once again.

Action:

No matter how busy the week becomes, find time to clear your mind and invite God's guidance.

Prayer:

Thank you, Lord, for forgiving our inattention. Lead us daily, making us clean and new and joyful at Your loving guidance. Amen.

MARCH 16

Lessons in Kindness
BY MYRA BIERNAT WELLS

John 13:34-35

A new command I give to you: Love one another. As I have loved you, so you must love one another. By this everyone will know that you are my disciples, if you love one another.

Even though I live a scant few miles from "The Happiest Place on Earth," in one of the most beautiful areas of the country, needy people are everywhere. They may not necessarily be the homeless on the roadside. They may be friends and coworkers, desperate for someone to care. They maybe acquaintances or folks we interact with throughout our day who are simply crying out for some compassion and understanding as they work through their pain.

More people come to Christ during a crisis than at any other time in their lives. Often redemption is found because someone took the time to listen and offer consoling words when the wounded cried out for someone to care.

As Christians, our eyes should be searching for those in pain around us. They walk by us every day, but most of the time we don't see them. Sometimes, I am too busy to notice the broken lambs the Good Shepherd sends my way. They become a frustrating distraction. Often, I'm so self-absorbed, it is tough to see the needs of another.

Hebrews 13:2 states, "Remember to welcome strangers, because some who have done this have welcomed angels without knowing it." How many angels have we missed because we were too busy? Or maybe the problem is simply that we don't care enough.

Throughout the Bible, Jesus confirms if we really love God, we will really love each other. We are never more like our heavenly Father than when we choose to weather the storms in another's life with kindness and love. Our compassion and empathy are directly related to the health of our personal relationship with Jesus Christ.

It is possible to be very religious and not care enough. Our mercy and tenderheartedness should not be limited. They should be searching for opportunities to spread God's love.

Action:
Galatians 5:14 states, "For the entire law is fulfilled in keeping this one command: 'Love your neighbor as yourself.'" How do you share the love you have for

yourself with others? During this next week, do something practical to show a neighbor the love of God. (Bring them food, mow their lawn, take them out for lunch, etc.)

Prayer:

Father, today I ask You to break my heart for what breaks Yours. Give me the eyes to see those around me in pain. Show me how to encourage them and love them with Your love. Fill my heart with Your compassion and give me strength to share it with others. In Jesus' name. Amen.

MARCH 17 - ST. PATRICK'S DAY

Banishing the Snakes
BY SHERRI GALLAGHER

Luke 10:1-20

I have given you authority to trample on snakes and scorpions and to overcome all the power of the enemy; nothing will harm you. **Luke 10:19**

Many people celebrate Saint Patrick's Day by eating boiled dinners and drinking large quantities of beer. It has become the day to celebrate all things Irish. The city of Chicago even dyes the river green. But who was this Saint Patrick?

Saint Patrick was an arch-apostle or archbishop who is credited with bringing Christianity to Ireland in the fifth century A.D. He was captured by Irish raiders when he was sixteen and was a slave for six years. During his captivity his faith grew and he prayed daily. After his escape he entered the church, was ordained, and returned as a missionary to Ireland. It was not an easy life. Patrick refused the gifts of kings and had no relatives in Ireland to protect him. He was beaten, robbed, and put in chains. Still he baptized thousands, converting wealthy women who became nuns in the face of family opposition and also converted the sons of kings. March 17th is the anniversary of his death. His birthday is not known.

Saint Patrick is credited with driving the snakes out of Ireland, but Ireland never had snakes. One suggestion is that "snakes" referred to the serpent symbolism of Druids. Saint Patrick converted the Druid followers to Christianity thus driving out their leaders or snakes.

So how should we celebrate Saint Patrick's Day? First and foremost, we should look at Luke chapter 10 where Jesus tells his disciples the harvest is plentiful but the laborers few. He sent appointees out ahead of Himself to where He planned and gave them power over the enemy. Their mission was to go and spread the good news. Saint Patrick came after Jesus, but he too spread the word of salvation, driving out paganism, self-centeredness, and idolatry. He converted the population of Ireland. So perhaps our goal should be toward evangelizing instead of drunken revelry.

Action:
Serve at a soup kitchen or homeless shelter today and share your joy in following Jesus.

Prayer:
Thank You, Lord, for the example of people like Saint Patrick for showing me the way. Help me to identify where I have let snakes enter my heart and then to trample them under foot. Amen.

MARCH 18

Thank You
BY SHERRI GALLAGHER

1 John 4:11

Dear friends, since God so loved us, we also ought to love one another.

If we have the opportunity to be generous with our hearts, ourselves, we have no idea of the depth and breadth of love's reach. **Margaret Cho**

I was having a bad day. My son had left for college and I missed him. There wasn't a glimmer of a consulting contract to be seen and the dogs were on a break. I'd finished writing my most recent novel and had the standard author's let down at saying goodbye to characters I'd enjoyed creating. Nothing was seriously wrong, I just felt useless and blue.

Then I collected the mail and found two envelopes with unfamiliar return addresses. Opening them, I found notes of encouragement from total strangers who had read something I had written months earlier. I wrote to serve others, not for praise or thanks or recognition. The true power in the words came from God; I was just an instrument for Him to use. Yet, in guiding me to serve others, He also guided others to minister to me when I needed it most.

Action:
Smile at someone, offer a kind word, reflect God's perfect care.

Prayer:
Lord, thank You for the gift to serve and in so doing be served in return. Amen.

MARCH 19

The Adventure
BY MYRA BIERNAT WELLS

Psalm 94:18-19

When I said, "My foot is slipping," your unfailing love, Lord, supported me.
When anxiety was great within me, your consolation brought me joy.

Our adventure was supposed to be fun. Traveling by car from Chicago to California, the goal was exploring as many sights as possible. I mean, isn't it exciting to say we saw the world's biggest ball of yarn or the world's largest rocking chair? As we rolled into our first overnight stop in Missouri, the fun abruptly ceased. The unpredictable January weather turned against us and a blizzard was closing in on tomorrow's route.

My husband suggested we hole up in our Missouri hotel until the storm passed, but I've never been a sitter. I want action; I want to feel like I'm moving forward. So, despite his misgivings, we packed up and headed right into Mother Nature's worst. Several hours, but only 50 miles later, I had to sheepishly admit my husband's plan was pretty good. Unfortunately, that was no longer an option – the only alternative was continuing on.

The greatest adventure in life is not conquering the weather. It isn't climbing the highest mountain or taking on sharks – or any of a dozen things thrill seekers do. The most breathtaking quest in life is the journey we take to God's heart. That's because with your faith firmly placed in Jesus, you become a child of the Heavenly Father. He loves you with the most stubborn love. His devotion is so strong; He will never leave your side. Paul told us we can never escape, never be separated from His love. Oh, yes, we can doubt it. We can ignore it, say it doesn't exist. We can question it. But the solid truth is we can never be separated from it—not if you are His!

Driving through the blinding snow, our feet, like the Psalmist's, were slipping. We succumbed to a heated argument in Chickasha, Oklahoma. Nearly out of gas and unable to pump it because the electricity was down, we finally prayed, laying down our fears and anxieties before the Lord. The anger lifted because His perfect love drove out the fear.

Before sleep overtook me that evening snuggled in my Texas hotel bed, I thanked God for the joy of His support, for His comfort, for the adventure of trusting in Him.

Take a moment to center your heart, soul, and mind on Christ right now. Worship Him. Praise Him. Pray that He will help you live the great adventure of your faith today.

Prayer:
Father, let me enter into the adventure of Your love. Thank You for loving me just as I am. Remove anything in my life preventing me from experiencing Your love today. Amen.

MARCH 20

Comfort
BY BETH DUMEY

Psalm 119:76

May your unfailing love be my comfort according to your promise to your servant.

Some people have comfort foods. I have comfort socks. The thick, they-must-wear-these-in-Canada type of socks lined with fleece inside and tightly woven wool on the outside. No parka or insulated coat makes me feel as warm as these socks. On a wintry day, nothing comforts more than a cup of hot chocolate and my Sherpa-lined socks. While they are likely designed for skiers or winter sports types, I am neither. I like to wear them indoors, as I settle into a challenging crossword puzzle.

Comfort often appears in unexpected places. That warm, taken-care-of feeling may surface in the car when the toll booth attendant informs you the driver speeding away has paid your fee. It might arise on a train, when your luggage is too heavy to hoist on to the center rack and a young man leaps out of his seat to perform the task. It might show up in a compliment from a stranger who has no agenda or motive, just kind words.

Christ, as the creator of comfort, knows how to comfort his children. He brings people, situations, and, yes, even well-made socks to us as reminders of His presence and provision. Sometimes He prompts us to act as the provider of His comfort. In a store, when the clerk needs a smiling face and a timely word of encouragement to pick her up. In an airport, when a traveler has too many bags and needs a hand to help to carry the load. Perhaps it is necessary in a restaurant, when the waiter has been on his feet for many hours and is aching for a break but gets a table of ten instead. How can we bring God's comfort to those around us?

Think about how Christ has comforted you recently. Did you recognize it at the time?

Prayer:
God of all comfort, thank You for caring about my needs and providing for them so graciously. Help me to be a conduit of Your comfort to others. Show me how You would like to use me in this way and prompt me to respond. Amen.

MARCH 21

You Have No Power
BY CATHY HARVEY

John 19:10

". . . Don't you realize I have power either to free you or to crucify you?"

The steps of power are often steps of sand. **Edward Counsel**, *Maxims*

The scene is the palace of the Roman governor, Pontius Pilate. Jesus had been arrested the night before in an olive grove by Judas' betrayal. It was meant to be. The Father knew. Jesus knew (Jn. 18:40). It was all part of a greater plan, an eternal redemptive plan.

Jewish officials had arrested Jesus. A detachment of soldiers with its commander bound him and brought him first to Annas, then to the high priest, Caiaphas. A night of questioning, illegal proceedings, unbelieving hearts. A rooster crowed and it was early morning.

Pilate goes out to the courtyard to learn the charges against Jesus. He tells the Jewish crowd to judge Jesus by their law, but they declare they have no right to execute anyone. Pilate returns to the palace, summons Jesus and has a compelling conversation with him. Back to the people Pilate claims he has no charges. Under pressure from the now crescendoeing crowd, he releases Barabbas, has Jesus flogged, and the soldiers make a mockery of him with a crown of thorns and purple robe. Pilate presents Jesus to the crowd and the Bible records, "As soon as the chief priests and officials saw him, they shouted, 'Crucify! Crucify!'" (Jn. 19:6)

Once again Pilate claims he has no basis for a charge, but when the Jews insist Jesus must die because he claimed to be the Son of God, the Bible says Pilate was afraid, "even more afraid" (John 19:8). Back in the palace he again questions Jesus. He demands, "Where do you come from?" But now, Jesus is silent. It's been a long sleepless night, shuffled from one palace to another, tortured, questioned, always the questions. There is nothing left to say. He preached openly. He did what

His Father sent him to do. He is silent, and Pilate is now the tortured one—tortured in conscience. He is afraid, unsure of the situation, perhaps curious about this man, and under pressure to do something.

When Jesus refuses to speak to him, Pilate pulls his trump card. Rising to his full height, mustering an air of confidence and Roman righteousness he asks, "Don't you realize I have power--?" Ahh, the power card! "…power to free you or crucify you?" And Jesus finally speaks. He pulls his trump card, "You would have no power over me if it were not given to you from above" (Jn. 19:11).

There was a plan in place from eternity past to eternity future, and Pilate was not in charge of it. Nor were the religious leaders, nor were the Jews, nor the Romans, or you, or me. We have no power, but that which comes from above. So, we need only look up. Look up! For our redemption is coming—and has come! Easter is just around the corner.

Action:

Consider the element of control of your life. Are you in the seat of power, or have you relinquished your heart to the One who is in control from eternity past until eternity future? Make the choice today, if you haven't already, to turn your life over to the crucified One who died for you!

Prayer:

Heavenly Father, help me hand the power for my life over to you, so I may be redeemed by the blood of Christ. Jesus, be the Lord in all areas of my life. In Your holy name I pray. Amen.

MARCH 22

First Come, First Served
BY SHERRI GALLAGHER

James 2:1-5

Prejudice is the child of ignorance. **Hazlitt**

I stepped into the restaurant and joined the line to get on the waiting list. The lady in front of me was obviously a foreigner. She was oddly dressed and her English was broken. Both of us were women alone. The hostess took my name and I took a seat. Things moved smoothly and people were called pretty much in the order they had arrived, except my name was called before the foreign lady. The hostess picked up a menu and started to march off, expecting me to follow. She was quite annoyed when I didn't. I asked about the other lady and was told, "We'll set up a table for her soon." The waitress looked at me like I had three heads when I said I could wait my turn. They seated the other lady and I was expecting a very long wait for antagonizing the hostess. Give the girl credit; five minutes later, I was led to a table and able to take my meal.

I suppose I could have gone merrily along, and the other lady wouldn't have known she had been discriminated against, but God would have known and so would I.

Action:
Be watchful and make sure you are not unwittingly party to discrimination.

Prayer:
Please help me to be vigilant and recognize when others are not being treated fairly. Give me the strength to stand fast for what is right in the face of prejudice. Amen.

MARCH 23

Born Equal, Lord?
BY MAUREEN LANG

Matthew 20:12

'These who were hired last worked only one hour,' they said, 'and you have made them equal to us who have borne the burden of the work and the heat of the day.'

Our envy always lasts longer than the happiness of those we envy. **Heraclitus**

I like to take walks in my neighborhood. One morning I left my house bright and early and noticed two women down the street, well behind me. While I've never considered myself an especially competitive person, it crossed my mind that they were so far back they'd be behind me for my whole walk if we chose the same streets ahead.

It was barely a few minutes before they weren't behind me anymore—they passed me right by as if I were out for a leisurely stroll. I panted and grumbled to the Lord. "You give them blonde hair *and* long legs? We sure weren't born equal."

Our Declaration of Independence reminds us we're all created equal, but come on—are we *really* created equal? The Bible is full of messages that God loves us all equally, but it's hard to accept this when some are born just plain smarter, or more talented, or more beautiful or more, more, more…

But did you catch the important part? *We're equal in value to our Creator.* In the story from Matthew (20:1-16) those who worked longer hours grumbled over being paid the same amount as those who worked a much shorter day. But the Master wasn't looking at it the same way. He made a bargain with each and every worker and was looking at it from an obedience angle. All the workers did what they were hired to do and deserved to be paid.

Perhaps one of the lessons to be learned here is to thank God for the gifts He's given us and use them obediently. That probably means I won't be winning any foot races, but when I use the gifts I *have* been given…who knows what will be won?

Action:

Delight in the gifts God has given you and use one today!

Prayer:

Help me, Lord, to concentrate on the tasks You've assigned to me, and devote less time comparing myself to others. Amen.

MARCH 24

Playing by the Rules
BY SHERRI GALLAGHER

PSALM 19:7-10

The law of the LORD is perfect, refreshing the soul. The statutes of the LORD are trustworthy, making wise the simple. The precepts of the LORD are right, giving joy to the heart. The commands of the LORD are radiant, giving light to the eyes. The fear of the LORD is pure, enduring forever. The decrees of the LORD are firm, and all of them are righteous. They are more precious than gold, than much pure gold; they are sweeter than honey, than honey from the honeycomb.

Play by the rules but be ferocious. **Phil Knight** (founder of Nike)

Dogs like rules. If you want your dog to be happy, make rules and insist on them at all times. Either the dog can always get on the sofa or he can never get on the sofa. You set the rules. You tell him how to act and he is happy and comfortable following your guiding hand. You are his leader and lord. If he follows your rules, he doesn't have to fear consequences. The rules generate trust. Just remember, as his leader, you are responsible for your dog's safety. If he obeys the rules, you must protect him.

When I call my dog to the heel position, he looks up into my eyes and obeys my commands, shutting out the rest of the world. He can do that because I am responsible for keeping him safe. When I first got Lektor, 100 pounds of intensity and protection trained, he thought he always had to protect me. He thought he was in charge of making the rules. I took him for a walk and the neighbor's Rottweilers came out to challenge him. He was ready to charge forward and take on two beasts as big as he was, but I called him to heel. I could see him struggle with the decision and slowly obey. As we backed away, one of the Rottweilers tried to circle in and attack Lektor. I jumped between them and kicked and yelled at the dog driving it off. While I don't read minds, Lektor's expression was priceless. From that day forward, if I gave the heel command, no matter what was going on, Lektor obeyed.

The psalmist tells us in Psalm 19 the ordinances (rules) of the Lord are true and righteous. They bring rejoicing to the heart, enlightenment to the eyes, and they endure forever. They are more desirable than gold and sweeter than honey. When I do my very best to obey God's laws, even when it is scary or seems to be the exact opposite of what I want to do, life is easier and much more pleasant. I don't have to worry. God is in control and I can trust Him. Just like Lektor, I can relax and not be afraid. God is my protector.

Action:
Read the ten commandments every day this week (Exodus 20:2-17). In your prayer time look at your decisions and see if you applied God's rules.

Prayer:
Thank you, Lord God, for the rules that make my life simpler, safer, and happier. Help me to apply them in everything I do. Amen.

MARCH 25

Entirely
BY MYRA BIERNAT WELLS

Matthew 16:24-25

If anyone would come after Me, he must deny himself and take up his cross and follow Me. For whoever wants to save his life will lose it, but whoever loses his life for Me will find it.

Founded in 1776, the Mission at San Juan Capistrano was a Christian outreach to the area's indigenous people. While visiting, I sat in the peaceful courtyard, drowning out the traffic noise of modern civilization, easily lulled into imagining how pleasant life was when the mission was surrounded mostly by vineyards.

I envied the slower pace of earlier inhabitants. They didn't have to deal with an over-flowing email box, schedules so crowded an electronic device is needed keep it all straight or the frenetic speed of the crazy traffic on the interstate. I imagined them working lazily in the fields, enjoying nightly community dinners where laughter and music abounded, plus strolling through the garden drinking in its aromatic beauty while deep in prayer.

That feeling stayed with me all the way to the parking lot, but abruptly ended the minute I turned over the ignition in my car. I had to ask myself, "Who was I kidding?" These folks worked hard; their days were longer and filled with more drudgery and exertion than mine.

And yet, every Lord's Day, they stopped everything to worship at the Mission. They listened to Mission bells calling them in from the fields at night, gave up working on Sundays to partake of the Eucharist, spent years building the church – meaning they hauled stones sometimes by hand from over six miles away! Which started me wondering, do I merely tack Christ on to my busy life? Or do I give Him everything I am?

Their Christianity was not a half-in existence, nor should mine be today. Christianity is all-in, devoting your life to Him and Him alone. Making Jesus the Lord of your life requires dedicating all you do to God. Jesus warned his disciples, "If anyone would come after Me, he must deny himself and take up his cross and follow Me. For whoever wants to save his life will lose it, but whoever loses his life for Me will find it." Matthew 16:24-25.

As a Christian, He becomes *your* life. This is sometimes hard to determine in mine, given my unwillingness to find the time to daily study His word, prioritize solitude to be with Him and listen to His still small voice. I don't ever wish to make my relationship with Christ something I just check off my list and neither should you. Let Him have all of you.

Action:

Unplug all your electronics for a short period of time and rededicate your life to God.

Prayer:

Seek me out, Lord. Help me to give myself, my life entirely over to You. Amen.

MARCH 26

Effortlessly
BY BETH DUMEY

Romans 12:3

For by the grace given me I say to every one of you: Do not think of yourself more highly than you ought, but rather think of yourself with sober judgment, in accordance with the faith God has distributed to each of you.

When reading through magazines, I often come across reporters describing a celebrity as "effortlessly" beautiful or a fashion ensemble as "effortlessly" chic. This tends to register on my radar because very few things in life, if any, are effortless. Getting out of bed in the morning requires effort, driving to work, toiling at a job, taking a test; all elicit some degree of effort. That celebrity that is effortlessly beautiful? It is likely that tanning (real or spray), hours in the gym, and a sophisticated skin care regimen all went into this "effortless" look.

Which is why it seems so foolish to add "effortless" to any description. It implies the desire not only to set the subject above everyone else, but also to show this eliteness required absolutely no exertion.

This hyperbole is in stark contrast to Scripture, which is mired in truth. Paul reminds us in Romans 12:3 to maintain sober judgment, not thinking too highly or too lowly about ourselves. This sober judgment frees us to merely tell the truth, whether we are referring to our appearance, relationships, family life, accomplishments, or even faith. Of course, this truth extends to how we think of others as well. Instead of assuming others are blessed with areas of their life that are "effortless," we can take a sober view that informs us that nearly everything involves effort and commitment.

Action:

Think about this: Do you tend to exaggerate or underestimate areas of your life? Journal about why this may be.

Prayer:

Father, each of us wants to feel special. Help us to see ourselves, and others, through Your eyes and rest in Your approval. Amen.

MARCH 27

The Empty Cross
BY SHERRI GALLAGHER

I Corinthians 15:55-57

"Where, O death, is your victory? Where, O death, is your sting?"
The sting of death is sin, and the power of sin is the law. But thanks be to God!
He gives us the victory through our Lord Jesus Christ.

My father called religion "pabulum of the masses." If I was caught going to church, I would face a lengthy diatribe about the ignorance of blind faith. Christians were obviously too stupid and uneducated to know that the cross was an instrument of torture. It was his job to make sure I knew better than that.

A popular book recently brought my father's words back to mind and I wished I could tell him Christians don't worship a torture device. The empty cross on the altar is the reminder to us that God, through Jesus' sacrifice, has taken the worst and given us the power of victory over death. It is not an object of worship but a reminder of sacrifice.

Christians know the cruelty of what our Savior accepted for our sakes and have the intelligence to accept God's loving gift. Thinking we are too smart to accept God is not knowledge or intelligence, but an eternal death sentence. Faith in God's love is victory over torture and death.

Action:

Research atheists' arguments denying God's existence and then research how to answer them.

Prayer:

Thank You, Lord, for victory over death. Please open the eyes of those who do not understand and are blinded by self-worship and a dedication to reason. Amen.

MARCH 28

The Thief
BY MYRA BIERNAT WELLS

Psalm 33:21

In him our hearts rejoice, for we trust in his holy name.

Her words stung. Though sweetly spoken, their meaning was venomous. I was left thinking, "How could a close friend say such hurtful things about me? What had I done to deserve this?" Because of our tight relationship, she knew all the nerves to hit, so when the phone call finally ended, I was angry. Actually, I was beyond anger – I was incensed. But more importantly, I was deeply wounded.

One of my first thoughts was, "How am I ever going to get over this?" To be honest, a small pity party started there in my family room. Other painful experiences from my past welled up inside of me further shadowing what had happened today. Yet the more I talked to myself, the more bitterness began to take root; the louder a tiny voice warned me not to become a victim. This was not my first experience with a thief, a joy stealer, and it most certainly would be not my last. And that's when I flee to God, the one and only source of joy. He repairs what the thieves in our lives take away by saturating every circumstance with His presence.

I was tempted to simply write: When the thief comes, choose joy instead. But I know from experience life is sometimes so painful even the very thought of being joyful is beyond our grasp. And writing those words would seem shallow and foolish. Because what you are facing can be so distressing; especially when the ones causing us our anguish are close to us.

Despite the thief who tempted to steal my joy, I knew God is in control. And as His children, joy is ours to claim. Unfortunately, our search for joy generally takes us to all the wrong places: to complaining, to gossip, to wail in self-pity. There is only one right place, a personal relationship with God. With Him, we find shelter, comfort and security—the type no joy stealer can embezzle from us.

How about you? Are you looking for joy in the protection only God can give? Are you letting Him apply salve to the bitterness in your life?

Action:

Recognize God is the only source of real joy. Make a list of the people or circumstances that steal your joy. Pray for wisdom and discernment on the next steps for each item on your list.

Prayer:

Father, apply your comfort to all my wounds. Be near to me, ever so close. In every circumstance, especially the ones threatening my joy, let me choose You. Show me the steps to eliminate my life's joy stealers so I can rest in Your glorious presence. Amen.

MARCH 29

Discipline
BY BETH DUMEY

Acts 10:2

He and all his family were devout and God-fearing; he gave generously to those in need and prayed to God regularly.

A fitness and health guru advised lifting weights for eleven minutes every day. This was to be as a supplement to regular workouts to increase strength. With my three-times-a-week fitness routine already sapping my time and energy, I was reluctant to take on more. Yet, unlike the hour of daily workouts that some programs recommended, eleven minutes seemed within reach. So, I pulled my weights out of the back of my closet and started lifting. Sometimes my eleven minutes took place in the evening, sometimes in the morning. My schedule varied, but I got my eleven minutes done. Every day.

The guru was right. I felt stronger. My arms felt leaner. To fill in the eleven minutes, I added new moves and developed new muscles. While it shouldn't surprise me, the discipline of being consistent made my body better.

Discipline can sound harsh. After all, the word is used as a synonym for punishment. It has connotations of rigor and duty. Yet, I've found creating disciplines has positive reverberations in my life. Take spiritual disciplines. Unless I set up a routine to regularly pray, regularly read scripture, regularly meet with my small group, it rarely happens. The haphazard approach just doesn't have staying power. To instill those activities that will be a catalyst for spiritual growth requires some intentionality on my part. And intentionality usually includes a consistent schedule and follow-through. Though sometimes this feels like a heavy weight, more often than not it delivers the results I am seeking. And I grow stronger.

Action:

Review how you go about your spiritual disciplines. Do you need to re-schedule or re-commit to some that have lapsed? Determine how you can best implement these in your weekly schedule.

Prayer:

Lord, I desire to honor You with my time and energy. Help me to arrange my commitments so that I can devote myself to knowing You more. Help me to remove any obstacles that may prevent me from doing so. Amen.

MARCH 30

Searching a Swamp
BY SHERRI GALLAGHER

Ephesians 6:5-9

The secret of joy in work is contained in one work – excellence. To know how to do something well is to enjoy it. **Pearl Buck**

On a recent search I was given the task of searching a swamp, in the rain. The police officers that were to accompany me were not prepared for what we faced – grass taller than our heads and sharp as a razor, hidden logs that made each step treacherous, and vegetation that broke under foot plunging us into two feet of icy water. We shared our gear as much as possible and helped each other where we could.

It would have been easy to grumble. The area was dense, and no evidence indicated our subject had been anywhere near this location. However, watching my dog made everyone smile. His first step dropped him into a murky pool of water. He swam across and calmly showered us while wearing a canine grin. We followed him into a stand of cattails and were rewarded by his tail wagging when he returned with a beach ball he'd found. He plunged through the vegetation searching with a thoroughness that never waned.

By the time we finished the search, the dog pranced in happiness and we all laughed instead of complained about our soggy situation. His sheer joy at having an opportunity to do the work he loved made all our tasks a little easier to bear.

Action:

The next time you take on an onerous task, find something about it to enjoy or make those around you laugh.

Prayer:

Thank You, Lord, for the people and creatures that teach us to enjoy the world around us. Amen.

MARCH 31

God the Rock Star
BY MYRA BIERNAT WELLS

Zephaniah 3:17

The LORD your God is with you, the Mighty Warrior who saves.
He will take great delight in you; in his love he will no longer rebuke you,
but will rejoice over you with singing.

Without worship, we go about miserable. **A.W. Tozer**

Who is your favorite rock star? To what song do you play a mean air guitar? Which song do you love so much that you always feel the need to sing along with it at full volume?

Would it surprise you to learn that God doesn't just listen to the heavenly choir, but He sings also? "The Lord your God is with you, the Mighty Warrior who saves. He will take great delight in you; in His love He will no longer rebuke you but will ***rejoice over you with singing.***" Zephaniah 3:17 (NIV) God loves you so much He rejoices over you with singing! God, the rock star, backed by a choir of heavenly hosts, is singing over you! Right now, tomorrow, next year.

The image of God singing when He looks at me brings more than a smile. It lifts my heart and makes me realize there is a power working with me and in me that is stronger than anything life throws at me.

He knows my frustrations and He sees my hurt more than anyone else can. God knows my future, so He whispers into my ears – sometimes it is a warning, often it is a word of comfort, many times it is a command to follow. God knows my fears and He wants me to turn them over to Him. God also knows my faithfulness and sees all the good things I do.

The fact that God knows everything means nothing I face will hinder His ability to help me; nothing will catch Him by surprise. Nothing I fear will be too big for God's strength; and nothing I do in His name is ever done in vain.

Always remember this – in the middle of your life, God is singing over you! Doesn't the thought of your heavenly daddy singing over you uplift you?

Action:

When burdens weigh you down, consider the song God is singing over you.

Prayer:

Jesus, help me fully comprehend the depth of your love. May I walk in a joyful, new direction as I contemplate the beauty of You rejoicing over me with singing. Help me hear Your encouraging, loving voice. May this day, this week be filled with new, joyous perspectives. Amen.

APRIL 1 - APRIL FOOL'S DAY

Oh, Yes They Do!
BY JUDY KNOX

Romans 1:18-32

There is a time for everything, and a season for every activity under the heavens.
Ecclesiastes 3:1

There is a story that circulates on the Internet this time of year about the atheist who became so incensed over all the attention given to the Easter and Passover holidays that he decided to do something about it. He contacted a lawyer who helped him bring to court a complaint of discrimination. Christians, he argued, have Christmas and Easter, and Jews have Passover and Yom Kippur, but atheists do not have a holiday to celebrate.

The judge dismissed the case. The lawyer, objecting to the ruling, complained loudly, once again listing all the various religious holidays. Atheists, he declared, are discriminated against because they have no holiday on which to celebrate. The wise judge then exclaimed, "Oh, yes, they do! It's April First!" and he quoted Psalm 14:1, "The fool says in his heart there is no God."

There is apparently no court record showing that this ever actually took place, but it does illustrate an important truth. God has made His existence apparent even through the natural world He created. "The heavens declare the glory of God. The skies proclaim the work of His hands" (Psalm 19:1). In Romans 1 Paul speaks about our own conscience giving evidence of God's existence.

The Bible has much to say about fools. We may think of April Fool's Day as a time to make silly jokes or play harmless pranks, but foolishness is not really something to celebrate. The fool spoken of in Psalm 14 does not refer to a person lacking in intelligence, but rather one who has chosen to deny God's existence, ignoring the evidence of his own conscience and the world around him.

Many atheists, when asked why they choose to insist there is no God, readily admit that a belief in God would make them accountable to that God. They deny God to escape the condemnation of their conscience and free themselves from the moral constraints they think a relationship with God would bring. Romans 1:18-32 describes the downward progression a person will find himself on once he has chosen to turn His back on his Creator. One of the steps in this process is, "Although they claimed to be wise, they became fools" (v. 22).

Instead of running and hiding and denying, how much simpler and more satisfying to turn to the Creator, receive His forgiveness and grace, and enjoy the love He is continually pouring out on us!

Action:

Do something that declares your faith in God.

Prayer:

Father, thank You for all the evidence You have given us that You are real. Help me to live in such a way that my life will be further evidence of Your existence. Amen.

APRIL 2

Do Not Make Another Stumble
BY SHERRI GALLAGHER

Romans 14:13-15

Therefore let us stop passing judgment on one another. Instead, make up your mind not to put any stumbling block or obstacle in the way of a brother or sister. I am convinced, being fully persuaded in the Lord Jesus, that nothing is unclean in itself. But if anyone regards something as unclean, then for that person it is unclean. If your brother or sister is distressed because of what you eat, you are no longer acting in love. Do not by your eating destroy someone for whom Christ died.

As the winter concert approached for my high school band, the baritone saxophone player met with the band director. His religious beliefs wouldn't allow him to play Christmas Carols. He believed in Christ, but his religion taught that the true date of Jesus' birth was hidden for a reason. Only the resurrection should be celebrated. The band director arranged to group the carols at the end of the program and allowed the young man to quietly leave the stage.

The band director understood the quandary faced by his student. To this boy, playing carols was a sin. The director showed his love by supporting another Christian's desire to follow God's direction, even when those beliefs were different from the majority present. If the band leader had insisted the boy play carols, the maestro would have been committing the sin of making another stumble. Not because playing carols was a sin, but because the student believed it was a sin.

Helping others to grow in faith and understanding is every Christian's responsibility. When another is acting out of a desire to please God, it is the responsibility of every Christian to support them and help them to grow in understanding—not place stumbling blocks in their paths.

Action:
Think about the things you do at work or school. Would any of them give someone a bad opinion of Christians? If so, what can you do about it?

Prayer:
Where there is hatred, let me sow love. Where there is injury, pardon. Where there is doubt, faith. Amen. (**St. Francis of Assisi**)

APRIL 3

Most People
BY MYRA BIERNAT WELLS

Isaiah 43:18-19
Forget the former things; do not dwell on the past. See, I am doing a new thing! Now it springs up; do you not perceive it? I am making a way in the wilderness and streams in the wasteland.

Enjoy your own life without comparing it that of another.
Marquis de Condorcet

Most people don't do what you do, love what you love, have the gifts you have. We're in pretty good company if we feel we're not like most people. After all:

- Most people don't…build an ark.
- Most people don't…lead people through the desert to the Promised Land.
- Most people don't…die on a cross to save the world.

If most people don't do what you do, and you're passionately pursuing Jesus with your life, then it's not just a human plan. The heartbeat of God is in it.

By following Jesus, you've already started making the world better every day with your hands and your resources and your love and your willingness and your belief! Isaiah 43:18-19 states God is going to restore the desolation, renew what has been lost. He asks me (and you) the probing question, "Will you not perceive it?"

He doesn't just ask us; God showers us with ways to perceive the freshness and grace He gives each of us with every new day. We need you, just you, to fulfill God's purpose, bring your gift(s) to our world in a way no one else can.

Most people don't…but you do.

Action:

Thank God for the spiritual gifts He has given you. Continue to or find a new way to share these with others in a way that glorifies God.

Prayer:

Jesus, help me to trust that You will never leave me as I walk this crazy earth. When my story is scary, grant me peace. When it's mundane, help me to rejoice in normal. When I fret, lift my eyes to You. When circumstances swirl out of my control, steady my mind to trust in You. Be near. I know that Your presence is what blesses me. Amen.

APRIL 4

Packing by Faith
BY JUDY KNOX

Hebrews 11:1-3, 6

Now faith is the substance of things hoped for, the evidence of things not seen. For by it the elders obtained a good testimony. By faith we understand that the worlds were framed by the word of God, so that the things which are seen were not made of things which are visible. But without faith it is impossible to please Him, for he who comes to God must believe that He is, and that He is a rewarder of those who diligently seek Him.

Take the first step in faith. You don't have to see the whole staircase, just take the first step. **Martin Luther King, Jr.**

How exciting! After praying and seeking God's direction, we had let a few people know that we wanted to sell our house, and by the next day, without even putting up a for sale sign, we had sold the house, and for a great price. God had truly done something amazing in our life, doing abundantly above all we had asked or expected. We had heard testimonies of such miracles happening to other people. Now it had happened to us!

The excitement wore off somewhat when the buyer told us he would need to postpone the closing date due to some business difficulties, but a two- or three-week delay didn't seem so bad. When 3 weeks had passed with no action, we received another call. The buyer apologized for the delay and offered to let us stay in the house rent-free for a month after closing while we looked for another house. The weeks dragged on with one delay after another, always with a promise to close "soon" and another rent-free month.

Our exciting testimony began to ring a little hollow. God had sent a buyer, but the buyer didn't appear to be buying the house. Our faith would waver, then we would hear an encouraging message or read a helpful scripture and once again we would declare our belief that God had not fallen asleep or gone out of town. We knew He had sent that man to buy the house, and we knew that God does not play tricks on His children, but it was perplexing.

Then one morning a realization struck me. We were waiting, hoping and praying, but our actions were not lining up with our words. I told my husband that if we truly believed the house was sold and God was working things out behind the scenes, then we had better get ready to move. We bought some packing boxes that day and started filling them up. A few days later we got the call telling us that we had a closing date.

Did our starting to pack move God? No. But it changed our hearts. Instead of hoping, we had moved into the realm of true faith. We gave substance to what we hoped for, and our actions were evidence that even though we didn't see it yet, God was working behind the scenes. Our excitement about moving had returned. By the time we got that call, it was almost anti-climactic because it had already become real to us.

Our faith does not move God, but our "acts of faith" move us. They bring us into position to be ready to receive. They move us out of the way to allow God to move. And they may also keep us from doing or saying dumb things that could interfere with receiving the answer to our prayers.

Action:
What situations are there in your life where God just does not appear to be answering your prayers? Find an action you can take that will give substance to what you believe.

Prayer:
Lord, I believe You are truly at work behind the scenes, even though I can't see the results yet. Help me to line up my actions with my faith. Amen.

APRIL 5

Keep Running
BY SHERRI GALLAGHER

Matthew 25:1-13

Plans are only good intentions unless they immediately degenerate into hard work.
Peter Drucker

I loathe running. In the summer it leaves me slimy as a dead fish. In the winter the cold air punishes me with headaches. I am great at excuses not to run. My favorite, "There is so much to do and not enough time; I'll run tomorrow." Just as the brides in the reading thought there would be enough oil for the lamps.

In the same way it is easy to ignore prayer and Bible study. The pressures of the day close in. There is the frenzy of getting off to school or work, or the need to get a dinner on the table and help with homework.

After I run and revive in a hot shower, I do get the benefit of better breathing. I can focus better on my work and stay at it longer. When I do my devotionals and prayers in the morning, getting up a half hour earlier for that tiny piece of quiet conversation with God, my whole day goes better, and I have more patience with the world.

Don't be like the foolish brides who thought they had enough oil in their lamps or like my sneaky inner excuse maker. Make sure you find the time to exercise spiritually and physically, so you are fully energized and ready for whatever tomorrow brings.

Action:
Start an exercise program.

Prayer:
Lord, give me perseverance. Amen.

APRIL 6

Backdrop
BY MYRA BIERNAT WELLS

Luke 1:14

He will be a joy and delight to you, and many will rejoice because of his birth.

Pizzazz. That's what I was searching for. An attention getter. Most importantly, I wanted the photograph to capture the special bond between me and my dog, Rascal. A picture illustrating our tight connection that would also bring me comfort and healing since Rascal was recently diagnosed with terminal cancer.

So I went hunting for backdrops. Something to make us stand out yet was in line with our personalities. When I found something remotely workable, I'd pester my husband to take a few pictures. Summoning every creative molecule in his body, he'd snap away, but the results would be less than spectacular.

It seemed I'd never find the perfect backdrop to make Rascal's black and white fur stand out and my blue eyes sparkle. Honestly, looking back it was an exercise in futility. No picture could ever give me what my heart longed for—more time with my dog.

When my life's hurts become overwhelming, I don't have to go searching for the appropriate scenery. Soothing comfort is found in God's backdrops. In a lowly manger, God came to this world, and other than the angels singing that night to the shepherds, his birth went widely unnoticed by the inhabitants of Israel.

This was the beginning of many more backdrops: a merciless cross, an empty tomb and eternity itself. His movement through these settings changed life forever. Christ showed us joy is created by flourishing in God's presence despite life's circumstances.

Life's storms will teach us God is faithful and will provide the strength to stand firm. Christ didn't come to eliminate the storms of life. He came to fill them with His presence. Joy is the presence and power of God in the one life we have been entrusted with—deeply connecting with God in its minutes, hours and days.

Each storm brings the victory waiting to be claimed—the awesome privilege of clinging tightly to the hand of God.

Action:
Take a moment today to stand still before God—no music playing, TV, etc. Take the time to exchange your burdens with His peace.

Prayer:
Lord, Your backdrops fill my life with grace and goodness. Align my heart with Yours. Quiet me today with Your love, direction and tranquility. Amen.

APRIL 7

Glorious Transformation
BY JUDY KNOX

2 Corinthians 5:17, 2 Corinthians 3:18
Therefore, if anyone is in Christ, he is a new creation; old things have passed away; behold, all things have become new.

But we all, with unveiled face, beholding as in a mirror the glory of the Lord, are being transformed into the same image from glory to glory, just as by the Spirit of the Lord.

There is nothing in a caterpillar that tells you it's going to be a butterfly.
Buckminster Fuller

Butterflies are among the most amazing wonders of the natural world. I remember studying about butterflies in third grade, but not from a book. Our teacher brought a terrarium into the classroom. Among the greenery were a few branches and three fat, ugly caterpillars. I found them disgusting, but fascinating, nonetheless. We would walk by the terrarium and stop to watch them crawl around on the branches, chomping on the weeds. We noticed them getting bigger and fatter, but our teacher gave us no clue what to expect next.

One morning a caterpillar was missing, but we did see, hanging from one of the branches, a strange green bag-like object. The teacher told us that was a cocoon, and that the caterpillar was resting in there. Soon the other two caterpillars also formed cocoons, although we never saw how they did it. These bags were not very exciting to third graders, but the teacher told us to keep watching them.

I will never forget the day I walked in and saw a beautiful butterfly in the terrarium. How did that get there? The teacher pointed to the open cocoon. When we had all seen the butterfly, she released it out the open classroom window. The next day we got to observe first-hand as the second butterfly worked its way out of the cocoon, and a day later the last one came out.

The teacher explained that what we had observed was called *metamorphosis*, a complete transformation. She told us that while the caterpillars were resting in the cocoons, they were being changed into butterflies. The new butterflies would live for a few weeks, feeding on nectar from flowers, and then would lay eggs. Those new eggs would hatch as tiny caterpillars and the whole cycle would start again. Amazing, and hard to believe, but we had seen enough of the process with our own eyes that we believed it.

When we invite Jesus into our lives, we also go through a metamorphosis. We become new creations in Christ. Our life cycle is different from that of the butterfly, however, because our transformation continues to unfold day by day as we follow Christ and renew our minds. We are being changed into His image with ever-increasing glory. Our caterpillar lives are a thing of the past. We never need to return to them again. As we "fix our eyes on Jesus, the author and finisher of our faith" (Hebrews 12:2), He will continue working in us to make us more like Himself.

Action:

Watch an online video about the life cycle of a butterfly, thinking about how this relates to our new identity in Christ.

Prayer:

Lord, I thank You for making me a new creation in You. Help me to keep my eyes on You, so that I will be transformed into Your image, more and more, day by day. In Jesus' name. Amen.

APRIL 8

A Swelled Head
BY SHERRI GALLAGHER

Matthew 19:23-26

Then Jesus said to his disciples, 'Truly I tell you, it is hard for someone who is rich to enter the kingdom of heaven. Again I tell you, it is easier for a camel to go through the eye of a needle than for someone who is rich to enter the kingdom of God.' When the disciples heard this, they were greatly astonished and asked, 'Who then can be saved?' Jesus looked at them and said, 'With man this is impossible, but with God all things are possible.'

You are the salt of the earth, but if salt has lost its taste, how can its saltiness be restored? **Matthew 5:13**

Hollywood stars claim to have plenty of food, glorious mansions, and designer clothes as a result of their hard work. They chase after the latest religious craze, yet never credit God for their success. They demonstrate why it is so difficult for the wealthy to get into heaven.

It's easy to sneer at the stars. We'd never be like them. We're not looking for wealth, just enough to care for our families and help those in need. However, if we claim that big bonus came from our hard work and don't credit God working through us, we're just as bad as the movie stars. We've lost our "saltiness," that little zinging reminder of God adding flavor to all we do.

He made it possible for us to learn and have the skills to be successful. When we're blessed, we must remember it was God, not us. Giving thanks and remaining humble is very difficult. Turning down recognition when we have worked hard for years isn't easy, but it is required if we are to be the first fruits. A simple prayer of thanks is the salt God loves and expects from us.

Action:
Each time you receive a check or payment, stop and offer a prayer of thanks to God for making it possible.

Prayer:
Please, God, help us to be humble and remember all good things come from You. Amen.

APRIL 9

Goal or Trivia
BY SHERRI GALLAGHER

Ephesians 5:15-17

Be very careful, then, how you live—not as unwise but as wise, making the most of every opportunity, because the days are evil. Therefore do not be foolish, but understand what the Lord's will is.

In the absence of clearly-defined goals, we become strangely loyal to performing daily trivia until ultimately we become enslaved by it. **Robert Heinlein**

As I shut down my lawn mower my phone vibrated. I yanked it out of my belt holder while removing my hearing protection and had to laugh. My smart phone wasn't so smart. My health app had mistaken the vibrations of the riding lawnmower as steps walked and notified me I had reached my goal. It did make me think about the number of silly goals I set for myself. While walking 10,000 steps daily is a great wellness goal, how many times did I let things sidetrack me and then take credit for accomplishing a task I didn't really do?

I set a goal to read a daily devotional, but if all I do is read it and move on to the next task on my to do list, how much good has it done me? Without taking the time to meditate and consider how the story and scripture readings can be applied to me, the reading becomes just so much trivia to fill up the day.

In Ephesians Paul looks at this problem a slightly different way. "Look carefully then how you walk, not as unwise but as wise, making the best use of the time, because the days are evil" (Eph. 5:15). When I get bogged down with tasks versus focus on the importance of God in my life, I am using my time unwisely and can get led astray. Only when I keep my focus on the goal, pleasing God, am I successful.

Action:

Take a step back and look at your day. Are you busy being busy or using your time wisely?

Prayer:

Heavenly Father, thank You for small reminders which keep my focus on You and not trivia. Amen.

APRIL 10

A Present Help in Time of Need
BY JUDY KNOX

Matthew 6:7-8, 33-34

Since you were precious in my sight, you have been honored. And I have loved you; therefore I will give men for you, and people for your life. Fear not....
Isaiah 43:4-5 (NKJV)

In the ten years following my retirement my husband and I eased into a comfortable division of labor where each of us had taken over certain responsibilities. When it came to the car, he drove and I navigated. Other than the occasional jaunt to the grocery store or mall, I did not drive. In the three years since we had bought the car, I probably logged less than 300 miles. He liked driving; I liked being a passenger. I paid little attention to the workings of the car. We ambled along smoothly until he was suddenly rushed to a hospital forty-five miles from home and underwent major surgery, and I became responsible for the car.

While he lay incapacitated, I began venturing forth as necessary. Though life in the hospital was stressful, I was doing fine with the whole driving thing until the morning I walked out the door of the house where I was staying to discover a windshield covered with sticky seed pods brought down by rain during the night. I turned on the wipers, which only created a gooey mess. Oh well, I would turn on the windshield washers. No problem, except I didn't know how. The owner's manual was no help. I did what I thought it said, but obviously had not understood the instructions. In a hurry to get to the hospital, I headed on down the street peering through streaks. I knew it would not be safe to make the return trip that night in the dark.

With the stress I was already dealing with at the hospital, I did not need the added stress of this dilemma. I tried to think of someone I could call to ask about it, but no good answers came to mind. Only then did it occur to me to pray for help, and my prayer was not eloquent: "Lord, thank You that You will show me who I can ask about this."

Approaching the parking garage, I saw a car exactly like mine enter the line just a few spaces ahead of me. I pulled into my usual slot, and the other car pulled in on the other side of the dividing wall. Instead of walking toward the hospital entrance, the driver walked in the opposite direction, around the wall, and right toward my car. I rolled down my window and as he came near, I asked if he would mind showing me how to work the windshield washer. Nothing to it when you know how!

All that morning I rejoiced over God's perfect, simple answer to my simple, heartfelt prayer. Once again, the Creator of the universe had shown me His love and care in a tangible way. I'm glad the owner's manual didn't make sense because I needed a touch of God that day more than a clean windshield, and I ended up with both.

Action:

Can you think of a time when God gave you a direct, simple and tangible answer to a prayer when you were in need? Share the story with someone.

Prayer:

Father, Your love is so awesome. Not only did You send Your Son to die for our sins, but You are always active in our lives. Thank You that our small problems are not insignificant to You. Amen.

APRIL 11

I Am with You
BY SHERRI GALLAGHER

Joshua 1:1-9

Believe in yourself! Have faith in your abilities! Without a humble but reasonable confidence in your own powers you cannot be successful or happy.
Norman Vincent Peale

When I was in college, the thought of standing up in front of a crowd and speaking terrified me. Who was I to stand up and tell anyone anything? Finally, a professor imparted a gem of wisdom after observing my fear. He said standing up and telling people what you know was the same as giving them a gift. Maybe they already had the same gift but hearing about it from someone else might give them a new insight. If it was new, then you had given a true treasure. Trust God and speak from your heart.

Joshua had a difficult job filling Moses' place of leadership. Certainly, he had to feel horribly inadequate for the task. Then God told him, "As I was with Moses, so I will be with you; I will never leave you nor forsake you." (verse 5) God also told Joshua, "Be strong and courageous. Do not be terrified; do not be discouraged, for the Lord your God will be with you wherever you go."(verse 9). With that promise Joshua could go forward with confidence.

Action:
The next time your confidence is shaken, repeat Joshua 1:9 to yourself.

Prayer:
Be with me, Lord, and I cannot fail. Amen.

APRIL 12

Practicing Gratitude
BY MYRA BIERNAT WELLS

Philippians 4:11-12

I am not saying this because I am in need, for I have learned to be content whatever the circumstances. I know what it is to be in need, and I know what it is to have plenty. I have learned the secret of being content in any and every situation, whether well fed or hungry, whether living in plenty or in want.

When it comes to life, the critical thing is whether you take things for granted or take them with gratitude. **G.K. Chesterton**

In order to pass his class, my high school German instructor required each senior to teach a complete class entirely in German. The topic was of our own choosing, so I picked Richard Wagner, the great operatic composer. For weeks, I practiced my talk in a language other than my own until I could practically say that speech forwards and backwards.

Practicing gratitude is much like learning a new language. You cannot become fluent unless you practice. In Philippians 4:11-12, Paul writes, "I have learned how to get along happily whether I have much or little. I know how to live on almost nothing or with everything." As with a foreign language, the more we use it, the more fluent we become.

It's a life-long journey: we come into this world as babies demanding our needs to be met. I would like to think people eventually outgrow this self-centeredness, but sadly, never do. We don't have to live self-absorbed lives. We can learn God's language of gratitude.

The rewards of gratitude are many. It is the most effective way to deepen your consciousness to the fact that you are the object of God's affection and love. Giving thanks awakens your senses to see God, to hear God and see He is good. When you *feel* far from God, gratitude will be the ramp to get you back on the right road.

Every day we speak words of gratitude helps remove our blinders to see glimpses of His glory, and as we discover and practice the beautiful language of gratitude, our native tongue of self-focused dissatisfaction begins to fade. To make the tongue of gratitude your heart language requires the practice of living and moving in Him with a grateful heart.

Action:

Practice gratitude. Find three people today and tell them why you appreciate them or why you are thankful for them. It could be as simple as telling someone "thank you" for how they helped you or encouraged you.

Prayer:

Lord, my desire is to become a grateful person. Help me to search out ways to show gratitude to You and to others. Convict me when I'm ungrateful. Help make gratitude my mother tongue. In Jesus' name. Amen.

APRIL 13

Limitations
BY BETH DUMEY

Isaiah 40:28

Do you know? Have you not heard? The LORD is the everlasting God, the creator of the ends of the earth. He will not grow tired or weary, and his understanding no one can fathom.

At the end of a long week, feeling bone-tired, energy-less and wrung-out, I wonder how much it will take to feel refreshed. A nap will not be enough; sometimes twelve hours of sleep will not be enough. This type of weariness needs more than a weekend. Perhaps a two-week vacation lounging somewhere far away might suffice. Even better is a sabbatical for a few months. At times, my weariness transcends my physical body and I need to be spiritually and emotionally replenished.

Being aware of my own limitations makes me even more in awe of God's lack of limitations. He never tires, never gets overwhelmed, never crashes on to the sofa for a weekend "retreat." His sovereignty never ceases and His power never wanes. He tells His children to lean on Him, for He "gives strength to the weary and increases the power of the weak" (Isaiah 40:29).

When I am feeling exceptionally limited—facing a day of work on little sleep, tackling unknown health issues or simply enduring the daily grind of life—it helps to know I can draw strength from Him who always has it and is willing to grace me with it.

Action:
Read Isaiah Chapter 40. What do you rely on to give you strength? While food, sleep and relaxation are all healthy, they are also all finite. Where do you get unlimited strength?

Prayer:
Lord, help me to remember Your promise to fuel my strength when I turn to You for it. Help me to cast my cares upon You and allow You to renew me. Amen.

APRIL 14

Everyday Gifts
BY SHERRI GALLAGHER

Proverbs 23:24-25

The father of a righteous man has great joy; he who has a wise son delights in him. May your father and mother be glad; may she who gave you birth rejoice.

I watched my son and husband serve communion. I do not think I could have been given a better gift than to sit in a pew and observe them. Both wore gray suits, my husband in a traditional white shirt and red tie while my son sported a dark striped shirt and white neck wear. Both stood straight and tall and strong. The day when my son toddled on unsteady feet and clung to his father's hand was past. The day when my husband would need to lean on his son's strong arm has yet to come. For a space, for a moment in time, I was given the greatest joy a mother and a wife could have: to watch the man she loved and their son honor God and serve the congregation.

Ecclesiastes tells us there is a time for everything and a season for every activity under heaven. There can be great joy in small moments such as these. Remember to stop and savor the everyday gifts we are given; a child's laughter, the expression of enlightenment on a student's face, a heartfelt hug.

Action:
Pull out your old photos. Look at how things and people have changed.

Prayer:
Lord, thank You for the gifts You have given us. Help us to treasure them. Amen.

APRIL 15 - TAX DAY

Taxed to Death
BY JOANNA BRADFORD

Romans 6:22

*For the **wages of sin** is death, but the free gift of God is eternal life through Christ Jesus our Lord.*

Kill the tax cuts! Slash the tax rate! Cut capital gains! Many of us are sick to death of taxes. Even in death there's no escape, as there is the "death tax," charged against our estate. While there isn't one complete answer to the tax dilemma, there is a certain way to avoid eternal death against our souls. Even better, someone volunteered to pay what we owe. Peter, one of Jesus' disciples, discovered this when confronted by the tax man.

No sooner had Jesus and his disciples set foot in Capernaum than the collectors pounced. "Doesn't your teacher pay the temple tax?" they asked Peter. While Peter replied, "Yes," he really wasn't sure. Jesus told him to retrieve the tax payment from a fish's mouth. Jesus not only paid the tax for himself, but also for Peter. Just as Christ paid this tax, he also pays the death tax owed for our sins.

Let's face it: there's just no getting around taxes. And, there is no getting around a life free of sin, either. But, there is a way to escape *eternal* death, which is the price of sin. By accepting that Christ volunteered to pay what we owe, we're guaranteed a complete write-off.

Action:
Think of the ways, such as good works, in which you've tried to pay God for your sins. Now, tear up the list!

Prayer:
Lord, there is no way I can pay for my sins. I thank You for Jesus Christ, the perfect sacrifice for me to escape eternal death. Amen.

APRIL 16

Morning Tea
BY MYRA BIERNAT WELLS

Isaiah 40:31

but those who hope in the LORD will renew their strength. They will soar on wings like eagles; they will run and not grow weary, they will walk and not be faint.

Faith sees the invisible, believes the unbelievable and receives the impossible.
Corrie ten Boom

My very British aunt taught me the joy of tea. She would drink it almost all day long, but I remember distinctly whenever anything was bothering her, she'd "have a spot of tea." Because of her, I drink tea in the morning instead of the American standard of coffee. I crave my first sip and relish the warmth of the cup in my hand. Mornings just would not be the same without my tea!

Even though I'm far from a morning person, I desperately try to wake up each morning running to God, to be in His presence, to listen to Him, to savor Him the way I savor my morning tea. A fresh-brewed faith strengthens us, renews us and enables us to "mount up with wings of eagles, to experience the power of God in our lives, run and not grow weary, to walk and not faint." (Isaiah 40:31).

But like many mornings, there are times when my faith is sluggish—times when trusting Him does not come easy. Times when my faith needs more of a jump start than one cup of tea could give it.

During those times, I remember the things God has brought me through in the past. The victories I have tasted in Him help me build my confidence for present deliverances. We can face whatever giants litter our lives with great confidence simply by pausing to remember God's goodness to us in the past. Remembering that goodness and choosing to trust God will bring us through what we face today.

Action:
Brew yourself a cup of your favorite coffee or tea and then find a quiet place to enjoy it. As you sit, think about a specific time God moved greatly in your life. Thank God for His favor during this trying time. Celebrate this by telling a close friend about it.

Prayer:
Dear God, You have brought me through so many challenging times. Please remind me of Your faithfulness in the past so that I may have fresh, equipping faith

to live today in Your strength. Help me to trust You, and keep me from leaning on my own understanding. In Jesus' name. Amen.

APRIL 17

A Slap in the Face
BY SHERRI GALLAGHER

James 2:14-26

We make a living by what we get, we make a life by what we give.
Sir Winston Churchill

The man stormed defiantly into the meeting. While he had a place at the table, he was pretty sure the group would reject and mock him. He felt he was owed an apology; the people in that room had brought him to the point of begging and begging didn't come easy. Anger and hurt were emotions he could show, but humbly asking for help wasn't his style.

The time for him to speak came. He stood and tried to read his prepared speech. Tears choked his throat and cut off his words. He crushed his pride and asked for money, because his family needed it. The room remained silent. Many knew his pride and failures had brought him low. He had earned the crushing financial blow with earlier actions.

He walked out of the meeting in silence. He was still in the parking lot as I left the gathering. I gave him money to buy his family food. Whether he used it for that or not, I don't know. I only know he had come to us as James had indicated in chapter 2:14, naked and hungry and I couldn't just say, "Go in peace and be full" without taking some action to help.

Action:
The next time you see someone who is hungry because of their own foolishness, feed them.

Prayer:
Lord, watch over and forgive us as we fail You and ourselves, and help us learn to forgive others' failures. Amen.

APRIL 18

The Pause That Refreshes
BY MAUREEN LANG

Psalm 44:8

*In God we make our boast all day long, And we will praise your name forever.
Selah.*

Take rest; a field that has rested gives a beautiful crop. **Ovid**

Have you ever noticed the little word that comes up after many of the verses in Psalms? *Selah.* Although the exact meaning of the Hebrew word is uncertain, it's believed to have something to do with pausing…either musically for the Psalm as a song or perhaps just to stop long enough to dwell on the preceding words.

Time is such an uncontrollable thing. It can work for or against us. The other day I had the strangest thing happen. One of my clocks needed a new battery, and when I installed it, the clock faithfully started ticking again—backwards! My husband laughed when he saw it and told me he was feeling younger already.

As a kid I thought summer lasted forever, that Christmas would never come, that Easter Sunday must be a lot farther than just forty days beyond Ash Wednesday, but the older I get, the faster all those times arrive. Busy days fly by. Before I know it one day falls into the next and another week is gone, then another month. Another year. I once asked my mother if it ever changes, if time ever went back to that slow-moving kind of a child. She just smiled and shook her head. No, time never slows, not even when your body does.

Not unless we do something about it. Our own Selah moments are just waiting for discovery if we become purposely aware of our happy moments. Pause and notice God's creation—in a sunset or in nature, in the smile on another's face—perhaps one inspired by the smile *you* offer first. God fine-tuned creation just for us, so we could fellowship with Him. If we take a Selah moment between our busy moments, we will recognize God's presence in our days. Time will never go backwards, but maybe we can slow it down just a little.

Action:
Take a Selah moment and thank God for one of the blessings He has sent to you today. Repeat as necessary throughout your day!

APRIL 19
HOLOCAUST REMEMBRANCE DAY

May We Never Forget
BY MYRA BIERNAT WELLS

Exodus 12:1-14

All that is necessary for the triumph of evil is that good men do nothing.
Edmund Burke

One of the most important Jewish holy days is Passover. In Exodus chapter 12 we read how God directed the Israelites to remember that day for all generations to come. It was a time when God stepped in and freed his people from slavery. God was with them and to this day Jews remember and celebrate God's loving protection with the Passover meal. Sometimes we too must remember times when the world experienced and was freed from the tyranny of evil and pass on a remembrance to the next generation.

Following the end of World War II General Dwight D. Eisenhower witnessed firsthand the horrific scenes of the holocaust. He ordered that they be documented with photographs, videos, and written accounts. Since that time, survivors of the concentration camps have been video recorded, recounting what they lived through and saw. Just 60 years later, Mahmoud Ahmadinejad, President of Iran, refused to acknowledge the holocaust occurred. Were it not for the foresight of General Eisenhower, future generations might doubt the Nazis tried to eliminate anyone who was Jewish.

Action:
Google or search in the library for the stories of holocaust survivors. Watch any available videos them and determine an age appropriate discussion of what you saw for your children and/or grandchildren. Tell family history of what WWII was like. Make sure they know, remember, and will speak out before ever letting anything similar happen.

Prayer:
Loving and protective God, give me the wisdom to identify prejudice and the bravery to speak out against it. Amen.

APRIL 20

Pas Auf
BY SHERRI GALLAGHER

1 Peter 5:6-11

As I pulled into the parking lot of a local restaurant, I spotted a man dressed in a dirty overcoat and acting strangely. Warning bells went off in my head, but I silenced them. "I'm being judgmental. It is lunch time and this is a good neighborhood."

I turned off the SUV and glanced in the rearview mirror. My newest canine partner, a two-year-old male German Shepherd, sat in the cargo section, his head darting from side to side watching the activity through the windows. For the first time I realized the value of his protection training. "Pas Auf," I commanded, telling him to watch out for danger. I felt a little silly, what could hurt me here?

I climbed out and leaned into the back seat, trying to scrape my scattered papers together and prepare mentally for my meeting. Deep threatening barks and growls exploded from the cargo section and the vehicle rocked from side to side as the dog bounced against the glass trying to get out. I jumped back just in time to see the strange man bolt away from me and my vehicle. The dog had spotted trouble sneaking up behind me and scared it away.

Just as I had warned the dog to be watchful, Peter reminds us to be on the lookout for trouble, ready to sneak up on us when we let our guard down. Our lives are much like that situation. Things are going well. We are distracted by our work and families. Trouble seems far away, and we get lulled into thinking Bible study and prayer can wait until tomorrow. Going to that restaurant lulled me into a false sense of security, but trouble snuck up behind me. If not for my watchful dog the result could have been much different. If not for my daily time with God, I could be led from His safe paths. Find the time for reading your Bible and listen to the subtle warning voice that keeps you in God's paths.

Action:
Watch for the dangers that turn you from God.
Prayer:
Thank You for watching over us and giving us those who protect us from evil. Amen.

APRIL 21

Fire!
BY MYRA BIERNAT WELLS

Isaiah 43:2

When you pass through the waters, I will be with you; and when you pass through the rivers, they will not sweep over you. When you walk through the fire, you will not be burned; the flames will not set you ablaze.

The most powerful weapon on earth is the human soul on fire. **Ferdinand Foch**

One of the Old Testament's most enduring stories is that of three young Jewish men: Shadrach, Meshach and Abednego. Refusing to bow down to King Nebuchadnezzar's idol, they were sentenced to be thrown into a fiery furnace. Appearing before the king just before facing their fate, they explained, "The God we serve is able to save us from it, and he will rescue us from your hand, O king, that we will not serve your gods or worship the image of God you have set up." (Daniel 3:17-18).

That's real faith: God can deliver me, but if He chooses not to, I'll serve him anyway. God can heal me, but if He doesn't, I will love Him regardless.

This so infuriated Nebuchadnezzar, he ordered the furnace to be heated seven times hotter than usual. Some of the strongest soldiers in his army tied up the young men and tossed them into the flames, which were so hot, the soldiers died in the heat. The King stood at a safe distance watching.

He soon grew confused when he saw four people walking around in the furnace. "Didn't we throw three men in the furnace? Look I see four men walking around in the fire, unbounded and unharmed and the fourth looks like a son of the gods." (Daniel 3:25). This quickly caused the king to have a change of heart. He ordered the door opened and the three young men walked out of the furnace unharmed.

When walking through the fiery trials of life, we are never alone. As with Shadrach, Meshach and Abednego, God is always right there with us. The smoke and fire of our lives does not bother Him one bit!

Action:

Do you desire friends like the three men in the story–ones who are willing to walk through fiery trials with you? If so, spend the day in prayer asking God to send you one or two friends you can lock arms with who have a strong faith in Him.

Prayer:
Dear Lord, thank You for walking with me through the fiery trials in my life. You promise You will never leave me, and I cling to that truth today. Thank You for the friends who have walked through the flames with me; they are my most treasured gifts. Amen.

APRIL 22 - EARTH DAY

Reduce, Reuse, Recycle
BY SHERRI GALLAGHER

Matthew 25:14-30

Then God said, "Let us make humankind in our image, according to our likeness; and let them have dominion over the fish of the sea, and over the birds of the air, and over the cattle, and over all the wild animals of the earth, and over every creeping thing that creeps upon the earth." God said, "See, I have given you every plant yielding seed that is upon the face of all the earth, and every tree with seed in its fruit; you shall have them for food. **Genesis 1:26, 29**

God gave us dominion over the plants and animals of the earth, but have we been good stewards? In 1969 the idea of holding an awareness celebration to remind people around the nation that God left us as stewards of the earth was started. The concept was to teach that a good steward conserves, protects and strengthens. The concept of Earth Day has grown until it is celebrated around the world, and some communities make it a weeklong event including tree planting campaigns and huge recycling collections.

The question remains, have we done enough to care for the world God gave us to manage? We can take some guidance from a phrase that was birthed from the early environmental movement - *reduce, reuse, recycle.*

The most recent Green Revolution has focused on utilizing renewable energy and recycling. The good news is, even throwing in the cost of collection and sorting, we use less energy resources by recycling than throwing something away and making a new one from scratch. But whether we make a replacement item from scratch or recycle the old, there is still a consumption of energy to make what we already had and threw away. That is why the phrase starts first with reduce, and then reuse, and only recycle as a last resource.

Some of the ways we can reduce our demand on resources is to purchase concentrated items. A small bottle of concentrated laundry detergent will wash twice as many loads as the big watered-down bottles. Purchasing the bulk container of powdered drink mixes uses less than a third the materials of the individual packages. Of course, bulk containers aren't always convenient and that is where the reuse portion comes in. By keeping a small stock of containers, we can dispense the bulk contents into easily manageable items.

One of the most significant things we can do is to stop buying our drinks in disposable containers. Instead of the buying bottles of water while on that road trip, carry an insulated cup or glass and refill it at the drinking fountains. Both your pocketbook and the planet will benefit. When buying that cup of coffee at the specialty shop, invest is one of their re-useable cups. I bought one in 1992 and the company still gives me a discount every time I use it!

There are many ways we can use our skills and abilities to help the earth. Some of us have the muscles to plant trees; others have only the strength to utilize a re-useable cup. God knows what talents He gave us. It is up to use to use them to the best of our ability to help the earth He gave us.

Action:

Identify one item you use and throw away repeatedly that you can re-use all year long.

Prayer:

Thank You, Lord, for this beautiful planet. Please give us the talents to protect and heal it and leave it in better shape for our children than when we received it. Amen.

APRIL 23

Waiters
BY BETH DUMEY

Psalm 13:1

How long, Lord? Will you forget me forever? How long will you hide your face from me?

Curiously, I've found myself saying "I can wait" quite a bit lately. It's perplexing because most of my life I couldn't. I graduated from high school early and completed college in three years. I've scheduled international trips one day after moving. I sometimes respond to e-mails before I've finished reading them. Usually, I can't wait.

Because God knows me better than I know myself, He puts the brakes on many of my plans. As painful as this is, I must admit it cultivates a patience in me that previously did not exist. Gaining an appreciation for God's sovereignty and timing frees me from needing to move forward so quickly. The waiting, the endless enduring that marks so much of our lives, has not become an enjoyable pastime. Yet the wisdom mined in the waiting time is a welcome companion. And the peace that accompanies it is golden—so much better than the pacing and the clenched fists.

Most of us are waiting for something—someone's health to improve, or a deal to come through, a job offer or a marriage proposal, a financial breakthrough or a positive pregnancy test. Once our waiting is over this time around, a new season of waiting will begin. Once we receive what we are waiting for—or find out definitively that we won't—we shift to the next item on our list. We are all just waiters. Because we are kingdom waiters, we can look up to see what God is doing in us rather than just watching the clock. What is His purpose for this time?

Action:

What are you waiting for right now? Reflect on what are you learning in this season of waiting.

Prayer:

Father, as short as life is, sometimes it seems so long, especially when we are awaiting Your response or even Your blessing. Help us to yield to Your timing. Help us to grow in knowing You and trusting You during our seasons of waiting. Amen.

APRIL 24

Always Take the High Road
BY MYRA BIERNAT WELLS

Galatians 6:9

Let us not become weary in doing good, for at the proper time we will reap a harvest if we do not give up.

The high road is always respected. Honesty and integrity are always rewarded.
Scott Hamilton

I don't know about you, but it's always tempting to embellish my stories a little; to tell a little white lie here and there. Puffing myself up feels good. And when I'm under stress, it's easy to fall into this trap. To make myself feel better I brag a little; we all do. I forget that even a small indiscretion is unholy to our holy God.

That's why one of the most powerful phrases Jesus uttered was: "Follow me." Paul teaches us in 1 Corinthians to follow Christ's example. Follow Him. Imitate Him.

Paul wasn't just talking about becoming a Christian; he was writing about a way of life. Christ wants us to follow His values, model His integrity, sacrifice as He sacrificed, love as He loved.

Jesus completely transforms a situation. Nothing, absolutely nothing, is hopeless when you invite Christ into it. He restores us when we work to become more like Him. His very presence covers us with an all-encompassing love and a radiant hope to fill our lives with energy and purpose.

Ensure God's blessing on your life by making the noble decision – the one that honors God the most, the one that blesses the most people, the one that helps us become living, breathing, walking displays of His glory. Proverbs 4:27 states, "Don't turn off the road of goodness; keep away from evil paths." Take the high road whenever possible. Even if it seems tough in the moment, the blessings will follow.

Just remember: all of us are just one step of obedience away from the next great, godly adventure and the mountain top moments that come from pleasing God.

Action:

Consider Psalm 32:8: "The Lord says, 'I will guide you along the best pathway for your life. I will advise you and watch over you.'" What comfort does this verse give you about God's plan for your life? How can knowing God honors the "high road" choice alter your decision-making ability?

Prayer:

Father, forgive me for the times in my life when I haven't stayed on Your path. Give me the strength and wisdom to make right choices that please and honor You. In Jesus' name. Amen.

APRIL 25

Get a Different Dog
BY SHERRI GALLAGHER

Psalm 118:22

The stone that the builders rejected has become the chief cornerstone.

"My dog doesn't fetch, she plays tug." I handed the national evaluator my dog's toy and stepped back to watch her work with my puppy. The woman petted the dog, waved the toy and threw it. Belle trotted out picked up the toy and sat down.

"I'd get rid of that dog and not waste time trying to train her." After two minutes of evaluation the so-called expert on search dogs made that comment and walked away. At six months of age, this woman would flush my puppy out of the search and rescue program. It is something I've run into more and more in both search and rescue and sport competition. The person handling the dog has a method for training; if the dog doesn't learn using that method, they get rid of the dog and buy another one.

Just as the chief builders would reject a stone rather than work with it, just as Jesus was rejected for not conforming to current thinking, my dog was rejected as unworthy. Thankfully the decision was mine to make. Belle stayed in our training program and became my "go to" dog. She earned extensive titles scoffers had told me were beyond her. She searched for a suicide victim turning up clues other dogs had missed. Her tracking skills have experts shaking their heads in amazement.

But how different am I from that evaluator? The truth is I'm not. I can be stubbornly set in my ways, sure mine is the only right way. I have to work at opening my mind and heart as Jesus taught us with his lessons. Training Belle wasn't easy. It took patience and persistence. I had to learn what motivated her. I had to "think outside the box." In the same way when I stand in judgment of someone because of their appearance or education, I am no different from the evaluator toward my dog or the Pharisees toward Jesus. I need to look beyond the obvious and find the value in the person I'm talking to. Generally, if I talk to a person instead of lecture or talk down to them their value becomes obvious.

Action:

The next time you are sure there is only one way to do something, listen to someone who offers an alternative.

Prayer:

Lord, forgive me my ego and help me to be open to the suggestions of others. Amen.

APRIL 26

Live Blessed!
BY MYRA BIERNAT WELLS

Mark 5:25-29

We must accept finite disappointment, but never lose infinite hope.
Martin Luther King, Jr.

Frustration grew as I rushed to get to an appointment the other day. After putting the car in drive, I prepared to back out of my driveway when my cell phone rang. I shoved the car back into park and answered the phone. It was a dear friend of mine from graduate school; her voice was heavy with hurt. Recently, she had suffered two deaths in her family and just last night, her mother-in-law had suffered a terrible stroke and was not expected to live.

Her sorrow broke my heart. I wanted to reach through the phone and hug her. I yearned to lift her up, to take away her grief. I couldn't do any of that, so I listened and prayed.

Do you feel overwhelmed today? Discouraged by the complicated challenges in your life? There are so many burdens being carried by souls weary of the task. So many people are desperate for a miracle from God.

God knew we would struggle with difficulties. That's why so many times the Bible points us back to the hope of Christ. In Mark 5:25-29, for example, we learn of a woman who had been bleeding for twelve years. She heard about Jesus and thought, "If I just touch his cloak, I will be healed." After He healed her, I love how the *Message* gives Christ's response, "Live well, lived blessed."

Like this woman, the best thing you can do is take your needs to Jesus. Purposefully place your faith in the Faithful One. When you pray, He will strengthen you. But if you try to handle things in your own strength, you will remain weak and ineffective.

If you are desperate for healing, help and hope, ask God to increase your faith today. Make a determined choice to trust Him. He sees what you are going through. He sees *you*. Look for His reassurance. He will whisper comfort to you, "I am here. Now live well, live blessed."

Action:
Meditate on Matthew 11:28-30, "Come to me all you who are weary and burdened and I will give you rest. Take my yoke and learn from me, for I am gentle and humble in heart and you will find rest for your souls. For my yoke is easy and my burden is light." Then call, email or send a card of encouragement to a friend who is hurting. Speak life and hope into his or her heart.

Prayer:
Heavenly Father, You are a mighty God and I need Your power in my life. Please fan the flame of faith today. I trust You are in control and ask that You would sustain and strengthen me to face every challenge. In Jesus' name I pray. Amen.

APRIL 27

Waiting
BY MAUREEN LANG

Psalm 27:14

Wait for the Lord; be strong, and let your heart take courage; yes, wait for the Lord.

Patience is not simply the ability to wait—it's how we behave while we're waiting.
Joyce Meyer

As a writer, I learned early that much of an author's time is spent waiting. Once we type "The End" on a manuscript, we often feel like zipping it off for immediate feedback rather than taking time to let it sit a while, so we can come back to it with a fresh eye days or weeks later. I'd much rather ship it right out to an agent or editor, or at least to friends or family. We'd like it if those friends dropped everything to read our work, and find themselves so engaged they would get the book quickly edited (for surely it just needs a tweak!) so I can get it off to publication and reach readers in record time. What a dream!

Waiting is an exercise we all must practice, sooner or later: from those who hurt and are waiting for healing to simpler waits like a cook waiting for water to boil. When I bristle against

the waiting times of life, I remind myself that time was God's idea. Waiting doesn't really affect Him, because He's outside of time. He created time for us, so He must want us to learn something from it. Although the phrase "this too shall pass" isn't from the Bible, it does offer comfort during times of suffering, but it's also a reminder that the good times will pass, too.

So, what should we learn by waiting? Patience? Endurance? Wisdom? It's how we spend our waiting time that reveals our character.

Action:
When you find yourself waiting, ask yourself what God might want you to learn during this period.

Prayer:
Lord, help me to take the time to appreciate the wait, to use the time wisely, to gain what insight I can during the process. Amen.

APRIL 28

Take What You Need
BY SHERRI GALLAGHER

Revelation 1:4b-6

...to the seven churches in the province of Asia: Grace and peace to you from him who is, and who was, and who is to come, and from the seven spirits before his throne, and from Jesus Christ, who is the faithful witness, the firstborn from the dead, and the ruler of the kings of the earth. To him who loves us and has freed us from our sins by his blood, and has made us to be a kingdom and priests to serve his God and Father—to him be glory and power for ever and ever! Amen.

There is no calamity greater than lavish desires. There is no greater guilt than discontentment. And there is no greater disaster than greed. **Lao-tzu**

Bob was upset. ROTC paid a year of tuition while the students decided if they wanted to make a commitment to the military. Several of Bob's friends took advantage of this loophole even though they actively protested the military. All of them were capable of paying for their college education. This was their way of getting more for less.

He pointed out that their actions increased taxes, reduced available benefits to the military personnel, and ignored God's guidance for how to treat others. His friends laughed at him. Their tactics were legal, and they were proud of using a loophole to get something extra for themselves.

God looks at our intentions. Taking advantage of loopholes may have been legal, but it provided abundance for some and prevented those in need from having enough.

Action:

Think about your activities for the last week. Did you take more than you needed simply because it was available?

Prayer:

God, open our eyes to places where we can be content with less so other have an opportunity to benefit, too. Amen.

APRIL 29

Sunrise!
BY MYRA BIERNAT WELLS

Psalm 63:2-3

*I have seen you in the sanctuary and beheld your power and your glory.
Because your love is better than life, my lips will glorify you.*

If you want to be reminded of the love of the Lord, just watch the sunrise.
Jeannette Walls

I bounded out of bed at 3a.m. that day, which is about as unusual as snow in Miami in June! I was living my dream: to watch the sunrise over Maui's Haleakala Crater, then ride a bicycle from the summit down to the sea. Predawn cold at this height dropped the enthusiasm level of our fellow riders. But I had followed the brochure's instructions, packed winter clothes and dressed in layers that day. Freed from the cold's distraction, my husband, Richard, and I explored the crater's east-facing pinnacle.

Soon, tiny hints of orange and pink punctured the dark. Within minutes, brilliant, magnificent colors spread through the sky. A fiery orange ball started rising on the horizon. Someone with a ukulele softly began to sing Hawaiian songs. For about twenty minutes, we were treated to an incredible show as dawn's colors stretched across the landscape of the national park. The experience was breathtaking, captivating and unforgettable.

I began to reflect on the graciousness of God in that sunrise, how He put on this awesome display day after day just for us. As the first rays of that morning hit my face, I sensed His presence. I felt bathed in His pleasure as I reveled in His intense love for me. Despite my excitement of the downhill ride to come, I felt a peace and serenity that was profound.

That sunrise was a love letter as God reminded me how much He cherishes me, how Christ bought my salvation on a cross and how, in setting my heart free, He changed me forever. As I separated myself from the crowd, I whispered to Him, "I love you."

I admit in the chaos of work, family and life, it is a constant struggle to free up time to just sit with God and worship. This is what God desires most: our love, our adoration. Have you *really* savored your Savior lately? Have you paused to tell Him you love Him?

Today, praise Him for the day – not just for sunrises that demand a prayerful response. Praise Him for the peace He brings when you are frazzled. Praise Him for the joy He showers on you in the little things, like the brush of your dog's whiskers across your face or the smell of freshly brewed coffee in the morning.

Action:

Write a love letter to God listing at least 10 reasons why you love Him. Or, write a love note to someone in your life you feel led to bless. Pray that God would lead you in this.

Prayer:

Heavenly Father, there are so many reasons why I love you! Please forgive me when my busyness crowds You out. Hear my heart today as it tenderly whispers, "I love you." Amen.

APRIL 30

Heroes
BY MAUREEN LANG

Matthew 11:11a

Truly I tell you, among those born of women there has not risen anyone greater than John the Baptist;

It is surmounting difficulties that makes heroes. **Louis Pasteur**

History reveals Christ to be a teacher and healer, someone who ultimately died on the cross an innocent man. Such truths make even the hardest heart soften just a bit, at least enough to call Jesus a hero among mankind, even if they don't accept His deity.

But did Jesus Himself acknowledge heroes in His life? The verse above suggests John the Baptist could have been someone Jesus would call a hero.

Our society loves a hero. We extol everything from comic book to sports heroes and have even created a few who've done little more than somehow achieve fame just for being pretty or the offspring of famous parents. What about our own personal heroes? We all know people who

may never make the news but who have in some positive way impacted our life for the better.

While I was growing up, I never thought of anyone I knew as a hero. Everyone was just so ordinary, even the unsung English teacher who inspired me to write; or the neighbor who drove a burning fuel truck away from a residential street to prevent sure disaster; or my dad who served honorably in the Navy, survived the Death March and nearly three and a half years of captivity in a Japanese camp.

I have better appreciation for all such people now that I'm older, and it's made me look at the ordinary people around me today and realize some of them are heroes.

Action:

Think about the people in your life who might be unsung heroes for you, then thank God for them—and consider letting them know how you feel.

Prayer:

Lord, please let me recognize the hero-potential in those around me, to make me truly grateful for those You have placed in my life. Amen.

MAY 1-MAY DAY

Work
BY MYRA BIERNAT WELLS

Ephesians 6:8

Remember that the Lord will reward each one of us for the good that we do.

Last night I rushed to the grocery store to pick up five needed items. I cruised around the market quickly placing the necessities in my shopping cart until I rounded the aisle near the iced tea display. A spill had occurred and two young men were mopping up the liquid, so I gingerly walked around the area.

The two employees were talking and while I didn't mean to eavesdrop, I couldn't help but overhear one of them say, "You know how I get through this job? I do the bare minimum. I get by with the least amount of work that is expected." And I immediately felt very sad for this teenager.

It can't be easy working in a grocery store: dealing with the public, keeping the place clean, making sure all the items are stocked correctly, that carts are available for everyone. Deliberate, mundane actions performed repeatedly become tedious. Every job has this same pitfall.

But the fellow was missing the bigger picture, so I hope you don't. I sometimes forget there is a hidden advantage in each minute of work. That is the ability to glorify God. That's the real opportunity in every workplace.

Colossians 3:23 states, "Whatever you do, work at it with all your heart as working for the Lord, not for human masters." In every one of our chores, even the ones that frustrate and make us weary, our work becomes a gift to God and others. No matter what job you have, you can become a little blessing to others; a person who multiplies joy and through it makes the world a brighter place – even when you don't feel like completing the task.

The daily grind makes this difficult, almost impossible. But we are called to be overcomers and we do that when we do everything with the love of God. We can let the hard things we must accomplish become holy things when we etch our work with love. We are put on this earth to make a difference, to give away what was freely given to us.

Unfortunately, that young man has a hard lesson to learn ahead of him. God did not create us to goof off, to be lazy, to just get by doing the bare minimum. He created us to serve. Our lives become significant when we minister to each other through our work, when we understand our labor is a holy endeavor. Serving others with untamed abandon refines our character, growing grace and wisdom in us. More importantly, we become reminders of the nails of service on the cross of Christ.

Action:
Read Ephesians 6:8 (above) once more. Think of ways you can bring joy to your coworkers. Develop a short action plan to do those things in the upcoming weeks.

Prayer:
Jesus, be with me as I work – whether it be outside the home or the housework inside. I give You permission to correct me when I lose sight of the fact that my labor should glorify You. Help me not to get so discouraged I forget my purpose— to proclaim You. Keep my feet firmly planted on the Rock. I need you. Amen.

MAY 2

What's Your Temperature?
BY MYRA BIERNAT WELLS

James 3:3-6

One kind word can warm three winter months. **Japanese Proverb**

Over the weekend, I served on the data entry team at my church. As research for future sermons, our Senior Pastor asked the congregation to answer three questions on preprinted cards made just for the occasion. My team took over the responsibility of entering all the responses into the computer. That afternoon, a team member brought his little dog into the classroom, which meant the doors had to be shut, so the little fellow wouldn't escape. But with all the computers generating heat, the temperature rose. None of us minded because we came to enjoy the companionship of our littlest worker.

At night, when I swung the door open to leave, I was surprised by the coolness of the evening. The temperature change from inside the room to the outside was quite dramatic – almost one extreme to the other. As I walked to my car, I realized the temperature of my life also swings back and forth.

I admit, there are times I can be the sweetest person one moment, then turn into a raging, angry woman the next. I've gotten up early, laid in bed praising God, only to end the day guilty of speaking unkind words to someone or about another person. I've screamed at clerks trying to do their job and I've yelled at my husband in moments of deep frustration.

However, the Bible instructs us to a higher, nobler, more consistent temperature of living. James 3:9–10 states: "With the tongue we praise our Lord and Father, and with it we curse human beings, who have been made in God's likeness. Out of the same mouth come praise and cursing. My brothers and sisters, this should not be."

We are accountable for our behavior and for the way we respond to circumstances. How we live outwardly reflects who we are inwardly. Our actions mirror our faith. But, if we center the thermometer of our hearts on Christ, we will become examples of His perfect love.

Action:
Write down the wisdom found in Proverbs 3:3, "Let love and faithfulness never leave you; bind them around your neck, write them on the tablet of your heart." What one new truth has God given you about how to better respond with His love?

Prayer:
Lord, please forgive me when my responses are unkind and do not reflect Your love. Please forgive the times when I over-react and under-love. Have Your Holy Spirit bring me the power to moderate the temperature of my heart and my responses. In Jesus' name. Amen.

MAY 3

Inheritance of Loving Kindness
BY MAUREEN LANG

Deuteronomy 7:9

Know therefore that the Lord your God is God; he is the faithful God, keeping his covenant of love to a thousand generations of those who love him and keep His commandments.

This is all the inheritance I give to my dear family. The religion of Christ will give them one which will make them rich indeed. **Patrick Henry**

I once had a conversation with my brother about how we'd received so many good genes from our dad: skin that tanned instead of burned, wavy hair. Good teeth!

That was before we knew I'd inherited something else from him—a genetic disorder called Fragile X Syndrome, the leading cause of inherited mental retardation. My dad and I are both carriers, but until my middle child was born with this condition, none of us knew it lurked in our DNA.

My son is now twenty years old but functions like a two-year-old. Without some kind of medical breakthrough, he's not likely to progress beyond this stage. But at least he's a happy two-year old in that young man's body.

I've often pondered (okay, complained) about Fragile X in my family. When my son was first diagnosed, I questioned whether God loved me. If He did, why would He allow such limitations for my son and the rest of the family who loves him? Fragile X didn't feel like an inheritance of loving kindness.

And yet it wasn't long before I was reminded of something Paul wrote in the book of Romans: Since God did not spare His own Son, but gave Him up for us all, won't He also give us what we need? Paul goes on to remind us that nothing can separate us from God's love.

Jesus Himself told us our faith won't spare us from troubles, but there are many promises of His faithfulness toward us, especially in our times of trouble.

On those days my son and I are most challenged by Fragile X, I strive to remember God's loving kindness and faithfulness…another "genetic" condition inherited by God's children. Instead of focusing on the problems, I can make a choice to remember that God didn't spare Himself of suffering, and He is there to turn to for hope.

Action:
Remember God's loving kindness and faithfulness is our best inheritance!

Prayer:
Remind me of Your love, Lord, and the sacrifices You made so the sufferings here will be forgotten in eternity. Amen.

MAY 4

The Front Cover of Dog World
BY SHERRI GALLAGHER

Romans 8:27-30

And he who searches our hearts knows the mind of the Spirit, because the Spirit intercedes for God's people in accordance with the will of God. And we know that in all things God works for the good of those who love him, who have been called according to his purpose. For those God foreknew he also predestined to be conformed to the image of his Son, that he might be the firstborn among many brothers and sisters. And those he predestined, he also called; those he called, he also justified; those he justified, he also glorified.

Have you ever been criticized and ignored for doing what you were called to do? Have you ever had someone defame you at work so they would get advancement instead of you? That happened to me when the State disaster response team started. I had to question if I followed the path God wanted for me or a path of my own choosing.

After a lot of prayers, I continued to serve the daily needs of the community with canine search and rescue. Those who'd blocked my path earned accolades and were pictured on television, in newspapers and magazines. Five years later, those people have moved on having never been on a real search or used their dog to help another person.

God had a different plan for me. I searched for missing hunters, accident victims, and suicidal people. I helped to give closure to families. I haven't been on the cover of "Dog World," but God knows what I did and has blessed me with wonderful experiences, loving dogs, and an opportunity to serve the body of Christ. He is with you when others take your work and glory. They can't take your memories or your calling.

Action:

The next time someone takes credit for your hard work, thank God for the opportunity to store treasures in heaven.

Prayer:

Take heart, stay strong, and walk God's chosen path. The cruelty of this world passes. God's loving guidance doesn't. Amen.

MAY 5

Become the Hero of Your Own Story!
BY MYRA BIERNAT WELLS

Psalm 27:3

...Even if I'm attacked, I will remain confident. (NLT)

"You just don't understand," she said softly in the phone. "I wasn't like you. High school was a terrible time for me." With those words, she politely declined the invitation to a reunion luncheon.

But I really didn't understand. There were times in high school when I was hurt, when I had doubts, when losses and failures filled my days. There were decisions that took me down paths of destruction. A lifetime of self-recrimination abounds in those four years.

I knew she didn't see the big picture for it was one that I missed many times. Sometimes I still miss it. There will always be battles. There will always be wounds. Life will always attempt to strip you of your confidence.

When my memories are so terrible I don't wish to relive them, I say to myself, "That may have been a dark hole in my life, but I am better for it. I survived it and I grew from it. I'm the beautiful, strong, caring individual I am today because of this pain. I will not be defeated by this. I am an overcomer."

For us to break through our regrets, our vision must be cast far beyond our restrictions, pain and obstacles. They must be placed on the One who created us to be His masterpiece, His child and His beloved. It is only then we can live with wild abandon, to rejoice unshackled from our regrets and to abundantly embrace life.

There is nothing in this life that is bigger than God: no problem, no painful memory, no opposition. If He can't be defeated, neither can you.

Hold tightly to your confidence and refuse to let anyone or anything take it away from you. God is even more powerful than you can imagine so you're stronger than any memory in the past. Don't allow anything or anyone make you into a victim; instead, become the hero of your own story, for with Him on your side, victory is assured.

Action:

Memorize Romans 8:37, "Now in all these things we are more than conquerors through Him who loved us." On a sheet of paper, write down a few regrets. Then with big, red magic marker, write this verse over all your words.

Prayer:

Jesus, bring clarity of vision when we remember our past with shame. Heal these places. Fill our hearts instead with the lavish love You have for us. Amen.

MAY 6

Capacity
BY BETH DUMEY

Colossians 3:12

Therefore, as God's chosen people, holy and dearly loved, clothe yourselves with compassion, kindness, humility, gentleness and patience.

As a basement owner, I need to be vigilant about monitoring my sump pump. The threat of a thunderstorm with accompanying flooding downpours is enough for me to reevaluate my schedule. The ever-present danger of water seeping over the edge and into the carpet and furnishings keeps my mind focused on weather reports. Because my sump pump has a limited capacity, I know its limits can be exceeded.

Often, though, this guarded awareness is confined to potentialities with immediate consequences. Drenched upholstery and submerged electronics have a direct budget impact and time cost attached. To avoid these consequences, I keep a careful watch.

This vigilance, however, does not extend to my own physical and emotional capacities. I've noticed during frustration-laden workdays or weekends full of errands my emotional reserves may run low. Often, I need to take a break or eliminate something from my list, but I usually don't. If I snap at the retail clerk or mutter under my breath in the car, the consequences are much milder.

Or are they? Over time, not recognizing my own limited capacities and inviting more margin in my days has spiritual consequences. God's goal for me, according to Colossians 3:12 is to grow in compassion, kindness, humility, gentleness, and patience. This is difficult to accomplish when I'm teetering on the edge of fatigue, hunger, depletion. When my reserves are empty, I have little patience for others and my compassion levels register in the red zone.

A reversal is needed. I need to be as vigilant about myself as I am about the basement. Likely, the carpet could be replaced with much less effort than repairing the damage to my developing character and my relationships. By recognizing the oncoming symptoms earlier, I can divert my energies and prevent an overflow from weakening my spirit.

Action:
For a few days, keep a diary noting when you are starting to feel weary. What difference do you notice in your behavior and attitude during these times? How can you re-focus?

Prayer:

Lord, help us to better assess our mental and physical capacities and manage them better. Our goal is to become more like You. Increase our awareness of those areas in which we need to grow. Amen.

MAY 7

The Chicken or the Egg?
BY SHERRI GALLAGHER

Romans 1:16-17

For I am not ashamed of the gospel, because it is the power of God that brings salvation to everyone who believes: first to the Jew, then to the Gentile. For in the gospel the righteousness of God is revealed—a righteousness that is by faith from first to last, just as it is written: "The righteous will live by faith."

The gospel to me is simply irresistible. **Blaise Pascal**

Paul writes in Romans, "For in it [the Gospel] the righteousness of God is revealed through faith for faith; as it is written, "The one who is righteous will live by faith." Romans 1:17. The phrase "through faith for faith" makes me catch my breath. I must have faith that the Gospel is God's words and through that faith I will learn and grow my faith in God and the salvation His son, Jesus Christ, offered. If I have faith, I will study the Gospel and use it to live a life that is puts others before myself. I learn how to do things because they are the right thing and not for accolades. I learn to accept as equal those I would hold as a different lower class. I learn to forgive those who hurt me and to return good for evil. I learn how to identify false gods such as wealth and security. And by my faith, I learn to trust that God is God and has loved me so much He has saved me from eternal death.

Which came first? My faith in God or my faith the Gospel came from God? Does it matter? Yes, I know there were other gospels written by other disciples of Jesus. Yes, I know that around 300 AD leaders of the church came together and selected what text became the Holy Bible. Conspiracy theorists would hold with Dan Brown's "The Da Vinci Code" that the Holy Bible was merely the result of groups of powerful men manipulating religion to uphold their own agenda and to control the multitude. I wasn't there but I will hold with the theory and have faith that the Bible is God-inspired and guided. I cannot know, and so by faith I will trust, the Bible is the Gospel, a thing that is absolutely true. I will trust by faith for faith.

Compare Matthew 19:13-15, Mark 10:13-16 and Luke 18:15-17. How are they the same and how do they differ? Does this influence your faith in the Bible?
Prayer:
Holy God, thank you for the guidance the word of the Bible gives to my life. Help me to live as You would wish me to do. Amen.

MAY 8

At the Foot of the Cross
BY MYRA BIERNAT WELLS

Psalm 142:5

Then I pray to you, O Lord. I say, "You are my place of refuge. You are all I really want in life." (NLT)

The other day, I had to stay overnight in the hospital for routine tests. I wondered if I would sleep that evening. Who really sleeps in a hospital? But I felt confident Richard and my dog, Lily, would sleep well – especially since Lily could stretch out on my side of the bed.

However, nothing could have been further from the truth. Lily didn't understand my absence. She went downstairs, crawled into the couch closest to the back door leading into the garage and waited. Several times during the night, Richard went downstairs and shooed her upstairs back into bed with him.

Finally tiring of this game, Lily went downstairs and sat in our living room in front of the three large windows that look out on the street. From there, she started to woof softly but plaintively. Richard told me it was almost as if she was trying to say, "Myra, where are you? I miss you. Come home to me." Obviously, she wanted me near her. Ever since she was a little puppy, she'd given her heart to me.

When I think back, the times I have felt the most disconnected from God was when I withheld my heart from Him. Unlike me leaving Lily for the night, God is always there beside me. I leave Him when I want nothing to do with Him or don't take the time to ask Him into my life. Conversely, I've felt the closest to Him when I desired God more than anyone or anything else.

Wanting God is not a decision, but a deliberate pursuit. It is a daily focus. Giving our hearts to Him requires face time through Bible reading and prayer. Maybe that sounds hard, but living without God is the harder life. For just like Lily with me, you can't receive the comfort of Jesus unless you get close to Him. God's answers to your questions, your pain and your longings are always at the foot of the cross.

Action:
Get out a piece of paper and write down times when you've felt God close to You. Then offer up a prayer of thanksgiving for His nearness and comfort.

Prayer:
Dear Father, I need You. Move my heart towards You. Tether me to Your truths and Your love. Help me to set aside a daily time to talk to You, to get close to You and to learn Your ways. Today, I commit to doing whatever it takes to want You the very most. In Jesus' name. Amen.

MAY 9

Desires of Our Hearts
BY JUDY KNOX

Jeremiah 29:11-13

For I know the plans I have for you," declares the LORD, "plans to prosper you and not to harm you, plans to give you hope and a future. Then you will call on me and come and pray to me, and I will listen to you. You will seek me and find me when you seek me with all your heart.

Trust in the Lord and do good; dwell in the land and cultivate faithfulness. Delight yourself also in Him; and He will give you the desires of your heart.
Psalm 37:3-4 (NASB)

Does God really give us the desires of our heart? What if we are longing for something outside of His will? I used to be confused about this scripture, since it seems to promise us whatever we want. That didn't sound like the way God works. On the other hand, some people say that God will call us to do the very thing we really *don't* want to. That didn't seem right to me either.

When we read the whole passage, it makes perfect sense, revealing a beautiful picture of the process God uses to work in a believer's heart. First, we trust in Him and "do good," doing what His Word says. We dwell in the land, wherever we are right now – church, workplace, marriage – and cultivate faithfulness. As we trust Him to work in our current situation, being faithful and looking for evidence of His faithfulness, we naturally begin to move to the next step, delighting ourselves in Him.

In my life, this is the point where I begin to see things happening. As I move beyond the circumstances and focus on enjoying God and His goodness, something happens in my heart. I find myself less concerned with my personal wants and wishes. My desires begin to change. I may find I am losing interest in something I thought I wanted, or I may feel strongly drawn to something new. Most times, however, God simply solidifies and refines my conviction about a direction in which I am already going.

What *does* happen every single time is that when God gives me a desire, He also fulfills it. How exciting! As Philippians 2:13 (NLT) says, "For God is working in you, giving you the desire and the power to do what pleases Him." He gives us the "want to," and then He equips us to act. The key is focusing on Him, not myself. If I trust in Him, and delight in the time I spend with Him, I find that what I want begins to line up more and more with His plans for me. So, does God give us the desires of our heart? Yes, if our heart is yielded to Him, He does.

Action:

Identify what your heart desires right now and ask God if it lines up with His will for you.

Prayer:

Father, I want to have the same desires for myself as You have. I invite You to change any that don't line up with Your plan for my life. Amen.

MAY 10

Success from a Strong Effort
BY SHERRI GALLAGHER

Psalm 132:1-5

LORD, remember David and all his self-denial. He swore an oath to the LORD, he made a vow to the Mighty One of Jacob: 'I will not enter my house or go to my bed, I will allow no sleep to my eyes or slumber to my eyelids, till I find a place for the LORD, a dwelling for the Mighty One of Jacob.'

As an engineering student, my son has stayed up all night working to complete an assignment on more than one occasion. He has set a difficult task for himself. When the day-to-day fears close in around him, he focuses on the job he will be able to obtain when he gets out of college, prays for strength, and focuses on the task at hand.

Likewise, David also set a difficult task for himself in preparing to build the temple. He knew the work would rob him of sleep, but he also knew the ultimate goal was worth the effort. He kept a vision of the joy the temple would bring to Israel before him to overcome the day-to-day fears and struggles.

Action:

What is your goal? Create a picture or detailed journal description and carry it with you to help overcome the obstacles. Tell God about it.

MAY 11

Dangerous Curves
BY MYRA BIERNAT WELLS

Proverbs 3:6

in all your ways acknowledge him, and he will make your paths straight.

Verdant rainforest, flowing waterfalls, plunging pools and dramatic seascapes provide a beautiful backdrop on Maui's Hana Highway. Despite this awesome display of nature, this wiggle of a road is known more for its 620 curves and fifty-nine bridges. The narrow highway was carved by pick-axe wielding convicts in 1926, but since it was paved in 1962, it now boasts over 1,000 cars per day; visitors aching to taste the adventure of its dangerous curves.

While they might be fun on the one way fifty+ mile trip from Paia to Hana, when our lives make dangerous curves, we feel the sting of pain, the uncertainty of difficulties and the weight of excruciating grief. Our souls become restless with questions. "Why, God? I want it to make sense. Why doesn't this make sense to me?"

Submitting to God doesn't just mean obeying Him. It means getting to know Him intimately, to be familiar with Him and to be deeply acquainted with Him. When we do that, He is quick to make our paths straight. Not because life is easy. Hardships sting and life is complicated. Not because all we experience is just. Much of life is unfair.

No, our paths become straight because when we know God, we can access His strength in our weakness; His comfort meets us when we mourn; His grace forgives our depravity; His peace calms our unrest; His joy wipes away our sorrow; His redemption brings beauty to our brokenness, and His love binds us to Him. Because we know Him, we trust He will provide all we need to process life's pains, heal our wounds and propel us forward in strength, grace and peace.

Amidst the dangerous curves of life, we grow to trust Him. The key to making the curves in our lives straight is way less about the challenges we face, but way more about the God we know.

Action:
Take some time this week to acknowledge the times when God has made the dangerous curves in your life smooth. Give thanks to Him for His intervention and write down a prayer asking God to increase your trust in Him.

MAY 12

The Tale of Two Tomato Plants
BY JUDY KNOX

Mark 4:3-9

Others, like seed sown on rocky places, hear the word and at once receive it with joy. But since they have no root, they last only a short time. When trouble or persecution comes because of the word, they quickly fall away. **Mark 4:16-17**

A science teacher once brought two terrariums into his classroom. Into one he put about twelve inches of soil, and into the other he put about one inch. Then, in each container he planted a tomato seed. Both seeds came from the same packet. In a few days, the seed planted in the shallow soil began to sprout. The plant was several inches tall before the second one began to peek through the soil. Both plants continued to receive the same sunlight and water. The students were amazed at the first plant. It looked great, with a strong, sturdy stem and bright green leaves. The second plant gradually caught up and was almost as tall. Then one morning the students arrived to find the early-sprouting plant had fallen over and its leaves looked withered and forlorn. Soon the plant died. The second plant continued to grow.

The teacher explained that because there had been so little soil in the first container, the plant had no room to develop a strong root system, so it had put all its energy into growing above the ground. Its tiny root system could not deliver enough water and nutrients to sustain continued growth. In the beginning, while the first plant had appeared to flourish, the second one had been putting down sturdy roots. By the end of the school year, the healthy plant had become strong and tall, and it produced a number of juicy red tomatoes.

In the parable of the sower (Mark 4:3-9) Jesus depicts four types of soil. He explains to His disciples that the types of soil represent four conditions of the human heart in response to the Word of God. The second type of soil, which Jesus calls the stony ground or rocky places, describes those who, when they hear the Word, receive it with gladness, but because they have no root lack endurance. When it becomes inconvenient or uncomfortable to obey the Word, they fall away.

We have all seen new believers who come to Christ with great excitement. They're at church every time the door opens. They sign up for every activity. Then almost overnight, they disappear. Why? Possibly, like the first tomato plant, they did not put down a strong root system. All the "growth" was on the outside. When trials came, they had not developed the faith needed to overcome the problems, and they returned to their old way of life.

There is only one way to put down roots and establish the Word of God in our lives, and that is to spend time reading and meditating on it. Songs, sermons and fellowship can encourage us along the way, but they are a poor substitute for putting time and effort into developing our own personal relationship with God and becoming strong in His Word. If we know the Word of God for ourselves, then when our beliefs are challenged, we can meet and overcome the difficulties, and we will become strong and productive.

Action:
Choose a verse or passage in the Bible that you would like to see growing and bearing fruit in your life. Spend time every day meditating on that Word.

Prayer:
Father, I want my heart to be good ground that lets Your Word penetrate deeply and take firm root in my life. Help me to spend time every day deepening my understanding of Your Word. In Jesus' name. Amen.

MAY 13

Hugs from God
BY SHERRI GALLAGHER

John 8:12-20

I was at our summer cabin and realized I was so busy coping with problems I wasn't listening for God's guidance. I was in the "do it myself" mode.

The air was thick with pine resin, the sun warm on my skin and the sandy soil cool under my bare toes. I walked to the dock and sat down to watch the eagles ride the wind currents and a mink swim passed.

Warmth gradually filled me like I had been given a loving hug. All the worries crowding my mind, were no longer mine but given to God. The situations were still there but they were no longer insurmountable. By listening for God's voice in the silence, I'd found peace and patience to deal with my problems.

Action:
Clear your mind and picture God's light pouring down on you. If a concern tries to crowd God out, push it away and listen for God's guidance.

Prayer:
God, thank You for giving us hugs in the darkness of our fears. Amen.

MAY 14

I've Got It!
BY MYRA BIERNAT WELLS

Psalm 56:3

When I am afraid, I put my trust in You.

In grammar school and high school, I loved playing volleyball. Each volley across the net was thrilling. As a player, the delicate dance of digging for the ball was exhilarating. Plus, the sport taught me a lot about working as a team. When someone called, "I've got it!" we got out of her way and let her handle the ball. We didn't try to take it from her. We didn't push her out of the way saying, "Oh no, you don't." Instead we trusted her to legally strike the ball.

No matter what you are going through today, I know one very important fact. God is not surprised or worried. He's got it. God is always right there with us – no matter what. And sometimes the godliest thing we can do is get out of His way and trust Him with our lives. He knows how to handle whatever comes our way. The God of the universe is never stymied by our past, shocked by our present or troubled about our future.

God wants us to trust Him in every trial and every difficulty – with the entirety of our lives. The best thing you can do is take your needs to Jesus. Place them in His capable hands. Then purposefully put your trust in the Faithful One. When you do, He will meet you at the place of your hardship and carry the load of your burdens for you.

God's got this! He has shown His faithfulness to you in the past. He will continue to do so even now. He holds the key to unlock every difficult situation, the resources to provide for every need and the balm to heal every hurt.

Action:
Try to think of one thing you are going through today that God can't handle. When you find this impossible, throw away your worry meter and let God handle it.

Prayer:
Dear Heavenly Father, hallelujah! There is nothing in my life that You can't handle. You are under me, supporting me, surrounding me and protecting me. I am not going to worry today or tomorrow because I know You've got this. In Your precious Son's name. Amen.

MAY 15

Oh, Those Pesky Weeds!
BY JUDY KNOX

Mark 4:3-8, 18-19

Though I delight in blessing My children, it grieves me when My blessings become idols in their hearts. **Sarah Young**, *Jesus Calling*

I am not a gardener. Though I love to see flowers with lush, green foliage blooming profusely in my yard, I don't look forward to the tasks needed to get and keep them that way. One of my least favorite tasks of all is pulling weeds. Yet, over the years I have learned that weeds do not become easier to pull out when they get bigger. If you ignore them, they will rob the good plants of needed water and nutrients, eventually taking over and choking out the more desirable plants. When we moved into our house, the flower border along our driveway, once a neighborhood showpiece, had grown into a tangle of weeds due to two years of neglect. It was difficult even to find the beautiful plants that had once graced the edge of the driveway. So, like it or not, if the good plants are to grow, we must remove the weeds, and the sooner the better.

According to Jesus in his parable of the sower, there are weeds that can grow up in our hearts and choke the Word, keeping it from flourishing. Left to themselves, they can take over our thoughts and attitudes until the fruit of the Spirit that should be evident in our lives is hard to find. Jesus very clearly spells out what these weeds are: the cares of this world, the deceitfulness of riches, and desires for other things.

Have you ever stopped to analyze these weeds? Nowhere does Jesus mention sin or evildoing. No, He says that our common, everyday activities and concerns can crowd into our hearts and stunt our growth. Such seemingly innocent things as entertainment, hobbies, friends, even – gasp – church activities can take up so much room in our minds and consume so many hours in our day that we devote little time or attention to our relationship with God. While these pursuits aren't sinful or evil in themselves, and they may even be things He has led us to do, we need to keep our lives in balance.

Satan does not need to get us to commit "big" sins, or even "little" ones, to render us ineffective. All he has to do is distract us from what should be our primary focus, our relationship with our heavenly Father. The cares and concerns of this world can easily take up all our waking thought. The deceitfulness of riches or desires for other things can also vie for our attention, causing us to ruminate over the things we don't have instead of reflecting with thankfulness on what we do have.

The solution, of course, is first to redirect our thoughts, bringing them "into captivity to the obedience of Christ" (II Corinthians 10:5). Second, we need to examine our activities to be sure that whatever we do, we are doing "as unto the Lord" (Colossians 3:23). With Christ at the center of our focus, and the weeds removed from our hearts, we will be that good soil that enables the fruit of the Spirit to bloom and grow in our lives.

Action:
Set aside a specific time and place every day to focus completely on God and His Word.

Prayer:
Father, please help me to examine my activities and my everyday cares and concerns to be sure I am not allowing anything to interfere with my relationship with You. Amen.

MAY 16

Selah
BY SHERRI GALLAGHER

Psalm 1:1-3

Blessed is the one who does not walk in step with the wicked or stand in the way that sinners take or sit in the company of mockers, but whose delight is in the law of the LORD, and who meditates on his law day and night. That person is like a tree planted by streams of water, which yields its fruit in season and whose leaf does not wither—whatever they do prospers.

Such is the generation of those who seek him, who seek your face, O God of Jacob. Selah **Psalm 24:6**

Amen is a declaration of agreement, or "so be it." When someone gives a beautiful musical performance at church, saying "Amen" means you agree it is a worthy gift to God.

Reading through Psalms, I came to the word "Selah." I couldn't figure it out from its context and not wanting to lose the meaning of the verse, I assumed it meant something like "Amen" and kept reading. The second time I came to the word "Selah," curiosity got the better of me and I decided to it look up.

"Selah" is direction to the reader to pause and meditate on the previous phrase. Where "Amen" expressed agreement, "Selah" directed me to stop and think. If I truly wish to pursue God's direction for me, I will not only read the words, I will think on them.

Take the time to learn one verse in the Bible, think about how it applies to you and carry it out.
Father, I pray for those who read but don't understand. Amen.

MAY 17

Lost on the Subway
BY MYRA BIERNAT WELLS

Psalm 10:1

Why, O Lord, do you stand far off? Why do you hide yourself in times of trouble?

When I was a youngster, about once a month, my mom would take my sister, brother and me downtown. I loved riding the subway, savoring the excitement of the Loop and lunch at the Palmer House, but especially the last item on our trip: picking out a book at the bookstore just before we boarded the subway back home.

On one of these trips, however, the three of them got off the train and were standing on the platform when the train door closed trapping me inside and separating me from them. I was panic-stricken; as a five year old, I had no way of knowing how to get home. I started to cry and pound the door with my little fists. Fortunately, a fellow rider hearing my wails and realizing what had happened pulled the emergency release lever, so I could be reunited with my family.

Have you ever felt separated from God like that? Have you ever wondered as you go about your routine, "God, do you see me? I feel all alone. I could use some help. You're nowhere to be found."

When we feel abandoned, it isn't because God walked away from us. It's because we have strayed from Him. It's so easy to get distracted by all the items on our to do list or the burden of one huge problem. Instead of pressing close to Jesus and squeezing His hand tight, we take our eyes off Him. We let the train door of life separate us leaving us to handle our challenges alone instead of with Him.

Even though we feel separated, His gaze has never left us. He is not standing away from us; He is right beside us, and you can always walk back into the warmth of His presence – even in the crowded subway or wherever you find yourself today.

Action:
Sometimes we get it backwards. We say to Jesus, "Here's what I'm doing. Please follow me and bless me," instead of saying, "Lord, take the lead; I'll follow You

today." Write a prayer of surrender to God. Include a line of thanksgiving because He will never abandon you.

Prayer:
Father, thank You that You always see me – that You will never leave me stranded. Lead me today. Shine Your truth into my life as I make the conscious choice to follow where You lead me today and always. In Jesus' name. Amen.

MAY 18

Sounding Like Janice
BY JUDY KNOX

Ephesians 4:17-24

Therefore be imitators of God, as beloved children; and walk in love, just as Christ also loved you and gave Himself up for us, an offering and a sacrifice to God as a fragrant aroma. **Ephesians 5:1-2** (NASB)

One summer during high school I began spending a lot of time with one particular girl, Janice. We had a great time hanging out, shopping, swimming, talking about boys, and just being silly. As the summer progressed, without realizing it, I began to take up some of her mannerisms and pet phrases. Undoubtedly, she also picked up some of mine.

During one "discussion" with my dad over some task I had failed to complete to his satisfaction, I made the flippant remark, "That's just the way the cookie crumbles!" He was not impressed. In a very disgusted voice, he said, "You're starting to sound just like Janice!" She was not the role model he would have chosen for his daughter.

I remember this vividly because it opened my eyes to the fact that we, as humans, tend to become like those we spend time with. Frequently my daughter and I are told, "I knew you were her mom (or her daughter) because you are so much alike." Since we don't closely resemble each other physically, we know it is the similarity in mannerisms they're talking about. And haven't you seen people who through the years come to resemble their mates or their pets?

Knowing this, then, we should give some attention to who we hang out with. Although we do not always have the choice in the workplace, or in other situations, we can choose to spend our free time among people who are a good influence on us, people who encourage us to love and good deeds (Hebrews 10:24).

Jesus has invited us to hang out with Him. We can do this in many ways: Bible reading, worship and praise, prayer, or just enjoying the peace of His presence. We can come before Him with singing (Psalm 100:2). "In [His] presence is fullness of joy; at [His] right hand are pleasures forevermore" (Psalm 16:11). Best of all, just like with any other friend, as we spend time with Him, we gradually, without even realizing it, become more like Him.

How awesome it would be to hear someone say, "You're starting to sound just like Jesus!" Wouldn't it be great to pick up His mannerisms, to react as He would react, and to speak as He would speak? I want to spend more and more time with Jesus and become more and more like Him. I think my dad would have approved of that!

Action:
Take some time every day to "hang out" with Jesus. Read the Gospels to learn more about what He was like. Picture yourself going through your day with Him by your side.

Prayer:
Father, I want to become more and more like Jesus. Show me some fresh, creative ways to spend time with Him so that His character will rub off on me. Amen.

MAY 19

Streams of Water
BY SHERRI GALLAGHER

Hebrews 10:19-25

Connecting with those you know love, like and who appreciate you restores the spirit and gives you energy to keep moving forward in this life. **Deborah Day**

My jogging route runs around a small man-made lake. It was created by damming a stream and flooding a marshy area. After a big storm, water gushes over the dam washing away silt and algae. Over time as the land dries out, the flow of water slows to a trickle and eventually stops altogether. When that happens, the lake becomes stagnant. Green algae blooms on the surface and the water itself becomes murky and smelly. It stays that way until the rains come and increase the flow of water over the dam once more.

Our spiritual lives can be much like that man-made lake. We start out excited and dive into scriptures, finding new meanings, guidance and ideas. But over time those same ideas become less and less helpful until we are so weighed down and tired of the same old thing that we are ready to give up and walk away. What we need is a fresh infusion of rain, and one of the best places to get that is at church. The sermons feed our spiritual needs flushing out stagnant ideas. Our friends encourage us, flowing their love over us in a soothing stream. The more we attend, the more abundant our energy, until we are overflowing with possibilities.

Go to church and try staying for the coffee hour after the service. Catch up on all that is happening in the life of our church.
Prayer:
Lord, help me to be more faithful in going to church to let Your guiding words flow over me in an ever-strengthening stream. Amen.

MAY 20

Victory over Your Fears!
BY MYRA BIERNAT WELLS

John 5:6

When Jesus saw him lying there and learned that he had been in this condition for a long time, he asked him, "Do you want to get well?"

My heart shattered as the doctor read my test results. Some negative words stood out: "Life-threatening;" "requires immediate treatment." He also spoke positive words: "totally treatable;" "caught early;" "no permanent damage – yet." While I suspected the news would not be easy to hear, I didn't expect the dire undertone of the results. The treatment would be arduous, repugnant and would probably last for the rest of my life. I was stunned.

My anger grew against God. All the way home, I wanted to journal bitter, accusing words to Him. "Why did You let this happen?" "Why couldn't You have protected me?" But before I could put thoughts to paper, I attended my church's midweek service.

The speaker was unfamiliar to me. Because my anger was still roiling at God, at first, I tuned the pastor out. Suddenly, his tone changed more somber, forcing me to listen. As a law student, he received an expulsion letter. Overcome by the fear of his future, the speaker's first response was to climb onto the roof of a six-story building with the intention of jumping. As he contemplated how much it would hurt to hit the pavement, he also reached out to Jesus. And in one momentous decision, he grabbed hold of the power of our Savior.

As I listened to this pastor, God, in another radical moment, spoke to me. "Do you want to get well?" Just a mere few seconds later, the same words were proclaimed from the stage! "Do you want to get well?" God was clearly trying to get my attention through this five-second delay. Jesus raised the same question to a lame man who sat for over thirty-eight years by the side of the pool at Bethesda. His hope was when the waters stirred, he would be the first person in the pool. According to the beliefs of the day, healing would occur. God went further with me. "You can go home and write angry page after page in your journal. Or, you can reach out to Me and let Me give you the strength to be healed. Do you want to get well?"

Not such a strange question. Often, we get used to being sick and wear it like a shroud. Emotionally we are the walking wounded – victims who pick at scabs – not allowing them to heal. Like the speaker, I reached out to Jesus and let Him heal me emotionally. That day, I chose to walk in Christ's freedom liberating the fears holding me captive.

Our freedom is more than shedding fear. Jesus set us free to live the abundant life by being all He created us to be and accomplishing His plans for us. Do you want to get well? Reach out to Jesus, the only one who can give you victory.

Action:
Are there fears you doubt God can remove from your life? Write them down on a sheet of paper. Then write a big "Yes" or "Amen" over your words and trust God to help you overcome them.

Prayer:
Dear God, I am sick and tired of being sick and tired. I reach forward today to receive my healing. Yes, I want to get well. Give me the faith to walk in freedom and victory. In Jesus' name. Amen.

MAY 21

What You Say Is What You Get
BY JUDY KNOX

Proverbs 18:20-21

A man's stomach shall be satisfied from the fruit of his mouth; From the produce of his lips he shall be filled. Death and life are in the power of the tongue, and those who love it will eat its fruit.

Keep your words short and sweet, because you never know which ones you will have to eat. **Anonymous**

In everyday conversation "eating your words" implies having said something wrong and now needing to admit it. But according to the Bible, eating our words denotes something quite different. It means receiving the results of what we have said.

"This is not going to work. Everything I do turns out badly." How many times have we all made such declarations? This is certainly not the way we want things to go, yet without realizing it, we negatively influence our lives and situations for negative results. The Bible makes it very clear that we set things in motion with our words. According to Proverbs 18:20-21, every time we open our mouths, we speak forth either life or death. When we understand the significance of this fact, we realize how important it is to watch what we say. To see positive things happening in our lives, we must speak positive words.

Why are words so powerful? The answer can be found in Genesis 1 where the events of creation are described. Over and over in this chapter -- 9 times -- we read, "then God said..." And every time God spoke, what He said came into being: light, continents, sky, oceans, plants, sun, moon, stars, animals, and finally people. He created man "in His own image, in His likeness" (Genesis 1: 26-27), and then He spoke a blessing over the whole creation and gave man authority and dominion to rule the earth. The creative force God used was the spoken word.

Because we are made in His image and likeness, our spoken words also bring things into existence. Most of us really don't pay much attention to our everyday words, and as a result, without knowing it, we speak a hodge-podge of life and death into our lives.

God has not only given us the power to create blessings and good fruit in our lives through our spoken words, but He has not kept this fact a secret from us. Proverbs 18:20-21 tells us "From the fruit of their mouth a person's stomach is filled." In fact, this passage states three times that we will indeed eat the results of what we say. When we make negative comments, we bring forth death. When we speak positive comments, we bring forth life.

The best words to speak are those that line up with God's written Word. Jesus said, "The words I have spoken to you—they are full of the Spirit and life" (John 6:63). When the words we speak agree with what God says, we set powerful spiritual forces in motion on our behalf. When we find Scripture applicable to our situation and speak that over it, we release the power of life into it. What kind of "food" are your words feeding you and the others around you? Speak life, and then you will be blessed when you eat your words.

Action:
Choose one area of your life where you would like to experience better results. Find Scripture that applies to it, and then begin speaking that Word into the situation, avoiding negative comments.

Prayer:
Lord, I thank You that I can have a powerful influence in my life just by monitoring my words and keeping them lined up with Your Word. Help me use the power of my tongue to speak life and not death. Amen.

MAY 22

Cousin Sean
BY SHERRI GALLAGHER

John 18:33-38

My cousin, Sean, was the only child of Uncle Gerry and Aunt Flo. They adored him, daily thanking God for their boy. He was nineteen when he died protecting a woman from a mugging. He didn't plan to sacrifice himself, there was just no time to save the other person and dodge a fatal blow.

My aunt and uncle were devastated at first, but they found solace knowing that thanks to Jesus' sacrifice, they would be re-united with their son. Their faith gave them a reason to continue and escape the morass of anger and depression.

Jesus was God's much-loved son. Unlike Sean, Jesus knew he would sacrifice himself long before it happened. He accepted death to save Sean and all of us. He accepted death to give Uncle Gerry and Aunt Flo comfort. Because of Jesus' sacrifice we know the worst tragedy can be overcome.

Action:

Take time to tell your child or parent you love them.

Prayer:

Lord God, thank You for the sacrifice of Your son to save us and our children. Amen.

MAY 23

Change
BY MYRA BIERNAT WELLS

Isaiah 40:31

But those who hope in the LORD will renew their strength. They will soar on wings like eagles; they will run and not grow weary, they will walk and not be faint.

While I have beautiful memories of my wedding day, there is one that stands out well above the rest. It was after the ceremony, after the greeting line, when my new husband, our bridal party and family went back into the chapel for pictures. I stood on the altar steps and was so filled with love, sweet expectation and joy that I didn't want the moment to end. I wanted to live on that altar forever.

The problem is, no matter how lovely a moment is, we can't stay in it for all eternity. If I remained at the altar, I'd have missed even more stunning moments: trips with my husband, Richard, creating new family traditions, his comfort when I was grief-stricken with pain – especially after the deaths of many I loved deeply.

No matter how lovely the moment is, we can't stay stuck in it. We must make the decision to move on. Change is a sign of growth, life and health.

Just as I had to step off the altar and into a new life, God may be asking you to step out in faith and make a change in your life. He wants only the best for you, so He has already mapped out a route and prepared every step along the way for you. This is risky because the future is unknown to you. But only to you…God is well aware of who you are, what you need and how much strength to supply. God may be asking you to ditch your old memories, eliminate destructive habits and forsake actions that do not breathe life into your activities.

The step that God is inviting you to take might not be as exciting as stepping off the wedding altar and rushing with eager anticipation into a new life. But God is waiting for you to take a step. One step. Faith does not come all at once. It is a step-by-step process that begins with one small movement towards His will and increases as you move closer to Him.

Action:
Is God asking you to make changes in your life? Write them down. Then next to them, create a list of the reasons you can trust God – even when facing uncertainty.

Prayer:
Father, I come to You in faith. Help me to make the needed movements to come closer to You. Help me to give up control of my life and make the changes You are asking me to make. In Jesus' name. Amen.

MAY 24

In All Things Give Thanks
BY JUDY KNOX

Colossians 3:15-17

And let the peace of God rule in your hearts, to which also you were called in one body; and be thankful. [16] Let the word of Christ dwell in you richly in all wisdom, teaching and admonishing one another in psalms and hymns and spiritual songs, singing with grace in your hearts to the Lord. [17] And whatever you do in word or deed, do all in the name of the Lord Jesus, giving thanks to God the Father through Him.

Give thanks in all circumstances; for this is God's will for you in Christ Jesus.
I Thessalonians 5:18

After five wonderful five days with my sister and her family in Arizona, I entered the luxurious resort where I was to spend four days at a Bible conference. At check-in the clerk asked if I would like a lift to my room in a golf cart. Fortunately, I said yes because my room was half a mile from the main building in a villa I would never have been able to find in the darkness. Nor could I have carried my heavy suitcase up the stairs to my second-floor room. This was not the setting I had expected.

When the bell person left, I assessed my surroundings. The clerk had given me a map with my villa circled. I studied it, trying to orient myself. I ventured outside, found myself in what looked like a back alley, and quickly retreated to my quarters. I texted friends who were also attending the conference, but they did not respond. Then I discovered there was no coffee maker in the room. For some reason, that suddenly loomed as a big issue.

After looking forward to my stay in this elegant place for months, I felt like the victim of some evil trick, isolated and disoriented, without even my comforting morning coffee to look forward to. What a bummer!

My old familiar enemy, self-pity, had come to pay a visit. At first, I listened to the old lies: nobody cares about me, I'm all alone, this is a disappointment. I began unpacking my suitcase.

As I pulled out my Bible, I realized that my thoughts and feelings did not line up with the truth it contained. Immediately I apologized to God and began thanking Him for all the good things He had done and there were many. My vacation so far had been absolutely wonderful.

The more things I thought of to be thankful for, the sillier I felt for my earlier thoughts. Peace and joy returned, and I delighted in the time alone with Him in this magnificent place. I ordered coffee from room service to be delivered at 6:30 AM, and after a nice sudsy bath in the lavish bathroom, I climbed into the comfortable bed and enjoyed a peaceful night's sleep.

The next day, after savoring my coffee and some time with God, I dressed and made my way to the main building. The map made total sense in the daylight. I had turned the wrong way the night before and walked to the back instead of the front of the villa. A brief walk in the Arizona sunshine took me where I needed to go. After a tasty breakfast I found my friends. The entire conference turned out to be a wonderful experience where God did exceedingly, abundantly beyond all I had asked or thought (Ephesians 3:20), and heaped blessings upon blessings.

The enemy sent self-pity to steal, kill and destroy. That attitude would have made me crabby and unable to recognize or appreciate the blessings God had for me. I would not have been fun for other people to be around. Jesus, on the other hand, came to give me abundant life (John 10:10). A thankful attitude readied my heart to be receptive to the many blessings He wanted to bring my way.

Action:

When things do not seem to go the way you expected, look around for blessings to thank God for. They will be there. Then turn to Him in thankfulness and praise.

Prayer:

Father, I know that Your desire is to bless me. Help me to see this when the circumstances are trying. Help me to be thankful for all the good You have done for me. Amen.

MAY 25

Be Prepared
BY SHERRI GALLAGHER

Genesis 41:54

...There was famine in all the other lands, but in the whole land of Egypt there was food.

I grew up in snow country. At least one week of the year, drifts and densely packed snow closed the roads and cut off electricity. I learned as a child to always be prepared. Instead of being cold and hungry, our family cooked delicious filling meals in the fireplace and slept snug and warm in the living room.

My son laughs at my stock of non-perishable food. He's never lived through a "snow day," but God warns us to be prepared for natural disasters that are typical of our area. For example, He sent Pharaoh a dream warning of the famine in Egypt so the Egyptians could store food. In the same way we should also be prepared to care for ourselves and others in an emergency, such as a hurricane, earthquake, tornado or blizzard.

Action:

Choose one of these: set up a disaster kit, discuss family plans in case of evacuation, take a Community Emergency Response Team course (www.citizencorps.gov).

Prayer:

Thank You, Lord, for Your bounty that will carry us through lean times. Amen.

MAY 26

Bright Beginnings
BY MYRA BIERNAT WELLS

Psalm 25:5

Guide me in your truth and teach me for you are my God and Savior and my hope is in you all day long.

Everything that is done in the world is done by hope. **Martin Luther**

As a child, one of my favorite games was tug of war. My neighborhood friends would gather on warm summer nights and we'd play for bragging rights. The pressure would mount as the advantage would volley from one team or to the other until one finally gained enough traction to win the game.

We live out a different type of tug of war each day – a faith adventure. The enemy is on his side of the rope ready to pull us into a pit of fear, despair, doubt, guilt, insecurity, comparison and lies. On the faith side of the rope, standing firm and ready to fight are: confidence, identity in Christ, compassion, forgiveness, competence and truth. In John 16:33, Jesus brings this issue into sharp focus for us: "In this world, you will have trouble. But take heart, I have overcome the world."

Unfortunately, because life *is* a tug of war, God made sure we are not without the strength and hope needed to give us traction to win, even when it feels like the other side has the advantage. As we move into a new year, remind yourself what side of the rope you would like to be on? Isn't the faith side of our Father, our Abba, the best place to be? Because with Him, we receive all we need to win every battle in life.

Action:
Read Hebrews 6:19 (NLT), "This hope is a strong and trustworthy anchor for our souls." Make a short list of some of the ways you feel pulled down by this world. Then balance it with a list of places God is working in your life. What is the first step of faith you need to take today? How does knowing God is on your side give you hope?

Prayer:
Lord, surely there is a battle raging around me. At times, it knocks me down and hits me hard. Please be the anchor of hope and strength I need right now. Hold me secure and pull me through each trial I am facing. Help me to remember who I am in You. In Jesus' name. Amen.

MAY 27

Walking in Good Counsel
BY JUDY KNOX

Romans 6:5-11

Blessed is the man who walks not in the counsel of the ungodly, nor stands in the path of sinners, nor sits in the seat of the scornful; but his delight is in the law of the Lord, and in His law does he meditate day and night. **Psalms 1:1-2**

When I retired, I looked forward to spending more time with my husband. It was fun sharing the grocery shopping, household chores and yard work. There was, however, one thing I had a hard time getting used to: his passion for talk radio. For at least three hours every day, the booming voice of the talk-show host droned throughout our house, garage, and car. Wherever we went, whatever we were doing, this man was there with us, expounding on the events of the day, especially the political events.

Wanting to be a good companion, I tried to share my husband's interest in all of this, but I never cared for the host's wit and sarcasm. Although I usually agreed with his opinions, I felt as if I were being lectured to all the time. My suggestions about reducing our listening time did not go over well.

Gradually I noticed that while we started out most days in good humor, by the end of the radio program we were usually somewhat grouchy. I did not make the connection immediately, but eventually I began to suspect that immersing ourselves in negative thinking, even if the information itself was true, and the jokes and song parodies were funny, had a negative effect on our moods.

Then one day my husband declared, "You know, listening to all this stuff is like walking in the counsel of the ungodly, standing in the path of sinners, and sitting in the seat of the scornful. I think instead of listening to talk radio, we should be reading the Bible. Instead of worrying about all this political stuff, we should pray for our government the way the Bible says we should."

While I agreed with him, I was surprised he was able to go "cold turkey" on radio listening. We rarely listened again. Occasionally when a major event occurred, he turned on the radio to see what his favorite host had to say about it, but after 15 or 20 minutes he would say, "That's enough of that!" and turn it off.

The talk show host was not "ungodly" in the sense of being evil, but listening to him was not "encouraging us to love and good deeds" (Hebrews 10:24). Instead of setting our minds on the Spirit, which is life and peace, we were setting them on the flesh, which the Bible tells us is death (Romans 8:6).

After we stopped listening to all the negativity, household projects were accompanied by nice music. In the car, we actually engaged in meaningful conversations. Life was more fun, and our thinking became more positive. Retirement held more of the joy I had looked forward to.

Action:

Examine the input that is coming into your home and your mind through various media. Determine which one has the most negative impact and try giving it up for a week.

Prayer:

Father, help me to be more conscious of what kind of counsel I am walking in, and help me to eliminate things that are standing in the way of my relationship with You. In Jesus' name. Amen.

MAY 28

Slow to E-mail
BY SHERRI GALLAGHER

James 1:19-21

My dear brothers and sisters, take note of this: Everyone should be quick to listen, slow to speak and slow to become angry, because human anger does not produce the righteousness that God desires. Therefore, get rid of all moral filth and the evil that is so prevalent and humbly accept the word planted in you, which can save you.

Someone started an accusatory e-mail over an e-group. My first thought was to send off a cutting reply. Instead, I wrote an e-mail reminding people that written words could be taken with the wrong perception and create strife. Several salvos ricocheted between group members. Another member caught on to what I was doing and also called for calmer, kinder words. This discussion ended on a happier note. People realized how inflammatory their words had been and they'd hurt other people's feelings. Apologies circulated avoiding a potential rift between good friends.

James tells us to be quick to listen, really listen to what the person is trying to say. He also tells us to be slow to speak, slow to anger. In this day and age of instant communication we need to be extra careful of what we write or say, and when offended, slow to anger and slower still to voice that anger.

Before we fire off that sarcastic reply, we need to stop and think. If you were on the telephone or face to face, would you say those words? If an exchange is escalating in callousness, stop. Pick up the telephone or go visit. It's well worth the effort and a time-saver in the long run.

Save strongly worded e-mails to draft and re-read them a day or two later and before you hit the send button!

Please help me to wait before I respond in anger and slower still to anger, and thank You for the delete key. Amen.

MAY 29

White House
BY MYRA BIERNAT WELLS

2 Corinthians 5:17

Therefore, if anyone is in Christ, the new creation has come. The old has gone, the new is here!

It was well past 2:00 a.m. when my husband and I pulled into our hotel in White House, Tennessee for the night. On the road from Savannah to our home in Lake Zurich, we stopped to visit friends in Atlanta. The fun we shared with them kept us longer than anticipated. When we finally arrived at our hotel, we quickly brought a very few things into the room and promptly went to sleep.

In the morning, when we awoke and went outside, we were surprised by the sights that greeted us. White House is filled with lush meadows, mature trees, beautiful houses, lovely neighborhoods. We'd been unable to see the beauty around us because the night had been dark, and we had been so tired. Yet it was there, right outside our door.

God is all about beautiful transformations. He is an active, deeply personal, infinitely caring God who restores us on a heart level with masterful changes. When we come to Him in repentance unable to see the beauty around us because of our darkness, He takes away the stain of our sin and replaces it with beauty.

His word says a lot about what happens when we turn to God. "Those who look to him are radiant; they are never covered in shame" (Psalm 34:5), and "Forget the former things; do not dwell on the past. See, I am doing a new thing! Now it springs up; do you not perceive it? I am making a way in the wilderness and streams in the wasteland" (Isaiah 43:18-19).

God gave His life so you and I could be surprised by the transformations in our lives. We can live beyond our disappointments, beyond our biggest mistakes and beyond our deepest pains. He bore a cross so we could be forgiven and made new. The good news of the Gospel is simple: when we call out to God and seek

His heart and forgiveness through Jesus Christ, He does a new thing! Every morning we wake up to His mercy, His forgiveness and His blessings.

Action:

Where do you need the most transformation in your life? Write it down, then pray about it once per day for a week.

Prayer:

Dear Lord, I am so grateful You love makeovers. You know my messes, failures and wounds. Please create a new heart in me today, Lord. Would You do a new and beautiful thing? In Jesus' name I pray. Amen.

MAY 30

Faith without Works
BY SHERRI GALLAGHER

James 2:14-24

And the scripture was fulfilled that says, "Abraham believed God, and it was credited to him as righteousness," and he was called God's friend. You see that a person is considered righteous by what they do and not by faith alone.
James 2:23-24

It is a denial of justice not to stretch out a helping hand to the fallen; that is the common right of humanity. **Seneca**

We had just returned from a search for a drowning victim, and I had called to tell my sister about it.

"Enough of the good works, you can't earn your way into heaven, you have to have faith." Sis was right. Yes, I had faith but how did that help anyone but me? We demonstrate our faith by helping others.

James tells us, "If a brother or sister is naked and lacks daily food and one of you says, "Go in peace; keep warm and eat your fill," and yet we do not supply their bodily needs, what is the good of that? (James 2:15-16) It's our responsibility to help others. Contributions to the shepherd's fund are good works. Teaching Sunday School, helping at service, or visiting shut-ins and those in nursing homes are all ways to demonstrate faith. But there are other ways to serve. You need to follow your calling. Can you write a letter for a visually impaired person? Clean gutters or run errands for the elderly? Address Christmas cards for an overworked mom? Doing what helps, big or small, is what matters.

Action:

Identify one thing you could do to help someone else besides giving money.

Prayer:
Lord, lead us to a path where we can help someone else. Amen.

MAY 31 - MEMORIAL DAY

Memorial Day
BY MAUREEN LANG

John 15:13

Greater love hath no man than this, that a man lay down his life for his friends.

Older men declare war. But it is the youth that must fight and die.
Herbert Hoover

Memorial Day is one of those holidays that, for me as a non-military-person, is often associated more with mattress sales and the end of the school year than with the actual significance of the day. I admit that with regret, more so since my Navy-vet father passed away.

Recently I was shopping in an area that's near the same naval base where my father trained. I saw several boys in uniform walking along the sidewalk and thought: *My goodness, those sailors are young!* But then I remembered my own dad volunteered when he was only seventeen years old, so he would have been about their age or perhaps even younger. It's a fact that has me simultaneously wondering how the country's security could be entrusted to such young hands and yet realizing that's exactly where it's best served: in people young enough to be trained to listen and obey the orders of their superiors, yet old enough to carry out those orders with strength, agility and speed.

Seeing the youth of those boys in uniform also reminded me of the thousands before them who sacrificed their lives while protecting our country. So many lives cut short! A quick online search tells me well over a million American lives have been lost in battle since the Revolutionary War. Being reminded just *how young* many of them were certainly compounds the loss—so many futures never to be lived.

So today, as I reflect on the great sacrifices of so many men and women who died while in the service of our country, I'm grateful not only for the amount of time I've been blessed to live, but especially so in light of those who sacrificed their lives for the freedom I enjoy every day.

Action:
No matter how many years you've been blessed with life, recall today those who paid the highest price to protect the freedom and way of life each of us in America enjoy.

Prayer:
Father, help me to cherish the gift of life that You gave me, whether we're under sunny skies or gray—knowing that our lives are in Your hands. Amen.

JUNE 1

Where Is the Duct Tape?
BY SHERRI GALLAGHER

Proverbs 4:10-27

This is part of the essence of motherhood, watching your kid grow into her own person and not being able to do anything about it. Otherwise children would be nothing more than pets. **Heather Armstrong**

Watching my son grow up and become an adult has been a pleasure. For the most part he has been easy to raise; an individual who would listen and discuss a situation and generally make a good decision. Of course, he isn't perfect. There has been more than once when I have watched him willfully ignore my advice. On occasion, the urge to talk sense into him has been extreme but I've known he won't listen. The only alternative was to walk away or at least duct tape my mouth shut. I've cried more than a few tears as hard knocks have sent his dreams spinning away from him. All I could do was let him know I still loved him and wait and watch and pray he would recover and find the right path back.

The more I watch him the more aware I am of how I must vex God. He has given me straightforward guidance and I have turned my back on it, quite sure that I know better. I know He cried for my pain and felt joy when I turned back to paths He would have me follow. Being a parent is to know great joy and great pain. It is a combination of pride and fear. While I am not sure if God feels either of those emotions, Luke 15 tells me He rejoices when I come back to His ways.

Action:
How have you strayed from the path God would have you take? Take stock and pick one way to reform and please God.

Prayer:
Heavenly Father, thank You for your love and guidance. Forgive me when I have left Your ways to travel the paths I thought were best, but You knew better. Thank You for loving my willful self and forgiving my sins. Amen.

JUNE 2

The Master Plan
BY MYRA BIERNAT WELLS

Jeremiah 1:5

Before I made you in your mother's womb, I chose you. (NCV)

It is difficult to make a man miserable when he feels worthy of himself and claims kindred to the great God who made him. **Abraham Lincoln**

There have been times in my life when I doubted my worth and value. Yet, I felt I could fix this self-confidence issue on my own. That sounded good, but it got me nowhere. I can never be good enough, do enough to earn the love and favor of God. The good news is, I don't have to be!

My journey, like yours, began in the heart and mind of God. Before we even took our first breath, God wanted, loved and planned us. We are not accidents. We were created in response to God's love and according to His plans. My worth and value rest in the fact that I am God's very own child. Like you, I am loved, wanted and cherished by God Himself. He supervised our formation so we could enjoy an intimate relationship with Him.

You and I were not only created in response to the love of God, but He also has a plan for us. He didn't accidentally create us and then step back in alarm and say, "Oh no, I created her. What am I doing to do with her?"

Labeling yourself as anything other than a child of the King is so limiting! Understanding you are cherished by the Creator of the universe who delights in you means His perfect plan and highest purpose for your life will naturally unfold before you each day. Always remember, in His eyes, you are special, and His plan for your life is simply for you to get good at being you.

Action:
Do you really believe God loves you unconditionally? What proof of that belief exists in your life? Do you consider yourself worthy? Why or why not?

Prayer:
Father, I want to know You and live Your plan for my life. I choose to see myself through Your eyes of love, forgiveness and grace. I want to be the person You created me to be. Thank You for loving me. Help me walk each day in the knowledge that I am in Your child. In Jesus' name. Amen.

JUNE 3

Shepherd in a Green Jacket
BY JUDY KNOX

Psalm 23:1-4

I am the good shepherd; I know my sheep and my sheep know me. **John 10:14**

I recently went on the trip of a lifetime – a thirteen-day tour of Alaska. I was flying alone to Fairbanks, where I would meet up with my sister-in-law Ruth and her senior citizens group from Huntsville, Alabama. As I cleared security, I learned Ruth was unable to make the trip due to illness, so now I would be flying more than 4,000 miles to connect with a group of people I had never met. However, the coordinator of the senior citizens group assured me I would be fine. "When you get to the baggage claim area, just look for the people in the green jackets. Those are our leaders."

Two flights and ten hours later, I landed in Fairbanks and headed for baggage claim. Before I even reached the carousel, a young man in a bright green jacket greeted me. "You must be Judy," he said. "Welcome to Alaska." His name was Barry, and he would be the guide for our group of fifteen plus twenty others throughout the trip. He said the Huntsville group had been delayed and would not arrive for at least another hour; he got me onto the shuttle for my hotel and gave me instructions for the next day.

Every morning Barry met us in the hotel lobby and escorted us to our bus. He rode along and explained the plans for the day. Often our bus driver would tell us about the sights along the way, but Barry also shared tidbits of information that enhanced our understanding and enjoyment of the area. When we got off the bus for further sightseeing, Barry kept a watchful eye on us. Every evening when we arrived at the day's destination, he handed each of us an envelope with our room keys and information for the next morning.

On one occasion we disembarked, only to discover the restaurants and shops were closed. One couple, however, had managed to get off the bus and into a building up the street, having no idea we were leaving. When Barry counted and found two were missing, he didn't have to check the list. He knew who they were and went looking for them, leaving us safely waiting on the bus. When they returned, we all rejoiced that they had been found.

Barry knew the area well, so he was able to direct us to the good restaurants and warn us about overpriced, junky gift shops as well as any dangers we needed to watch for. He gave us his cell phone number in case we needed his help. Everywhere we went, Barry was there to serve us, lead us, and watch over us. The more I saw him putting our needs before his own, the more secure I felt under his leadership. Although I was traveling alone, as a member of the group with Barry at the helm I felt completely safe.

After returning home, I recognized many similarities between Barry and various images of the Good Shepherd in the Bible. Now I understand why sheep are so peaceful and secure. All they need to do is stay with the flock and follow the shepherd. And that is what God wants us to do. He does the organizing and planning. He knows the area where He is taking us and will show us the green grass and still waters. He will lead us and keep us safe. He will even come after us if we stray. I have a better picture now of what it is like being cared for by the Shepherd after being part of Barry's group. Little did that man in the green jacket know God would use him to show me new insights into scriptural passages I have been reading all my life.

Action:
Do a study of passages about the Good Shepherd, especially John 10, Psalm 23 and Psalm 95.

Prayer:
Father, I thank You for being my Shepherd. Help me learn to follow and trust You more through understanding this relationship. Amen.

JUNE 4

The Search That Wasn't
BY SHERRI GALLAGHER

James 3:13-18

No man is wise enough by himself. **Titus Maccius Plautus**

Sometimes the phone rings and our search and rescue team can't help. A recent call asked for skills beyond the capabilities of our training. We could have gone and might have been a help. We also could have obliterated clues a properly trained team needed to be successful. We recommended people with the training and stood down. Walking away from that call was not easy. There was a need. We had trained and wished to serve, but the call was for someone else with different training. It took experience, learning and wisdom to walk away when we all wanted to do was go.

In the book of James, the question is asked, "Who is wise and understanding among you? Show by your good life that your works are done with gentleness born of wisdom." Leaders are constantly under pressure to make decisions and take action or answer questions on a broad range of topics and speak before they've had the opportunity to consider the situation in depth. Yet speaking or acting from ignorance only causes problems. Just look at the latest sound bite mocking a politician and take a guess how much they wish they could call those words back.

It is a heady feeling to be considered an expert or a leader. Getting lost in that feeling leads to boastfulness and selfish ambition. That can be disastrous. Wise leaders take things to the appropriate committee or discuss it with others who may have experience or knowledge with a similar situation. Being slow to act or speak is wise.

Action:
The next time you are asked a question, count to 10 and decide if you are the right person to answer it or if more thought is needed.

Prayer:
Heavenly Father, guide our leaders. Give them the wisdom to know when to speak, when to seek guidance and when to stay silent. Amen.

JUNE 5

The Canyon on the Prairie
BY MYRA BIERNAT WELLS

Psalm 91:1-2
He who dwells in the shelter of the Most High will rest in the shadow of the Almighty. I will say of the Lord, "He is my refuge and my fortress, my God, in whom I trust. (NASB)

A mighty fortress is our God. A bulwark never failing. **Martin Luther**

I love downtown Chicago. What a humbling place it is! As you walk through the streets in the Loop, even in the daytime, you are engulfed by the shadows of gargantuan skyscrapers that blot out the sun. The city is enormous in every way.

God is just like that!

The Scripture above says you can reside in Him. You find sustenance, love, beauty and trust in Him. He is a city unto himself. **Dwell in Him.**

He shelters you. He can protect you from whatever life throws at you. He is so big and sovereign that nothing can touch you except what He allows. **Hide in Him.**

He is so significant and His shadow is so vast that it falls on everything, everywhere and everyone on earth. No matter where you find yourself in the world and no matter what condition you are in, you can always rest in His shadow and find the help you need. **Rest in Him.**

God is unbeatably strong, preeminently vast and unstoppably powerful. He truly is our fortress and refuge. **Trust in Him.**

If life is getting you down, go to the City of the King and take refuge in His greatness, rest in His shadow and rely upon Him to see you through. **He will never fail you.**

Action:

Think about the past few days, weeks and months of your life. Where has God sheltered you? Where has His unfailing love been your fortress? Spend a few moments in praise thanking Him for what He has already done for you.

Prayer:

Father, thank You for being such a powerful God. Thank You for the rest found in Your shadow and the comfort in Your strength. In Your power, I find hope. Amen.

JUNE 6

Big Shoulders
BY BETH DUMEY

Matthew 11:30

For my yoke is easy and my burden is light.

Like many women, I carry my handbag on my shoulder when I am out and about. Or, at least I try to. Often, it slips down my arm or hangs half on and half off until I correct the imbalance. Because I apparently have narrow shoulders, I am constantly struggling with my handbag. It occurred to me, during a months-long season of crises, that my shoulders did feel unusually small; not strong enough to handle the traumas of life. I needed bigger shoulders.

The Lord knows each of us will reach times in our lives when the demands are too great for us to shoulder. He makes it clear in Scripture that relief comes directly from him, the God of big shoulders. In Matthew 11:30, He reminds us "my yoke is easy and my burden is light." Whatever we can't handle, He can.

If we release our challenges and difficulties to Him, trusting that He can take on our monster burdens, he will work in and through them. They may not be removed or resolved immediately, but over time we will sense his power whittling away at them. And our shoulder muscles can relax.

Action:

Take an inventory of the burdens you are currently carrying. When was the last time you prayed, "Father, this one is Yours. I am releasing _____ to You."

Prayer:

Lord, thanks for taking on my yoke and my burdens. In my own power, I am limited at best. In Your power and with Your strength, I can handle any challenge You allow to enter my life. Help me to remember to always turn to You. Amen.

JUNE 7

American Biker Girl Doll
BY SHERRI GALLAGHER

1 Samuel 16:5-13

But the LORD said to Samuel, "Do not consider his appearance or his height, for I have rejected him. The LORD does not look at the things people look at. People look at the outward appearance, but the LORD looks at the heart."
1 Samuel 16:7

Beware so long as you live, of judging people by appearances. **La Fontaine**

I had a business meeting downtown and waited at the Metra Station for the train. For once I was professionally dressed instead of in my muddy and worn dog training clothes. As I waited several people struck up a conversation with me, identifying themselves as professors. When the train pulled in, we all piled into the first nearly empty car. I plunked myself down in a seat near the door, determined to make the best use of the hour ride, but all the instructors turned quickly and left the car, glancing over their shoulders as they hurried away.

Two men, one of them clearly a biker wearing his colors and sporting several tattoos sat about mid-car, talking quietly. I thought about leaving but couldn't see how to do it without appearing rude. I was close to the door, if violence erupted, I could escape quickly.

A childish voice floated from the upper level, "Daddy, my doll's braid came out."

The biker rose, "Okay hand it to me and I'll fix it."

A vision in pink shirt with sequins, jeans and light-up sneakers trustingly bent down to hand over her Barbie to this hulking man. He quickly and efficiently went to work braiding the doll's hair. While she waited the little girl look over at me and informed me her daddy was taking her to the American Girl Doll Shop and was going to let her pick out a new doll. The biker finished his task and the three of us discussed just which doll should be selected.

Later I wondered if the other passengers would have been as polite and engaging to me if I had been wearing my everyday clothing. How nice would I be to someone else wearing muddy, worn garments? Just like Samuel looking at David's brothers, I didn't have a clue as to the person inside and left to my own judgment would have mistakenly ignored a person of value.

Action:
Resolve to sit and really listen to a person you would normally rush by.

JUNE 8

God Will Never Leave You!
BY MYRA BIERNAT WELLS

Hebrews 13:5

I will never desert you, nor will I ever forsake you. (NASB)

Loneliness and the feeling of being unwanted is the most terrible poverty.
Mother Teresa

It took a while after my beloved Rascal dog passed away before I'd even think of getting another dog. I was so heartbroken I couldn't imagine getting a new pet. I didn't want to face that kind of pain ever again.

With time came healing. And when I was finally ready for a new dog, I narrowed my selection down to two German Shepherds – a four-year old and a puppy. What tipped the scales in favor of a puppy was not the cute face or the adorable wiggles. No, it was that she was alone. My Lily dog came from a large litter. One by one her litter mates were bought and sent home to their new owners. Soon it was just Lily in the large cage they once all shared. My heart broke for it seemed as if no one wanted her.

Sometimes, we can feel the same. All alone – abandoned by friends, deserted by a spouse, forgotten by family and unseen by society.

The good news is that even on those days when we feel deserted, on those days when we feel like we have been abandoned, God is with us. We are never far from God's heart and He is right there beside us.

When we feel discarded, it is difficult to imagine that the God who created the universe is there for us, but He is. His greatest desire is to draw you close to Him. This is why He created you. So, when you are feeling like no one cares, call on the Lord to show Himself in your life. His love never fails. He wants nothing more than to be there for you.

Action:
Think of one person in your life who might feel all alone; who feel God has abandoned them. Do one thing (a friendly phone call, an encouraging email, a short visit, a gift of flowers) to brighten their day and make them feel less lonely.

Father, thank You that You are with me always. Remind me in the lonely moments – in the times when I feel like the world has abandoned me – that You are there right beside me. Remind me that I am Your child and that I am never alone. Amen.

JUNE 9

Good Lunch – Bad Idea
BY JUDY KNOX

Hebrews 12:5-11

But solid food is for the mature, who by constant use have trained themselves to distinguish good from evil. **Hebrews 5:14**

Meeting at the restaurant/bakery seemed like a great idea. My niece and her two children had a day off from school and she wanted me to meet her friend Susan, the mother of two young boys. We had never been to that restaurant before, but Susan had, and she suggested the place.

Prior to lunch, the two young moms had taken the four children to the park for a couple of hours of swings, slides, and monkey bars. When they arrived at the restaurant, although the children's faces still flushed from their active morning, it was obvious the four-year-old was not happy to be there. He was angry about having to leave the park.

Inside the restaurant, we got into line to order. The line crept alongside a huge glass-fronted case resplendent with a tantalizing array of cookies, cupcakes, and pastries. The young mother asked her four-year-old what he wanted for lunch. He pointed to the two most brightly colored cookies in the case.

A tired, cranky boy, staring into a case full of sugar-laden treats, is not likely to be excited about a grilled cheese sandwich. In order to keep him quiet, she bought the two cookies, telling him he could have them after he ate his sandwich. The "lunch" ended with Susan dragging two boys, lunches uneaten, out of the restaurant. She and I never did have a chance to get acquainted.

Susan was not trying to withhold cookies from her child; she purchased them for him. But she knew a load of sugar on a tired boy's empty stomach would not give him what he needed to make it through the rest of the day. She was thinking beyond the moment; he did not have the maturity to understand her motives, so conflict was inevitable.

After they left, my niece expressed surprise that her friend would suggest this place, knowing we would have to stand in front of all the tempting desserts to order our food. Even I, who seldom order dessert in a restaurant, had trouble resisting those goodies, which the owners know look even more enticing when you're hungry.

Sometimes I find I am like that four-year-old, seeing something I want, and wanting it now, regardless of what might be in my best interest. However, God knows what's best for us. He is not trying to withhold good things from us. His Word gives us principles to follow, which are intended for our benefit. We need to be mature enough to realize that doing things God's way will give us better results in the long run.

When things don't go our way, do we stomp our foot and whine, insisting on the cookie, or do we "man up" and obey God's Word, trusting that only He sees the big picture?

Action:

Take a few minutes to consider the things you think you want right now, but don't seem to be readily coming your way. Ask God to show you if He has a better plan.

Prayer:

Father, although sometimes I don't outwardly throw a tantrum when I don't get my way, there are times when I keep thinking about the thing I want instead of trusting Your timing and realizing You know what's best for me. Help me to be mature, more interested in what You want for me than what I want. Amen.

JUNE 10

Consistency
BY SHERRI GALLAGHER

Matthew 22:35-40

The first duty of a leader is to make himself be loved without courting love. To be loved without 'playing up' to anyone - even to himself. **Andre Malraux**

I don't train dogs professionally. I train my dogs for the joy of interacting with them and for the service we can perform to the community. When people ask me to come help them with a dog training problem, I quickly look for excuses to bow out and refer them to people who are paid professionals. It is not that I don't want to help, the problem is they may not like my help when I give it.

That is not to say I don't end up helping train sometimes. A friend needed help with a young dog still in training. He was a strong dog and she was no match for his strength and speed. I walked her through the process. Step 1: get the dog's attention. Step 2: give the command. Step 3: give a correction if the command is not followed. Step 4: Give the command again. Step 5: reward obedience. Repeat as necessary. We started to walk and the dog surged forward jerking her, so she almost fell. I directed her to give a correction and she refused because she didn't want to hurt the dog. Nothing I said could convince her that not giving the correction would hurt the dog more in the long run. She could not accept that eliminating the consequences for breaking the rules made him a danger to himself and the people around him.

God gives us two very simple rules: Love the Lord your God with all your heart and love your neighbor as yourself. When we fail to obey them, we face the consequences of our actions. Ignoring these rules can lead to lonely, empty lives. Following them gives us the wealth of joy and love that no amount of money can buy.

Action:

Using colored pens, pencils, paints or other craft materials you like to work with make a small sign or plaque quoting Matthew 33:37-39. Hang it near your desk or place of prayer.

Prayer:

Thank you, Lord, for these two simple rules that make my life richer and happier. Help me to apply them in everything I do. Amen.

JUNE 11

Who Is Walking Beside You?
BY MYRA BIERNAT WELLS

Matthew 28:20

.... And surely I am with you always, to the very end of the age.

Later on the same day the women discovered Christ's tomb was empty, two disciples were walking to the village of Emmaus, seven miles from Jerusalem. As they traveled talking about the unusual events of the past week, another man began to walk beside them.

"What are you talking about?" the man queried.

Dismayed by his lack of knowledge, they asked, "Are you the only visitor in Jerusalem who doesn't know about what happened there these past few days?

"What things?" he asked.

Then the two disciples gave their fellow traveler an account of Jesus' arrest, crucifixion, burial and disappearance from the tomb. As they talked, their eyes were blinded by despair and they didn't realize that hope was walking right beside them. All they saw was the tragedy.

When they came to the village, the disciples asked this stranger to join them for dinner. There Jesus took the bread, gave thanks, broke the bread and passed it to the men. A flood of memories returned upon seeing the nail-scarred hands that held the bread. "Their eyes were opened and they recognized him, and he disappeared from their sight." (Luke 24:31)

Have you traveled down your own dusty road to Emmaus with circumstances leaving you confused, troubled and depressed? If so, remember that just because you cannot see Jesus or sense His presence does not mean that He is not there. He is walking the path with you. He assured us, "Never will I leave you, never will I forsake you (Hebrews 13:5). He gave His word. He gave His life.

Action:
Take time today to consider this question: How does the realization Jesus is always walking beside you change your reaction to disappointment and broken dreams?

Prayer:
Dear Lord, I know You are always with me. Forgive me when I whine about being all alone. Forgive me when I complain no one understands my problems. I know You understand all things and that You are my hope, who will never leave me. Amen.

JUNE 12

Spending Time
BY BETH DUMEY

Ecclesiastes 3:1

There is a time for everything and a season for every activity under heaven.

While I've never considered myself a techie, I am somewhat of a news addict. Because of this, I limit the number of television channels I receive so I don't spend entire days watching 24-hour cable news. However, with an unlimited number of online venues to mine for news, I find myself surfing the various network sites, independent news, and related web sites for hours at a time. On one hand, I find this relaxing, on the other it leaves me feeling like I just ate a whole bowl of cotton candy. It's too much of something that should be taken in measured doses. And like junk food, it is a poor replacement for what could have been much better for me, such as community, journaling, reading scripture, or even soaking in the tub.

We have many choices about how we spend our time and we may have seasons in which more down time is needed. How we spend this time though will either build us up from the inside out or leave us empty. I find that taking in too much news leaves me feeling a bit depleted. While there is nothing objectionable about staying informed, maybe it is just too easy to turn on the laptop. Perhaps reaching for the phone and connecting with a friend would fill me up more. Possibly writing through some of my thoughts and feelings would lead to greater insights. Likely, what would really satisfy my soul is seeking God in this time and spending it with Him. While we have much freedom, Matthew 3:10 reminds us "every tree that does not produce good fruit will be cut down…"

Action:

What habit or time-zapper would you like to limit or remove from your life? Share this with a trusted friend.

Prayer:

Lord, our time on this earth is limited. Help us to spend it in fruitful ways, taking in those things that are edifying and eliminating those that do not give us life. Help us to discern between the two. Amen.

JUNE 13

Maybe I Will, Maybe I Won't
BY SHERRI GALLAGHER

Hebrews 12:4-13

It is our choices that show what we truly are, far more than our abilities.
J.K. Rowling

I love my dog Belle, but sometimes she makes me want to scream. She was the most independent dog I've ever met. This is probably because the majority of her training was done through motivation, she obeyed because she got something she wanted. Sometimes her actions made me laugh, but more often than not her disobedience was dangerous. If I saw her running into the path of a vehicle, she had to stop on my command not make her own decisions about obeying. Eventually I added an electronic collar for corrections to my motivational training and Belle became a trustworthy canine partner that could be used for search work.

I could be very upset at Belle's attitude, but I realize I do the same thing to God. Much as I try, I do not give Him the blind obedience I demand from my dog. When I come to a problem, I frequently evaluate it from my skills and abilities to deal with it instead of turning to God for guidance. When God is sure I understand and am ignoring Him, He may offer a kind correction to make me realize I need to listen. Hopefully I change my actions with His equivalent of a verbal correction and don't ignore God until he puts a shock collar on me.

Pray before acting. Make sure you are obeying His commands
Prayer:
Lord, thank You for your patience when I am disobedient. Amen.

JUNE 14 - FLAG DAY

I Pledge Allegiance
BY CATHY HARVEY

Psalm 60:4

But for those who fear you, you have raised a banner to be unfurled against the bow.

I pledge allegiance to the flag of the United States of America and to the Republic for which it stands, one nation under God, indivisible, with liberty and justice for all. **Francis Bellamy** ("under God" added by Congress, 1954)

My father was born during the Roaring Twenties era of our American history. His parents sailed here from northern Italy, checked in through Ellis Island, and settled in Chicago where my dad and his siblings grew up. Somehow, they made it through the Depression. At some point my grandfather left the family, so my dad started driving when he was twelve years old so he could take his sister, my aunt, to her many doctor appointments. She had Cerebral Palsy—she was lucky, the doctor said; she had the "good type," because the part of her brain that was affected only disengaged her legs from working properly and did not affect her mind.

World War II arrived and with all the loyalty and patriotism of the time, my dad joined the Navy at age seventeen, faithfully lying that he was eighteen in order to enlist. Perhaps after Pearl Harbor was bombed the Navy was in too much of a hurry to check such details, or perhaps my immigrant grandmother had no birth papers to disprove his age. He served on the USS Denebola and I am privileged to have the memorabilia from his Navy years.

I learned patriotism from my Dad. He never lectured about it; he simply lived it. He was a hard-working family man with a devoted spirit of service. He and a friend ran a car dealership together. His friend ran the front-end sales and my dad managed the body shop. He was not a mechanic, but a good leader and his shop was spotless. More than once we heard customers say, "I could eat my lunch off that floor!" It was true. He sealed and polished the concrete floors. He ran a clean, tight ship and no car left the body shop without a car wash and cleaning.

I have a memory of my dad's personal Saturday morning routine. Every summer weekend, without fail, unless it was raining, he would hoist an American flag at the front of our property. After setting it in place, he would pause and stand for a moment of silence. If we were to visit his business partner's home for a cookout, they would perform the same silent ceremony together at the start of their visit. They never invited anyone to join them, I never saw them speak about it, they just did it—out of love for America, respect for what our flag stood for, and in joint camaraderie having served in the same war together. I watched from a distance and learned respect for our flag, our country, and our veterans by his unassuming practice.

Action:
Attend a local ceremony honoring Flag Day or display our country's flag at your home. Replace it if it is worn and dispose of it properly if need be.
http://www.united-states-flag.com/displaying-flags.html
http://www.united-states-flag.com/flag-disposal.html

Prayer:
Heavenly Father, as your Son sacrificed His life for my eternal freedom, help me to always show respect to those who have fought for our flag and what it stands for and the earthly freedoms I enjoy because of their sacrifice. Amen.

JUNE 15

I Give Up
BY SHERRI GALLAGHER

Psalm 132:1-5

LORD, remember David and all his self-denial. He swore an oath to the LORD, he made a vow to the Mighty One of Jacob: "I will not enter my house or go to my bed, I will allow no sleep to my eyes or slumber to my eyelids, till I find a place for the LORD, a dwelling for the Mighty One of Jacob.

Have patience with all things, but chiefly have patience with yourself. Do not lose courage in considering your own imperfections but instantly set about remedying them - every day begins the task anew. **Saint Francis De Sales**

"I give up. I can't do anything well. I am a total failure." This has been a hard year and those words have run through my brain more than once. I wrote a novel, but the work to market it and make it a success consumed more time than I had to spend. I have a new dog. He needs focused training to deliver a long-term reliable result, but it requires many hours every day. I have a search and rescue team that looks to me to organize our trainings, develop the programs to bring each dog to its maximum potential, identify ways to raise funds, and process government and insurance forms. I have two websites to maintain. I have a consulting firm to market, as well as prepare and submit reports and government required documentation, and do the projects to bring in an income. I need to exercise as age deteriorates my muscles and my stamina. And I need to write. I can't seem to find enough time to do any of it well and I can't find either the people to help or figure out which tasks I should drop. Instead, I judge my performance and find it wanting.

It is easy to slip into a morass where nothing you do is good enough. Depression crawls in and whispers in your ear. "What is the point of trying?" I take comfort I am not the only person feeling this way. David recognized he wasn't perfect and wished to do better. He turned to the right source for comfort and strength, he turned to God.

With so many paths it is easy to focus on the failures and become discouraged, but when instead I focus on the successes, I have the energy to do more. Using my engineering talents, I developed a list of over 80 potential speaking engagements to promote my book and sent requests to all of them in an hour. Each hour I take a ten-minute break and work a single command with the puppy. It gives my tired eyes a rest and the dog eagerly watches for his "fun-time" in which we can focus on perfection for that one little command. I set a single day a week to update websites. I set up a specific timeframe to market each day on LinkedIn. I squeeze in writing when my tired brain can't face another numerical question, or my husband is traveling so cooking is no longer a priority. I pray in the morning for guidance and at night give thanks for what I have accomplished. Ultimately what is truly needed will get done well enough to make a difference, and making a difference is all that really matters.

Action:
When the "to do" list is overwhelming take it in small chunks and reward yourself for the successes instead of focusing on the failures.
Prayer:
Lord, be with me and guide me to perform the tasks that best serve others. Amen.

JUNE 16

Replace Trying Harder with Loving More!
BY MYRA BIERNAT WELLS

1 John 1:9

If we confess our sins, Jesus is faithful and just and will forgive our sins and purify us from all unrighteousness. (NLT)

Two of Satan's greatest weapons against Christians today are shame and condemnation. He knows that because of the finished work of Jesus Christ and His work of redemption in your life, you are deeply loved, completely forgiven, thoroughly cleansed, eternally saved, fully pleasing and totally accepted by God. All Satan can do is *try* to convince you it isn't true. He can do nothing to make you unclean. All he can do is make you *feel* unclean. And if you believe his lies of shame, then back into the bushes you'll go – hiding like Adam and Eve as God walks and calls out, "Where are you?"

We all fail God. We all sin. We all fall short of the glory of God, of what He intended us to do, to be back in the Garden. But here's God's promise, "If we confess our sins, Jesus is faithful and just and will forgive our sins and purify us from all unrighteousness" (1 John 1:9).

What do you do when you fail God? If you're like me, after I have repented and asked forgiveness, my natural tendency is to tell God I'll try harder next time. *Try harder.* Is that really the solution? Do I really need to buck it up and try harder? Is that what Jesus would say?

On the contrary, Jesus said, "If anyone loves me, he will obey my teaching" (John 14:23). Perhaps the solution to our tendency to disobey God is not trying harder but loving more. Perhaps an intimate relationship with Jesus, one in which we *live and move and have our being in Him* in every aspect of life, is key to obedience. When we love deeply, we are more likely to obey Him.

Jesus has a wonderful way of restoring us when we fail Him. He doesn't humiliate, berate or criticize us. Rather, He takes us aside and asks us to reaffirm our love for Him.

"Do you love me?" Jesus asked Peter three times.

"Yes, Lord, you know that I love you" (John 21:15-17). **No more questions!**

It's hard for us to understand because sometimes grace just doesn't make sense.

Write down some sins from the past you have difficulty forgiving yourself for. Pray over the list giving all these back to the Lord. Then destroy the list to release these from your heart.

Prayer:
Jesus, I affirm my love for You today. Yes, Lord, I love You. Convict me when I'm trying harder to perform well but neglecting to love more. Thank You for loving me even when I mess up. I pray this in Your name. Amen.

JUNE 17

Restoring the Default Settings
BY JUDY KNOX

Psalm 23: 1-6

Thou wilt keep him in perfect peace, whose mind is stayed on thee: because he trusteth in thee. **Isaiah 26:3** (KJV)

When an electronic device comes from the factory, all its settings have been programmed for "optimal values" which enable it to function most efficiently. Most settings have options that can be adjusted to suit the needs and preferences of the user. One example would be font styles in an e-mail program. These settings are also referred to as "default values" because the device will automatically go to them unless instructed differently by the user.

The purpose of default settings is to make the device useable upon taking it out of the box. Over time many of these settings are changed by the user or by various software applications. Usually these changes do no harm, but occasionally things can get "out of whack" and the device will need to be restored to its factory settings. Returning to the default settings causes the device to function once again as it did when it was new.

In some ways, we are a little bit like those electronic gadgets. When we were born again, we became new creations in Christ. God filled us with His Spirit, and we were programmed with the fruit of His Spirit, including love, joy and peace. This love, joy and peace are always in us. However, as we go about living our daily lives, we are bombarded with circumstances, relationships, and problems. In our attempts to cope with our trials and temptations, we make adjustments. Little by little our hearts and minds, distracted by the cares of the world, drift farther and farther from our default settings. We find we are no longer functioning optimally.

So how do we get back to our "factory settings?" The answer can be found in Psalm 23:2-3 where we read the beautiful description of Jesus, our Great

Shepherd. "He makes me to lie down in green pastures, He leads me beside the still waters, He restores my soul."

Picture a sheep in a cool, green pasture beside a still, quiet pool of water. And what has the shepherd told the sheep to do? to lie down; to be still. The sheep has only to rest. David's word picture shows us how our Shepherd wants to restore us in our deepest part. We are to "Be still and know that I am God" (Psalm 46:10). As we focus on our awesome, loving God and Savior, He will refresh us with the cool water of His Spirit. He will restore our soul to the love, joy and peace that are always in us.

Action:
Set aside time to simply be quiet and rest in God's presence.

Prayer:
Lord, I come to You in quietness, resting in Your presence, drinking in the cool water of Your Spirit. Thank You for restoring my soul. Amen.

JUNE 18

Feed Me!
BY SHERRI GALLAGHER

Deuteronomy 8:1-6

Never again clutter your days or nights with so many menial and unimportant things that you have no time to accept a real challenge when it comes along. This applies to play as well as work. A day merely survived is no cause for celebration. You are not here to fritter away your precious hours when you have the ability to accomplish so much by making a slight change in your routine. No more busy work. No more hiding from success. Leave time, leave space, to grow. Now. Now! Not tomorrow! **Og Mandino**

I have a bad habit of getting so involved in a project I forget to eat. I remember to feed my family, but if they aren't around and I'm buried in documents and spreadsheets, the world, including hunger, ceases to exist. After a couple of days, I start to get dizzy and cranky. About that point, the project fails to develop, and frustration builds until I take stock and realize I need to step away and nosh.

There is another kind of hunger, spiritual hunger. When I forget to feed my soul, I find I have a very negative mindset. I'm suspicious and miserly and not a person I like very much. The best way I have found to prevent spiritual hunger is to read daily devotionals and study the Bible. On a radio program the guest speaker invited people to memorize scripture, starting with Psalm 1. After following that advice, I find I now can reflect on scripture even when my Bible isn't handy.

Deuteronomy 8:3 is often quoted, "Man shall not live on bread alone, but on every word that comes from the mouth of God." The text around that passage is important, too. It explains that we must diligently observe God's commandments in order to prosper. Just reading the Bible or going to church once a week isn't enough. We must study, learn and integrate the text into who we are as people. We must become a living example to others.

Action:

Memorize Psalm 1.

Prayer:

Thank You for the words to feed my soul and make me a better person. Amen.

JUNE 19

Choose Forgiveness, Not Gossip
BY MYRA BIERNAT WELLS

Proverbs 17:9

Love prospers when a fault is forgiven but dwelling on it separates close friends. (NLT)

I couldn't believe she did that – blew me off again! A friend promised me she'd help me out with a project, but then failed to live up to her commitment. This particular friend is one half of a pair of identical twins. Forgetting for a moment that no matter how much they looked alike, these twins were still two separate people, I wanted so much to pick up the phone, call the other twin and say, "Do you know what your sister did to me?"

It is an honest reaction. When someone hurts or upsets us, the first thing we do is tell someone else. We want to feel their affirmation. We crave this so much it is difficult to stop. It may feel good when we call someone and spread the word about what happened to us, but it is also unloving.

Gossip is incredibly destructive and so easy to fall into. All we want to do is feel better about ourselves, but in order to get that support, we belittle another. Our words are not just damaging to the person who hurt us, they are also harmful to churches, families and businesses. Gossip can destroy even the closest of relationships.

It is even detrimental to you. The worst thing about gossip is that the person who hurt you wins! You allow them to control your conversation. They start to rule your emotions. Gossip just continues the hurt meaning the person who upset you wins.

Refuse to participate in gossip. Take your cue from 1 Peter 3:9: "Do not do wrong to repay a wrong and do not insult to replay an insult. But reply with a blessing because you yourselves were called to do this so you might receive a blessing" (NCV). You will ultimately feel better for doing so.

Action:

Take some time this week to think about and write down some personal ways to avoid or confront gossip. Learn not to share anything unless it passes the THINK test. (It is true, helpful, interesting, necessary and kind.) How can you replace gossip with encouragement or with a blessing?

Prayer:

Jesus, please give me courage to avoid gossip and confront it when others try to engage me in it. Please help me be the kind of friend You want me to be so that Your love can flow through me in my relationships. Amen.

JUNE 20

Identity Crisis
BY JUDY KNOX

Ephesians 4:17-24

For it is God who works in you to will and to act in order to fulfill his good purpose. **Philippians 2:13**

When a butterfly emerges from its cocoon, do you suppose it goes through an identity crisis? The fat, unappealing, worm-like being has been transformed into a delicate, beautifully colored creature of magnificence whose beauty touches our hearts. As it stretches its wings and flies away, it leaves the cocoon behind, never to return. The rest of its life it will flit gracefully among the flowers. I'm sure it never gives a thought to what its life was like when it was a caterpillar.

The Bible tells us that when we put our trust in the finished work of Christ on the cross, we become a new creation. Like the caterpillar transformed into a butterfly, we are changed. However, unlike the butterfly, we may experience an identity crisis. The Word of God says we are new, but we find that most of our problems remain with us after we have been born again. We look the same, feel the same, and act pretty much the same. So, are we new creatures, or are we not? I wondered about this for years.

The answer is yes and no. According to 1 Thessalonians 5:23 we are made up of three distinct parts: spirit, soul and body. The moment we accepted Christ, our spirit was joined to His, and we became one with Him. Our spirit became new, changed completely. But our soul, consisting of our mind, will, and emotions, does not change instantly. This transformation is an ongoing process, and the Bible tells us to how it happens. "Be transformed by the renewing of your mind" (Romans 12:2). We renew our minds by learning what God's Word says about us and putting our trust in that truth. Renewing our minds is our responsibility. Nowhere does Scripture say God will do it for us. Yes, the transforming part is His doing, but it is up to us to fill our minds with His truth, supplanting the old ways of thinking that came with our old nature.

God tells us, "See, the former things have taken place, and new things I declare" (Isaiah 42:9). "Forget the former things; do not dwell on the past. See, I am doing a new thing!" (Isaiah 43:18-19). Too much thinking about our old life keeps us from seeing our new identity. As our thoughts become more like God's thoughts, our emotions and actions will change as well. Like the butterfly that is no longer thinking about its former state of existence, step by step we will walk away from our caterpillar-like ugliness into the beauty of who God created us to be.

Action:
Look up scriptures on "new creation in Christ" and picture yourself walking in that reality.

Prayer:
Lord, I thank You that I am a new creation in You. Help me shed the old ways of thinking about myself and identify with the new person You have designed me to be. Amen.

JUNE 21

But I Want It Now
BY SHERRI GALLAGHER

Mark 8:14-21

Learn the art of patience. Apply discipline to your thoughts when they become anxious over the outcome of a goal. Impatience breeds anxiety, fear, discouragement and failure. Patience creates confidence, decisiveness, and a rational outlook, which eventually leads to success. **Brian Adams**

"I will sell you this dog, but you must promise no protection training until he is a year old. Give him time to grow up. Give him time to be a puppy." With that sage advice, Orex's breeder loaded my new six-month-old German Shepherd into my SUV for the long drive home from Nashville. This wisdom was counter to what I had done in the past, puppies were started at eight weeks old learning how to grip and chase. I took Orex to a new facility to do obedience. They were appalled at how far behind he was. They even went so far as to suggest I return the dog.

I was frustrated. Belle's bad hip, Lektor's failing muscles and now a puppy that couldn't be worked. What was I doing wrong? About the time my patience had run out I read Mark 8:14-21. Jesus had been with the disciples a long time and had given the Sermon on the Mount and they still didn't get it. However, he continued to patiently teach and explain what he was saying to them over and over again. I took it as a direction, grit my teeth and continued to give Orex time to grow up and time to be a puppy.

On his first birthday we started protection training and Orex made us all believers in patience. Within a month he had surpassed all the other dogs his age. His grip strength, confidence and focus make him a force to watch and the helper that suggested I return him now tells people, "Watch this dog. He is amazing." When I take Orex onto the field we still have a lot to learn, but hopefully, I now have the patience I need to make us a success.

Action:
What task has been frustrating you? Pour yourself a nice cup of tea and consider taking a small break to enjoy the project and not worry if a goal has been met. It will come in good time.

Prayer:
Thank You, Lord, for the guidance Your word offers even when we apply it to the small and unimportant tasks. Amen.

JUNE 22

Remember the Best, Forget the Rest!
BY MYRA BIERNAT WELLS

Philippians 1:3

I thank God every time I remember you.

High school reunions – people either love them or loathe them. I put one together recently and I was amazed at the laughter generated. It seemed everyone had a funny story or tender memory of someone in our class. For whatever reason, all us women (yes, I attended an all-girls school) took the Apostle Paul's advice – remembering the good things about people, focusing on the good times we had and recalling the positive experiences.

When Paul wrote the verse above, he was in very difficult straits. Acts 16 tells us that when Paul went to Philippi, he was illegally arrested, whipped, humiliated and thrown into prison where he was chained to a guard 24 hours a day. When he was finally asked to leave town, he says, "I thank God every time I remember you." If there was someone who could have dwelt on the negative, it was Paul. He certainly had painful memories, but he chose not to remember those, focusing instead on the things that brought gratitude to his heart.

Have you been hurt in the past by a parent or friend? Are you holding on to that hurt? Are there individuals you can't stand being around? You are still focusing on the negative.

Instead try being grateful for the good in people. Pleasant memories are a choice. You can choose what you remember about the past. This isn't to say that you can deny the hurts you've had or that you excuse the weakness in others. This is psychologically unhealthy. But if you focus on the good and chose to emphasize the strength, overall, you'll be a happier person.

I often hear my girlfriends say, "I love my husband, but…" That simple 'but' moves the conversation from positive to negative. Be grateful for what you've got. Mr. Perfect does not exist. And for you husbands, Mrs. Perfect doesn't exist, either.

If you want to enjoy others, you've got to focus on their strengths and not their shortcomings. With some folks, it takes a lot of creativity, but you can find something good in everybody.

Action:

Release the painful memories keeping you from showing full love to others by praying for them throughout the week.

Prayer:

Jesus, please heal the relational messes in my life. Bring reconciliation. Give the gift of forgiveness and the ability to move on. Heal and renew me so I can keep loving people, keep risking and keep sharing. Shine amid my inability to find the very best in people. Amen.

JUNE 23

In Contact
BY BETH DUMEY

1 Thessalonians 5:17

Pray continually.

During my recovery from surgery, when I was weak in spirit and lonely for company while everyone seemingly was at work, one constant I could look forward to was my daily phone call from my friend Julie. Family and other friends checked in regularly, but Julie called every day on her way home from teaching school. She asked how I was, how I slept, how my day went. Sometimes my answers were mundane, but somehow the conversation was always a highlight. I knew someone was checking in with me.

I wonder if this is how God feels, I thought, when we pray every day. Just checking in God. Here's how I'm doing. Here's what I need. Thanks for being there and listening. Simple prayers, really, that don't fit any formula or structure, but express my daily needs, offer thanks, and humbly acknowledge my relationship with my Lord and Savior. Staying in contact, even if I say the same things over and over, and the conversation seems trite.

Praying continually may not be eloquent but it is consistent, and this is more valuable. What I say is less important than whom I am saying it to and how often I am saying it. As a child of God, placing myself in His presence daily keeps me in close connection with my creator.

Action:

Take a quick overview of your prayer life. How often do you pray? Are you held back by the desire to be eloquent or sound wise or fresh? Resolve to release these limitations and approach the Lord regularly.

Prayer:

Lord, I come into Your presence seeking Your wisdom, Your provision, and Your majesty. Help me to remember I am Your child, humbly before You, seeking to pray continually. Amen.

JUNE 24

Fear Itself
BY SHERRI GALLAGHER

1 Corinthians 2:2-4

For I resolved to know nothing while I was with you except Jesus Christ and him crucified. I came to you in weakness with great fear and trembling. My message and my preaching were not with wise and persuasive words, but with a demonstration of the Spirit's power,

Remember that fear always lurks behind perfectionism. Confront your fears and allowing yourself the right to be human can, paradoxically, make you a far happier and more productive person. **Dr. David M. Burns**

Test anxiety is a fact of life for many people, myself included. The question running through the back of our mind is, what if I fail? Faced with a recent testing situation, my stomach in knots and my hands shaking, I had to find a way around my fear.

I have always been a perfectionist, a people pleaser. If a test was worth 100 points, I would get distraught over a score of 97 and focus on the few points I lost. My dog trainer says in testing we start with 100 points and then see how many we give away. He directs us to be points hoarders and drills us on the minutia to keep as much of the 100 points as possible. That doesn't help perfectionists like me. I know every point that can be lost and how I will probably lose it, until I am sure I will never pass. My nerves ratchet up and I create a self-fulfilling prophesy of failure.

Struggling to overcome my fear, I settle for procrastination and cruise through Facebook to avoid thinking about the situation. Then a post popped up which answered my question. It read, "Jacob was a liar, Moses stuttered, David was an adulterer, Rahab was a prostitute, Esther was an orphan, yet God used them, He can use you too."

Many of the people God used in the Bible were flawed. Certainly, they had rather huge stigmas attached to their names, and yet God used them to do great things. Surely, I could accomplish such a small thing. I started thinking about where I would lose points and tried to find a positive. If an exercise was worth ten points and I was sure I would lose two then turning my viewpoint around I could be sure to earn eight and that was a better than passing score. By the time I was through with my analysis I had convinced myself I could score in the high 80's, more than enough to pass and all I needed to do.

God made me human. He knows I am not perfect. I know I am not perfect, but until I looked at how God uses us imperfect people, I was crippled with fear. Now when that interior perfectionist creeps up and whispers in my ear, you aren't good enough, all I need to remember is I am as good as God needs me to be.

Action:

If you are counting your imperfections, turn them around and show yourself how they are positive.

Prayer:

Father, You love me just as I am with all my imperfections. Please help me to love myself the same way. Amen.

JUNE 25

Are You Stuck in Spiritual Neutral?
BY MYRA BIERNAT WELLS

Ephesians 1:4-5

Even before he made the world, God loves us and chose us in Christ to be holy and without fault in his eyes. God decided in advance to adopt us into his own family by bringing us to himself through Jesus Christ. This is what he wanted to do, and it gave him great pleasure. (NLT)

One day, a woman in my small group called and said, "I'm a Christian, but I don't feel like I'm growing spiritually. I'm kind of stuck in neutral." So I asked, "What do you think the problem is?" She responded, "I think my problem is that I just don't love God enough."

The Holy Spirit gave me insight to reply, "I'm not sure that's your problem. I think you don't understand how much He loves you." Love is always a response to love. The Bible says, "We love because He first loved us" (1 John 4:19).

To understand your life's purpose and calling, you must begin with understanding God's nature. God is love. It is the essence of His nature. The only reason there is love in the universe is because of God. Love is the proof of God. Since we are made in His image, we can love.

You are alive because God wanted to love you. The very purpose of your life is to be loved by God. Yes, it is important to serve Him, obey Him, trust Him, but your most important endeavor is simply to love Him. Let that sink in. Your first duty is not to do *anything*, but just *be loved by God*.

Action:
What was your response to the truth that your first calling is to enjoy a relationship with God? Do you long to feel close to God but feel like there's something missing? Try to identify where it becomes more about rules, regulations and rituals than love. Then during the week, work on replacing those areas with love.

Prayer:
Jesus sometimes I'm so very tired of life. Forgive me when I don't put my relationship with You first. Please give me the joy to walk more closely with You. I want so much to be grounded in Your love. Thank You so much for loving me. Amen.

JUNE 26

Protection
BY BETH DUMEY

Ephesians 6:11

Put on the full armor of God so that you can take your stand against the devil's schemes.

On my key chain I carry a symbol of the warrior described in Ephesians 6 who wears the helmet of salvation and carries the shield of faith. The passage continues by referring to the breastplate of righteousness and the sword of the Spirit. All of this imagery is of one who in some way is at war and needs protection. While the round medal I carry is merely a symbol, it is comforting to me. Because as much as I value peace and tranquility, I have to acknowledge the evil that is in this world and pray for protection from it.

And as easy as it would be to think that the evil is "out there' somewhere away from me, sometimes it appears right in front of me in the form of plotting, one-upmanship, and gossip. At times, someone's ego is on the line, so it rears up or a need for control surfaces and it is right there. It may even invite me in to participate. I need my warrior key chain to remind me to seek protection from the Lord and the "armor" He has provided for me.

I pray nearly every day for protection from evil but honestly thinking too much about it frightens me. I often don't feel very warrior-like and instead, ill-equipped to deal with unknown schemes that could harm me. So, I trust in the "mighty power" of the Lord, leaning on His strength and provision, and the discernment that helps me flee from evil when I encounter it.

Action:

Read Ephesians chapter six. What thoughts come to mind? Journal your impressions.

Prayer:

Father, protect me from evil in every form. Help me be wise and give me discernment to stay away from evil schemes. Help me to control my tongue and guard my heart and my mind. Amen.

JUNE 27

Teach Your Children Well
BY SHERRI GALLAGHER

Psalm 78:1-8

Teach your children well, their father's hell did slowly go by, and feed them on your dreams the one they picked, the one you'll know by. Don't you ever ask them why, if they told you, you would cry, so just look at them and sigh and know they love you.
Crosby, Stills, Nash, Young, *Teach Your Children*

The babies I taught are having babies; boy do I feel old. The pastor announced the birth of a baby and smiled as he told us mother and child were doing well. I was more than a little happy. The mother had been one of my Sunday school students when I taught the three to five-year olds, eons ago. It took a little while for a more important and happier message to sink in. This child had learned her lessons well. Through all the angst of growing up, she had held onto her belief in God. She still attended church regularly, only this time it was of her choosing, not because her parents insisted she be there. And through her this new child had been welcomed into our church family to be loved and guided to follow in her mother's footsteps.

The psalmist tried to warn the Israelites how important it was to teach their children. In verse four he says, "We will not hide them from our children, we will tell the coming generations the glorious deeds of the Lord," and in verse eight, "that they should not be like their ancestors, a stubborn and rebellious generation." And in Matthew 19:14 Jesus said, "Let the little children come to me, and do not stop them; for it is to such as these that the kingdom of heaven belongs."

Teaching your children about God isn't easy. Sometimes, as they reach adulthood, they decide not to attend services and may walk a dangerous path that causes their parents many tears and sleepless nights. Be patient. Love them and live the example. You may find that they must have children of their own in order to value your lessons on the love of the Lord.

Action:

Volunteer to teach one short session of Sunday school; you may be surprised at how much you learn.

Prayer:

Lord, watch over your children whether they are hours or decades old. Guide their steps as lovingly as the Father you are. Amen.

JUNE 28

From My Sick Bed
BY MYRA BIERNAT WELLS

2 Corinthians 1:3-5

Praise be to God the Father of our Lord Jesus Christ, the Father of compassion and the God of all comfort, who comforts us in our troubles so that we can comfort those in any trouble with the comfort we ourselves receive from God.

The illness struck me hard, making me so weak that getting from my upstairs bedroom to my downstairs family room couch expended all my energy. I felt I was running the mile in less than *three* minutes! Wheezing and unsteady, I'd collapse in the couch wondering if this were the beginning of the long goodbye.

Several friends brought me great comfort. They'd call, offer to get groceries, check in on me, send me cards or funny emails. As I slowly began to recover, I realized in the eight weeks I had been unwell, the Lord worked a miracle. Not a physical one, but an emotional one. Being desperately ill taught me how traumatizing it is to be sick. My distress made me more empathetic towards those suffering with an illness plus enhanced my ability to comfort others.

God will always use your hurts, even your illnesses. He will send someone your way who needs a person who understands. Who better to comfort a woman struggling with a wayward teenager than a mother who has welcomed a prodigal home? No one can encourage a woman struggling with depression like the woman who has come out of that same darkness and into the light.

And in my case, no one can truly rally around someone who has lost their freedom or mobility from an illness than one who has risen from their sick bed. What have you gone through that made you uncomfortable? Today, use your wisdom and experience to bring comfort to someone in a similar situation.

Action:

I love reading different versions of the Bible. Each seems to bring out a new truth to ponder. Read 2 Corinthians 1:3-5 in several different versions and ask God to reveal a new aspect of His truth.

Prayer:

Lord, I thank You for being the God of all comfort who has reassured me time and time again. This week show me someone who needs to know the comfort You have given me. Help me be a hope to someone who needs to know You are their hope. Amen.

JUNE 29

An All-Round Bad Day
BY SHERRI GALLAGHER

1 Thessalonians 5:16-18

Rejoice always, pray continually, give thanks in all circumstances; for this is God's will for you in Christ Jesus.

If we had no winter, the spring would not be so pleasant: if we did not sometimes taste of adversity, prosperity would not be so welcome. **Anne Bradstreet**

June 29th was a very bad day for me. It was the day I took my canine partner, Lektor, to the vet and said good-bye. This dog had been my constant companion for eight years, protecting me from danger, giving me reasons to laugh and love, and spending hours and hours of searching in good and bad conditions to save lives or bring closure to grieving families. He was in pain. Horrible pain. The only way to combat it was to give large doses of drugs that had other nasty side effects. For the last eight years he had trusted me to protect him and now it was time to release him from his pain. I held him to the last and then gave in to my own pain.

How could there be anything good in this day? But there was. I was held in the deep love of my friends and my pastor. I arrived home to a search team cooking and caring for all my needs. Pastor Alex came by with Henry. Watching that happy little boy and playing with him in my yard brought a healing I never expected. Every night I give thanks for the love that was shown to me that day.

The passage in 1 Thessalonians tells us to rejoice always in all circumstances. I didn't understand how that could be until June 29th. My very good friend was gone, but he was also freed from horrible pain, and I got a better understanding of how much love surrounds me at all time. No other dog will be exactly the same as Lektor. No other dog and I will have the same experiences. I will always remember that canine partner, and through losing him I have a little better understanding of how to rejoice in all circumstances.

Action:

When something has you hurt or sad or angry, call to mind one good friend and remember all the blessings your friendship has brought.

Prayer:

Thank You, Lord, for the love of friends and our church family that holds us up from the pit of despair in times of need. Bless them. Amen.

JUNE 30

Golf
BY MYRA BIERNAT WELLS

Psalm 139:1

You have searched me, LORD, and you know me.

Many people call themselves golfers. They own a set of clubs, they hit the driving range from time to time and they understand the basic rules of the game. They might even make it out to an actual golf course once or twice a year.

Then there are those who are passionate about the sport. They practice often. They take lessons. True golfers own special equipment to hone their skills: golf shoes, hybrid clubs, laser range finders, and a myriad of other equipment.

Isn't Christianity a bit like that? There are many who call themselves Christians, but who haven't been inside a church in months, maybe even years. They pray, but only in those dark, desperate no-way-out situations. Their Bible is collecting dust. And it is easy to point them out as wannabes.

Often when I find myself pointing a disparaging finger towards someone else, I force myself to take a good long look inside. When have I found myself too busy to read my Bible? Have my prayer times been deep spiritual conversations with God? And just how easy is it for me to occasionally skip out of church services?

And then I racket it up a notch. Daniel 9:3 says, "So I turned to the Lord God and pleaded with him in prayer and petition, in fasting, and in sackcloth and ashes." When was the last time I fasted? Or had a day of solitude?

The reality is we were specifically designed by God to crave Him in a deep, meaningful way. Fasting, prayer, solitude and journaling are important tools to build a deeper relationship with Christ. It's in the Bible we learn we are fully and uniquely accepted. It is through prayer we can look back on the Lord's faithfulness to us. In fasting and in journaling, we can discover how to love God with all our hearts, souls, minds and strength.

All those things have a powerful influence on us. We experience the joy of God's love. We can articulate our salvation passionately and boldly and find delight in speaking words of blessing and encouragement to those around us. But most importantly, we find the unfading beauty of God's gentle spirit and His grace that makes us worthy in His sight.

Action:
Pick a spiritual discipline and practice it this week. (A great book on the subject is Richard Foster's *Celebration of Discipline*.)

Prayer:
Jesus, please give us courage to search ourselves and see You amid our doubts. Help us seek You every day in new ways, so that Your love will set us free. Amen.

JULY 1

A Day of Remembrance
BY TONJA BRICE

1 Timothy 2:1-4

I urge, then, first of all, that petitions, prayers, intercession and thanksgiving be made for all people for kings and all those in authority, that we may live peaceful and quiet lives in all godliness and holiness. This is good, and pleases God our Savior, who wants all people to be saved and to come to a knowledge of the truth.

All temporal power is of God,
And the magistratal, His institution, laud,
To but advance creaturely happiness aubaud:
Let us then affirm the Source of Liberty. **Samuel Adams**

Three times a year my mom would pull down a tattered old cardboard quilt box full of family pictures. We would sit on the couch in the living room, my sister on one side, me on the other, and we would go through each and every photograph. My mom would talk about her grandparents, one of her great-grandparents, and even stories of my dad's side of the family that had been handed down to her. For hours my sister and I would sit, mesmerized, listening to the family lore. Those days are some of my fondest memories.

Remembering is a key verb with God. As soon as God brought the Israelites through the Red Sea, Moses built an altar of stone – to remember that God had brought them through to safety from the Egyptian army. In the Shema, a very well-known prayer in Deuteronomy 6:4-9, God doesn't simply ask the Israelites to remember what He has done for them – He commands it. He needs his people to know the history of His mighty acts lest they forget about their need for Him and in forgetting lose hope, purpose and identity.

In much the same way, we need to remember our heritage, the heritage of fighting for independence, fighting for equality and fighting for freedom. Only 40 years after the signing of the Declaration of Independence, John Adams lamented in a letter to James Madison that America was losing its history. He lamented this because of the factions and parties that were showing up and causing turmoil in the struggling new government. He longed for unity and saw that only through unity could the nation sustain varying opinions. But it wasn't until 1870, nearly 100 years after the Declaration, that Congress first declared July 4th to be a federal, national holiday. We had just been through one of the biggest tests to our democracy that we would ever face – and we needed to remind ourselves of the reasons that America exists, reasons that would unify us.

The Declaration of Independence established a free, democratic nation. Among other reasons, it is free because it gives us the right to freely worship God without fear of persecution – something that had never happened before in the history of the world. It is important for our nation to collectively remember these reasons and why this nation has been a beacon of hope and prosperity ever since. Certain parts of our world today no longer accept religious freedom as a basic human right, and these nations are becoming more and more violent, particularly against Americans. Unless we remember the reasons why we fought in 1776, we will never understand why we should continue to fight today. As each new generation grows up, they need to discover and understand freedom, take it to heart and fight for it with all their might.

Action:
Share with your loved ones what God means to you – and do so without fear. In the Old Testament, altars serve as a visual reminder of some great act that God had performed. America has altars – the Washington Monument, the Lincoln Memorial, etc. – take time to teach the children in your family about those altars and their importance. Take this one step further and build an altar to remember how God has acted in your life and celebrate the freedom you have to worship the Living God.

Prayer:
Dear Lord, we thank You for the freedoms we have today that were fought for over 200 years ago. We are still fighting for these freedoms. Please be with all our

servicemen and women who are serving this country and fighting for our freedom. Amen.

JULY 2

Arctic Morning
BY SHERRI GALLAGHER

Mark 14:66-72

Immediately the rooster crowed the second time. Then Peter remembered the word Jesus had spoken to him: "Before the rooster crows twice you will disown me three times." And he broke down and wept. **Mark 14:72**

It is impossible to live without failing at something, unless you live so cautiously that you might as well not lived at all. In which case, you've failed by default.
J.K. Rowling

I stretched tired muscles and huddled in the warmth of my sleeping bag while watching the daylight gradually increase. We had one more day to try and find a missing caribou hunter. My search dog was injured. My ankles were bruised and my knees ached from the rough terrain. My next assignment was to search caves around a nearby lake. A headstrong greenhorn was to accompany me. Worry stole my sleep. I crept softly into my clothes and slipped from the cabin. The weight limit for our packs had prevented me from bringing my Bible. I watched the sun rise and thought about the hunter's family and all they had done to get us here. How could we go home empty handed? But when the float plane came to get us the next day, there had been no sign of their loved one in the 15,000 acres we had searched.

The family waited for us in Montreal. We arrived empty handed exhausted, wearing dirty clothes, coated in bug spray and sweat, and they hugged us and thanked us. They had hoped for a different outcome, but they accepted our failure without judgments or rancor. I don't think I could have been that generous; I certainly wouldn't have wanted to hug a person that smelled as bad as I did.

We all had a hard time accepting our failure. It wasn't until I read Mark 15 where Peter denies Jesus that I felt any better. Peter failed spectacularly and yet went on to lead the church. If he could get over what he had done, I could accept a failed search and move on.

Action:
When you fail at a task, remind yourself of Peter.
Prayer:
Lord, help us to forgive ourselves for the things You have already forgiven. Amen.

JULY 3

Record-breaking Heat
BY MYRA BIERNAT WELLS

Psalm 51:12

Restore to me the joy of your salvation and grant me a willing spirit, to sustain me.

With eager anticipation, I welcomed this weekend. It would be one devoted entirely to prayer at a stunning retreat center hugging the foothills of southern California. But as the day grew closer, a significant worry began to form – the area was experiencing record breaking 100+ degree days. The center's main building, the original owner's ranch house, was built in the 1920s, long before home air conditioning was in vogue. None of the participants, least of all me, wanted to swelter in the heat while drawing close to God.

Thankfully, the retreat center was air-conditioned, but as we finished the Friday night session, the director invited us to enjoy a fire built in the outdoor pit. Just what we needed – more heat! Despite the late hour, the temperature still hovered in the low 90's.

I sensed God calling me to sit still and reflect on knowing Him and being known by Him. Freeing my thoughts, I sat beside the fire and listened. I heard the crackle of the wood, but also the sounds of crickets; the wind causing the palms to gently sway and then the cry of an owl, probably looking for prey on this warm night.

The spectacular beauty of the evening stirred my heart deeply. Its splendor seeped into my spirit – not a very attractive place. So God whispered very gently, "You are not your past sins. You are not defined by your current struggles. I will use these shards of brokenness to redefine you – to make you lovely like this night."

True beauty will never be found this side of heaven. But during our time on earth, God is transforming us from broken into beautiful. The process is neither easy nor instantaneous. It demands a heart that is melted, yet it comes with great reward. God uses the heat of His abundant love to mend the broken pieces – our scars, shame, insecurities, disappointments and failures.

As I walked away from the fire that night, I felt the work had begun: that our creative Lord was starting a beautiful new work in me; one requiring all my broken pieces to complete.

Action:

When is the last time you intentionally made time to listen to God's creation? Join God in your backyard, in a forest preserve, in nature. Take a pad of paper and jot down your thoughts.

Prayer:

Father, please take the broken pieces of my life and use Your refining fire to mold me and shape me into a beautiful reflection of Your glory. In Jesus' name. Amen.

JULY 4 - INDEPENDENCE DAY

"AMERICA, I LOVE YOU!"
BY EMO DESIDERI

Hebrews 11:14

...looking forward to a country they can call their own.

In 1977, after the 60's decade of hippie rebellion, my father felt compelled to pen his feelings for our country which was being bombarded with criticism. This is how a local Wisconsin magazine, *Exclusively Yours* (March 12, 1977) prefaced his personal essay, with the article following.

> *A middle-aged American, of sound mind—*
> *A local businessman. . .*
> *A family man not a professional commentator, liberator or agitator—*
> *states some observations and personal feeling you might care to share.*

America, I love you! How long has it been since you heard someone make that remark? As it happens, I've heard quite a few people say it. But then, they were people who had just returned from overseas. After having been out of the country for a while, and seeing the rest of the world, they're unanimous in stating "America looks pretty good to me. We may have troubles, but we have fewer problems than any other country I've seen. I'm really happy to be back in the good old United Sates."

Perhaps we should stop being so super-critical of everything American, and start looking at the positive side of this wonderful country of ours. We've some serious problems, but then no country is perfect, and in America the common man has risen farther and faster than in any other civilization the world has ever known.

Just for starters, let's give a hand to some of the fine, dedicated politicians and government workers (including the police) who make our country, our state, and our cities run. Let's also acknowledge that there are many ordinary citizens in business and industry doing their jobs in a quiet, dignified, upstanding manner, and they, too, make America run. These people, all of them, are the backbone of our country. They're our unsung heroes.

In reality we're one big family. From time to time most families have differences of opinion, but they're usually ironed out, and then they learn to live together. That's what we're learning now.

This country has a fantastic future. So let's learn to be a bit more objective about our demands on ourselves. Let's make our voices a bit less strident. Self-improvement is always to be sought, but let's not expect perfection among men or nations. I am very tired of our apparent national inferiority complex . . . constantly nourished by an often negative press.

I remember being in a foreign country during World War II, and watching our flag being raised over a new base. There wasn't a dry eye among the Americans present. America could stand a little of that patriotic feeling right now.

We could also stand some happy songs like George M. Cohan's "Grand Old Flag." I've heard enough wailing and crying songs. I'd like to hear some happy songs about the good things in our national life—and there are quite a few good things. I'm convinced that the large percentage of American people is smarter and more perceptive than given credit for. . . .

This is the greatest country in the world . . . . So let's stop demanding instant perfection. Let's all work harder at our jobs and try a little harder to get along with each other. Then we can all realize and share in the full potential of America's great future. AMERICA, I LOVE YOU!

Action:
Give yourself an attitude check about how you speak of your homeland and what you post on Facebook. Are you part of the problem or the solution?

Prayer:
Heavenly Father, thank You for the freedoms we have in the United States of America. We do have some serious problems, but please help our leaders turn to You, the only One who can truly solve our problems. Help me be a positive part of the solution. Amen.

JULY 5

Fireworks
BY MYRA BIERNAT WELLS

Psalm 141:2

May my prayer be set before you like incense; may the lifting up of my hands be like the evening sacrifice.

Fireworks are one of my favorite things in the world! I adore their pageantry, creativity and grandeur. Consequently, with childlike abandon, I look forward to the 4th of July, researching when all the fireworks displays will occur and trying to squeeze in as many as possible.

What I don't like, however, are folks who purchase their own and insist on shooting them off into the wee hours of the morning. Last night, I felt my house was under siege as the neighborhood booming and banging didn't stop until almost 2 AM. Who could sleep with all the ruckus outside my door?

Unfortunately, I don't do well when my sleep is interrupted, so today I am bleary-eyed and irritable. I've been fervently trying to gut it out without a nap, so I also ardently pray, "Lord, help me get through this day." Every few minutes I lift up this request because my eyes are droopy and my "to do" list is long.

Sometimes I feel a bit sheepish praying to God for something so trivial. I rationalize, "He has more important things to worry about like world peace, starving people or decaying morals. He doesn't care about my lack of sleep." But in 1 Samuel 1:15, Hannah states, "I am a deeply troubled woman. I was pouring out my soul to the Lord."

Now Hannah had some real problems. She was infertile in a time when women were judged by the number of children they bore. She was one of two wives – a cultural norm at this juncture in history – and was experiencing a rival wife problem. I'm sure these challenges left her feeling frustrated and devalued. But Hannah poured out *all* her problems, her entire soul, to God. Not just the monumental concerns, but the entirety of them.

It is easy to believe God is not interested in my sleeplessness, but God cares about everything. He is faithful and longs to fill our souls with peace regardless of what is bothering us. When we explain our feelings to Him, He bears our burdens. What is important is not the size of our problem, but the time we spend with Him. For it is in His presence we are changed.

My sleeplessness may pale in comparison to your concerns. Maybe you are dealing with financial woes, relational difficulties, a bad medical report. Your life may be peppered with seemingly impossible situations that won't be solved by a good night's rest. But when you pour out your soul to God, when you get really honest with Him, He will faithfully replace your emptiness with His fullness, regardless of whether He removes your burdens or allows them to remain. Only in prayer do we experience the One and Only life-altering God.

Going to God with whatever is causing your head to ache reminds us that God is able. He is powerful. He is caring. To get through the worries, fears and hurts bring them to Him. So, when you are feeling alone, scared or just plain tired, pour your soul out to God and experience the relief of divine arms wrapping themselves around you.

The best way to pray is with honesty. To gain that transparency, pray often, frequently opening up your life to God. Even if all you are praying for is a little sleep.

Action:

Read Jeremiah 29:12, "Then you will call on me and come and pray to me, and I will listen to you." Think of a few times when God has answered your prayers. Before you go to sleep tonight, thank Him for His faithfulness to you.

Prayer:

Jesus, You care about every aspect of my life – even the trivial things. Help me to be more honest, more transparent when I pray to You. I trust Your faithfulness. Stay close to me, Lord. Amen.

JULY 6

Navigating Between Swamps
BY SHERRI GALLAGHER

Psalm 23:2-4

He makes me lie down in green pastures, he leads me beside quiet waters, he refreshes my soul. He guides me along the right paths for his name's sake. Even though I walk through the darkest valley, I will fear no evil, for you are with me; your rod and your staff, they comfort me. (ESV)

Every day you may make progress. Every step may be fruitful. Yet there will stretch out before you an ever-lengthening, ever-ascending, ever-improving path. You know you will never get to the end of the journey. But this, so far from discouraging, only adds to the joy and glory of the climb. **Sir Winston Churchill**

On a search near the Arctic Circle, I acted as support for another dog handler. It was up to me to navigate and keep us on a straight line while the handler concentrated on his dog. Caribou flies were attracted to the red-gold fur on the canines. Part fly, part bee they bit viciously. A swarm attacked the dog. The poor creature dropped to the ground rolling to free himself from the painful bugs. We had no choice, we dosed him with Deet, a poison that would affect his nervous system if left on him too long. I had seconds to identify the exact direction back to the cabin before we took off as fast as we could run. We were a mile and a quarter away. We had to get to a 100-yard strip between two swamps to get the dog to safety. A very long fifteen minutes later we arrived on the plateau behind our campsite and saved the dog.

Sometimes trying to follow in the path God wants us to take feels the same way. The pressures of life force us to rush forward and we are keenly aware that the slightest veer to left or right will dump us in a swamp we'd rather not enter. Thankfully, we have His Word and His Spirit and our church leaders to help navigate between the dangers.

Action:
Make a practice of reading the Bible daily.

Prayer:
Lord, thank You for Your guiding words. Amen.

JULY 7

A Pure Heart
BY MYRA BIERNAT WELLS

1 John 1:9

If we confess our sins, he is faithful and just and will forgive us our sins and purify us from all unrighteousness.

Faith is taking the first step even when you don't see the whole staircase.
Martin Luther King, Jr.

Before my father would even consider taking me, as a teenager, to the DMV to take my driver's license test, he insisted I learn some basic car maintenance tips. I had to know how to change a flat tire, how to check the fluids in the car and how to change my oil. Regular oil changes to him were practically a religion. He knew when dirt gets in the oil, it can cause engine wear. Without these regular changes, an engine will be seriously damaged.

Our souls need to be kept clean on a regular basis. Purity matters to a holy God. Are you like me? Too often in my prayers, my concentration is on the "God, please help me," or the "God please give me," parts of the prayer, instead of saying, "God forgive me for my sins today. Keep my life pure for Your sake."

John's verse reminds us how valuable maintaining a pure heart can be. And it is so easy. The verse promises us if we confess our sins, we will be forgiven. It also says that if we confess, we are renewed and made pure before God. He does this because He is faithful to us. He is also a gracious God who has the right and authority to cancel every debt your sinfulness has cost you now and forever.

So if you feel weighed down by sin like the dirt in the engine oil, confess. If you feel worn out, confess. If you want to experience the blessings of God on your life, confess. And God will take care of everything else.

Action:
Write down three to five benefits you'll experience when confessing your sins to God. Then thank God for canceling your debt.

Prayer:
Lord, I confess my sins to You today. Please forgive me for my impure heart. Please give me the faith to believe in the promises in Your Word and the strength to take the first step of obedience. Thank You for Your provision for purity in my life. Amen.

JULY 8

Construction Zone
BY JUDY KNOX

James 1:1-5

He who began a good work in you will carry it on to completion until the day of Christ Jesus. **Philippians 1:6**

The intersection near my home has been under construction for more than a year. At first, the closed lanes and tied-up traffic annoyed me, but I recited the mantra of my fellow residents and local business people: "It's going to be awesome when it's finished." Yes, the final product – double lanes each way – will make for enjoyable driving.

For the first month or two I drove through the construction zone focused on staying in my lane and hoping to arrive at my destination on time without scraping my car on the cement dividers or knocking over an orange and white striped barrel. I paid little attention to the work itself. But eventually I became aware of some of the details. I began to marvel at the engineering and planning that obviously went into the project before the first worker or piece of equipment ever arrived on the scene. The construction company had a system and specialized pieces of equipment for every task. As the workers followed the engineer's plan and operated according to the system, a beautiful new road began taking shape.

Then one day, just as the new road was finished and I thought it was almost over, a bright orange sign announced, "Caution. New traffic pattern." The lanes had been moved, and now I found myself driving in a narrow lane on nice new pavement. The road I previously drove on was being torn up so they could build two new lanes there. Surprisingly, I did not find this new turn of events terribly upsetting. Having adjusted my schedule long ago to accommodate possible delays I had become more aware of the construction process. Each trip along that piece of highway revealed interesting sights.

I saw many similarities between road building and the process of spiritual growth in our lives. We may not notice every change occurring in ourselves on a moment-by-moment basis, but periodically as we revisit an area, we see evidence of transformation. Sometimes we arrive at a new level of understanding, only to find that the lanes have been moved and new work has started. Since we are transformed by the renewing of our minds (Romans 12:2), old habits or ways of thinking may need to be torn out to make way for the new.

Just like the highway, we have a Master Planner who knows how to get the job done. God's plan, spelled out in His Word, is available to us; He is always on hand for consultation; and He equips us for the task He has assigned to us. We naturally look forward to how awesome our lives will be when He has completed the work, but if we open our eyes and hearts, we can enjoy our journey through the construction zone as well. As we observe and cooperate with the changes in our lives, instead of being frustrated, we will be amazed at how well He has designed and is executing His plan.

Action:
Reflect on the last year or two and look for evidence of the transformation that is taking place in your heart.

Prayer:
Father, I thank You that You are always at work in my life, even when I can't see anything happening. Help me to enjoy the process and notice the changes along the way as I look forward to the final results. In Jesus' name. Amen.

JULY 9

Waltzing Orex
BY SHERRI GALLAGHER

Luke 15:1-10

If we had no winter, the spring would not be so pleasant: if we did not sometimes taste of adversity, prosperity would not be so welcome. **Anne Bradstreet**

I love my new puppy Orex and he adores me, but training him can be an exercise in frustration. It is a dance of two steps forward, one step back. We have great eye contact and focus for obedience at home but take him to the pet store and forget it - his nose is on the ground checking all the scents, investigating the treats, and greeting the strangers. We work on it for weeks with all the patience I can muster, but frustration builds until I am ready to give up. Suddenly we get to that point where we can walk into the store and have the puppy focus on me and obey my commands. It makes me want to shout for joy!

Sometimes I think I must be to God like Orex is to me. Dancing around in circles all excited to focus on Him and then distracted by a new scent and wandering off on a tangent that frustrates the Lord. It happens over and over again. Thankfully, God has infinite patience with a slow learner like me. Sometimes He has to give me a little correction, like I have to do to Orex, to get me back on the right track. I just hope when I make progress on my spiritual journey, I give Him the kind of joy I feel when Orex takes two steps toward being the dog I want him to be.

Action:
Identify one area of spiritual growth you wish to work on and make it a priority for the next 21 days.

Prayer:
Thank You, Lord, for forgiving me my lapses in focus. Amen.

JULY 10

Be Still, My Screens
BY MYRA BIERNAT WELLS

Psalm 46:10

Be still and know that I am God; I will be exalted among the nations. I will be exalted in the earth.

The conference speaker made what seemed to be an unusual request. She gave us a hashtag and asked us to tweet comments throughout the conference. Her command was sweetened by explaining if we tweeted, we'd be entered into a drawing for prizes! Little did we realize the speaker was making us guinea pigs in a social media experiment – to see how many people we could engage during the day-long conference. Sixty-one of us eventually touched 117,000 people in the six-hour tweeting experiment.

As impressive as that statistic sounds, a more important question swirled in my brain – admittedly a query counterintuitive to one showing the power of social media. Are we listening to the voice coming out of our smart phones and computers more that we are listening to God's voice? Have we traded stillness and silence for the thrill of online living?

If your life is touched by anxiety, stress, fear or fatigue, maybe it is time to still your screens. They often distract us from putting our focus on Christ. Unplug your modem, limit your time on social media, turn the television off. Take time, instead, to be still before the *God who calms the storms so its waves are still* (Psalm 107:29).

Think about the environment of your home. Is it a place where you can be quiet before the Lord to think about His goodness? Or is each room permeated by pixels, chimes and ring tones. Maybe it's time to still your screens. When you are still, you realize anew that He is God.

Action:

Throughout the day, silently repeat, "Be still and know that I am God." Then evaluate how dependent you are on your screens. Would you feel lost if you didn't have your phone and Internet connection for one day? Ask the Lord to help you put screens in their proper place.

Prayer:

Heavenly Father, give me wisdom regarding my screen time. Help me to make the most of my moments. Show me areas where I need to make changes. I need to tune into Your voice. I want to be still and know that You are God. Amen.

JULY 11

A Word from God
BY JUDY KNOX

Isaiah 55:12

For you will go out with joy and be led forth with peace; the mountains and hills will break forth into shouts of joy before you, and all the trees of the fields will clap their hands.

As I completed my packing for a trip to Alaska, the words kept coming to my mind, "You will go out with joy and be led forth with peace." At the airport, after passing through Security, I learned my traveling companion would not be able to make the trip. Although I would be with a tour group, the others in the group were strangers to me. Buoyed by the encouraging words about joy and peace, I proceeded to my gate, and once settled there I felt prompted to look up the verse. That was when I discovered the part about the mountains and trees. Because I knew I would be seeing lots of those, I knew God was using this verse to reassure me that although I would be traveling alone, He knew exactly where I was going and would be there with me.

As we approached Denali National Park the next day, our guide pointed out Mt. McKinley in the distance. After almost a month of rain and clouds, the weather had cleared just that morning. Not only was the mountain visible, but we could see the whole peak rising into a perfectly clear blue sky. The mountain had broken forth before me out of the clouds! I learned that although about one-third of all visitors get to see the mountain; usually part of it is hidden behind clouds. I was one of the five percent who gets to see the entire mountain the way we were seeing it.

The next day I went for a covered wagon ride. As we approached a bend in the road, the driver stopped the horses. She told us autumn was her favorite season in Alaska, and she wanted to share one of the reasons. In the fall, the bright yellow leaves on the aspen trees become dry. When the wind blows through them, they "quake," in a jiggling motion that causes the trees to shimmer in the sunshine. Then she said, "Listen to the sound they make. Don't they sound like an audience clapping their hands?" They did!

I was very excited to see that scripture verse come to life before my eyes. I had already felt God's joy and peace. The sheer joy of taking this long-anticipated trip, and the peace I experienced as I navigated airports and planes was amazing. When the mountain broke forth before me and the trees clapped their hands, I marveled at how specifically God can communicate with us through His living, active Word. The view of the mountain and the sound of the trees were a confirmation to me that as my journey continued, I could also expect to continue walking in God's joy and peace.

Action:
The next time a phrase or part of a Bible verse comes to your mind, take the time to Google it. You may be surprised at how specifically it applies to what is going on in your life.

Prayer:
Father, I thank You for encouraging me through Your Word. Help me to be attentive to what You are showing me. Amen.

JULY 12

Meditation
BY SHERRI GALLAGHER

Psalm 1:2

But his delight is in the law of the Lord, and on his law he meditates day and night.

It had been a hectic, miserable morning. It was one of those days we all have where errands and tasks pile up, and we spend the day rushing around only to end the day feeling as though our time was wasted. We accomplished nothing except our own exhaustion. I was extra frustrated because my morning time of prayer had been consumed by cleaning up a dog-created mess.

As I drove from one shop to another, I tuned in to a religious radio station. A lady was talking about just my kind of day and how to fit in time with God even under those circumstances. She suggested writing Bible verses on index cards and tucking them in your pocket or purse. When you were stuck waiting in a line at the checkout, pull out the index card and read and meditate on it until it is in your memory and you really don't even need the card any more to recall God's word. In the waning seconds of the program, the interviewer asked, "Where should you start?" "Psalm 1" she answered, then they cut to commercial.

The next morning, I turned to Psalm 1 and copied it on an index card. Those six simple verses seemed to say it all. Verse one told me how to be happy and made me wince a little when I remembered some of my mistakes from yesterday. Having time and a way to meditate on God's word no matter how hectic the day made me smile as I read verse two. Verse three brought visions of an oasis in a desert to mind. Verse five made me think of how warm and welcome I felt in our sanctuary. Verse six reminded me how God is always there watching over and protecting me.

Every time I read this psalm, I get something new and different. I really don't need the index card anymore. God's word is in my memory and in my heart. And, as I stand in line, I can call it up and meditate on His word any time of day or night.

Action:

Make your own index card of Psalm 1.

Prayer:

Thank you, Lord, for this wonderful woman who gave me a way to keep You close and take joy in Your presence even on hectic days. Amen.

JULY 13

The Incident in the Dog Park
BY MYRA BIERNAT WELLS

Philippians 4:14

Yet it was good of you to share in my troubles.

I've always wondered if I were threatened bodily harm whether Lily, my dog, would protect me. Oh, I flippantly tell everyone, "No one will bother me with Lily around." Honestly, who would want to tangle with a 4-year-old, 76-pound German Shepherd with sharp teeth? But what would she do if someone *did* bother me? She's never been trained in protection. Would her natural instincts and loyalty take over?

One idyllic afternoon in the doggie park that question was forever answered. While I read a book in the shade, Lily was whooping it up with her canine friends. None of them paid much attention when a white German Shepherd entered the park or even while the canine and its owners made their way to a bench near mine. As the couple seated themselves, they explained to me their dog, Lexi, had been roughed up during some recent trips to the park, so they temporarily stopped coming. After a brief hiatus, this was their first trip back to get Lexi re-acclimated.

Lily, ever the amicable peacemaking pooch, ambled over to check Lexi out. My dog's temperament must have soothed Lexi's fears for soon the two of them were running as a pair never venturing more than 30 feet away from her owners and me. Watching Lexi, a white German Shepherd, dart alongside Lily, a black German Shepherd, was captivating as they gracefully danced as a salt and pepper team. Weaving in and out, their powerful strides carrying them quickly through the green grass made a perfect picture of canine euphoria.

I've been told dogs sense fear. I can now tell you from firsthand experience this is true. After the two German Shepherds were frolicking for a short time, with

Lexi feeling a bit more confident, they slowly widened their circles around us. Just enough, unfortunately, to catch the attention of two pit bulls playing at the opposite end of the park. These pit bulls dashed over, separating Lexi from Lily. Extremely frightened, Lexi hotfooted it back to the benches, but for some reason, maybe because I was closest, charged straight towards me, not her owners. Within seconds, a dog fight erupted at my feet.

Sensing I was in dire trouble, Lily hustled over to my side. She promptly placed herself between me and the three other dogs. The pack was winnowed down to two as this action gave Lexi the time needed to retreat over to her owners. But the two pit bulls were not backing off; angrily snarling and with great menace lunging towards Lily. I tried to get the attacking dogs to withdraw, but they grew even more antagonistic.

I was scared for my dog, but Lily showed great courage. I've never seen her so agitated, so fiercely protective of me. The only way those pit bulls were going to harm me was over her dead body.

Love is not something you earn, but something you receive. It is a benediction, a blessing that is undeserved. We are protected, healed, uplifted when someone shows us love. We were not meant to walk this road alone. Amid the teeth baring, the vicious growling and the loud barking, my little lady turned into a warrior. Her bravery in the middle of this scuffle, despite my concern for her safety, made me proud.

Doesn't it bring you great joy when a friend becomes your champion? They reach out to you, hold your hand tightly, form a protective barrier around you and gently whisper to you, "You'll get through this. You'll find yourself once again in a better place. You'll laugh again, sleep well once more, find happiness. It will happen. I promise." They make a sacred space of your grief and mess.

Fortunately, the owner of the pit bulls finally came over and got them to back away. Once they left, Lily sat down quietly at my feet, still protecting me even though the danger had subsided.

When you sense a crisis, loneliness or pain overtaking the life of someone you care deeply about, take a lesson from Lily's action during this incident in the doggie park. Bathe them with goodness from God: comfort, protection and the firsthand knowledge that peace will follow seasons of turbulence.

Action:

Have you ever been bowled over by genuine love that was totally unexpected? What was that like for you? Take a few minutes to think about, or better yet, write down how it changed you – what long term effect did it have on your life?

Prayer:

Jesus, as much as I need champions in my life, please help me be a champion to another. Free me from my insecurities and vulnerabilities so that I can connect with someone who is in pain or embittered. Teach me, through Your world, to live open-hearted, caring and authentic. Amen.

JULY 14

The Seed Is the Word
BY JUDY KNOX

Mark 4:1-9

The LORD does not look at the things people look at. People look at the outward appearance, but the LORD looks at the heart. **I Samuel 16:7b**

Sneak a peek with me at opening day exercises for the faculty at a local high school. The scene is the same every year. The superintendent imparts words that he hopes will inspire the teachers and set the tone for the coming school year. He is delivering one message. Yet, as we look around, we see that not everyone is receiving it in the same way. Some listen actively, taking avid notes, responding with nods of agreement or even vocal assents. Others sit quietly, perhaps looking around to see what everyone else is doing. Still others are making their grocery lists, fiddling with electronic devices, or getting a head start on their lesson plans.

A low level of attentiveness in this case will probably have little effect on a teacher's success for the year. However, Jesus makes it very clear that our heart attitude when we hear the Word of God has everything to do with success and fruitfulness in our Christian walk. After He had talked to the multitudes about the sower and the seed, His disciples asked Him for an explanation. "Do you not understand this parable?" He asked them. "How then will you understand all the parables?" He wanted them to know this teaching held the key to understanding everything He was trying to teach them.

The disciples realized that Jesus was not teaching a lesson on farming. He was revealing important truths about the Kingdom of God. The seed, He told them, is the Word, and the soil describes the condition of the heart that is receiving the Word. Most of us, by the time we reach adulthood, have heard this story and its explanation so many times that we read or listen to it with the attitude of, "Oh yeah, I know what that's about," and we move on past the message without letting it penetrate our hearts. And yet, isn't this exactly what Jesus is getting at? The attitude with which we receive the Word has a major impact on our fruitfulness. No one else can prepare the soil for us. The condition of our heart is our responsibility. We must keep it fertile so the Word can penetrate it. Then the Word we have planted there can grow, and our lives will bring forth the fruit of the Holy Spirit.

Action:
Read what Jesus says in His follow-up to the parable in Mark 4:14-30. Which type of ground sounds the most like you?

JULY 15

Your Church or Mine?
BY SHERRI GALLAGHER

1 Corinthians 12:12-31

We must no longer be children, tossed to and fro and blown about by every wind of doctrine, by people's trickery, by their craftiness in deceitful scheming.
Ephesians 4:14

A few years ago, our church bought new hymnals. Much to the surprise of many members the words to some old favorite hymns had been changed. Our pastor could have been outraged on behalf of the congregation or he could have sternly insisted the congregation learn the new words. Instead he did something that represents a founding principle of our church, all- inclusiveness. He gave us permission to sing the hymns the way we wanted. If we wanted to use the wording learned when we were children, we should do so with joy. If we wanted to use the new wording, he invited us to sing out in happiness. He reminded us God knew what was in our hearts and God asked that we make a joyful noise not spout doctrine.

In Ephesians 4:14 Paul tells us not to be children tossed to and fro by every wind of doctrine. We are to work together to grow the church in love. We are to look past our differences to those things we have in common and build on those. We need to love each other because we are different. Each of us has a place in the church. 1 Corinthians 12 talks about gifts of the spirit and how each one is important just as the different parts of the body are important and each needs the other. We are directed to use our gifts for the good of all and rejoice in our differences as all are needed. Thankfully in our church all are welcome.

Action:
Think about the Lord's prayer (Matthew 6:9-16) and compare the different versions you have heard or learned. How are the meanings the same and how are they different?

Prayer:
Thank you, Lord, for all the different members of our church and for the differences that make us stronger as a group than if we were all the same. Amen.

JULY 16

Choose Wisely!
BY MYRA BIERNAT WELLS

Proverbs 3:5-6

Trust in the Lord with all your heart and lean not on your own understanding, in all your ways acknowledge Him and He will make your paths straight.

One of my favorite Old Testament books is that of Ruth. It tells the story of Ruth and Naomi: two women who faced difficult circumstances and an uncertain future. Following the death of her husband and sons, Naomi decided to return to her homeland of Israel. Though she freed her daughters-in-law to stay in their home country of Moab and re-marry, Ruth refused to leave Naomi's side. What a difficult choice to make!

Both traveled to Bethlehem as broken, depressed and hopeless widows, but each was comforted and restored there by the loving hand of God. He breathed hope back into their souls through their kinsman-redeemer, Boaz. Ruth eventually married Boaz and because of her faithfulness to God was included in the genealogy of Jesus.

Though our own natural tendency in hard times is often to try to go it alone, the lesson I've learned from Ruth and my own experience is that in turbulent times, it's vital we hold fast to our faithful God and to the ones we love.

Like Naomi and Ruth, I must choose to trust God. This is essential. But how do I make the choice? I decide in my heart. Then I bolster this decision by playing praise music, meditating on God's goodness, reading Scripture and praying. These things collectively renew my mind and strengthen my faith.

No matter what challenges you face today, take comfort that God knows every issue on your heart and is able to carry your burdens. Hold fast to the Faithful One. Your challenges will never fall out of the scope of God's ability to intervene. God is mysterious, powerful and able.

Action:

Read the book of Ruth today. It is only four chapters. Could you have left your homeland like Ruth did?

Prayer:

Father, You know exactly where I am right now, and You know the circumstances of my life. Please shower me with the courage to be gracious in my relationships and to trust You today and forever. In Jesus' name. Amen.

JULY 17

The Hard Re-set
BY JUDY KNOX

Matthew 11:28-30

Come to me, all you who are weary and burdened, and I will give you rest. Take my yoke upon you and learn from me, for I am gentle and humble in heart, and you will find rest for your souls. For my yoke is easy and my burden is light.

For thus says the Lord God, the Holy One of Israel: "In returning and rest you shall be saved; in quietness and confidence shall be your strength," **Isaiah 30:15**

I love my smart phone. More than just a phone, this tiny handheld computer can do more than the big, clunky desktop computer I spent many thousands of dollars for fifteen years ago. Because this little device can perform so many tasks so quickly, I've become dependent on it. Yes, I know, we all used to get along fine without cell phones; but in those days few people had them, so the expectations we had of one another were different. Now we expect friends and family to stay in touch by text or email, and they expect us to do the same.

Being able to look up an address, and find my way to it, is worth the price of the phone. And how about being able to look up definitions, Bible verses, historical facts? No question this handy gadget really makes our lives easier. Easier, that is, until the phone starts doing strange things. One time my phone just didn't make a sound when a call or text was coming in (and yes, I checked all the settings). Another time all the little symbols showed that I was connected to the Internet, but I absolutely was not. The smart phone is so smart that it keeps coming up with new and different way ways of being goofy, baffling me with new surprises for apparently no reason.

Very early in the cell phone using game I learned a way to solve almost every kind of weird phone behavior: the hard re-set. The first time a technician support person told me to do this, I nearly panicked. I pictured being unable to retrieve all my phone numbers and other data. However, I followed the directions and held my breath as the screen went blank. A minute later, I turned it back on, and voilà! Problem gone!

Sometimes, I find myself short-circuiting like my phone, not functioning the way I was designed to, not able to think straight. I've discovered that the re-set procedure that fixes my phone also works for me. I take a few moments to disconnect my thoughts from everything I'm trying to do. But instead of going blank, I turn my thoughts toward Jesus, take a deep breath, and picture him looking me straight in the eyes and telling me, "Be still, and know that I am God" (Psalm 46:10). Peace returns, and once again I am functional.

Action:

Next time you find yourself trying to do too many things at once, and not doing any of them well, stop and give yourself a hard re-set before continuing.

Prayer:

Lord, when I get into one of those states of mind where I function as if my wires were crossed, please stop me and help me to put You back at the center of my focus. Help me enter into the peaceful rest that only You can give. Amen.

JULY 18

Judge Me by My Fruits
BY SHERRI GALLAGHER

Luke 6:43-45

No good tree bears bad fruit, nor does a bad tree bear good fruit. Each tree is recognized by its own fruit. People do not pick figs from thorn bushes, or grapes from briers. A good man brings good things out of the good stored up in his heart, and an evil man brings evil things out of the evil stored up in his heart. For the mouth speaks what the heart is full of.

Say nothing of my religion. It is known to God and myself alone. Its evidence before the world is to be sought in my life: if it has been honest and dutiful to society the religion which has regulated it cannot be a bad one.

Thomas Jefferson

A client who had known my husband for years, found the Lord. She was filled with joy and felt a great need to share His promise with everyone she met. My husband attended a business meeting with her, and she witnessed to everyone there. The attendees listened, offering polite responses and went on with the business of the meeting. Later, she took my husband aside and asked if she could pray over him that he would find our Lord and Savior. He was very nice to her, expressing his happiness that she had found salvation. He then asked her why she thought he had not? She answered that he did not evangelize and therefore could not have found Jesus.

My husband could have been very mean. He could have been angry. Instead he asked her to look at how he lived and worked, because he showed people the way by example. He gently pointed out his actions in all his dealings, both business and personal. He reminded her of examples she had seen where he was honest and gave freely of his knowledge, experience, and connections even though it cost him additional business billings. He told her of his community service activities, something he didn't generally share with business acquaintances.

That night he came home worried that he had confused this client. She resigned before he saw her again and returned to her home country as a missionary. We do not know what impact his word had or didn't have on her.

Jesus gave us a way to measure our own actions and determine if we are acting in a manner befitting a Christian. Do we put the needs of others ahead of our own needs? Do we share what we have with those who are less fortunate? Do we live healthy lifestyles? Do we resist the urge to gossip or post cruel comments on Facebook? Do we go out of our way to listen and comfort people in need? Do we bear good fruit; in-other-words do our actions have a positive result on the lives of others. What is in our hearts will show in our actions and speech. If God is in our hearts, then it will show.

Action:

Decide on an activity that will help others and not bring you any accolades, like visiting a lonely neighbor or taking a bag of groceries to the food pantry.

Prayer:

Lord God, guide my actions that I may be worthy of the title Christian. Amen.

JULY 19

Whose Voice Do You Hear?
BY MYRA BIERNAT WELLS

John 10:27

My sheep listen to my voice; I know them and they follow me.

"Come" was never one of my German Shepherd's favorite commands. Lily would easily do "sit" and "down." She'd squirm on a "stay" sometimes, but not often. She loved "shake"…learning that command in a few hours. But "come," that was a huge difficulty for her. We worked on it quite a while and in various settings: in the house, at the park, on walks, in parking lots. But it was always a hit or miss command. My theory was that there were so many more exciting doggie things to do, to sniff and to explore. After months of inconsistent responses, I was quite disappointed, but still worked on it with her.

I knew she finally understood when one day, I tried an experiment. Lily was in the backyard. I was in the upstairs bedroom, the one with the balcony overlooking the yard. With the sliding door open, but in a conversational voice, I said, "Come!" I didn't want to look outside, but my heart leapt for joy when I could hear the jingling dog tags on her collar slowly move towards me. Into the family room, past the dining room, up the stairs, until my beautiful black dog was sitting beside me in the upstairs bedroom.

What activities do you put before listening to God's voice? Stress comes when we allow the distractions of everyday life to drown out the only voice that really matters: the voice of God. We can't obey every voice we hear. That leads to total failure, carrying a heavy load we were never meant to carry. Obedience to God is not a burdensome load; we don't have to bear it alone. God's strength and power uplifts us. And how do we learn to recognize His voice? Like Lily, we practice. We discover Him by spending time in the Bible and in prayer.

Action:

Through faith, accept the truth that God is always at work in your life and thank Him for His steadfast provision. Look back over the last few days of your life. Identify the voices you tend to listen to instead the voice of God. End by praising Him for all the things He has done for you.

Prayer:

Father, I come to You today, wanting and needing to hear Your voice. I am drowning in the expectations of others and I am so confused about the next step I need to take. Please give me Your direction and the strength to follow Your plan for my life. In Jesus' name. Amen.

JULY 20

Words Fitly Spoken
BY JUDY KNOX

Proverbs 25:11

A word fitly spoken is like apples of gold in settings of silver. (NKJV)

A couple years ago I began taking cello lessons. Although I had some musical background, the cello was completely new for me, requiring a whole new set of brain-body connections. In choosing an instrument, I looked for something that would not sound screechy, even if I did not hit exactly the right note. This definitely ruled out the violin! However, although not painful to the ears, my early attempts to produce those beautiful sounds usually associated with the cello were not too encouraging, and my first recital was definitely not something to be proud of.

Just as I was on the verge of giving up the whole idea, my pastor's wife invited me to join the church worship team. I came to the first practice with trepidation. I almost backed down when the sound engineer placed a microphone right in front of my instrument. But when we began playing the first song, to my delight the cello's sounds contributed a mellow smoothness to the music, balancing the more rhythmic sounds of the guitars, drums and bass. Eventually, I was called on to play little solo passages that added to the overall worshipful effect of the music.

As a member of the Body of Christ, it seems I am a lot like my cello. Most of the time I function in the background, adding depth and richness, making the sound of the whole team fuller without drawing attention to myself. Occasionally, the Holy Spirit prompts me to step out and play solo, or I am called upon to teach or share a testimony. As I follow His leading, my words are fitly spoken, encouraging and edifying to those who hear them. Whether I am producing background sounds or playing solo, my contribution to the team effort is important to the overall function of the body.

Everything a cello needs for producing music is already built into it. In order to bring out the sound, the player must draw the bow skillfully across the strings, and his fingers must be in the right position to play the correct note. With practice I have been learning to produce those mellow sounds and tones so they can bless the hearers.

Likewise, in our walk with God, His attributes are built into us and are always in us. He placed them there when we accepted Christ, and He wants to bring them out. We must practice listening to His voice, so when we are called upon to play a solo, we can speak what He would have us say. Then we won't be a screechy sound, but our words will be fitly spoken, bringing joy and blessing to those around us.

Action:
Join a ministry working in the background. Add your fitly spoken words to the orchestra that is the Church.

Prayer:
Lord, I want to be a blessing wherever I go, whether I am playing a supportive role or called upon to lead or speak. Let my words always be like golden apples in settings of silver, words of encouragement and hope. Amen.

JULY 21

Breaking with the Past
BY SHERRI GALLAGHER

Philippians 3:1-11

The definition of insanity is to do the same thing over and over and expect different results. **Rita Mae Brown**

It is very easy to fall back into old bad habits and much more difficult to create a new habit. A trainer once told me that a person needs to do the new habit twenty-one days in a row for it to become an automatic action. I was training my dog for the ausdauerprüfung (any wonder why English speakers just call it the AD?) It is an endurance test where the dog must run for twelve miles at an eight mile an hour pace. To correctly train, I needed to bike him every other day for six weeks, gradually increasing the speed and distance. I could find all sorts of excuses not to take that bike ride. It was too hot or too cold or I didn't have time. Playing with a toy in the backyard was so much easier and what we were used to doing, but it wouldn't help the dog prepare for the test.

Paul gives us guidance to grow spiritually through his letter to the church at Philippi. He warns against falling back into old habits of worship that had nothing to do with Christianity. Prior to finding Jesus, Paul had every reason to boast. His birth, education, and actions made him important; one to be emulated by other followers of Judaism. It would have been easy for him to be blinded by all his old habits of worship and not follow the plan God had for him. Instead he turned away, and while it cost him dearly, Paul understood he had more through Jesus Christ than he had by practicing strict rituals. By following Jesus Paul gained eternal life, something no human can earn through their actions.

Spiritual habits can be more difficult to analyze. A man I worked with would go to services with his family and then ignore the sermon. He would use the time to make notes and "to do" lists for his job.

Action:
What habits are you practicing that are a roadblock to following the Lord? Pick one and make a conscious effort to reverse it, leave yourself a note or ask a family member or friend to remind you of your plan.

Prayer:
Lord God, forgive me when I fall back into old habits. Please give me gentle reminders so I may be a better follower of You. Amen.

JULY 22

The Pain of It All
BY MYRA BIERNAT WELLS

Psalm 106:1

Praise the Lord. Give thanks to the Lord for He is good. His love endures forever.

Pain has been the major theme of these past two weeks. A friend's father died; another friend was hospitalized; a third is teetering on the precipice of home loss; a fourth is in the throes of serious financial crisis; a high school friend is dying of bone cancer. And on top of this, I was sick myself, unable to provide the level of kindness these situations demanded. Yet, in this world, there will always be someone who needs our attention. The list of wounded hearts and unmet needs is endless.

On top of these real sorrows, we often play an interesting game of "Life will be better when…" When I have more money, when I get a nicer car, when I go on that fantasy vacation, when I find that dream job. With so many people in pain, facing trials that seem impossible to handle, along with those of us who simply aren't content with where we are in life, thanklessness abounds in our world. But maybe that's because we try to find joy, contentment and peace in lifeless places and things.

Jesus Christ, our Redeemer is our life. He is Joy and Love. Because He took our place on the cross, we can give thanks even when it seems as if there is nothing to be thankful for. When the brokenness of the world and the pain of life become too overbearing for me, I run for my journal. It is there I write down my praises to God. Because the only way I can change my attitude about what is happening to me is by clinging tightly to the one who walks with me. 1 Thessalonians 5:18 states, "Give thanks in all circumstances, for this is God's will for you in Christ Jesus."

There is often little we can do to change the world with its challenges, sadness and pain, but today can still be a day of thanksgiving and prayer. Joy is possible during the storms as we worship our Redeemer. All we need do is celebrate the One who gave us victory over this life.

Action:
Memorize 1 Thessalonians 5:18, "Give thanks in all circumstances, for this is God's will for you in Christ Jesus." Then examine your heart for any traces of discontentment. Write down the good things God has done in and through you. Then praise Him for each blessing and celebrate Him.

Prayer:
Father, I come to You today, praising You for meeting my needs in ways I cannot even imagine or understand. Help me see Your hand of mercy and love on my life. Let me dwell deeply in Your presence and celebrate You as I also celebrate my life. Amen.

JULY 23

Appearances Can Be Deceiving
BY JUDY KNOX

I Samuel 16:7b

The Lord does not look at the things people look at. People look at the outward appearance, but the Lord looks at the heart.

I once had a boss who found my "piling system" very annoying. Though I had a private office where my messy desk affected no one else, its appearance bothered him. I tried many times to explain and even show him how organized I really was, but what looked to him like a sign of disorder continued to be a bone of contention. Eventually he admitted that I was very productive and there was nothing wrong with my work, so we agreed to disagree about the desk.

A few weeks later, he asked me to take charge of our department's purchase of new furniture and equipment for the following year. The school district had given us a large budget to update our surroundings. After many hours of hard work, I completed over a hundred purchase orders, and just before spring break I brought the stack of forms to my boss. All he had to do, I explained, was sign each one and then send the whole bunch to the business office. He thanked me profusely. "You've done yeoman's work!" he exclaimed.

I was glad to have been helpful and was looking forward to the new furniture that would greet us when we returned to school the next fall. Everything was great until the last day of school when I received a call from the business manager wondering why we had never ordered our furniture. He said my boss told him I had taken care of everything, but the business manager had never received the order forms.

I walked into my boss's office, sat down before his sparkling clean desk with nothing on top but a framed family photo and a pen set, and reminded him of the green forms I had given him three months before. He vaguely remembered that. Then he opened his bottom desk drawer, where instead of the expected tidy array of hanging file folders I saw a drawer piled to the brim with papers. "They must be in here somewhere!" he said and began digging through them until he unearthed the purchase orders. I thought of Jesus' remark to the Pharisees about whitewashed tombs full of dead men's bones.

Are we like the supervisor's desk, clean on the outside but a mess inside? Or do we allow God to work in our hearts, changing our attitudes and renewing our minds?

Action:

Are there areas in your life where your heart attitude does not match up with what you display to the world? Ask God to change that attitude.

Prayer:

Father, please shine Your light on my heart and reveal to me those areas where I am putting too much effort into how I look to others, and too little effort on following You, and help me to change. In Jesus' name. Amen.

JULY 24

OMG
BY SHERRI GALLAGHER

1 Timothy 1:12-20

Never use the name of the Lord your God carelessly. The Lord will make sure that anyone who carelessly uses His name will be punished. **Exodus 20:7** (GW)

The front cover of "People" magazine proclaimed in large letters "OMG! She's Pregnant Again." Why is it the magazine would never print, "Oh My God!" but thinks nothing of using the texting abbreviation OMG? Do they think it is less blasphemous? I will admit when angry to having something of a potty mouth; hang out in factories and with construction guys and it is easy to slip into bad language habits. But I do try very hard to curb my tongue and not use offensive language. It was not until I joined our Christian writers' group that I understood that just avoiding four letter words wasn't good enough. "Geez," "gosh," and "darn" are still offensive. The first two are still considered taking God's name in vain and the third is wishing evil on someone. I have taken to equating people who offend me to being a "turnip."

Have you ever heard of a vegetable that had a brain? And if I happen to hammer my thumb instead of a nail, I try really hard not to say anything stronger than "fudge." But is this really necessary?

Most of us are not strict followers of the laws of the Old Testament. In Ephesians 2:15 we are told, "He has abolished the law with its commandments and ordinances, that he might create in himself one new humanity in the place of two, thus making peace." That doesn't mean forget the ten commandments. It is a guide that we should put away ritualistic differences in order to love one another. Jesus gave us two commandments. The first was, "You shall love the Lord your God with all your heart and with all your soul and with all your mind" (Matthew 22:37). Taking His name carelessly is not a demonstration of love but rather of disrespect. Timothy turned Hymenaeus and Alexander over to Satan for blasphemy. Ouch, glad Timothy isn't around now, or I might be in big trouble.

We are also not to do things that offend others or cause them to be misled (Romans 14:13-23). Using God's name carelessly, whether in actual words or abbreviations or alternative words is offensive and should be avoided.

Action:

Consider if your texts, tweets, postings and words are accidentally taking the Lord's name carelessly. Reframe, review, and delete where possible.

Prayer:

Lord, help me to be more careful of my language and to only say Your name with respect. Amen.

JULY 25

An Awful Truth
BY MYRA BIERNAT WELLS

Psalm 34:18

The Lord is close to the brokenhearted and saves those who are crushed in spirit.

It was bright and blue and just the right size. I loved that umbrella. I'd carry it with me even when rain wasn't in the forecast. As a four-year-old, I was granted that concession. But it was also that umbrella that would teach me an awful truth. On one particularly windy day, the material was ripped from the frame. Trailing the remains beside me, I presented my busted up, but much beloved umbrella to my father, thinking in my childish mind he'd surely be able to fix it. He'd fixed so many things in the past!

But this time, he couldn't repair what was broken. I still remember my inconsolable tears. It must have been such a relief to my parents when they finally put me to bed, but my tears kept my pillow soggy throughout the night. I wasn't just crying about the umbrella. My dad had always been my hero; had always fixed the broken things in my life; had wiped away my little girl sorrows. Tears filled my eyes because of the truth revealed: I was disappointed because I now knew my dad couldn't fix everything.

My heart has been broken many times since then and for things more important than just an umbrella. With each disappointment, I've gained courage knowing God is drawn to broken people. In fact, God does some of His finest works in broken people. In their woundedness, their desperation, His Love and His grace fall through the cracks in their hearts and find fertile spots in which to grow.

Deuteronomy 6:6 says, "These commandments that I give you today are to be upon your hearts." Notice the passage doesn't say *in* your hearts. That's because I believe we can only place the truth on our hearts until our hearts are broken. Only once they are ruined can God's amazing love restore you.

Action:

Read Romans 8:28. Write the verse down on the top of a sheet of paper. Below it, write about the good things God has brought out of your pain. Where is your faith stronger because of what you have endured? Now use this list to think of someone you can encourage who has experienced the same pain. Reach out to them either by phone or card and let them know God is with them.

Prayer:

Father, I surrender all the broken places in my heart to You. Please heal them by allowing Your truth to sink in and bring restoration. I lay down my hardheartedness, my sin, and ask for Your forgiveness. Help me harness the power of my broken place to live for You. In Jesus' name. Amen.

JULY 26

Balloon Ride
BY JUDY KNOX

Hebrews 12:1-3, 2 Corinthians 4:17-18

May the winds welcome you with softness. May the sun bless you with its warm hands. May you fly so high and so well that God joins you in laughter and sets you gently back into the loving arms of Mother Earth. **Balloonists' Prayer**

On a recent trip to Arizona, I had the privilege of going for a hot-air balloon ride. I watched with fascination as the crew laid out the balloon so it could catch the hot air, and then started up the giant fan that filled the balloon. Slowly the balloon inflated and began to rise.

Once the balloon was filled, we climbed into the basket, the pilot gave the word, and the crew let go of the ropes. Up we went. At first, I didn't realize we were moving. There was no sensation of movement, but as I saw the ground gradually fall away from us, I knew we were on our way. People and objects below grew smaller, and the horizon expanded below us.

I was surprised that my hair wasn't blowing in the wind. In fact, I couldn't even feel the wind, yet I knew it was blowing because the balloon kept traveling sideways. The pilot could control our up-and-down motion by the amount of hot air he released into the balloon, but he had no control over the sideways direction. We were part of the wind, and whichever way it went, we went. Once we were in the air, the only sounds we could hear were our own voices and the hot air blower.

As we sailed along, I looked at the view below, the mountains beyond, other balloons in the air, and what the pilot was doing. We dipped down close to some people on their back patio who were waving at us, then swooped back up again trying to get to the place where our crew was heading to pick us up. The whole process was fascinating.

Later, though, I realized how much this was like our life in the Spirit. In God we live and move and have our being (Acts 17:28), but much of the time we are not aware of it. When we allow ourselves to dwell in God's presence, then wherever He goes, we go. We may not feel anything, but we are in the flow of the Spirit, just as in the balloon we were one with the wind.

I also thought of the old song that says, "Turn your eyes upon Jesus, look full in His wonderful face, and the things of earth will grow strangely dim in the light of His glory and grace." Just as I had been unaware of all the activity going on below me, and focused on the pilot, the balloon and what was going on in the basket, God wants us to focus on Him and what He's doing. Then our circumstances will fade. They may still be there, but we are transported to a place where we can see them from God's perspective. They become less important.

Who knew a ride in a balloon would really be a picture of life with God?

Action:

Think about a circumstance in your life that is troubling you. Sit quietly and picture yourself soaring above it, focusing only on Jesus and His promises.

Prayer:

Thank You, Lord, that You are always moving in my heart and life. Help me to focus on You and what You are doing instead of on my problems and cares. In Jesus' name. Amen.

JULY 27

Not the Best
BY SHERRI GALLAGHER

Matthew 25:14-30

Use what talents you possess: the woods would be very silent if no birds sang there except those that sang the best. **Henry Van Dyke**

A visitor stood nervously next to me in the pew as it came time to sing a hymn. I opened the hymnal to the page and turned to share it with her. She waved me away with a whispered, "I don't sing well." I whispered back, "God said make a joyful noise, not carry a tune." She nodded and joined in a little tentatively. She wasn't the greatest of singers. Once she realized that no one was offended by her poor singing skills she did sing with a little more confidence and a little more on key. While she would never make it to *The Voice* those around her took pleasure in her joy at being able to sing to the Lord.

How many times have we been like that visitor, afraid to attempt something due to a lack of confidence in our own skills? Writers tend to be a little shy. More than a few have joined our writers group and been afraid to submit a story or article to a publisher for fear of being rejected. We sometimes walk them through the results of the submission process. When submitting a story, it might be published, or it might be rejected. If it is rejected the author receives feedback on why the story wasn't publishable and what changes need to be made to get it published. By not submitting, we are guaranteeing not getting published and not getting better which is much worse than getting rejected.

When we fail to try, we are like the servant that buried his talent. We do not help others to grow. We do not grow ourselves. In essence we have wasted a gift from God and that is not what He wants us to do with our gifts.

Action:

The next time you have worked hard but are afraid to step out, ask yourself, "What is the worst that can happen? Is that worse than doing nothing?"

Prayer:

Heavenly Father, give me the courage to step out and display my talents giving glory to You. Amen.

JULY 28

Your Last Day
BY MYRA BIERNAT WELLS

Psalm 104:33

I will sing to the Lord all my life; I will sing praise to my God as long as I live.

He rushed out the door on his way to school, pausing just long enough to verify with his mother that she was making his favorite meal for dinner. Less than an hour later, his mother dashed to the hospital to be by his bedside as her son lay dying. A victim of a random shooting, he was dead before dinner time.

Ebony Ambrose didn't realize that morning would be his last. But when reading his story, the darkness of it grabbed hold of me. The futility of a young life with all its promise lost forever. But what about the promise still left in my life? How often have I looked forward all day to my favorite dinner? Did I make good use of the hours between morning and dinner time? Suddenly I felt God speaking to me, "Myra, if you knew you only had a short time to live, how would you spend your day?"

It was a poignant moment, but not a morbid one. A reminder of the brevity of life is never easy, but God also pointed out the beauty He placed around me and of His desire to make each of my days count for Him.

It got me to thinking of how my life impacts others. What seeds am I planting along my life's journey that will continue to bloom years after I am gone? What have I been putting off that will bring bright sunshine into someone else's life? Write a letter to a friend? Plant a rose garden? Call an elderly relative? Take someone to church with me? Memorize a few verses in the Bible so I can share God's Good News with ease?

I'm sure you, along with me, want the fragrance of your life to softly linger once you are gone. And so, I return to the question God asked of me, "What would you do today if you knew you only had a short time to live?"

Action:

How did you answer that question? Are you still pondering it? Make a list of three to five things you can do this week that are true, noble, righteous, lovely, admirable, excellent, praiseworthy. Then, don't wait - go do them!

Prayer:

Dear God, thank You for the gift of today. Thank You for reminding me life on this earth is short. Help me to live today and every day with a longing for home but with the purpose of making each moment count for You. In Your precious Son's name. Amen.

JULY 29

Pearls Before Swine
BY JUDY KNOX

Matthew 7:6

Do not give what is holy to the dogs; nor cast your pearls before swine, lest they trample them under their feet, and turn and tear you to pieces. (NKJV)

The paradox of gifts: I know what I have given you. I do not know what you have received. **Dr. Sam Wolf**

Jesus paints a vivid picture here. A woman takes valuable pearls that mean something to her, comes into the pigpen, and tosses them amidst the pigs. The pigs walk over to the pearls and sniff them. They don't smell like food, so they disregard them, eventually trampling them into the muddy ground, then they turn back to the woman and chase her out of the pen.

I have often contemplated this verse, wondering why a person would throw pearls to pigs in the first place. I believe Jesus uses this illustration because it is a very unlikely scene. Who would do something like that? And what about the pigs? Are they evil? No, those objects that have a very high value to people are of no use to the pigs, who are ignorant of their worth. They are just doing what pigs do.

We can all relate to this scene. How often have you spent time and effort on a special gift for someone, only to learn it wasn't very special to them. Or what about sharing some gem of wisdom that you were sure would help another person, only to have them trample it under foot by arguing with you about why the suggestion won't work. On some occasions a person may even become angry at what you told them and attack you.

I can think of many times when my efforts to bless another person backfired, or at least what I gave them was not valued. Just as the pigs, which are not evil, did not value the pearls because they were not what they were looking for, so the other person did not appreciate my offering. When you remember one of these situations, how does it make you feel?

God is continually blessing us with all manner of good things and speaking to us with beautiful words of wisdom for our comfort, encouragement, and guidance. Do we receive and prize what He is giving us, or do we disregard it because He did not answer our prayer exactly as we were expecting? When God reveals a problem in our life, do we embrace His instructions and follow them, or do we become angry or annoyed with Him?

I wonder how God must feel when He gives me pearls and I trample them underfoot.

Action:
Think of a time when through ignorance or rebellion you did not value what God was giving you and bring it to Him in prayer.

Prayer:
Lord, forgive me for those times I did not recognize Your blessings and advice as valuable gifts. Help me to become more sensitive to Your interactions in my life. Amen.

JULY 30

Time Out
BY SHERRI GALLAGHER

The LORD is good to those whose hope is in him, to the one who seeks him; it is good to wait quietly for the salvation of the LORD.
Lamentations 3:25-26

But the Advocate, the Holy Spirit, whom the Father will send in my name, will teach you all things and will remind you of everything I have said to you. Peace I leave with you; my peace I give you. I do not give to you as the world gives. Do not let your hearts be troubled and do not be afraid. "You heard me say, 'I am going away and I am coming back to you.' If you loved me, you would be glad that I am going to the Father, for the Father is greater than I. **John 14:26-28**

In the attitude of silence the soul finds the path in a clearer light, and what is elusive and deceptive resolves itself into crystal clearness. Our life is a long and arduous quest after truth. **Mahatma Gandhi**

When my son was in pre-school, the children were put in time out as a corrective measure. Keeping that small energetic body still for even a few minutes agonized most of the children, but not my son. The frustrated teacher came to me one day. "I can't put your son in time out. He likes it." Shane had learned the art of sitting quietly and being at peace.

The Bible asks us to do something similar. Some passages use "quiet", some use "peace" others use "rest". It means putting away distractions around us and inside us and listening quietly for God's guidance, love and joy to fill us. When we do, the worries and stresses melt away and we can leave our troubles in His capable hands.

Action:
Find five minutes to sit quietly and think about Gods gifts and blessings. Tell Him about your hopes and fears and trust Him.

Prayer:
God give patience and a sense of humor to the parents of very young children. Amen.

JULY 31

Queen for the Day!
BY MYRA BIERNAT WELLS

1 Peter 5:5b-6

All of you, clothe yourselves with humility toward one another, because, 'God opposes the proud but shows favor to the humble.' Humble yourselves, therefore, under God's mighty hand, that he may lift you up in due time.

My freshman year in college, I lived in a women-only dormitory. Men were allowed in the lobby and first floor sitting area of the building – never up in the rooms except on moving days. It was not my first choice, but it made my parents happy.

Fortunately, I made many female friends. Since our dorm did not have food service, on most days we walked the short distance over to Allison Hall for lunch. Our mail was delivered sometime right before lunch, placed in little slots in the wall right off the dorm's lobby. Often, we'd pick it up before heading for our mid-day meal. Normally, everyone in my group received mail, but on the odd day when someone didn't receive a card or a letter or even junk mail, we made her Queen for the Day.

There wasn't much to the distinction. The gal got to sit at the head of our table. One of us carried her tray from the cafeteria line. Made sure she always had enough to drink and if she needed or wanted seconds, someone would go back into the line and get what she desired. As our very last act of kindness, we'd bus her tray back to the dishwasher. It was a fun to do, but also a small way we could serve each other.

We learned a lot through this. We discovered how to humble ourselves and perform small acts of kindness – that giving ennobles both the giver and receiver. We realized when someone is troubled, we serve God by lifting their burdens, even in tiny actions. And that even a small five- minute favor can brighten a person's spirit.

A community where women were loved, were seen and were comforted grew from this. We both blessed other each and were blessed by others when disappointments came. I really appreciated this when I didn't have newsy letters to share at the table or tasty homemade cookies to pass around for dessert. And learned that even small things can bring great comfort to one who is disappointed or hurting.

Action:
Read 1 Peter 5:5-6 (above) once more. Think of a couple of five-minute favors you can perform this week to encourage your family and friends.

Prayer:
Jesus, please help me focus on Your greatness and not my own. Make me humble enough to share another's burdens and lift them up in times of discouragement. Open my eyes throughout the day to opportunities to serve others so that You might be glorified. Amen.

AUGUST 1

He Prayed for You!
BY CATHY HARVEY

John 17:20

"My prayer is not for them alone."

More things are wrought by prayer than this world dreams of.
Alfred Lord Tennyson

Jesus, as usual, was teaching His apostles. He had just finished explaining in John 16:33, "I have told you these things, so that in me you may have peace. In this world you <u>will</u> have trouble. But take heart! I have overcome the world." He had also assured them that it was <u>for their good</u> that He was going away because unless He went away, the Counselor (His Holy Spirit) would not come to them.

And then, He prays, out loud, looking toward heaven, and He prays for them! He talks to His Father about glory for Himself and for the glory He has brought to the Father. He prays protection for his followers. He prays about joy, sanctification, truth, unity, and love. And, if you are a true believer in Jesus Christ as Lord, He prayed for you! He said to His Father, while praying for His apostles, recorded in John 17:20, "My prayer is not for them alone. I pray also for those who will believe in me through their message…" So, He prayed <u>for you</u>—and for me!

Ponder that incredible truth: He prayed for you, before you were even born, hundreds of years and many witnesses later, connected by a chain of believers through the ages, you too, became a Christ-follower—or perhaps, need to become one. I don't know about you, but like the psalmist, that makes me want to shout, "Bless the LORD, O my soul: and all that is within me, *BLESS* HIS HOLY NAME" (Psalm 103:1)! And to the name of Jesus who will one day take His place at God's judgment seat, the Scriptures say, "every knee will bow before me; every tongue will confess to God" (Romans 14:11). My personal prayer warrior, and your personal prayer warrior, believer, is Jesus Christ the Lord to whom all the world will one day bow! Therefore, take heart, dear pilgrim, if you are struggling today. Jesus prayed for you, and prays for you still, through the Holy Spirit.
Action:
Meditate on this and know you are loved and on His mind and in His heart today. If you do not know Jesus as your personal Savior, why not put yourself under His care, prayer protection and power right now?

AUGUST 2

A Different Kind of Success
BY SHERRI GALLAGHER

Psalm 118:22

The stone the builders rejected has become the cornerstone;

Ultimately, we all have to decide for ourselves what constitutes failure, but the world is quite eager to give you a set of criteria if you let it. **J. K. Rowling**

As a writer, sales are everything. To even make the tail end of the best sellers list you need to sell several thousand books. If you want to have a second book published by a traditional publisher, the first had better sell over 15,000 copies. If you are on your third or fourth or however many books, your sales figures can't be lower than the previous book or the publisher will drop you. But is this how success is measured? Are dollars the way God looks at things?

A few years ago, a dog trainer I worked with opened up to me about his worries for his son. The boy hated to read and had to be bribed or threatened to pick up a book. It was becoming a real problem for him as the boy was falling behind in English class because he wouldn't read the required literature. He had finished the school term with a low "C" and his dad didn't know what to do. I gave him a copy of a teen novel I had written and asked him if his son would read it and send me a critique. I never heard anything more on the subject and we drifted apart.

Our paths crossed again at a recent dog event and the trainer asked me how my writing was going: had I written anymore books? My first book was not a big seller so the second in the series was never published. The trainer shook his head when I told him that. He told me after reading my novel his son started taking books out of the library and buying books. Now the boy's room was filled with all sorts of novels, and it was all because the book I gave him was fun to read.

This was not the first time I had been told that my book had turned a non-reader into a reader. My agent and I had discussed this more than once. He told me sometimes Christian writers needed to remember our role in life may not be a path to financial success but to change the life of a single reader and that is how God measures success.

Action:

How do you measure success? Is that the way God measures it?

Prayer:

God, guide me that I may be a success in Your eyes even if I am not a success in the eyes of the world. Amen.

AUGUST 3

Perfectly Loved
BY MYRA BIERNAT WELLS

1 John 4:18

There is no fear in love. But perfect love drives out fear, because fear has to do with punishment. The one who fears is not made perfect in love.

I have found the paradox, that if you love until it hurts there can be no more hurt, only more love. **Mother Teresa**

Salvador Dali, the great painter, once said, "Have no fear of perfection; you'll never reach it."

God teaches us we don't have to constantly strive to be perfect because we are perfectly loved. "There is no fear in love. But perfect love drives out fear," (1 John 4:18). We struggle with perfection; it is a human weakness, mostly because it seems like the ideal insurance policy against rejection, doesn't it? Yet all the time we know we are filled with faults, and will always be, this side of heaven. We simply get tangled up in the myth of perfection until suddenly God stops us in our tracks.

He gently tells us, "Beautiful child of mine, you don't need to be perfect. You are already perfectly loved." The truth is, God knows your defects and failures, but He still loves you unconditionally.

His response to our insecurity, faults and hurt is always the same – to call us back to confidence in Him, remind us of Whose we are and bring us back into the light of His love. That's a thought worth sharing—you are perfectly loved. And you only need to please the One who has already declared you are a delight to His heart.

Action:

Before you go to sleep this evening, write down five ways God showed you today that you are loved. Lift those up in a prayer of thanksgiving.

AUGUST 4

My Sheep Hear My Voice
BY JUDY KNOX

John 10:3-5

To him the doorkeeper opens, and the sheep hear his voice; and he calls his own sheep by name and leads them out. And when he brings out his own sheep, he goes before them; and the sheep follow him, for they know his voice. Yet they will by no means follow a stranger, but will flee from him, for they do not know the voice of strangers.

Our failure to hear His voice when we want to is due to the fact that we do not in general want to hear it, that we want it only when we think we need it.
Dallas Willard

My friend Kathy loves to tell about her experiences in Spain. While there she learned a lot about sheep. One of her favorite stories is about watching two shepherds with their flocks. The two men were walking in different directions and stopped to chat. As they conversed their two flocks of sheep milled around, nibbling on the grass, and mingling with each other until they had become one large group.

Kathy wondered how in the world the shepherds would ever be able to sort out and separate the groups. But when it was time to go, each shepherd began walking in the direction he had been going, and as they went, they each gently began talking to their sheep. As quickly as they had mingled, the group separated as each sheep followed the voice of his shepherd.

Jesus used the example of sheep and shepherds to illustrate how our heavenly Father wants us to relate to Him. God wants us to know His voice so well that we can distinguish it from all the other voices that clamor for our attention. Our everyday lives are so full of voices coming at us – the people around us, the media, even our own thoughts. Some of what we hear is from God; some is not. How can we tell the difference?

For sheep, it is easy. They have grown up from birth hearing their shepherd's voice. They know him intimately. For us, some effort is required. We must spend time with God and in His Word. If we know what the Bible says, we will then recognize incoming thoughts or words that do not line up with it. The more familiar we are with God's written Word, the more readily we will hear His voice.

God is always speaking to us, but we can't hear what He is saying unless we are really listening. When we are able to hear, discern, and follow His voice, He will be able to lead us to those still waters and green pastures we long for.

Action:

Spend some time every day prayerfully reading God's Word and asking Him to speak to you.

Prayer:

Father, I am Your sheep. Your Word says that Your sheep hear Your voice. Help me to be attentive to what You are saying to me, and to follow You. Amen.

AUGUST 5

Ricochet Rosie
BY SHERRI GALLAGHER

Exodus 4:10-12

Moses said to the LORD, "Pardon your servant, Lord. I have never been eloquent, neither in the past nor since you have spoken to your servant. I am slow of speech and tongue." The LORD said to him, "Who gave human beings their mouths? Who makes them deaf or mute? Who gives them sight or makes them blind? Is it not I, the LORD? Now go; I will help you speak and will teach you what to say."

If you think you can win, you can win. Faith is necessary to victory.
William Hazlitt

Rosie is our newest search dog in training. She has all the potential to make a great canine SAR dog. At one year she has boundless energy, tremendous focus and the drive to work long periods for a toy. She also has Insufficient Pancreas Syndrome. Her body does not produce the enzymes necessary to digest her food. Without our help she would starve to death. Most would say she should not be allowed to work, but with our help, I think she will be one of the best search dogs we've owned.

Moses had a speech impediment. Most, including Moses himself, did not believe he could be a spokesman for God, but he was one of the best leaders portrayed in the Bible. Moses went forward following God's direction even though he didn't think himself capable. He trusted God to make the necessary difference.

In Matthew 19:26 Jesus tells us, "With man this is impossible, but with God all things are possible."

Action:

The next time you are faced with an impossible situation, trust in God, believe you can and give all you have.

Prayer:

Lord, thank You for making the impossible possible. Amen.

AUGUST 6

Never Enough!
BY MYRA BIERNAT WELLS

Luke 12:15

Jesus said to them, "Watch out! Be on your guard against all kinds of greed; life does not consist in an abundance of possessions."

We live in a stuff-driven world. It doesn't seem to matter how much we have because it is never enough. We are told the more things we have, the more successful we are. We not only want what we possess, we want what our neighbors have. It seems the world is driven by the desire to have the best, be the best – making many of us unable to relax and celebrate who we are and what we do have.

Whenever I get caught up in wanting the latest gadget or getting depressed because someone has what I want, my thoughts turn to Corrie ten Boom. She was a godly Dutch woman who endured great persecution from the Nazis. During World War II she was an inmate in the notorious death camp known as Ravensbrück.

A devout Christian, she became a sought-after speaker after the war. During an interview following a talk, she once stated she learned how to hold everything *loosely* in her hands. When asked why, Corrie explained that after being a Christian for many years, she discovered that when she grasped things tightly, it hurt more when the Lord had to pry her fingers loose.

The choice is really ours to make. We need to hold our stuff loosely. We need to stand ready to give financial resources to eternal things. When keeping our gaze riveted to God's plan for our lives, instead of entering the all too familiar competition that plagues our world these days. To avoid greed, we need to change our focus from what we want to have to what we have and choose to be satisfied with whatever that is.

Many of us are in a never-ending and futile quest to accumulate here what is totally worthless in heaven. Our Father wants all of us to be wealthy. We just have to be careful not to settle for earthly money, possessions, human power and/or prestige instead of the eternal treasures only He can offer.

Action:

If you are brave enough, chose to give away a prized possession. What emotions did you have to deal with in making that choice?

Prayer:

Father, please forgive me when I value things over people and my relationship with You. Thank You for meeting every need in my life. I now surrender all my worldly goods to Your control. Help me to become a generous and joyful giver and use me to meet the needs of others so You will be honored and glorified. Amen.

AUGUST 7

Beside the Still Waters
BY JUDY KNOX

Psalm 23: 1-3a

The LORD is my shepherd; I shall not want. He makes me to lie down in green pastures; He leads me beside the still waters. He restores my soul;

When we are fearful and worried all the time, we are living as if we don't believe that we have a strong and able Shepherd who is tenderhearted toward us, who only leads us to good places, who protects us and lovingly watches over us.
Joseph Prince

When we think of shepherds, especially back in David's day, we probably think they have an easy job. All they have to do is lead their flock to food and water, then sit around playing the harp and writing psalms while the sheep munch away.

However, the shepherd's job is not that easy. He needs to understand the nature of sheep and know what they need. Still waters, for example. We picture an idyllic scene where the sheep are drinking from pools of crystal-clear water. In a still pool, all the sediments have settled to the bottom leaving the clean, clear water on top. Apparently, sheep have a delicate digestive system so God designed them in such a way that they simply will not drink moving water.

If the shepherd were to bring them to a gently flowing stream, even one with nice clean, clear water, they would not drink. They would stare at the water as if they had no clue what it was. They would die of thirst while standing inches from the water. Nothing the shepherd might do or say could convince them to drink that water. So, the shepherd knows he must find them the places where the water is perfectly still.

Sometimes we are like these stubborn sheep. God leads us and we follow Him, until the place where He has brought us doesn't look like what we were expecting. Because the water He has provided us comes in the form of a moving stream instead of a still pool, we balk, fuss, and refuse to partake. How frustrating this must be for our Great Shepherd.

How many times have we missed out on an answer to prayer because the answer did not fit our preconceived idea of how it would look? How often have we refused to partake of a blessing He has provided us because it did not look familiar? We need to learn to trust our Shepherd and understand that He knows our needs better than we do. We need to receive all He is providing for us, even if it is different from what we had in mind.

Action:
Keep a prayer journal. Note what you prayed for and how the answer came. In those instances where the prayers appear to be unanswered, examine them more closely to see if God has answered, but just not in the way you had expected.

Prayer:
Lord, help me not to be like the sheep who only receives water that is absolutely motionless. Help me to see Your hand in everything that goes on in my life and to recognize Your goodness. Amen.

AUGUST 8

The Table Is Ready
BY SHERRI GALLAGHER

Mark 14:22-26

Unless man is committed to the belief that all mankind are his brothers, then he labors in vain and hypocritically in the vineyards of equality.
Adam Clayton Powell Jr.

My birdfeeder fails miserably. It is a rough wood post with a single flat square board on top. It stands next to a bushy blue spruce tree, easy jumping distance for a squirrel. I go through a bag of seed in less than a week, much of it consumed by the fat, furry rodents. People have made suggestions on how to limit the visitors to my feeder to popular birds. They don't understand my feeder is open to all. The bright cardinals and the more subtle females, a huge blue jay, a flock of chickadees and sparrows, nut hatches and squirrels all feast there. There is a definite pecking order and their antics enforcing it make me laugh. If the weather will be bad, then all come and eat as much as they can, squirrel beside sparrow beside cardinal pecking order forgotten.

Our communion table is much the same. Everyone is welcome, rich and poor, strong or feeble. The love and salvation of God is for every one of us. All have value. The poor and weak matter to God and we should always welcome them extending a warm greeting and a helping hand. Doing so has its own rewards, just as feeding squirrels and sparrows can bring joy.

Action:
Deliver some groceries to the local food pantry.

Prayer:
Lord, help me to make all feel welcome in our church. Amen.

AUGUST 9

When You Don't Like the Story God Is Writing
BY MYRA BIERNAT WELLS

Psalm 77:7-8

Will the Lord reject forever? Will he never show his favor again? Has his unfailing love vanished forever? Has his promise failed for all time?

The seven long years waiting to realize my dream of living in California ticked by so slowly. Every day, I prayed to God asking Him to grant His favor and hasten the move. The answer always came back, "Not yet!"

The paramount reason for the delay was the high price of California housing. Richard and I agreed we would not be fiscally responsible if we spent the resources God gave us while prices were so elevated. Growing weary in the wait, I suggested we purchase a small condo. Every time we found one we liked and put a bid in, our offer was rejected. This only frustrated me even more. Ok, you guessed it: my anger roiled against God.

A few months into the process, the perfect house went on the market. With its charming décor and beautiful neighborhood, we knew love would move in with us. This family home was much better than my original plan. It was Ephesians 3:20 in the California real estate market: *Now to him who is able to do immeasurably more than all we can ask or imagine...*

Why didn't God lead us to this solution much sooner? Why did it feel like all my praying and seeking His will during those seven years were in vain? I'd like to think he was molding my character so when I finally moved, I'd appreciate both Him and Orange County just a little bit more. C.S. Lewis writes, "If you think of this world as a place intended simply for our happiness, you will find it intolerable. Think of it as a place of training and correction and it's not so bad."

God taught me a lesson in dependency, ripping away the cheap fabric of my self-sufficiency. He wanted to work a miracle in my life, so I more fully understood His power and love for me. During that long wait, I learned the dark places are opportunities to trust Him, to believe He knows the way. When the wait seems unbearable, it is the perfect time to hold tightly to Him.

Action:

Read all of Psalm 77. What did David do to remind himself of God's faithfulness? How does trusting God change the way you look at difficult situations?

Prayer:

Loving Father, thank You for always knowing and doing what is best for me. Forgive me when I don't trust You and forge ahead with my own plan. I know You have wonderful surprises in store for me when I simply trust You in all things. Thank You for being the Teacher. Help me be a much better student. In Your precious Son's Name. Amen.

AUGUST 10

CREEPY, CRAWLY THINKING
BY JUDY KNOX

Romans 8:5-17

"Know thyself" A maxim as pernicious as it is ugly. Whoever observes himself arrests his own development. A caterpillar who wanted to know itself well would never become a butterfly. **Andre Gide**

Do you ever have days when everything just seems hard, and every little task feels like a tedious chore? This happened to me recently. I went about my day, plodding along, trying to get things done. Where was the joy? I didn't feel close to God; I was not in a good mood.

I spoke Scripture verses aloud. Usually when I do this, after a while one verse will stand out and I can use that truth to pull myself up and out of the gloom. But for some reason, on that day this technique failed to work. Finally, in desperation I plopped down into my chair. "God, what is wrong with me? Where am I missing it?"

I closed my eyes, hoping for some sort of answer. As I sat quietly, a picture came to my mind of a beautiful butterfly flying gracefully from one flower to another. It lands on one flower, and as it does, some of pollen on the flower sticks to its feet. When it goes to the next flower, some pollen is deposited, and new pollen is picked up. It accomplishes its God-given purpose with very little effort, and it most certainly doesn't worry about pollen as it flits around.

Interesting, but I didn't see how it applied to me. Then in my mind's eye I saw a fat caterpillar slogging along on the ground. *Ugh!* I thought. Some day it, too, would be a beautiful butterfly, but for now as it lumbered along, I realized all it could see was the ground and a little of what was around it with no awareness of the sky above, or the trees or flowers. It could only go as far and fast as its stubby little legs could take it. Its existence, compared to that of a butterfly, was very limited and humdrum.

Aha! Being a new creation in Christ is like becoming a butterfly, and here I was, thinking like a caterpillar, focused on the mundane, right-in-front-of-me details, the work I needed to do, the meeting I needed to go to. Just saying Scripture verses without really meaning them was not enough. But taking the time to focus on my identity as a child of God, and seeing myself seated with Jesus in heavenly places – now I was able to become once again like the butterfly, soaring above those earthly tasks, effortlessly carrying out all I needed to do.

As my joy and peace returned, I became more productive, and I'm sure I was nicer to be around. I thought of Colossians 3:1-2, "Since, then, you have been raised with Christ, seek those things which are above, where Christ is, seated at the right hand of God. Set your minds on things above, not on things on the earth" (NKJV).

Action:
Next time you are stressed over all the work that confronts you, close your eyes and picture yourself seated with Christ in the heavenly places.

Prayer:
Father, I thank You that I am a new creation in Christ Jesus. Please help me to remember my true identity in You. Amen.

AUGUST 11

The Back Transport
BY SHERRI GALLAGHER

Philippians 4:12

I know what it is to be in need, and I know what it is to have plenty. I have learned the secret of being content in any and every situation, whether well fed or hungry, whether living in plenty or in want.

Self-control is the chief element in self-respect, and self-respect is the chief element in courage. **Thucydides**, *The History of the Peloponnesian War*

One of the exercises I have been teaching my dog Orex, is called the back transport. It simulates the dog and I escorting a criminal to the police car or station. The "criminal" is played by the helper and he wears a protective sleeve on his arm. My dog knows he will get a wonderful game of tug if he bites that sleeve on my command. However, he must wait for my command. If Orex goes before I tell him, he will be corrected, and we have to start over. This is one of the most difficult exercises as the dog needs to balance staying with the handler to listen for commands and running up to grab the sleeve and play with the helper. Eventually, when he masters the exercise, the dog will be allowed to run to the helper and grip the sleeve. For now, if he stays with me while watching the helper for a few steps, we stop, and the helper comes to the dog so they can play.

Sometimes I feel like God is trying to teach me balance. I have always been opinionated. Like the dog wanting to run forward and grab the sleeve, I have actively expressed my opinions without regard for others' feelings. That is not what He wants of me. I must learn to be quiet and wait for when it is the right time to speak. I must control my emotions and find a way to be clear but not aggressive. When I fail, I know God will give me other opportunities to try again.

Action:

Determine where you are out of balance, note the things that trigger this condition and set a goal to improve.

Prayer:

Lord God, help me to be more balanced and in control of myself. Amen.

AUGUST 12

You Did What?
BY MYRA BIERNAT WELLS

John 13:34-35

A new command I give you: Love one another. As I have loved you, so you must love one another. By this everyone will know that you are my disciples if you love one another.

One night while leaving an unemployment seminar, I offered a homeless man a ride. It was just him and me walking through the dark parking lot, then alone in the car while I drove him a few miles down the road to where he asked to be dropped off. Interestingly, I was never afraid or fearful until I got home. It was then I seriously doubted my actions, but it was too late to fear for my safety. I was already safe in my home. In the morning, when I told my husband, he read me the riot act asking me very loudly, "What if he had had a knife?"

God protected me that evening I believe because I stopped to show kindness to one of His beloved children. Needs constantly parade before us every day, but often we don't see them. The Good Shepherd sends His broken lambs to us every day. They might not be the homeless, but the person who needs a smile. Or the friend who needs a word of encouragement. Sometimes we simply view them as intrusions or annoying interruptions instead of God's divine appointments.

Hebrew 13:2 states, "Remember to welcome strangers, because some who have done this have welcomed angels without knowing it." How many angels do we miss because we were too busy? Jesus says that if we really love God, we will really love each other. We are never more like our Father than when we choose to show the kindness and compassion that well out of our personal relationship with Jesus Christ.

We can be very religious, but not care enough. Kindness does not look for reasons. Compassion doesn't ask for limitations. It searches for opportunity. It may not mean giving a homeless man a ride, but it could mean offering him a meal. Noticing the need always proceeds the act of kindness.

Action:

Sit down this week with a friend and share a story of how someone showed you God's compassion. Be sure to examine how you felt and use those feelings as inspiration to help someone else this week.

Prayer:

Father, I come to You today, asking You to break my heart for what break Yours. Give me the eyes to see those around me who are in pain. Show me how to encourage them and love them with Your love. Fill my heart with Your compassion and give me the strength and courage to share that compassion with others. In Jesus' name. Amen.

AUGUST 13

Picture of Grace
BY JUDY KNOX

Ephesians 3:20-21, Timothy 6:17

*When God puts you in the **right place** at the **right time**, you can't help but get blessed. You will meet the **right** people, do the **right** things and even escape danger!*
Joseph Prince

The portrait of Jesus caught my eye as I stood at the counter of the Christian bookstore. It was the picture from *Heaven Is for Real* by Todd Burpo. I had seen and admired it in the book, and now here it was, a little larger than life-sized and in full, rich color. "Wow! I would really like to have that," I exclaimed, but it was expensive. I handed the clerk my twenty percent off coupon and completed my purchase which was a gift for a friend.

The clerk pointed me to a smaller version of the same picture on a back wall. I looked but was in a hurry, so I let it go. But it didn't let me go. I kept thinking how nice that painting would look on my bedroom wall. A few days later, not wanting to be extravagant, I returned to the store with my last twenty percent off coupon and bought the smaller, more affordable picture. However, my prized purchase turned out to be too small for the space on the wall.

I began asking God if I was being silly, or if the bigger portrait was something He wanted me to have. Eventually, I came to feel that it was meant for me. The day I decided to go and buy it, I also needed to get an upgrade on my cell phone, and the phone store was near the bookstore. Very handy indeed!

But when I walked out my door, I had an uneasy feeling, as if something was not quite right. Assuming it was only my usual trepidation over any change in my technology I kept walking toward my car – until my phone rang. My daughter wondered if I had gone to the phone store yet. "There are some things I wanted to tell you before you go," she said. So, I went back to my apartment and sat down while she explained the procedure and admonished me to back up the phone to my computer. Backup completed, I walked out the second time with confidence. Instead of the uneasy feeling, I felt the peace of God.

All went fine at the phone store, and then I went to the bookstore, proceeding directly to the checkout line. When it was my turn, I pointed and said, "I would like that picture right there." As the clerk wrapped it, I told him I was sorry I had used up all my coupons. He agreed that a twenty percent coupon would have been a big help. Just then the lady behind me asked, "What's that on the floor by your foot?" I could see it was a thirty percent off coupon. Bending over to pick it up I commented, "It's probably expired." To my amazement, however, it did not expire for a couple more days.

I drove home with my beautiful portrait of Jesus in the back seat and tears in my eyes, overwhelmed at the love and grace He had just poured out on me. The more I thought about all the intricacies of His timing that morning, the more overwhelmed I became. And to think, it all started when I went into that store to buy a gift to bless someone else.

Action:
Think about a time when all of the details worked together so perfectly you knew it was the hand of God. Share the story with someone.

Prayer:
Father, help me listen carefully to Your voice so I will end up in the right place at the right time. Amen.

AUGUST 14

The Spirit of Prayer
BY SHERRI GALLAGHER

Ephesians 6:10-18

Pray in the Spirit at all times in every prayer and supplication. To that end keep alert and always persevere in supplication for all the saints. **Ephesians 6:18**

I'm a list kind of person. If I have my "to do" list, I accomplish a lot. Certain things are on the top of every "to do" list – read my devotionals, pray, train dogs.

We're warned not to just pray but to pray in the Spirit, which means the words must come from our heart. It is two-way communications with a quiet place for God to reach out to us, not a task to be completed and checked off the list.

One day, my prayers sounded more like a "honey do" list than a heartfelt communion with God. The thought crossed my mind, "I'll do better tomorrow." Later that day I tried to find a passage in the Bible for an article when my eye fell on Ephesians 6:18. I froze in place. There had been no spirit in my prayer; it had simply been a task to complete. I stopped what I was doing, cleared my mind of all that had to be done, and prayed from the heart and with the Spirit.

Action:

When you pray or say grace make it an original prayer that relates to what is happening at the time, not a memorized collection of words without meaning.

Prayer:

Let us find the peace of Your love in prayer, stepping away from our busy schedules to pray in true communion with You. Amen.

AUGUST 15

Pick Me!
BY MYRA BIERNAT WELLS

1 Corinthians 1:27–29

But God chose the foolish things of the world to shame the wise; God chose the weak things of the world to shame the strong. He chose the lowly things of this world and the despised things to nullify the things that are; so that no one may boast before him.

If God were to appear beside you and ask, "I am looking for a great woman to help accomplish My plans and fulfill My mighty purposes," would you feel qualified? Not many of us would raise our hands shouting, "Pick me, pick me!"

When the angel of the Lord came to call Gideon to be the leader of the Israelite army, Gideon was hiding in a winepress threshing wheat, Judges 6:11-13. Just so everyone is clear, you don't thresh wheat in a winepress. You thresh it by throwing the wheat up into the open air and letting the chaff blow away while the heavier grain falls to the ground. (Don't be embarrassed if you didn't know that – I had to look it up.)

So why is Gideon in the winepress? He is hiding. He was so terrified of the quickly encroaching enemies that he hid. And yet, when that same angel of the Lord addressed Gideon, the angel called the scared wheat thresher, "a mighty warrior" Judges 6:12. Can you imagine the shock on Gideon's face? He probably looked to his left, then to his right and asked, "Are you talking to me?"

It's a great reminder that God doesn't see us as we see ourselves. We tend to look at what we can accomplish in our own strength, but God looks at what we can accomplish in His. Think about some of the great heroes of our faith. Moses was a stutterer; David was a shepherd; Rahab was a harlot. The Samaritan woman was a five-time divorcee. Peter was a fisherman, while Paul was a murderer.

Even though they might not be what the world would choose to lead a nation or a great movement, they were exactly what God needed and chose to fulfill His purposed in their lifetime. But they were only able to accomplish great things through His power.

Action:
Read Judges Chapter 6 and note how God spoke to Gideon's fear. Especially note verses 14 and 16.

Lord, I don't know why you have chosen me to do mighty works for You, but I do know this: I am not qualified, but You are. Give me strength in my weakness. Give me faith in my fear. Give me power in my powerlessness. On this, I am trusting You. Amen.

AUGUST 16

Heavenly Heart Surgery
BY JUDY KNOX

Psalm 139:1-4, 23-24

I will give you a new heart and put a new spirit within you; I will take the heart of stone out of your flesh and give you a heart of flesh. I will put My Spirit within you and cause you to walk in My statutes, and you will keep My judgments and do them.
Ezekiel 36:26-27

I followed the gurney as the nurses and orderlies pushed it toward the operating room. I kissed my husband and told him I would see him later. The metal doors clanked shut and there was nothing for me to do but wait and pray. Alan would be undergoing open- heart surgery.

The process was pretty scary. The doctors would cut open his chest, remove a defective valve, and replace it with a new one. Then they would take veins from his leg to replace arteries the angiogram doctor had said were like cement, clogged with calcified plaque. Scary as it was, the surgery was a success and Alan emerged with the equivalent of a new heart, free of clogs, functioning as it was designed to function.

This is a graphic analogy of what God does in our lives, going into our hearts to change things that are defective and make us new. However, there are a few differences between God's surgery and what the doctors do. First, in order to have God do this open-heart procedure, we must open our own hearts. God does not do it for us. We must choose the surgery and then make our heart available to the Holy Spirit.

Instead of using a scalpel or knife, God uses a spiritual laser, shining the pure light of His love, goodness and grace into the dark places where evil lurks, burning away the impurities. Whatever needs to be removed – rebellion, fear, or a lie we have been believing about ourselves – once He shines His light on it, it has to leave.

There is no anesthetic for this operation, and at times it may be painful, but it will never be more than we can bear, plus the results are well worth it. In the natural realm, heart surgery usually takes place once or twice in a person's life, but God's open- heart surgery is an ongoing process. The more often we allow Him access to our heart, the more benefits we gain.

If God were to reveal all of our faults at once, it would be too overwhelming for us, so He patiently and gently shows us, a little at a time, areas where we are holding things in our heart that do not line up with His will or His Word. As we yield a heart open for correction, He will fix the problem.

Are you ready to open your heart to the Great Physician?

Action:

Ask God to show you an area in your heart that needs His laser surgery, then yield it to Him.

Prayer:

Father, I open my heart to You. Show me those areas that are not fully yielded to You, and help me give them to You. Amen.

AUGUST 17

Bite Your Tongue
BY SHERRI GALLAGHER

1 Corinthians 13

America isn't easy. America is advanced citizenship. You've got to want it bad, cause it's going to put up a fight. It's going to say, "You want free speech? Let's see you acknowledge a man whose words make your blood boil, who's standing center stage and advocating at the top of his lungs that which you would spend a lifetime opposing at the top of yours.
Andrew Shepherd in *The American President*

There have been a number of hot button issues in the news lately. People have picked these up on social media and tempers have clearly flared. Friendships have suffered for the simple reason people cannot agree to disagree and remain friends. More and more there is discussion of being politically correct and a lot of finger pointing and name calling. Each side insists that their way and only their way is acceptable. But is that wise, reasonable or even Biblical?

In this country, the Bill of Rights gives us permission to speak our opinion without fear of reprisals. Multiple court cases have proven that specific point. We may find the words of another abhorrent, but they have the right to voice them just as we have the right to stand and voice the opposing view.

What do we read in the Bible? "If I speak in tongues of men or of angels, but do not have love, I am only a resounding gong or a clanging cymbal" (1 Corinthians 13:1). The Bible does not tell us to be silent. It doesn't even tell us to be right. What it tells us is to speak with love, but how do you show that love? By remaining silent? By accepting everyone else's opinion as right and subjugating your thoughts and beliefs? Perhaps it is saying, love the other person enough to let them have a different point of view.

James 1:26 reinforces this, "Those who consider themselves religious and yet do not keep a tight rein on their tongue deceive themselves, and their religion is worthless." It doesn't say remain silent, but it does say choose your words carefully. No one can choose their words carefully if they are spewing hate through angry words. To love is to accept the person as they are. That means accepting that two people will not always agree on everything and each has a right to keep their own opinion.

Action:
The next time someone expresses a view you disagree with, think of how you would feel if they never spoke to you again, then decide how you will express your opinion.

Prayer:
Wise and loving God, help me bridle my tongue and speak in love not anger, accepting we are different with different experiences, thoughts and needs. Help me to love those I disagree with, accept our differences and find common ground. Amen.

AUGUST 18

When Times Get Tough, Thank God!
BY MYRA BIERNAT WELLS

Philippians 4:4

Always be full of joy in the Lord. I say it again – rejoice. (NLT)

When the apostle Paul writes, "Always be full of joy in the Lord," he doesn't say only be joyful when everything is going well. Even when times are tough, the Bible teaches we can be joyful if we follow this simple strategy.

Don't worry about anything. Worrying doesn't change anything. There are no such things as born worriers. Worry is a learned response. You learn it from those around you. Here's the good news: the fact that worry is learned means it can also be unlearned. How do you unlearn it? In Matthew 6:34 Jesus says, *"Therefore do not worry about tomorrow for tomorrow will worry about itself. Each day has enough trouble of its own."* He's saying don't open your umbrella until it starts raining. Live one day at a time.

Pray about everything. Instead of worrying, use your time for praying. If you prayed as much as you worried, you'd have a lot less to worry about. Is God interested in your car payments? Yes. He's interested in every detail of your life. That means you can take any problem to God.

Thank God in all things. When you pray, pray with thanksgiving. The healthiest human emotion is not love, but gratitude. It actually increases your immunity. It makes you more resistant to stress and less susceptible to illness. People who are grateful are happy. But those who don't practice gratitude are miserable because nothing makes them happy. If you cultivate an attitude of gratitude, of being thankful in everything, it reduces stress in your life.

Think about the right things: Another way to reduce stress in your life is to change the way you think. The way you think determines how you feel. And the way you feel determines how you act. The Bible teaches that if you want to change your life, you need to change what you think about. This involves a deliberate, conscious choice to think about the right things. We need to choose to think about the positives in our lives and to meditate on God's word.

What is the result of not worrying, praying about everything, giving thanks, and focusing on the right things? We will "experience God's peace, which exceeds anything we can understand. His peace will guard your hearts and minds as you live in Christ Jesus" (Philippians 4:7, NLT).

Action:

What do you worry about? Spend time today talking to God about your worries and honestly tell Him why you worry.

Prayer:

Jesus, we worry so much when Your peace is readily available to us. Help us to rest in Your strength and to be grateful for all the blessings in our lives. We give You all our worries. Take them all, Jesus, and give us a new sense of peace. Amen.

AUGUST 19

Bearing Fruit
BY JUDY KNOX

Psalm 1:1-3

The "fruit of the Spirit" has also been misinterpreted as characteristics that believers should somehow manufacture in their lives. But the key to understanding these qualities is in the name. "Fruit" is the natural result of growth. And "of the Spirit" explains exactly Who causes that growth—it's not our striving or straining, but the power of the Holy Spirit. **www.gotquestions.org**

A seed is an amazing thing. This is why Jesus used the image of the sower and the seed to illustrate our spiritual growth.

Picture an apple seed, for instance. That tiny seed contains everything necessary for producing a mature apple tree. With the right soil and growing conditions, within just a few years that tree will develop and begin producing a crop of apples.

When we become born again, we receive the incorruptible seed, God's Word (1 Peter 1:23). The fruit God intends us to exhibit in our lives is the fruit of the Spirit: love, joy, peace, longsuffering (patience), kindness, goodness, faithfulness, gentleness, and self-control (Galatians 5:22-23). How do we become a fruitful tree producing a bountiful thirty-, sixty-, or hundred-fold crop of these traits?

We begin preparing the soil by opening our hearts to God and minimizing distractions that keep us from hearing His voice. This will allow the Word to penetrate, take root and grow. As a new believer I thought it was up to me to produce the fruit. I tried to be more loving, more patient, more peaceful. I tried to have more self-control. I frequently asked God to help me be more joyful, or kinder or gentler. It was frustrating when I continually found myself falling short.

After years of trying to grow the fruit of the Spirit through my own efforts, I heard a message in which the speaker talked about producing fruit. He asked us to close our eyes and envision a mature apple tree with apples beginning to grow on it. Was the tree grunting and groaning and struggling to produce apples? No. Was it worrying about whether the apples would ripen? Of course not. The tree simply took in water and nutrients and continued to grow. Eventually, as a natural result of the tree's growth, the apples would mature into the beautiful fruit God had designed it to bring forth.

So, it is with the fruit of the Spirit that grows in our lives. Exhibiting the fruit of the Spirit is not a process we have to work at. Rather it is accomplished as we allow God to work in us (Philippians 2:13). The fruit was placed within us in seed form when we accepted Christ. Our efforts must be put into preparing the soil (our hearts) and caring for what is growing there, being especially alert for weeds that can spring up and choke the growing plant.

As we do that, we will begin bearing spiritual fruit every bit as effortlessly as an apple tree bears apples, as a natural result of the changes taking place within us. Without our even realizing it, as we spend time with God and in His Word, He will change our attitudes, making us more like Jesus. Before long we, and those around us, will begin to notice that our lives are bearing spiritual fruit.

Action:

Find a scripture about a spiritual fruit you would like to see your life producing more of and begin meditating on it.

Prayer:

Father, I want to be a good tree that produces a bountiful crop of spiritual fruit. Thank You that it is not something I have to struggle with, but the natural outcome of spending more time in Your presence. Amen.

AUGUST 20

Shh! Pass It On
BY SHERRI GALLAGHER

2 Timothy 1:1-14

The whole problem with the world is that fools and fanatics are always so certain of themselves, but wiser people so full of doubts. **Bertrand Russell**

I sometimes wonder what it would have been like to grow up in a household of faith. Would I have come to the Lord or been rebellious? My father told us religion was the pabulum of the masses and tried to raise us without God. However, God used Dad's love of Africa to expose my sister and me to His presence. (That little fact always made me believe God has a sense of humor.) The local minister had done mission work in the Congo. When Dad brought us to services, the minister would spend Sunday afternoon telling stories of Africa.

I was around six when I accepted the Lord into my life, and nothing could shake that belief. Forty years later it took a Christian writers group to teach me about daily devotionals and how to write them. I use my experiences to share how the Bible guides me in daily living.

On Sunday mornings I look around the pews and I see so much learning and understanding in the faces around me, I'm almost ashamed to write what little I know. How wonderful it would be if the members would share their experience and what they have learned.

Action:
Can you write a paragraph or two explaining why you believe God is still speaking and relate it to a scripture? Try it. Pass on what God has taught you.

Prayer:
God, remove the fear from our members and help them to share their wealth of knowledge and experience. Amen.

AUGUST 21

5K

BY MYRA BIERNAT WELLS

Psalm 68:4

Sing to God, sing praises to His name; cast up a highway for Him who rides through the deserts; whose name is the Lord and exult before Him. (NLT)

A few years ago, I completed my second 5K. This particular walk was held in Disneyland prior to its daily opening. Despite the gorgeous surroundings, being welcomed by Disney characters and a confetti start, there were times during the walk when I just didn't feel like finishing. To combat this, I would talk to myself. "Myra, you can do this. Legs, just keep on going. Think how close you are to the finish. Don't give up now." And then it struck me, we need to have the same attitude about praising God.

Scripture tells us to give God praise. Not only when we feel like it. Not only when we don't feel like it. Not only when we want to give up. Not only when we feel we can conquer the world.

We are to praise God in all circumstances. Do you know what the word *all* literally means? It means everything. No matter what crisis we find ourselves facing, we are to choose to give God praise. No matter how dark or painful the storm may be, we are to choose to give God praise. Praise is not an emotion. It is a choice.

We are not necessarily praising God for the trial, crisis or storm. We are choosing to give God praise and thanks because of who He is…despite the painful circumstances we are facing.

Praise provides a highway upon which the Father conveys deliverance and blessing.

Praise invites God to take up residence amid our messy lives.

Praise becomes a free-flowing conduit to God's very presence and power at work in us.

Don't miss the life-changing truth that we can enthrone God in every situation of our lives by giving Him praise. Praise converts our everyday surroundings into His dwelling place. It is from that throne of praise God dispenses victory and peace and joy. Praise tunes us into His sovereignty and allows us to experience the reality and power of His presence.

So, no matter where you are today, take charge of your heart and soul by telling Him you love Him. No matter how tired or frustrated you are, remember God is with you. Choose to give Him praise.

Action:

Look for the opportunities throughout the day to praise God – then voice that praise aloud. When you can't seem to find the right words to pray – go to the Word of God and pray Scripture. Psalm 150 provides a great prayer of praise.

Prayer:

"Praise the Lord. Praise God in His sanctuary; praise Him in His mighty heavens. Praise Him for His acts of power; praise Him for His surpassing greatness. Praise Him with the sounding of the trumpet, praise Him with the harp and lyre. Praise Him with dancing, praising Him with the strings and pipe, praise Him with the clash of cymbals, praise Him with resounding cymbals. Let everything that has breath praise the Lord. Praise the Lord." Amen.

AUGUST 22

Guarding Our Minds
BY JUDY KNOX

2 Corinthians 10:5

We demolish arguments and every pretension that sets itself up against the knowledge of God, and we take captive every thought to make it obedient to Christ.

As I was having lunch with a group of ladies from church, one of them made a comment to me, questioning my behavior in a particular area. "How can you call yourself a Christian and do that?" she asked, adding that apparently I must not be "sanctified." For some reason, her remark hit a nerve; my feelings were hurt. On the way home, instead of thinking about the good food and fun conversation we had all enjoyed, my mind kept going back to this one remark.

Who does she think she is, judging me? I know she doesn't like me. I just won't go to lunch with these people again if she's coming with them. Really mature thoughts, right? On it went, one negative thought rolling into the next. I had failed to guard my mind. A few more minutes of this would have found me wallowing in my old, familiar stronghold self-pity for the rest of the afternoon.

I was about halfway home when I recognized the old pattern of thinking. Knowing I needed to bring those thoughts into captivity, I immediately chose to forgive this lady, and then turned on some praise music to help me refocus my attention on the goodness of God. When I stopped mulling over the unkind remark and my feelings about it, and began thanking God for His goodness and grace, my joy and peace returned. By the time I arrived home, I was free from self-pity, ready to enjoy the rest of my Sunday afternoon.

I have read that ninety percent of all spiritual warfare is fought between our ears. Controlling our thinking can go a long way toward gaining control over our emotions. We are the gatekeepers of our minds. Thoughts may come from any number of sources: God, our own minds, the enemy, or things we see or hear in our environment. The thoughts I was entertaining were certainly not from a good place.

We can't keep thoughts from coming to us, but we do get to decide whether or not to let them in. As Martin Luther once said, ". . . we cannot prevent the birds from flying over our heads, (but) there is no need that we should let them nest in our hair." If a thought comes into our mind that does not speak life, peace, or hope to us, we need to boot it out. The secret to shooing unwanted thoughts away is to replace them with something else. By refocusing on Jesus and His obedience in going to the cross for us, we flush out the negativity. We are the ones who ultimately get to decide how we will think, and this will affect how we feel.

Action:

Examine your emotions. If you are feeling something negative, try to determine what thoughts may have led to feeling that way. Ask God to help you redirect your thinking toward Jesus and the good things He has done in your life.

Prayer:

Father, I want to be a good gatekeeper of my thinking. Help me recognize when I begin to entertain unproductive thoughts and help me turn them over to You, so that I may walk in thankfulness and forgiveness. In Jesus' name. Amen.

AUGUST 23

Worry Wart
BY SHERRI GALLAGHER

Matthew 6:25-34

Instead strive for His kingdom and these things will be given to you as well.
Luke 12:31

Before we left on vacation, I had a terrible time writing. I put words on the page, but they weren't interesting enough to keep a reader's attention. Frustrated, almost everything I had written for a month ended up in the fireplace. I gave up forcing the words and packed my bags.

Once we got there a nervous feeling kept welling up inside of me. I should be doing something productive, not lounging. Then I remembered the words from

Matthew, "Which of you can add a minute to your life span by worrying?" I took a deep breath, laid back and looked at the big fluffy clouds overhead. I started playing the childhood game of visualizing shapes and figures in the clouds. There was a bunny, a football player, a lobster.

As I relaxed the writer's block disappeared. The words to make the next chapter interesting were right there. I had gotten too dependent on me and not dependent enough on God. The next time worrying distracts me from progress, I will stop, take a deep breath, and wait for His guidance. God knows what we need and will provide it in His own good time.

Action:

Taking time for you is not a waste. Do some activity every day that recharges your spirit.

Prayer:

God, help me to trust more and worry less. Amen.

AUGUST 24

To the Brim
BY MYRA BIERNAT WELLS

John 2:7

Jesus said to the servants, "Fill the jars with water"; so they filled them to the brim.

Shortly after Jesus was baptized, He attended a wedding reception in the town of Cana in Galilee. Jesus felt very comfortable at such a party. Can you imagine Him laughing, mingling and having a good time with His friends? Near the end of the festivities, the servants let Mary in on a dilemma: they were out of wine. To run out of wine at a Jewish wedding celebration was an embarrassment and disgrace to the hosting family. Mary turned to her Son and said, "They have no more wine" (John 2:3), as if she expected Him to do something about it. Did she say this with a mischievous twinkle in her eye or out of a deep concern for her hosts?

Jesus answered, "Dear woman, why do you involve me? My time as not yet come" (John 2:4).

Mary turned to the servants and said, "Do whatever He tells you." Mary seemed to understand Jesus' power before anyone else.

Jesus told the servants to fill six large thirty-gallon stone pots with water. So, they filled them *to the brim*. Then He told them to draw some out and take it to the master of the banquet. When they did so, the master tasted the water that had been turned into wine. He then called the bridegroom aside and said, "Everyone brings out the choice wine first and then after the guests have had too much to drink, the host serves cheap wine; but you have saved the best till now."

Besides wondering what the wine tasted like, I also often ponder what would have happened if the servants had filled the pots half full or three fourths full. I imagine Jesus would have transformed exactly what they put in. But the Bible is very specific that the servants filled them to the brim. I think this is noted because God will transform just as much of our lives as we give Him. I want to "fill it to the brim;" – to give Him all of my life, every bit of it: my ministry, my finances, my relationships, my schedule, my decisions. Filled to the brim.

Reflecting on where Jesus was at the time of this miracle, I also want to give Jesus all of my marriage…filled to the brim. So then when our winter years are upon us, my husband and I can agree…we saved the best until now.

Action:

How much of your life do you want Christ to transform? How much have you given Him? Think about that throughout your day, then list four or five ways you can give Him more of your life.

Prayer:

Dear Lord, I pray I will be like the servants who did exactly what You told them to do. My desire is to obey You fully…to the brim. Help me not to hold back anything but give You all of me, so You can transform me totally. In Jesus' name. Amen.

AUGUST 25

Be Still
BY CATHY HARVEY

Psalm 46:10

He says, "Be still, and know that I am God; I will be exalted among the nations, I will be exalted in the earth."

As often as I could, I placed myself as a worshiper before Him, fixing my mind upon His holy presence, recalling it when I found it wandering from Him.
Brother Lawrence

As a little girl in church school our class was encouraged to stop every hour on the hour to simply pray, "I love You, God." I have not followed through on that hourly prayer, but am trying to pause in my workday, get up from my desk and walk to a quiet corridor, pause at a window, or step outdoors. I stop, slow my breathing from the pace at work (or home), and take a moment to notice nature's beauty and consciously admire His handiwork. When I do this—engage in a moment of stillness, a simple prayer, an act of worship—it is difficult to explain the peace from God that fills me, peace that brings my soul to a place of quiet rest with the assurance that God is taking care of everything in spite of circumstances.

No matter how hurried, stressed, or chaotic my day may become, when (if!) I remember to stop and be still, when I close my eyes and just think of Him, I am filled with calm. A sense of satisfaction, something deep and incomprehensible realigns my core. I feel refreshed without a nap and re-energized without caffeine. I feel . . . love.

In *The Practice of the Presence of God,* the 17th century monk known as Brother Lawrence explains how he struggled to practice the discipline of expressing his love to God in the common and mundane tasks he was assigned in the monastery kitchen. Doing something as simple as picking up a piece of straw, peeling potatoes, or scrubbing pots became for him a life of love and service. Moment by moment he lived to please his Lord in his humble and obscure sanctuary.

Isaiah 30:15 reminds me, ". . . in quietness and in confidence shall be your strength. . ." It is up to us to create the moments we need to sense His presence in the quiet or the clatter of our days.

Action:

Be aware that your place of work is a sanctuary. Set a reminder at home or work to stop and pause several times a day to release your burdens and love to the Lord, to gain a sense of His presence, peace, and love for you. Make even the mundane and common tasks an act of love for your Savior.

Prayer:

Heavenly Father, I love You. Help me consider my days and build in pauses to still my heart and reflect on You and Your great love for me. Let my devotion to You be intentional no matter the task. Help me live out Isaiah 30:15 and Psalm 46:10. Amen.

AUGUST 26

An Early Morning Walk
BY SHERRI GALLAGHER

2 Samuel 23:1-7

Is not my house like this with God? For he has made an everlasting covenant ordered in all things and secure. Will he not cause to prosper all my help and my desire?
2 Samuel 23:5

My favorite time to be outside is at sun rise, especially when it is crisp and clear after a night of rain. The dust is washed from the air; as I walk, I can smell the rich earth and the scent of crushed grass. Late night worries over income and regrets of sharp words spoken in anger disappear as God's promise to be with me is as evident as the rising sun and renewed fields.

David expressed similar feelings. He had periods where he struggled to feed his men and slept in caves and other times he lived in a palace. Always he felt secure in his everlasting covenant with God. Through all his mistakes, he knew God loved him.

Action:
Take a walk in the early morning and rejoice in the glory of being given a new day to walk the path God has chosen for you.

Prayer:
God, thank You for each new sun rise. Amen.

AUGUST 27

A Freshly Brewed Faith
BY MYRA BIERNAT WELLS

Isaiah 40:29-31

He gives strength to the weary and increases the power of the weak. Even youths grow tired and weary and young men stumble and fall; but those who hope in the Lord will renew their strength. They will soar on wings like eagles, they will run and not grow weary, they will walk and not be faint.

Every morning, my husband practically runs straight to the coffee pot. He is totally hooked on the stuff. He struggles to function without his first *cups* of coffee. In fact, when we were first married, he issued the edict, "Don't even talk to me until I've finished my first pot of coffee." His mornings would be dreary, sad times without his warm, savory brew.

As Christians, we should have the same attitude about our faith. We should wake up each morning bursting at the seams to be with God, to be in His presence, to listen for His still small voice. A faith that is brewed fresh daily strengthens us, renews us and enables to mount up with wings like eagles.

This energizing, percolated faith is readily available to all those who ask God. How can you experience this power in your life? By getting alone with God, reading the Bible and listening for His voice each day.

Like a morning without coffee, there are times when we are sluggish in our faith. Life drains us and we literally need a shot of God-caffeine in our day, a spiritual espresso. What can we do during these times? Are there things in the Scriptures that tell us how we can strengthen our trust muscles and jump start our faith? Absolutely!

One practical way to build your faith is by remembrance. When David was just a shepherd boy, he had the courage to face a giant partly because he remembered the previous victories the Lord gave him. He approached King Saul with great confidence, saying, "The Lord who delivered me from the paw of the lion and the paw of the bear will deliver me from the hand of this Philistine" (1 Samuel 17:36). His past victories fueled his faith and helped him to trust God for his present deliverances. Ours do the same. We can face our giants with equal confidence when we pause to acknowledge God for His past deliverances.

What has God brought you through in the past? Think on these things and choose to trust Him to bring you through all you face today and tomorrow. When you rely on God with a fresh shot of faith, He will be your Strength, your Sustainer and your Hiding Place, so you can run and not grow weary, walk and not be faint.

AUGUST 28

Oh No! I Left My Cell Phone in the Restroom!
BY JUDY KNOX

Psalm 34: 6-9, 17-19

The cell phone has become the adult's transitional object, replacing the toddler's teddy bear for comfort and a sense of belonging.
Margaret Heffernan

I can't believe I left my cell phone in the restroom at the airport, but I did! Having flown from O'Hare Airport in Chicago to Des Moines, Iowa for a business meeting and two days of visiting with family, I had already suffered two days of embarrassment over leaving my wallet at home. I managed okay because my driver's license and credit card were in the tote bag I carried with me, but having no cash and no ATM card had led to several awkward situations.

Now I was relieved to be heading home. I arrived at the airport in plenty of time and relaxed at the gate. The plane was delayed, and nowhere in sight. When it finally pulled up to the jet bridge, I followed my usual right-before-boarding procedure – a quick dash to the restroom. When I came out, the passengers were boarding and the line was moving fast! I entered the plane, found my seat, and tucked my tote bag under the seat in front of me. As I started to sit down, I patted my back pocket to assure myself that the cell phone was there… and it wasn't! Nor was it in the tote bag. Grabbing my boarding pass, as soon as the aisle cleared, I rushed toward the door.

I told the flight attendant I would be right back; I just needed to grab the phone I had left on top of the toilet paper holder. She informed me that if I left the plane, they might close the door before I got back. They could not hold the plane for me. Visions flashed through my head of staying on the plane, then trying to get a cab from O'Hare Airport with no phone, let alone trying to manage the rest of my life. The thought was daunting.

I said, "I have to try! It's in that restroom right there on the end."

"Do you have your ID?" she asked.

"No, but I have my boarding pass." I waved it at her.

"We won't be able to let you back on the plane without your ID."

I hurried back to my seat to grab the whole tote bag in case I did get left behind. I would have to make arrangements for another flight, which probably wouldn't be till the next day, and would need the credit card, my ID, and everything else in the bag. Reaching for it, I sent up a quick, not very eloquent, prayer. "Lord, I need Your help. I don't know what to do!"

As I started back down the aisle, the flight attendant came toward me holding up my phone in its bright pink case. "Is this it?" she asked. She had called the gate attendant, who had sent someone to retrieve the phone and bring it to her. I thanked her profusely.

In my seat once again, I thanked the One who was really responsible, whose angels encamp around those who fear Him and rescue them (Psalm 34:7) – even when they do really dumb things!

Action:

Think of a time when God answered a prayer when you thought the situation was impossible. Thank Him again for His loving care and protection.

Prayer:

Thank You, Lord, for watching over us, even when we make mistakes – *especially* when we make mistakes – and that when we cry out to You, You hear us and deliver us out of our troubles. Amen.

AUGUST 29

We Failed
BY SHERRI GALLAGHER

Psalm 118:13

I was pushed back and about to fall, but the LORD helped me.

You may be disappointed if you fail, but you are doomed if you don't try.
Beverly Sills

I had put everything I knew into getting my dog Orex his first title. I had worked hard in all weather and with impressive trainers. I had driven hours to practice on the testing field. Repeatedly. And I had prayed that if it was God's will we would pass. We failed.

Discouraged doesn't begin to cover what I felt. I am really good at calling myself names and mocking my own efforts. Comparisons to people who didn't work as hard as I do, whose dogs don't have Orex's natural talent but were more successful came to mind. I was a mess.

I reminded myself that I had asked God, if it was His will, that we pass. I had done all I could so perhaps this wasn't the path He wanted me to follow, but where did He want us to go? As one of the few Christians in our raucous training group, I was surprised I failed, and those who did not follow Him, passed. But as a Christian it was up to me to accept His will.

What did he want me to do? Orex has the drive and skill to be a great search and rescue dog, but not the right personality. One out of two dementia patients will attack and hit and kick the search dog; Orex will probably not respond correctly in that situation. My dog's build is all wrong for agility, and after a bout with water poisoning, he hates to swim so dock diving is out. Did God want me to step away from attempting high level competition? Maybe. It certainly had taken a toll on my nerves.

The next time I trained with my club, they were very supportive—or most of them. One lady demanded I tell them our scores which were dismal. Sharing the numbers hurt. As I continued to train and tried to figure out God's plan, I gained some information. First, the testing I wanted would be more available in the fall and closer to home. Second, I learned that all those people who I thought had passed without working at it, hadn't passed. They just let everyone think they had.

What does God want me to do? I still don't know. I continue to pray and train. I do know I have found closer friendships with some of the club members and the lady that embarrassed me finally admitted she had failed, too. Maybe I was His instrument to teach her it is okay to fail. I will continue to wait on His timing, train my dog and schedule to test for national and club level competition for the fall to see if the path He wants for us becomes clear. At least I stopped calling myself names, and maybe that was the lesson I needed all along.

Action:
Think about the last time you failed at something. What did you learn? Do you need to apply that lesson to something in your life right now?

Prayer:
Heavenly Father, forgive us when we are upset that Your will isn't always the same as our will. Give us Your comfort and guidance to the path You want us to follow. Amen.

AUGUST 30

Greeting the Dawn
BY MYRA BIERNAT WELLS

Psalm 23:1-3

The Lord is my shepherd. I shall not want. He makes me lie down in green pastures, He leads me beside quiet waters, He restores my soul.

Anyone who knows me knows I am not an early riser. Don't get me wrong, I don't languish in bed until all hours of the afternoon. I love to stay up late and then welcome dawn on my terms. So, it would shock my friends to learn that on this morning, I was up before the sun rose, especially when I didn't have to be.

Honestly, I wanted to be awake! I was staying at a lovely retreat center and wanted to revel in the quietness of the early morning. I was giddy about sitting before the Lord, just to meet with Him, quietly, expectantly, to listen and to be restored. I had come on this retreat because my life was tied up in knots. Nothing horrific was happening in my life. The drudgery of daily chores, appointments and responsibilities just had strangleholds on my joy. As I sat in the cool still of the morning with the warming presence of God in my soul, the burdens of my heart began to drift away. Direction came. Joy resounded. Mercy reigned. And peace, beloved, sweet peace fell.

In that precious hour, the Spirit of God transformed my soul. I found myself repeating, "This is where they go. This is where my burdens go." For in the stillness, I realized I'd been trying to do life in my own strength. The time spent with God during that daybreak reminded me He is my Restorer. To know renewal, I need to take time out of my day to sit in wonder. Still. Quiet. In His presence.

Are you like me? When your life gets too busy, do you forget the power of quiet? The power of being still before God? The power of listening, expecting and receiving rest from your Restorer? Sitting in His greatness uplifts souls and never leaves burdens pressing down.

Action:

Take some time to power down and be still before Him right now. Remember the power of quiet as you accept the renewal invitation of Jesus to exchange your burdens for His peace and restoration.

Prayer:

Dear Lord, Your mercy is fresh each day and Your grace covers all my heart woes. Thank you, Lord, for Your love. Please align my heart to Yours. Quiet me with Your love, direction and peace today. In Your Son's precious name, I pray. Amen.

AUGUST 31

My Dad Called Them Co-Inky-Dinkys
BY JUDY KNOX

Proverbs 3:5-6; Romans 8:28

Trust in the LORD with all your heart, And lean not on your own understanding;
In all your ways acknowledge Him, And He shall direct your paths.
And we know that all things work together for good to those who love God, to
those who are the called according to His purpose.

Do you believe in coincidences? Einstein once said they were God's way of choosing to remain anonymous. While I agree that God is involved in every so-called coincidence, I don't agree that He wants to remain anonymous. I think His fingerprints are all over the things He does, and I believe He loves it when we recognize and acknowledge His hand in our lives.

Last winter I spent two months in a fifty-five-plus community in Arizona (residents call it the park). I rented a cello so I could play music with my niece who lived nearby. When I first arrived, I casually mentioned in a conversation with God that it would be really nice if there were also a musician in the park that I could play music with. I think I worded it something like "Lord, if there's someone here in the park who plays a string instrument or the piano, it would be really nice if I could connect with them." Then I promptly forgot about saying it.

A couple days later, I decided to check out the park's writers' group. Each of the members read something she had written. One woman read the New Year's letter she had written to family and friends. In it she mentioned that she and her husband played in a local orchestra. After the meeting, on our way out the door, I asked her what instrument she played. "Viola," she answered.

"Oh, really?" I said. "Well, I play the cello."

"Oh my goodness," she replied. "I've been praying for another string player in the park that I could play music with." Then I remembered what I had prayed.

We had a lot of fun playing music together and found that in addition to our shared interest in music and writing, we had many other things in common, too, including our Christian beliefs. She became a good friend who brought much enjoyment to my days in Arizona.

Was meeting this woman during my first week there a coincidence? Well, she had almost decided to read something else that made no mention of her music playing, but at the last minute felt prompted to read the New Year's letter. Had she not been sensitive to God's leading and read that letter, we could have gone the whole two months without ever discovering our mutual interest. Both of us would have missed out on a very rewarding friendship. Instead, she listened to God and read it.

As a result, we got to be the answer to each other's prayers. And we didn't let God remain anonymous. We told many people about how He had brought us together. This was no random co-inky-dinky!

Action:
Have you had experiences where many things fit nicely into place, and then said, "What a coincidence?" Take a few minutes to go back over these experiences and thank God for bringing everything together for you.

Prayer:
Lord, You work all things together for my good. Please increase my awareness of Your perfect timing in my life and help me remember to give You the credit instead of attributing it to coincidence. Amen.

SEPTEMBER 1

The Well
BY SHERRI GALLAGHER

John 4

For true love is inexhaustible; the more you give, the more you have. And if you go draw at the true fountainhead, the more water you draw, the more abundant is its flow.
Antoine de Saint-Exupery

Our first piece of property had an old, hand-dug, stone-lined well. It was not very deep, only fifteen feet, which was surprising since our lot was the highest point in the county and our neighbors' wells were several hundred feet down into the earth. We did some research and talked to some long-term residents. The well appeared on maps dating back to the Civil War and records indicated it was originally dug by Native Americans.

The old timers told us a terrible drought hit the area in the 1920's and everyone's wells dried up. People drove their cattle from miles around to our property to water them. It was the only water available and never ran dry.

The bottom of the well had several feet of silt when we bought the property. Using a trash pump, which is made to remove mud and dirty water, we pumped the well dry then let it refill. When we tried to pump it dry again, we couldn't empty it. The well filled faster than we could remove the water. Sweet, clean water continued to flow, and we never had to worry about the well going dry.

Jesus is our well of living water. We can drink and revel in the sweetness of His love knowing it will never fail us, and the more we draw on it the more that will be available. His love will never fail us. He tells us that in John 7:38, "Whoever believes in me, as Scripture has said, rivers of living water will flow from within them."

Action:

Think about what first drew you to become a Christian. Remember that giddiness of first love? Draw on that feeling as you go about your day.

Prayer:

Thank You, Lord, for a love that never fails us, that flows over and around us like a stream of fresh running water. Amen.

SEPTEMBER 2

A Heart of Thanks
BY CATHY HARVEY

1 Thessalonians 5:16-18

Always be joyful. Keep on praying. No matter what happens, always be thankful, for this is God's will for you who belong to Christ Jesus.

"Please," "thank you," and "excuse me for interrupting" - it's amazing how far those words carried me. **Sidney Poitier**

It seems the old-fashioned thank you note may be a thing of the past as e-mail, Facebook, Tweets and twitters dominate modern communication. Still, a personal hand-written or typed thank you, whether in a Hallmark or on a sheet of lined notebook paper can be a treasure.

I have a sister-in-law who lived in a small rural town where she and her husband pastored for many years. Besides a salary, every week there were people in this farming community who gave them produce from their farms or offered services of some type. Every Saturday before retiring for the evening, my sister-in-law sat down and wrote thank you notes to all who helped them out in some way that week. What a fragrant testimony of a loving, thankful heart! Surely, our Lord is well-pleased with this type of spirit. Here are the basic who, when, why, and how of this dying art form.

Who: Anyone who extends a thoughtful service, a gift, or a deed which took time, effort, or finances. This could include: a special speaker you heard, a teacher, mentor or pastor, a neighbor, relative, or how about your spouse or children once in a while?

When: As soon as possible after the deed or gift is given. However, in the event a thank you slips your mind, a thoughtful note with an apology for the delay will still be very much appreciated. The Lord often blesses the timing for the recipient no matter when it arrives.

Why: To write a thoughtful thank you nurtures an appreciative spirit and an others-oriented focus. It shows respect and gratitude to the person who offered something from their heart, finances, or efforts.

How: Be personal and detailed about the gift or act of kindness. Name the gift specifically and avoid a generic, "Thank you for the lovely gift," as well as an equally generic and cold closing such as, "We will get a lot of use out of it."

Try to limit the times you begin a sentence with "I," and replace it by restructuring it to focus on them. Instead of, "I was so surprised by…" you can say, "You really surprised me with …." Instead of, "I love the contemporary pattern…," you can say, "The pattern you chose is just what I love…"

Thank them for traveling if they came from out-of-town for a special event (showers, weddings, parties). Let them know it was special to have them there to celebrate with you. Let the Holy Spirit guide you in comments. Your relationship to the person will dictate the kinds of things you say about your connection to them.

Action:

Sit down and write, or if you must—e-mail—a long overdue thank you to someone who has blessed you. Do it today.

Prayer:

Father, You have done so much for me. Bring to mind those who have blessed me in some way and help me express my appreciation to them in a thoughtful way. Amen.

SEPTEMBER 3

Birthday
BY MYRA BIERNAT WELLS

John 10:10

I have come so they may have life and have it to the full.

This year, I celebrated a milestone birthday. My years have included both some extreme storms and some momentous jaw-dropping experiences. With the wisdom I've gained, I feel comfortable giving a few pieces of sage advice.

If you are younger, cherish every moment you have with family and friends. It is true – the older you get, the quicker the days fly by. If you have some distance between you and your birth, pat yourself on the back and celebrate your survival skills. I truly believe if you are still alive, even now God has a purpose and plan for your life. In the past I gave myself authority to do or not do something simply to please others and not because it was according to God's plan. My actions now are much more defined by the audience of One.

There are times I wish I were younger, but let's face it, my life is rich and full right now. And, honestly, there are places in my past that I do not wish to revisit. Yet I embrace my youth because it taught me some great things.

1.   Keep only cheerful friends. The grouchers pull you down.

2.   Keep learning. Learn more about the computer, crafts, gardening – whatever. Just never let the brain idle.

3.   Laugh often, long and loud. Laugh until you gasp for air. Laugh so much that you can be tracked in a store by your distinctive laughter. (I have and I'm not ashamed of it!)

4.   Tears happen. Endure, grieve and move on. The only person who is with us our entire life is ourselves.

5.   Surround yourself with whatever you love, whether it is family, pets, keepsakes, music. Display Bible verses throughout your home.

6.   Don't take guilt trips. Go to the mall, the next county, a foreign country – but not guilt.

7.   Tell people you love how much you love them every chance you get. Never assume they know.

8.   Whenever possible, life should be a pattern of experiences to savor, not to endure. Recognize these moments and cherish them.

9.   Don't save anything. Use your good china and crystal for *every* special event, such as losing a pound, unstopping the sink or new blossoms in your garden.

10.   *Someday* and *one of these days* should vanish from your vocabulary. If something is worth seeing, hearing or doing, go and see, hear or do it now.

What about you? Are you living each day to the fullest? Jesus is all about living an abundant life in the here and now – whatever stage you might be in. Eternity began the moment you accepted Him as your Lord and Savior. Life is not measured by the number of breaths we take but by the moments that take our breath away.

Action:
Look around you. What can you find in your life to celebrate? Get out the fine china and have a party.

Prayer:
Father, I want to live life to the fullest. I want everything You have for me. I don't want to miss a single blessing or trial that is for my good. Please help me keep my eyes on You and celebrate every day and all it holds. I trust You. Amen.

SEPTEMBER 4

Finally!
BY SHERRI GALLAGHER

Hebrews 12:1-4

If you wish success in life, make perseverance your bosom friend, experience your wise counselor, caution your elder brother and hope your guardian genius.
Joseph Addison

It took several years for my son to graduate from college, much to his embarrassment and dismay. He watched his friends either go from high school into the military or the workforce and get on with their lives independent from their parents. Over time other friends graduated college, some finishing four-year degrees in closer to three years than the expected four. After the planned four years he became restless, wondering what was wrong with him that he still had to depend on his parents for support and that he hadn't graduated when he thought he would. He looked at changing majors, but much of the course work he had already taken in math and science would not apply and the time he would save would also result in a lower paying job without much chance of future advancement. He continued with his engineering major and finally graduated. It was a very pleasant surprise for him to learn his starting salary was more than double what his friends were earning, even with their years head-start in the workforce. Perseverance had paid off and was a lesson he would not likely forget.

Paul talks about perseverance in Hebrews 12:1-2. He tells us to listen to the cloud of witnesses around us and throw off everything that hinders us from reaching for God's Holy kingdom. He reminds us to fix our eyes on Jesus Christ and continue to follow His teachings for the reward we will reach at the end. While my son's perseverance brought him financial success in this life, our perseverance to follow Christ brings us the much more valuable eternal life.

Action:
Set a Bible study goal for the coming year that is personally meaningful.

Prayer:
Thank You Holy Father, God, in heaven. You are with me always. Please give me the strength to overcome my weakness and despair at my lack of success and guide me to be a child that pleases You. Amen.

SEPTEMBER 5

The 3:40 A.M. Test
BY MYRA BIERNAT WELLS

Colossians 3:17

And whatever you do, whether in word or deed, do it all in the name of the Lord Jesus Christ, giving thanks to God the Father through Him.

It had been a sleepless night. Tossing and turning, trying to find a comfortable spot, I really never drifted off to sleep. Frustrated, I picked up my cell phone and tapped a message to my husband, who was out of town. "I feel," I texted, "like my actions aren't motivated by love. Instead of doing it all in the name of the Lord, I'm doing life begrudgingly."

The past few weeks had been very busy with ministry obligations. Somewhere I lost the joy of serving God. Every time I thought I'd finished a project, someone else would pile on another activity. I wasn't seeking all this work; it seemed like it was seeking me out! And I didn't have the backbone to politely refuse. The constant juggling of complicated relationships, crazy schedules and weighty challenges had drained me.

The truth is our exhaustion problems cannot be solved without God. I find comfort knowing we are not the first people to struggle with these feelings. Throughout Scripture, people got worn out and lamented about their tired souls. David wrote countless psalms about being weary and Elijah was so exhausted at one point he sank into a deep depression and lost his God-courage.

Jesus revealed the only sure-fire solution to our exhaustion problem. I love the Message version of Matthew 11:28-30, "Are you tired? Worn out? Burned out on religion? Come to me. Get away with me and you will recover your life. I will show you how to take a real rest. Walk with me and work with me – watch how I do it. Learn the unforced rhythms of grace. I will not lay anything heavy or ill-fitting on you. Keep company with Me and you'll learn to live freely and lightly."

Keeping company with Jesus, you live freely and lightly. Does that sound appealing to you? If so, then it is time to respond to His invitation. Whether you have thirty seconds or thirty minutes, pause now and turn to Him. Center your heart on His splendor and approach Him with reverence. While you are in His presence, empty your exhaustion out before Him. Tell Him the concerns on your heart and take a soul rest.

I'd forgotten that and when I finally laid my burdens down before Him, I got to sleep.

Action:

Read and meditate on the words Jesus spoke to His apostles when they were tired and weary, "Come with me by yourselves to a quiet place and get some rest" (Mark 6:31).

Prayer:

Heavenly Father, You are mighty to save and all I need. Thank You for reminding me I can always come to You and trade in my exhaustion for Your rejuvenation. I come to You today and ask that You would restore rest to my soul. In Jesus' name. Amen.

SEPTEMBER 6

De-cluttering
BY JUDY KNOX

Mark 4:7, 18-19

Other seed fell among thorns, which grew up and choked the plants, so that they did not bear grain. Still others, like seed sown among thorns, hear the word; but the worries of this life, the deceitfulness of wealth and the desires for other things come in and choke the word, making it unfruitful.

I love paper – all kinds of paper, especially gift-wrapping paper. It calls out to me in the store. Occasionally I will toss a roll of the captivating stuff in my cart "just in case." No wonder the closet in my spare bedroom became overrun with paper and gift bags.

The day I decided to organize that closet, I began by pulling out all the gift-wrapping materials. Yikes! Considering how few occasions I have for wrapping, I was amazed to see how much paper I had accumulated. Weeding out the pile and organizing the remaining papers gave me a great sense of accomplishment.

But that closet, and in fact my entire house, is not the only part of my life that needs de-cluttering. What about my time, and the activities that fill it? Many of them got into my days the same way the paper got into my shopping cart: they were appealing at the time, but I didn't really need them.

Such activities may be harmless; but taken to excess they eat up space in my day, just like the paper took up space in my closet. A few minutes here, a few minutes there, and then I wonder why I don't have time to do the things I had planned for that day. So many activities and relationships clamor for our involvement. It's a good idea to take them out occasionally, examine them, and ask God to help us decide which ones are really worth keeping. Then our days won't resemble a closet over-run with useless items.

Jesus warned about letting the cares of this world crowd out the Word of God in our hearts. When we start thinking we're too busy for the things God has called us to do, it's time to weed out other activities that are taking more than their fair share of time in our days. Time to get rid of the clutter!

Action:

Choose one activity that you engage in daily and keep a log of how many minutes you actually spend on it. Reduce the time in half the next day and spend the extra time with God.

Prayer:

Father, I know I am letting the cares of this world take up time that I could be spending with You. Please help me to spend less time with them and more time with You. Amen.

SEPTEMBER 7

Good Luck
BY SHERRI GALLAGHER

Romans 14:1-4

Rabbit's foot? Wasn't lucky for the rabbit! **Becky Hernley Brown**

My dog and I were going onto the competition field when one of the spectators called out, "Good luck!" I waved and smiled. Being more focused on my dog than the people around me, I didn't respond verbally. After I finished and came off the field the person walked up to me and apologized for using the term "luck." It seems a club member had taken them aside and told them I was a Christian, so they had probably offended me.

It was my turn to apologize for not responding. I told him I understood he meant, "I wish you well" and I appreciated the sentiment. He asked if I would have responded differently if I had been at church. When I explained my congregation was a pretty easy-going group and not given to those kinds of judgments, he skeptically asked where my church was located. He seemed disappointed to learn we were several hours drive away. As he walked away, I prayed he could find a local church near him that could accept him.

Whenever we treat another person with less respect than we would want for ourselves we are standing in judgment, but is that the only place the concept applies? Most of our interactions are not as sharply defined. Taking offense at someone wishing us "good luck" and judging them as "of this world" is still being judgmental. Paul uses the example of eating anything versus those eating only vegetables. He instructs us not to despise others no matter which meal we choose.

Look at what you do and how you do it. Is the example you are setting one of judgment or one of love?

Prayer:
Heavenly Father, let me see where I am standing in judgment of others and help me to be more loving and welcoming. Amen.

SEPTEMBER 8

Like a Cascading Fountain
BY MYRA BIERNAT WELLS

Matthew 5:7

Blessed are the merciful, for they will be shown mercy.

Mercy is the stuff you give to people who don't deserve it. **Joyce Meyer**

Thank God for His mercy. We certainly need it. He has shown us mercy at the cross when He took on the very punishment we deserve. The Holy Spirit continues to pour out His life giving, life sustaining mercy in our lives. Like a cascading fountain, "His mercies never come to an end; they are new every morning" (Lamentations 3:22–23, EVS).

God calls us to drink deeply of His mercy, to return to the fountain daily to become more intimately acquainted with His compassion. And as those who know the mercy of God, we are to be a people of mercy ourselves. As those who have been blessed with the mercy of God, we are to bless others with the same grace, patience and care we received from Him.

Do you want to be a person of mercy? If you drink deeply from God's fountain, then His mercy will overflow in your life. If you are aware of how much you need God's mercy, your heart will be softened towards others who also need it.

In the culture of His day, Christ's compassion towards sinners and social outcasts was a radical display of God's love. It's just as powerful – and unexpected – in our culture of self—centeredness and judgment today. As we extend mercy, grace, compassion and forgiveness to the forgotten, the marginalized and the rejected, we will point people towards the mercy of Jesus.

Action:
Other people in our lives need our leniency. Pray God would show you how to look at others with His eyes. Slow down today and work to really see the people who cross your path. Look for ways to show them God's mercy. Write down the

name of one person you expect to encounter today. Pray for that person, then offer them grace, compassion or forgiveness.

Prayer:

Jesus, allow us to show mercy to others. We don't want to live close-fisted, embittered. Set us free to love, to open our hearts, to forgive and show compassion. Teach us to care for others and able to extend mercy like you do – every day! Amen.

SEPTEMBER 9
GRANDPARENTS DAY

Pop's Oatmeal
BY JUDY KNOX

Matthew 21:16

... From the lips of children and infants you, Lord, have called forth your praise.

It was Grandparents Day at Precious Lambs Pre-school. Forty proud adults sat in child-sized plastic chairs surrounding the gathering of squirmy children sitting on the floor. "Circle Time" was one of the last activities of the day. My husband and I had watched four-year-old Luke play with toys and interact with other children. We had read stories, done crafts, and had our picture taken with him. We weren't surprised to hear the teacher say Luke's computer skills were very advanced, and we were impressed with her perceptive ability as she noted that he was indeed very bright.

Now we sat patiently in the uncomfortable chairs, trying not to be as wiggly as the children after the fun-filled but tiring day. The teacher was reading a storybook about the joys of staying at Grandma and Grandpa's house. Grandma and Grandpa might let you do special things. "They might even let you have ice cream for breakfast!" she read, showing us all the brightly colored picture of two children in pajamas smiling over bowls of the tasty treat.

When the book ended, the teacher asked, "Do you like to stay at your grandparents' house?" Luke's hand shot right up. "Yes, but I don't want ice cream for breakfast. I would rather have Pop's oatmeal." Suddenly the discomfort of the chairs and all my husband's tiredness vanished. Beaming from ear to ear like a little kid, he proudly pointed to himself and told all the people around him, "I'm Pop! That's my oatmeal he's talking about. I'm Pop!"

The oatmeal itself was nothing unusual, but it was one part of staying with us that Luke and Pop both looked forward to. It created a special bond between them. This public declaration of appreciation made Pop's day then and brought a smile to his face many times during the years afterward.

Thinking of this the other day gave me a little insight into my attitude toward God. Just like Pop's oatmeal, some things God does in our daily lives may not look like anything special. Sometimes they seem so ordinary that we hardly notice them. Yet, just as Pop delighted in fixing oatmeal for Luke, God delights in blessing us on a regular basis. How must He feel when we publicly acknowledge our appreciation? I think it must warm His heart.

Sometimes I waste my time and God's by looking for the "ice cream," hoping for some big spectacular answer to prayer or supernatural manifestation that will make an exciting testimony. But I want to have the same attitude as four-year-old Luke, being content with the wholesome goodness of everyday interactions with God. I want to value the special, unique ways He shows His love and care for me. When I publicly express thankfulness for the oatmeal, I think it makes God smile. "I'm God!" He says. "I gave her that blessing. That's Me she's talking about!"

Action:
Make a list of some of the special things God blesses you with on a continual basis. Then share your thankfulness publicly by telling someone about them.

Prayer:
Father, thank You for always providing everything I need. Give me that child-like awareness of all those special everyday interactions with You that are happening all the time. Amen.

SEPTEMBER 10

Louder Than Words
BY SHERRI GALLAGHER

James 2:14-26

Words without actions are the assassins of idealism. **Herbert Hoover**

I probably spend too much time on social media. I admit to liking to repost positive and inspirational sayings, along with the occasional political opinion, and status updates. I can spend hours checking out what my friends are doing, but just posting, "don't worry, be happy" sayings doesn't do much to help others unless I am willing to take action.

James was quite clear: "For just as the body without the spirit is dead, so faith without works is dead" (James 2:26). We are saved by grace, but we show our faith by works. Posting trite sayings and nothing more is as effective as faith without works; I might as well tell the hungry to go and be filled but not give them anything to eat.

So the next time I re-post something, I am going to also send a card to a shut-in or go buy a bag of groceries and donate it to the food pantry, or say a prayer for someone I know who is in need of my prayers. I will take it as an opportunity to show my faith and help someone else.

Action:

Each time you post on social media, say a prayer for those around you until it becomes a habit.

Prayer:

Heavenly Father, help me to see how I can help the people around me and give me the strength to accomplish what needs to be done. Amen.

SEPTEMBER 11 WTC REMEMBERED

God Never Forgets
BY SHERRI GALLAGHER

Isaiah 49:14-18

You have kept count of my tossings: put my tears in your bottle. Are they not in your record? **Psalm 56:8**

On September 11, 2001 2,996 people died when members of a radical Muslim group used four jet liners as weapons to attack two towers of the World Trade Center in New York City, the Pentagon, and thanks to the brave passengers, a failed attempt to attack the Capitol Building in Washington, DC. Beyond that, the dust from the collapsed towers was wildly toxic, containing asbestos, lead, and mercury as well as dioxin and PAH from the fires that burned for three months. Seventy percent of the first responders developed serious respiratory illnesses and cancer that can be linked to their exposure during rescue and recovery operations. Medical professionals estimate the rescue workers at ground zero lost 12 years of lung function. Most of the canines who responded died of cancer at a much younger age than normal.

A short decade later American protestors demand an investigation claiming the destruction of the world trade center was a controlled explosives demolition funded by the USA government so the American public would support the invasion of Afghanistan and Iraq. This is the widely held belief in Arab countries. Video of flights 11 and 175 crashing into the towers are claimed to be photo-shopped. So, who will remember and what will they remember? What will the history books report? Or will this incident be removed as too inflammatory or offensive to some segments of society? When the people who lived through the events of September 11, 2001 are gone who will remember? God will. In Isaiah 49:14 Zion says God has forsaken them, but in verses 15-16 God promises not to forget us; He has even inscribed us on the palm of His hands.

Everyone of those people lost that day and the days that followed, every tear they and their families shed are remembered by God. When each of us passes away and we are no more than a forgotten name on a family tree, God will remember everything about us. God loves us. We are his children. He will not forget. We have His promise.

Action:
Take the time to tell your children and grandchildren where you were on September 11, 2001. What did you see, hear, smell, taste and touch? Write it down in a letter to them or make a video or audio recording.

Prayer:
Loving God, knowing that You remember everything about a normal average person like me gives me the strength to get through the tough times. Thank You for making me Yours. Amen.

SEPTEMBER 12

Absolutely No Fishing!
BY MYRA BIERNAT WELLS

Micah 7:19

You will have mercy on us again; You will conquer our sins. You will throw away all our sins into the deepest part of the sea. (NCV)

God takes our sins – the past, present, and future, and dumps them in the sea and puts up a sign that says NO FISHING ALLOWED. **Corrie ten Boom**

I do it all the time. I come to a place where I want to face my sins. I go to God with a tender and repentant heart and lay that sin at His feet. Confident that my sin was dealt with on the cross – secure in His love and forgiveness – I walk away. Until something happens in my life that makes me question that forgiveness. I then beat myself up with my own thoughts of self-loathing. All for a sin that Jesus has forgiven and buried in the deepest trenches of the ocean.

We all need to quit fishing in the waters of our past. We must deal with our sin, but then we must leave it behind. The unconditional love and overwhelming forgiveness of God should stop our guilt right in its tracks.

Sin requires only one payment – and that was given on the cross when Jesus died for our wrongdoings. Instead of celebrating this fact, I often live with my negative self-talk and carry on as if what Jesus did on the cross was not enough. It is more than enough. It always will be.

Scripture clearly explains God's attitude when one of His beloved children seeks His forgiveness. Isaiah 1:18 says, "Though your sins are like scarlet, they shall be white as snow. Though they be as crimson, they shall be like wool."

Let today be the day your wrap yourself up in the glorious wool of God's forgiveness. Make today the day you quit fishing in the waters of your past.

Action:

Put away your fishing gear by spending some time in prayer asking the Holy Spirit to reveal any sin in your life. Confess that sin and leave it behind, never to go fishing in those waters again.

Prayer:

Father, I am so very tired of living each day carrying the baggage of my past. Please forgive me and give me the courage to turn away from each one, leaving them in Your tender hands. Thank You, Lord, for Your grace. In Jesus' name. Amen.

SEPTEMBER 13

A Dreaded Place I Love
BY CATHY AND JOSEPH HARVEY

Hebrews 12:11

No discipline seems pleasant at the time, but painful. Later on, however it produces a harvest of righteousness and peace for those who have been trained by it.

No matter how slow you go, you are passing everyone on the couch.
Posted in a gym

For three years I taught a Bible health class. It was an excellent program with solid principles. Besides Bible study and prayer, part of the program involved exercising five times a week for thirty minutes. Over six months I lost twenty-five pounds and reached my ideal weight. I did a variety of exercises to keep the process interesting, and I was amazed and pleased with the results. I felt great, I looked great, I had great energy. But, I dreaded every minute of exercise. Really. Every. Minute.

When I came across my son's homework essay while cleaning in his room one day, I completely understood the sentiments he expressed in his English 101 assignment, "A Dreaded Place I Love." Perhaps you can relate to his perspective also. He gave permission to share his high school thoughts below.

"Through thick, red, wooden doors is a large room with blue and white walls. It is enclosed with a door on one side, two on the other side, and a chain link fence dividing it from another room. Warm and stuffy, it smells strongly of sweat and foam rubber mats. A coach once said, 'that is the smell of heart and dedication.' Spend ten minutes in there during the season and one would know what he was talking about. Everyone who practices there dreads it every day, but loves it when the season is over, and knows it was worth every grueling second.

One can hear the screeching of shoes on the mat and groans of athletes somewhat painfully learning technique. For the ones who must be there, the sounds of shoes beating like drums on the mat, while athletes run sprints up and down them, is the sweetest sound in the world. This sound signifies the end to yet another exhausting practice. One look at the tired cringing faces of the athletes trying to squeeze out just one more rep to make them that much better, and you'll know why this room is thought of the way it is by the ones who train there.

'There is no glory without pain.' There is plenty of pain in this room, along with the excess blood, sweat, and occasional tears. This is why the wrestling room is the dreaded place I love."

Action:

Is there a discipline you know you need but struggle to incorporate? It might be physical discipline, or perhaps a spiritual one: a daily quiet time? Prayer? Fasting? Solitude? Could you manage fifteen minutes a day for just one week? Then, evaluate the value of it, and consider repeating it for another week. In three weeks, you might establish a healthy habit.

Prayer:

O God, I am sorely lacking in discipline for _____. I need Your help to overcome this lack, this laziness in my life. Please help me, one day at a time, to "get off the couch," not for vanity or pride, but to seek a closer walk with You. Use it to reveal Yourself to me and make me more like You. Amen.

SEPTEMBER 14

The Spare Coat
BY SHERRI GALLAGHER

Luke 3:11

In reply he said to them, "Whoever has two coats must share with anyone who has none; and whoever has food must do likewise."

My husband and I have a system. When the leaves start to crunch under foot and there's a tang in the air, my husband goes shopping. He brings home a warm, sturdy coat with a snug hood. It's hung in the closet to await bad weather.

He wears the coat once or twice, declares it "too warm" and goes back to wearing a well-worn coat from many years earlier. When spring arrives, I clean out closets and move the cold weather clothes into storage. In the autumn, I take last year's coat to Goodwill.

Early in our marriage, when money was very tight, I asked him about his annual shopping spree. He remembered a time when he couldn't afford a warm coat and his family didn't accept charity. If not for the Goodwill store, he would not have had a garment to keep himself warm. He had promised himself, when he could afford it, he would pass on a new coat each year. So, if our system means we eat a little more pasta and beans to give away a coat, it is a tasty dinner we share.

Action:

Go through your closet and send the gently used garments you no longer wear to Goodwill or the Salvation Army.

Prayer:

Thank You, Lord, for the experiences we have had to help us understand just how blessed we are and giving us the ability to share those blessings with others. Amen

SEPTEMBER 15

God Doesn't Compare
BY SHERRI GALLAGHER

Matthew 12:24-37

The surest route to breeding jealousy is to compare. Since jealousy comes
from feeling less than another, comparisons only fan the fires.
Dorothy Corkville Briggs

I have a hard time with comparisons. No matter what I do, I can always find someone better at "it" than I am. For example, I think I am a pretty good dog trainer, then I go to IPO (Internationale Prüfungs-Ordnung) a dog sport which requires functioning in tracking, obedience, and protection. I look at the other dogs' performances, and I feel that my skills are nowhere near their handlers' level. This undermines my confidence and I think bad things about myself, get discouraged and want to give up.

What I must remind myself is in IPO you are not competing against other people. You get a score as to how closely you met a standard. You don't have winners and losers, so everyone is cheering each other on and praying everyone has a good day. I should be analyzing if my dog is improving or not instead of making comparisons. Usually he is better than the last time we were there so instead of being discouraged I should be encouraged that we are making progress.

I never thought about this in biblical terms until a friend said, "God doesn't make comparisons." I knew in my heart this was true, but I wanted to find a Bible verse that said that. I did a search for "comparisons" and "inadequacy" without result. After a little diligent searching I found Matthew 12:36-37, "But I tell you that everyone will have to give account on the day of judgment for every empty word they have spoken. For by your words you will be acquitted, and by your words you will be condemned." When I thought bad things about myself, my words were empty and bitter and untrue. I was condemning and judging myself for things that were not true.

My dog is different from every other dog. So, where he does well or poorly has as much to do with his personality as my training. I was forgetting the things my dog excelled at that other people were struggling to achieve. I was focused on the negative. I was focused on empty words. That is not a place God wants me to be. He wants me to focus on what I can do well and do it. He wants me to be positive - positive that I am loved, positive that God doesn't make mistakes, positive that I have value.

Action:

The next time you are getting discouraged, stop and look for the improvements and positives. Name them and cheer yourself on.

Prayer:

Heavenly Father, thank You for loving me as I am, for making me in Your image, and for believing in the good in me. Help me to remember those things when the negatives try to overwhelm me. Amen.

SEPTEMBER 16

Huddled Masses
BY SHERRI GALLAGHER

I Timothy 4:1-5

There are, in every age, new errors to be rectified and new prejudices to be opposed.
Samuel Johnson

As a teenager, I searched to find a church. A friend took me to his church, and I tried desperately to fit in. I followed the rules to the letter, but I was always not quite good enough. My parents weren't church goers, so I was "the bad girl" to be looked down upon, if not shunned. Eventually I left. If they ever thought of me, it was probably to gloat over the belief that they will be in the resurrection and I will not. I wish I had read these verses from I Timothy about the "hypocrisy of liars" and that "everything that God created is good" it would have saved me a lot of pain.

It was many years later that I married, joined a mainstream church and started a family. Moving to Illinois brought a number of challenges, including finding a church where I felt comfortable. My teenage experience made me wary and nervous. Imagine my pleasant surprise when I walked through the doors of this church and was welcomed with open arms. I sometimes think we should put the inscription that is on the Statue of Liberty on the church door. "Give me your tired, your poor, your huddled masses, yearning to breathe free, the wretched refuse of your teeming shore, send these, the homeless, tempest tossed to me, I lift up my lamp beside the golden door."

Being accepting of everyone is at the heart of this church. "Nothing (no one) is to be rejected... and all are received with Thanksgiving." As long as we continue to exist there will be a church home for the people seeking God through Jesus.

Do you have a friend who feels they were rejected by another church? Invite them to services and introduce them around at coffee hour. Sit with them and make sure they feel they belong here, too.

Prayer:
Lord God, thank You for this small but loving congregation. Help us to find those who feel rejected and bring them here to show they are loved. Amen.

SEPTEMBER 17

Water Lily Pond
BY MYRA BIERNAT WELLS

Hebrews 4:12

For the word of God is alive and active. Sharper than any double-edged sword, it penetrates even to dividing soul and spirit, joints and marrow; it judges the thoughts and attitudes of the heart.

I'm in love with the Art Institute of Chicago and visit as often as possible. On one trip, I walked quickly through each room, surveying most of the masterpieces with a short glance. Priceless works of art got only a fleeting look. I was in a hurry to see one particular Monet – his famous Water Lily Pond painting.

When I finally found it, I sat down and examined it. The more I looked at the painting, the more I began to see: the playful curvature of the bridge, the multiple shades of greens in the water lilies, the graceful bends of the Willow tree, the delicate brush strokes needed to form the lilies, how the water looked more brackish than blue. The more I stared, the more I felt the excitement of the artist surrounded by the loveliness of his own garden.

As I sat there enveloped by the beauty, God began to speak into my heart. How I visited the art gallery that day is how I sometimes read the Bible. I dash through the Scriptures like my race through most of this museum – never stopping to see what the artist intended. Like my hasty sprint through the galleries, I sometimes grab my Bible and read a few verses before swiftly going on to something else.

But God's word is a masterpiece and He speaks through every stroke of the writer's pen. There are treasures stored on each page just waiting to be discovered. And like my examination of the Monet, the more time I spend in Scripture, the more God will reveal its marvelous truth.

No matter how long we live, no matter how many times we read the Bible, it will still come alive because God continues to speak to all of us through the pages of His Word. His words are living and they bring us life!

Action:

Today, pick one verse and ponder it. Just one. Try to find a new meaning in it – one you've never experienced before.

Prayer:

Dear Lord, slow me down when I read Your Word. Send the Holy Spirit, so I can find the wisdom in its pages. Fill my heart with the hope You have called me to. Cover me with Your incomparable strength. Let me know peace in the delicate brushstrokes of Your love. Amen.

SEPTEMBER 18

The Less the Better
BY MYRA BIERNAT WELLS

Colossians 4:6

Let your conversation be gracious and effective so that you will have the right answer for everyone.

Life has no remote…get up and change it yourself! **Mark A. Cooper**

During every writing conference I have attended, at least once each speaker has explained, "Write tight!" That means use as few words as possible. Less is more. When it comes to words with impact, being long-winded is not a value. But speaking exactly the right words can be life-altering.

Words are extremely powerful. We need not speak many words but must take the time to speak the right ones. Consider that:

- The Lord's Prayer contains 71 words.
- The Gettysburg Address contains 272.
- The Ten Commandments contains 139 words.
- The Declaration of Independence contains 1323.

Yet a US government order setting the price of cabbage contains 26,911 words.

How long we talk or how eloquent the words we use doesn't matter. Something simple like, "I'm here for you," can be a lifeline to a person drowning in sorrow. Words are like seeds. What we plant will grow.

The rights words—given at the right time and in the right way—can bring order amid confusion, light on a very dark path and wisdom to a questioning heart.

Read Proverbs 16:24: *Gracious words are a honeycomb, sweet to the soul and healing to the bones*. Consider how your words can be gracious. Put your ideas into practice.

Prayer:
Father, I come today asking for Your forgiveness for the careless words I have spoken. Please teach me the right words to say in every situation. Give me a holy desire to encourage and build others up with my words. In Your precious Son's name. Amen.

SEPTEMBER 19

Busy Work
BY SHERRI GALLAGHER

Mark 6:45-46

Beside the noble art of getting things done, there is a nobler art of leaving things undone. The wisdom of life consists in the elimination of nonessentials.
Lin Yutang

"Girl, just listening to you talk makes me tired."

As a fast-talking New Yorker, I have to laugh every time I think of my Arkansas friend's comment. Throughout my life I have valued always moving, always accomplishing many things. If there is a spare minute, I tend to fill it with work. While I was growing up, I was responsible for cleaning the house, doing the laundry and helping my sister cook and wash dishes. We both had to do all this and finish our homework before Mom and Dad got home from work.

As a working mother, the day started early and ended late with no thought of "down-time." Now as an empty nester, my days get consumed with work, dog training, writing and the regular chores of the house and the yard. If I can't list several items accomplished by the end of the day, I worry that I have been lazy and unproductive. But is that wise? There is a difference between important tasks and busy work.

Jesus took time to rest and pray. After the sermon on the mount He dismissed the crowds and went up the mountain to pray (Mark 6:45). The night of his betrayal, Jesus went to the garden to pray (Mark 14:32). Repeatedly, throughout the scriptures we are told to pray, and Jesus sets the example.

When I go to our cabin, I love to sit on the dock and look at all the beauty around me and give prayers of thanks for God's goodness, but that short visit isn't enough to sustain me. When I get too busy, I need to find the time to be quiet and pray. Without this time with God, all my busy work is a waste. God must come first and if Jesus needed to pray, then I as a sinner need it even more.

Action:

Look through the gospels and list all the verses where Jesus took time out to pray.

Prayer:

Lord God, thank You for the guidance Jesus gave us to find time with You. Guide my actions so I know when to work and when to rest in Your love, peace and comfort. Amen.

SEPTEMBER 20

Delight in the Law of the Lord
BY SHERRI GALLAGHER

Psalm 1

Learning is not attained by chance, it must be sought for with ardor and attended to with diligence. **Abigail Adams**

The first scripture I ever tried to memorize was Psalm 1. I wrote it on an index card and would silently practice it in the grocery line, while stuck in traffic waiting for a train to pass, and even in the shower. When I would get to verse two, "but their delight is in the law of the Lord, and on his law they meditate day and night" I would be filled with the hope that I was pleasing God.

Over time, I have read and studied the Bible and memorized various verses, but when I get nervous and wonder if I am heading in the right direction, I recite Psalm 1 to myself. It has become my calming mantra and made difficult meetings and hard decisions bearable.

Recently I noticed in my studies the importance and emphasis placed on studying God's word and living it. God's directive to Joshua was to be strong and courageous but also to act in accordance with the law (Joshua 1:7). Saul turned his back on God and did not follow His commands (I Samuel 15:11) so God withdrew His support. Solomon turned away from God's teachings and paid the price for his error (I Kings 11) as did Jeroboam (I Kings 14) and many other Kings and leaders.

Jesus set the example that it is still important to read and study God's Word when as a twelve-year-old he stayed behind in the temple sitting among the teachers listening and asking questions (Luke 2:46-47).

Action:

Select a verse or verses to memorize.

Prayer:

Loving God, help us to study and delight in Your word. Amen.

SEPTEMBER 21

Just Checking in…
BY MYRA BIERNAT WELLS

Psalm 145:2

Every day I will praise you and extol your name forever and ever.

My German Shepherd, Lily, is the happiest playing in a doggie park. She loves them so much that when I even say the words doggie park, she'll run to the side entrance of our garage, waiting expectantly to be transported to a canine's version of heaven on earth. Knowing these words trigger her, I've developed the habit of saying LP (for La Paws) and CB (for Central Bark) so there is no disappointment if we aren't headed for one.

Once in the park, Lily runs, romps and plays with all her canine friends. But she has this sweet habit. Every once in a while, she'll stop what she is doing and come back to me no matter where I am in the park. She doesn't stay long. She holds my gaze for a second, then scampers off to a new doggie adventure. It's as if in that moment, she's telling me, "Just checking in. I know you're here with me, but I'm just checking in."

While I'm told this is part of the breed's characteristic sense of loyalty, my dog is modeling for me what I should be doing with God. I want to walk with God. I want to journey through my days in tender conversation with Him, aware that He walks with me; that when I pray, He hears me; that as I rest, He carries me.

It is far too easy to get seduced by the busyness of the day. I forget that my life, my very happiness, is held together by Him. And so, I want to become like Lily, and take the time to say, "God, I know You are here. I'm holding my hand out to you. I want to walk with You. I'm just checking in."

So, I'm trying to circle back to God throughout my day because when I do even in tiny moments of prayer, my life is transformed by Him. In an instant, I am grounded with the reality of His love for me because through these holy encounters I see the work of God around me.

Action:
Spend one day checking in every hour with God. Set your watch or phone if you need to but use the reminder to talk briefly to our holy, loving God.

Prayer:
Father, thank You for loving me even when I don't check in. Help me develop this holy habit. Oh, how I desperately need to stay close to You. Amen.

SEPTEMBER 22

Maybe Next Year
BY SHERRI GALLAGHER

Luke 2:36-38

There was also a prophet, Anna, the daughter of Penuel, of the tribe of Asher. She was very old; she had lived with her husband seven years after her marriage, and then was a widow until she was eighty-four. She never left the temple but worshiped night and day, fasting and praying. Coming up to them at that very moment, she gave thanks to God and spoke about the child to all who were looking forward to the redemption of Jerusalem.

Patience is the companion of wisdom. **Saint Augustine**

I was positive I could get Orex, my male German Shepherd, ready for his first IPO test (*Internationale Prüfungs-Ordnung*) which is a three-part sport where the dog must perform in tracking, obedience and protection this year. We worked diligently several days a week if not every day in tracking, obedience and protection. Things were shaping up and I entered him in the last local event called a trial.

That was when things started to go wrong. First, the judge backed out and the replacement judge was not recognized in Germany. If I competed with him internationally, his titles could be called into question. I decided to go forward and repeat the title under a German recognized judge in the spring and sent in my entry fee.

Then, my dog decided to stop tracking. This dog which could find a golf tee in a heavily trampled soccer field wouldn't go ten steps without giving up and returning to my side. As we closed in on the trial date it became clear he would fail. I had to pull him from the test. I expected to be devastated, but I wasn't. I used to fall to pieces when things failed to work out on my schedule, but the true joy and gift was spending time with this dog and enjoying being with him as he learned. Maybe I am learning too—to be patient.

My patience with this dog is nothing compared to Anna, the prophet's, patience. She was eighty-four years old and waiting patiently to see the Messiah. She remained faithful, praying and fasting every day for not just years, but for decades. Her patience was rewarded when Joseph and Mary brought Jesus to the temple for purification. Anna saw and recognized Jesus as the redeemer.

I am sure many people scoffed and considered Anna foolish. They probably said behind her back, "What a waste of time! She could have been more effective performing works of faith and serving the poor." But Anna remained faithful and God rewarded her patience.

Action:

The next time a person, or dog, frustrates you and you wonder if you should give up, think about the patience of Anna and practice a relaxing breathing exercise, knowing God's timing will work out in the end.

Prayer:

Holy God, give me the patience to see me through the stresses and delays in my dreams and plans. I remember Your timing is perfect, even when it is different from what I want and expect. Amen.

SEPTEMBER 23

Focused Heel
BY SHERRI GALLAGHER

Hebrews 12:1-4

A dog is the only thing on earth that loves you more than he loves himself.
Josh Billings

In the dog sport of IPO (Internationale Prüfungs-Ordnung) the dog must perform in three phases; tracking, obedience, and protection. I felt that obedience would be Orex's and my weakest phase and have the lowest score simply because of his poor heeling.

For a very long time my dog wouldn't stay at the correct heel position - his shoulder at my left leg, eyes and ears focused on my face. His total attention on me. He would do this for ten or twenty steps, but then he would glance away. A slight sound or movement would distract him. He never left my side, but he wasn't focused on me. Every time he glanced away in a test, the judge could take away a point. Since the heeling pattern is over two hundred steps, we could lose a lot of points.

Observing my dog brought an uncomfortable truth about my life to light. I have sought after the Lord and even in my darkest times, I knew he walked with me. However, like my dog I find I don't keep my focus on Him. I am easily distracted by work, family, service activities or even computer solitaire. I try very hard to stay focused and it works, for a while, then I fall back into old habits and like my dog, glance away.

We have worked very hard to correct my dog's heeling. At first, if I could get twenty-one steps with focus, I rewarded him. We built to twenty-two steps and so on, until we are now at the point of sixty steps consistently even when surrounded by lots of distractions. I have decided to try the same thing with myself. I am working on building positives into my life for staying focused on Him. If a big project comes up and I still take my time to pray and perform daily studies of God's word, I give myself a little pat on the back. When I slip and glance away, I start over knowing God forgives. Unlike the judge at an IPO test, God doesn't take away points, He simply forgives and rejoices when I self-correct and focus on Him. God is eager to bless us through these moments, not punish us.

Action:

Step back and check out your actions. Are you giving God the attention He deserves or are you easily distracted? List your distractions and when one of them occurs make an extra effort to stay focused on God.

Prayer:

Heavenly Father, thank You for forgiving me my lack of attention. Give me the wisdom to see what distractions take my attention from You and how to overcome them. Amen.

SEPTEMBER 24

The Sign
BY MYRA BIERNAT WELLS

Luke 15

I was looking for something else, when I found them - three small ceramic horses I've had since childhood. I first saw them at the card store I passed on my way to and from grammar school. I wanted them so badly and finally got them as a birthday present when I was nine. Throughout my life, they have been carried from home to home, always given a place of honor. As a reminder of a happy childhood moment, they grow even more precious to me with each passing birthday.

Finding them was a holy moment. Anytime I find something lost, the moment is imbued with the sacred. It is more than just a hard-won celebration, but also knowing the frustrating search is over. Often, in that glorious moment of discovery, I remember the fifteenth chapter of Luke, where Christ tells the parable of the lost sheep, the lost coin, the lost son. My heart leaps with the understanding I serve the God who cares about lost things. He goes looking for the lost souls in the world, cherishing each and every life.

As Christians, we are to walk by faith, standing firm in our beliefs, not needing signs from God. But I fall more deeply in love with God when He sends a reminder of who He is. Exposed in those beautiful signs is the awareness He will keep all the promises He gave us in His word.

Finding a lost object is just one way He showers encouragement on me. Little reminders of His love are set in many ways - through His word, through faithful friends who pray for me, through the love of my husband. They remind me He understands my frustrations; He cares about my pain; He celebrates my joy. He is with me and He is for me. God will always find a way to tell me how much He loves me.

He will do the same for you. It might not be by finding a lost object. For you it might be in the hug of a friend, in an unexpected surprise, in a walk through a garden awash in color. God is crazy about you and He'll keep bringing good gifts into your life.

That's why, to me, finding a missing object is a sacred reminder that God is God. He is leading my life. He shouts out to me that He will never leave me or forsake me. He sends reminders of this promise throughout my day, if I just take the time to notice.

How is God reminding you of His love today?

Action:

Read Luke 15. How does knowing God will never leave you make you feel? Write down a short prayer thanking Him for His faithfulness.

Prayer:

Jesus, thank You for loving me even when I go missing. Teach me each day about the power of Your grace and forgiveness. Oh, dear Lord, I desperately need Your faithfulness. Amen.

SEPTEMBER 25

Knowing
BY BETH DUMEY

Genesis 2:17

But you must not eat from the tree of the knowledge of good and evil, for when you eat from it you will certainly die.

When most of us learned of the horror that took place at Sandy Hook Elementary School in late 2012, we were heartbroken. We mourned with the entire Connecticut town as they laid to rest 20 children and six adults who had been massacred at school. In the media coverage shortly after the tragedy, a child summed up the experience of those who survived the attack. "We know lots of things we shouldn't know," the young child murmured.

So much of what we try to preserve within our children is an age-appropriate innocence. What really separates children from adults, other than age itself, of course, is limited knowledge of what is evil and harrowing. The children of Sandy Hook received a premature glimpse of the terror that humans can inflict on one another. Even the young knew it was too much for them to process.

According to God's ideal plan, evil is more than any of us are meant to comprehend. As our heavenly Father, He sought to protect us from what would cause us loss, heartache, and the death of innocence. He issued an edict to stay away from the tree of the knowledge of good and evil. Yet, with the consequences of the Fall, our "knowledge" has expanded in ways few of us desire. As we scan our globe and witness outbreaks of conflict and war, starvation, corruption, scandal, and every form of evil, we are sickened. In our own hearts, we battle with pride, jealousy, superiority, greed, selfishness, and divisiveness. Like the child from Sandy Hook, many of us can echo, "We know lots of things we shouldn't know."

The only antidote to the knowledge of evil is perhaps the knowledge of good. Dwelling in God's word, seeking Him in prayer, studying Christ's life and imitating it in our own — this type of knowledge, rather than destroy and devastate, blesses and restores.

Action:
Think about a time when too much knowledge (perhaps gossip or ongoing news coverage of a tragic event) left you sickened. Identify how you processed those feelings. How do you respond to evil in our world?

Prayer:
Father, we live in a world often overrun by evil. Help us to see Your presence in the midst of this. Help us to counteract evil with good, in Your name. Amen.

SEPTEMBER 26

Martha or Mary
BY SHERRI GALLAGHER

Luke 10:38-42

The charity that hastens to proclaim its good deeds, ceases to be charity, and is only pride and ostentation. **William Hutton**

We had a lively discussion the other night about Martha versus Mary. Most of us were homemakers and responsible for seeing to our guests' comfort so we had a strong affinity for Martha. How many times had we hosted a party and been so busy making our guests welcome and seeing to their comfort that we were not able to enjoy the evening or enter the lively conversation? Each of us had seen where we were stuck with all the work in the background. Others were remembered as the life of the party with witty conversation but never lifted a finger to help. They got all the glory and attention when it was really our hard work that made it possible. If they had helped, even a little, we could have joined in the festivities. If Mary had helped with the preparations wouldn't Martha have had the same opportunity to learn and not been rebuked by Jesus?

One of the ladies pointed out that maybe Martha got carried away with the preparations and doing things like carving the animals for Noah's Ark from fruit and decorating the walls and trees to get just the right ambiance instead of setting out bowls of fruit, cheese and crackers and letting people serve themselves. After all, Jesus knew people needed to eat.

Martha invited Jesus into her home. She may have taken great pride in her entertaining. I know before I throw a party, I scrub the house from top to bottom and prepare complicated dishes. How hard is it to think Martha was the same? But Jesus wasn't there to see if dust bunnies existed under the bed or if the soufflé was perfect. He was there to teach and whether it was a field or a lake or a home His time was short and teaching more important than the surroundings. That is why Martha was rebuked.

Action:
Next time you host a small group meeting or church function, evaluate your preparations and see if they can be simplified.

Prayer:
Loving and forgiving Father, help me to stay focused on You and not how people view me. Amen.

SEPTEMBER 27

Pass the Baton
BY SHERRI GALLAGHER

John 4:31-38

Go confidently in the direction of your dreams! Live the life you've imagined. As you simplify your life, the laws of the universe will be simpler.
Henry David Thoreau

I didn't get to my desk until after lunch. I hadn't even had time to do my daily devotionals yet. My frustration built. I had so much to get done and there wasn't enough time. What could I cut from my routine? Exercising? Dog training? Caring for my house and family? Writing? Working?

I pulled out the "Upper Room" and "These Days" and focused on what was important; God. Feeling a little calmer, I tried again. A scary solution came to me. I needed to hand off some of the search team work to the other members. Collecting ink cartridges, writing articles and maintaining the website and

Facebook page, sending out notices and staying in contact with police and fire departments so they knew our capabilities and availability didn't need me to manage them. I had planted the seeds. We had four operational dogs and handlers; we were two-thirds of the way to our goal of covering the expenses of the team members while they search. The team members were well-educated business people fully capable of handling the tasks. It was time for me to let others reap what I had sown. And boy was it hard to let go.

It made me think about Jesus. He gave his life to build His church and He gave control over to His apostles, who really didn't seem ready to take up the challenge. It would take someone with God's strength and wisdom to do that. Of course, He did have the knowledge that he was sending the Holy Spirit to them. Thinking about the trust Jesus had in the apostles put my worry into perspective. Jesus was turning over teaching people about salvation to others. I was turning over fund-raising and promoting. That took the scary out of the decision.

Action:

What would you like to delegate but are afraid to give up? Help the person taking over to develop an effective plan and then let them run with it.

Prayer:

Lord, forgive my fear, give me the strength to trust others, and give them the guidance to be successful. Amen.

SEPTEMBER 28

True Self-worth
BY MYRA BIERNAT WELLS

2 Corinthians 5:17

Therefore, if anyone is in Christ, the new creation has come. The old has gone, the new is here!

Our culture can obliterate our self-worth. It tells us to get our self-worth from our accomplishments, the opinions of others or from our appearance. But when we do that, we crumble when someone gives us criticism, we are rejected by a person we love, or we have a bad hair day. We will always fall short in our quest to be better, accomplish more or look more attractive.

True self-worth, though, is not an issue of beauty, talent or intelligence. It is really an identity issue. When your identity is solidified in Christ and His redemptive work on the cross, it is unconditional, unshakable and unchangeable.

Your self-worth need not be at risk of collapse. As a child of God, you are chosen. You are deeply loved. You are created to fulfill a great purpose that God chose specifically for you. Your self-worth is bound up in the awesome power of the Holy God.

When you base your significance, self-worth or self-esteem on Christ, you can banish feelings of inferiority, insecurity and inadequacy by replacing them with God's overriding truth about your identity in Him and His power in you. You can trust who God says you are redeemed and loved. You are a chosen, holy, precious child of the most high God.

Action:
Read Romans 8:17. Then write down several ways being a co-heir with Christ can release you from any echoes from your past that squelch your self-worth.

Prayer:
Lord, help me base my self-worth on You and You alone. Let me always remember that according to Your Word, I am valuable, chosen, and dearly loved. Please anchor my identity in You and only You. Amen.

SEPTEMBER 29

Separation Anxiety
BY SHERRI GALLAGHER

1 John 4:17-18

This is how love is made complete among us so that we will have confidence on the day of judgment: In this world we are like Jesus. There is no fear in love. But perfect love drives out fear, because fear has to do with punishment. The one who fears is not made perfect in love.

Courage is fear that has said its prayers. **Dorothy Bernard**

I learn a lot from watching my dog. We are going through a rough patch right now and his breeder says it's a form of separation anxiety. To perform the tracking test my dog must follow footsteps through several turns for close to a quarter of a mile. He is on a ten- meter lead so I am about thirty-three feet behind him. Right now, he goes a little way, stops and returns to sit at the heel position, but that isn't what he is supposed to do.

The problem is I taught him a little too well that being at heel is a safe, fun place to be. If he is there, focused entirely on me, he will get a treat or a toy. Apparently being out there at the end of that ten-meter lead is a scary place where he is on his own without my support.

The truth of the matter is he is not alone, and I know what I am asking him to do is a safe exercise. I am trying to instill confidence in my dog by varying my distance from him as he tracks, sometimes close, sometimes further back, always with a lot of leash tension so he knows I am not far away.

In many ways I am like my dog in that I don't like to go out of my comfort zone. I have my studies and my routines; this is my safe place. Like my dog when I ask him to step out in front, when God asks me to step out in faith, my first thought is to run back to "heel" and be safe. But, just as my dog must learn to trust me, I must trust God and step out to follow His direction. Since God has infinitely more patience than I do, I know He will work with me, going back and forth on my leash and communicating His presence so I can overcome my fears and perform the work He expects me to complete.

Action:

When you are asked to step forward out of your comfort zone and you are scared, repeat the Lord's Prayer with emphasis on the "deliver me from evil."

Prayer:

Our Father who is in heaven, hallowed be your name, your kingdom come, your will be done on earth as it is in heaven. Give us this day our daily bread and forgive us our sins as we forgive those who have sinned against us and lead us not into temptation but deliver us from evil for yours is the kingdom and power and glory forever. Amen. (Matthew 6:9-13)

SEPTEMBER 30

Dance, Dance, Dance
BY SHERRI GALLAGHER

2 Samuel 6:14-15

David danced before the Lord with all his might; David was girded with a linen ephrod. So David and all the house of Israel brought up the ark of the Lord with shouting, and the sound of the trumpet.

Every day brings a chance for you to draw in a breath, kick off your shoes, and dance. **Oprah Winfrey**

I love getting my big, male, German Shepherd, Orex, out to go train. He is so excited and happy at the prospect of working that he jumps and spins and wags his tail. He will leap up and put his front paws on my arm and as I move, he dances alongside of me on his back feet. Even though he weighs in at a solid eighty-five pounds, the pressure on my arm is feather light.

Our work is not easy. He may have to track a scent for long distances or stay focused and obedient, ignoring a toy that is within easy reach. If he disobeys, and he will, since this is training and proofing (making sure he obeys no matter the conditions or provocations) there are always some corrections. However, he knows if he listens, he will get rewarded with playing tug or fetch. Overall, his joy at the prospect of time working with me outweighs any memory of the corrections I give him.

Have you ever felt like jumping and dancing for sheer joy in God? King David certainly did. His joy was so great at finally relocating in the ark of God that "David danced before the Lord with all his might" (2 Samuel 6:14). David made his share of mistakes and knew what it was to be "corrected" by God just as Orex knows what it is to be corrected in training. But David's joy in God couldn't be contained any more than Orex's.

Many of us were raised to believe we should be on our best behavior in church. Smiling, dancing, or stepping out in an unrestrained manner would draw frowns of disapproval. But is that really what God wants? Is that really what our church is about? David was "a man after God's own heart" (Acts 13:22) and he danced for joy while worshipping God.

Action:
Next time we pass the peace and Gloria Patri is played dance back to your seat.

Prayer:
Lord God, no matter my background, make me unafraid to show my joy at being able to worship You. Amen.

OCTOBER 1

Step Up
BY SHERRI GALLAGHER

Joshua 1:1-9

Stop seeing the obstacles you face as reasons why you can't do something. See them as a reason why you can. And celebrate your accomplishments on a daily basis. **Ali Vincent**

Can you imagine being Joshua? Your people have been led in the wilderness for forty years by Moses, and now it is your job to step into his place and lead. I think my first thought would be to run screaming in the other direction! Nope, not me. Not worthy. Not capable. Wrong choice. Talk about big shoes to fill!

God calling Moses, and Moses in Exodus 3 and 4, we get to read both sides of the conversation as Moses expresses his concerns about leading the Israelites. In Joshua 1:1-9 we hear God's directive but not Joshua's response. It is interesting to note that in both verses seven and nine, God tells Joshua to "be strong and courageous." In verse nine he goes even further, telling Joshua "Be strong and courageous; do not be frightened or dismayed, for the Lord your God is with you wherever you go." Maybe Joshua had some misgivings as to his abilities, too.

When are you afraid and feeling unworthy? One of those times for me was being asked to teach Sunday school. I didn't have the education to teach God's word. I had never had experience in a classroom situation. But the need was there and no one else to fill it so I stepped up and ended up teaching for several years.

Action:
The next time you are asked to serve on a committee or as a teacher pray for God to guide you and step up. You are needed.

Prayer:
Lord God, be with each member of the congregation as they work to fulfill and support the needs of our church. Give us the strength and courage to go forward and lead by following You. Amen.

OCTOBER 2

Weren't You Listening?
BY SHERRI GALLAGHER

Matthew 7:24-29

The Word of God is a Christian's instructions for life. God speaks to us through His word, so we cannot constantly be running on empty. **Monica Johnson**

"I know you were standing there when I told you what to do but I don't know where your mind was!"

Over a year ago, I was at an impasse with training my German Shepherd, Orex, to track. Frustrated, I drove to Nashville where his breeder, Gabor, was located and spent a weekend trying to absorb as much wisdom and experience as possible. At world competitions, Gabor always has one of the highest scores in tracking, so his instruction is extremely valuable. I took copious notes and had my husband make videos. After I came home, I followed the instructions Gabor had given me as best I could. At regular intervals or when I was having difficulties, I would have someone video Orex and me working to send to Gabor for commentary and instruction. Gabor's comments are very valuable, but you need a thick skin for negative comments. Hungarian born and German trained, Gabor is quite blunt. The worst part is he is usually right, but no matter how hard I try, I make mistakes and don't follow his directions.

The same is true of my Christian life. God gave very clear direction in a very thick book we call the Bible. If I could just follow these instructions, applying them to how I live, life would be so much better. Unfortunately, just as I have difficulty following Gabor's instructions, I sometimes have problems following God's directions.

Gabor hasn't given up on teaching Orex and me how to track competitively and thankfully God hasn't given up on my following His direction. Both know I am doing my level best to learn and grow and be obedient. Both Gabor and God forgive my lapses in judgment and offer me guidance how to get back on track. I keep working knowing that if I do, the lapses will be further and further apart.

There is one big difference between the two situations. Thanks to the blood of Jesus Christ I am forgiven when I fail to follow God's instructions. I won't get the same level of forgiveness from Gabor when it comes to tracking, but then he isn't God.

Action:

During your prayer time consider your actions, are there times you haven't followed God's instructions? Ask God for forgiveness and guidance on how to better follow his instructions.

Prayer:

Lord God, as much as I try, I am not perfect. Thank You for our Savior, Jesus Christ. Amen.

OCTOBER 3

Loving Generosity
BY SHERRI GALLAGHER

2 Corinthians 9:5-7

So I thought it necessary to urge the brothers to visit you in advance and finish the arrangements for the generous gift you had promised. Then it will be ready as a generous gift, not as one grudgingly given. Remember this: Whoever sows sparingly will also reap sparingly, and whoever sows generously will also reap generously. Each of you should give what you have decided in your heart to give, not reluctantly or under compulsion, for God loves a cheerful giver.

A kind gesture can reach a wound that only compassion can heal.
Steve Maraboli

My friends were out to dinner. It was Friday night and they had survived a long exhausting week of business travel and juggling parental duties. The restaurant was crowded and noisy and after placing their order they had settled in with a cool beverage and prepared to share all the news of the week. Their ten-year-old daughter suddenly piped up with the comment, "That lady looks like Nanna. Do you think she is visiting from heaven?"

The elderly woman sat at a small table eating while absorbed in a book. She did indeed look startlingly like "Nanna." The woman seemed quite content and not the slightest bit lonely, so my friends didn't want to disturb her. Instead, they asked the waiter to add her check to their bill but not to tell her which of the patrons had paid for her dinner. The evening was spent talking about all the wonderful memories of Nanna and my friends went home happy and relaxed and feeling like they had indeed been visited by their much-loved mother and grandmother.

They could have invited the woman to join them, but the noisy restaurant would have made conversation difficult and the woman seemed genuinely happy in her own space and activities. They also didn't want the woman to feel indebted to them. Only the waiter knew who made the generous gift: my friends weren't looking for accolades. They just wanted to show kindness to someone who had reminded them of some wonderful memories.

Action:

Pay a toll for the person behind you or pick up the tab for a senior citizen in the grocery store or restaurant just because you can.

Prayer:

Thank You, Lord, for the reminders of those we have loved and have gone home to You. Help me to be generous and anonymous. Amen.

OCTOBER 4

Broken
BY MYRA BIERNAT WELLS

2 Corinthians 2:10

That is why, for Christ's sake, I delight in weakness, in insults, in hardships, in persecutions, in difficulties. For when I am weak, then I am strong.

When I had only been married a couple of weeks, I tearfully sat down with my husband to explain a problem to him. I choked out only three sentences before he started telling me how to fix the problem. I started up again, sobbing about my difficulty, when he interrupted again with suggested solutions. Finally, desperate to be heard, I told him, "I don't want you to fix the problem. I want just want you to listen to me!"

I've learned throughout the years my husband is a fixer. If something is broken, he'll find a way to repair it. I'm amazed sometimes at how he figures out creative ways to mend mechanical breakdowns.

Watching him repair things reminds me of how God brings His healing to us. God loves broken. His light shines best through the broken places in our lives. While we are frantically trying to fix those damaged parts of ourselves, He asks us to stop, be still, rest in Him and let Him fill each wounded, broken part of our lives with His healing grace, love and forgiveness. And the amazing part of it is that if we do, He makes us stronger than we ever thought we could be.

Where can God work the most in us? In those broken places we cannot repair on our own. But be encouraged! Because of those shattered places, He allows us to bring joy into the lives of others who are also broken.

So, today embrace the pain in your life. Celebrate the broken places. Come crying and wailing from the pain but surrender your troubles to God and let Him heal them for your good and His glory.

Action:
Read Psalm 40:1-3: "I waited patiently for the LORD. He turned to me and heard my cry. He lifted me out of the slimy pit, out of the mud and mire. He set my feet on a rock and gave me a firm place to stand. He put a new song in my mouth; a hymn of praise to our God." Now circle all the action words in these verses. What does God say He will do? Are you willing to let Him be God in your life?

Prayer:
Father, I come to You broken, shattered and in desperate need. I come to You in complete surrender. Please heal my brokenness and show me Your way. In Jesus' name. Amen.

OCTOBER 5

Reiza
BY SHERRI GALLAGHER

Psalm 118:21-23

I will give you thanks, for you answered me; you have become my salvation. The stone the builders rejected has become the cornerstone; the LORD has done this, and it is marvelousin our eyes.

Everyone fears rejection. **Derek Jeter**

Reiza is a pretty, little, German Shepherd who greets everyone with kisses, a wagging tail, and a posture begging you to be kind. Considering the level of rejection she has faced in the three short years of her life, her abundant love sometimes makes me want to weep.

She was born of world class competitive parents, but when tested as a puppy it was determined that Reiza just didn't have what it takes to compete in IPO (Internationale Prüfungs-Ordnung) which is a three part sport where the dog must perform in tracking, obedience and protection. It wasn't that she wouldn't be competitive on a world stage; she wouldn't even do well in a backyard competition. She was sold as a pet—the biggest rejection in the IPO world for a puppy.

Reiza might have been happy with her new owner, but the owner's husband enjoyed intimidating the sweet little puppy and would drive her away. Whimpering, Reiza was rejected again.

The breeder took the puppy back and she languished in a kennel for months. She was clean, well-fed, and exercised but no one had time to love her. And Reiza was a bundle of love that wanted cuddles and pets and focused attention.

On a visit to the breeder, I fell in love with her so Reiza ended up in my SUV. I had been planning on retiring from search and rescue but Reiza changed all that. Search and rescue were a perfect fit for this dog. It took almost a year for Reiza to come out of her shell but when she did the results were inspiring. She had the work ethic, physical ability, and the natural gentleness to be a great success at wilderness search and rescue.

Every time we go out to train, she amazes me, and I can't help but think of Psalm 118:22, "The stone that the builders rejected has become the chief cornerstone." Reiza is a foundation stone the search team can build on.

There have been times in my life where I have desperately wanted something; a position on a FEMA team, a book on the best sellers list, a vice-president position in a corporation. None of them happened. I was rejected. Or was I? Did God want me to follow a different path? The FEMA team position would have put a strain on meeting all my other obligations and would have put my dog's life at risk. Being an acclaimed author would be nice, but knowing my book led a woman to seek a church home is much more important. Having a corner office with an impressive title would have meant missing out on important events with my family. In each case, like Reiza, it wasn't the right fit or the right place for me. Just like retiring from search and rescue wasn't right for me after all.

Action:

When you feel "rejected" stop, tell yourself you have actually been "selected" for something much more important to God. Search for all the opportunities you now have available.

Prayer:
Heavenly Father, we weep in anguish when cherished dreams fail to come true. Comfort us and guide us so we can find the path You dream for us. Amen.

OCTOBER 6

The Word of God
BY SHERRI GALLAGHER

Matthew 4:4

Jesus answered, "It is written: 'Man shall not live on bread alone, but on every word that comes from the mouth of God.'

The words that enlighten the soul are more precious than jewels.
Hazrat Inayat Khan

I watched a news program about orphaned boys in Sudan who walked for years until they reached a refugee camp in Kenya. They were predominantly Christian, and their villages were attacked by Islamic forces. Their families were murdered. The boys were outside the village tending the herds and were able to flee, but their journey was horrific. Many died of starvation and thirst. After a journey of a thousand miles they arrived in the refugee camp, but they didn't come empty handed. They carried books. They carried Bibles. One of the boys, Abraham Nial, now an adult, became an ordained minister. He still carries that same Bible. Abraham eventually returned to Africa and continues to feed his flock's hunger for the word of God.

I have been in some remote places where the weight of my pack mattered, and I carried what I needed to survive. I always make sure to pack the ten essentials; map, compass, sunglasses and sunscreen, extra clothing, flashlight, first-aid supplies, firestarter, matches, knife, food. After hearing this story, packing my pocket New Testament has added meaning. If these boys understood and suffered so much and yet still carried Bibles with them, I can certainly make the ten essentials, eleven, and include a Bible.

Action:
If possible, donate to an organization that provides Bibles to prisons or countries where they are scarce. I donate to www.americanbible.org

Prayer:
God in heaven, thank You for this country where households have multiple Bibles and daily opportunities to read your Word. Help me to be generous and provide the bread of life to others who are not as fortunate. Amen.

OCTOBER 7

Born to Be Wild
BY MYRA BIERNAT WELLS

Hebrews 12:1

Let us also lay aside every weight and sin which clings so closely, and let us run with endurance the race that is set before us.

My husband and I love visiting lighthouses. Their lone outpost and their strength against the ravages of the sea attract us. We knew when we visited Kauai, we'd be stopping at the Kilauea Lighthouse. What makes the lighthouse so amazing isn't that it was built in 1913 with the largest lens of its kind. Nor that it helped guide ships traveling to and from the Orient. What makes it so spectacular is that the lighthouse sits on a small finger of land jutting into the serene Pacific Ocean. The views are amazing.

The coastal inlet formed beside it provides a safe haven for the endangered Hawaiian monk seal, ('Illio-holo-i-ka-uaua), the green sea turtle (Honu) and the humpback whale (Kohola). During our visit, for hours we watched the antics of both the humpback whales and a pod of playful dolphins.

It was life-changing to see these animals up close, but still in their natural habitat. Their wildness reminded me that I was also born to be wild. Wild for Jesus. Wild with His purpose for me. Wildly surrendered to the will of God. Wildly obedient to His Commands. Wildly led by the power of the Holy Spirit at work within me.

Many times in my life I was so focused on my limitations, distractions and losses that I failed to see God's possibilities for my life. But standing on that volcanic cliff, leaning against the railing with the wind whipping through my hair while watching God's magnificent creativity in the azure waters below reminded me that to live the life I was born to live, my vision must be cast far beyond my restrictions and obstacles. It must be fixed on the One who designed us to worship with wild abandon…to live with wild freedom.

Action:
Think about a wild place you have visited. What did it teach you about the character of God? How can you live more wildly surrendered to Him?

Prayer:
Father, thank You for the wildness of the ocean and its creatures. Your love is wild, untamable and unstoppable. Thank You for promising redemption and renewal to all who call on You. Be my vision, Lord. Empower me to live in the wild freedom of Your grace and in the center of Your plan. In Your precious Son's name. Amen.

OCTOBER 8

Oops!
BY SHERRI GALLAGHER

Luke 8:4-8

You have to accept the plan and realize that if you slip, and you might, that you can't use that as a reason to give up or stop. **Jennifer Hudson**

My dog, Orex came from a good-sized litter of around eight puppies. The litter was bred to be champion working dogs. All the puppies had good focus and attention and a deep love of work. They will be five years old in September. Of the eight handlers who bought the puppies, I was the only one who was not a professional dog handler and competitor.

Orex was not the best of the puppies; his brother Ori was much more impressive. Early on Ori's handler made significantly better progress than Orex and I. They blossomed while we struggled. My inexperience, worry and fears caused setbacks they didn't run into. There were times I felt like giving up. My efforts were never going to see the kind of fruition developing in the other littermates. Still, we plodded along following the plan to prepare Orex for competition on a national level. Along the way, the other handlers dropped out of training. Ori became dog aggressive and it was easier to give up than to try and fix the problem. Each of the littermates or handlers hit a point of failure. Rather than accept the failure and find a way through, they gave up.

Looking at the progress of this litter reminds me of the parable of the sower. Some seeds fell on the path and were eaten by birds. Some of the seeds fell on rocks and withered from lack of moisture. Some fell into thorns and were choked out, but a few fell into good soil and produced a hundred fold. While I am not sure Orex and I rate the hundred fold, we are progressing and will eventually reach the goal.

Isn't this what our spiritual life is like? We are excited and focused to start. We dream of being leaders and teachers and active members of the church, making huge contributions. Then we come up against difficulties, a decision we disagree with, or an overbearing member of a committee who makes us feel our contributions are valueless. Some of us walk away and talk about our poor experience with organized religion. A few find a way to stay and day after day make steady contributions which make all the difference in the success of our church.

Action:
When things don't go as planned, make a new plan to reach the same goal.

OCTOBER 9

Obedience
BY SHERRI GALLAGHER

John 14:15-27

Obedience to God is the pathway to the life you really want to live. **Joyce Meyer**

I drill with my dogs on obedience almost every day. Before they get their dinners, they must sit quietly beside their bowls and on command turn away from their food and come to my side. Only then do I release them to eat. If I am walking to the kitchen and planning on giving them a treat, they must walk beside me watching my face until I free them instead of rushing back and forth to the treat jar and risking injuring themselves or me.

Orex is the best of the dogs at obedience and it only took four years. Time and again he has proven that he will obey my commands, even when it is so very counter to his desires. He does this because he knows a greater reward is coming if he follows my commands. I only wish I could be as obedient to God in as short a time as my dog has become obedient to me. God promised me a great reward if I follow His commandments, much greater than anything I could ever give my dog. But I still have trouble following His commandments.

God understood our human nature is to sin and disobey His commandments. To help us he promised the Holy Spirit would come and teach us and remind us of all Jesus taught us (John 14:26). If we listen and work to obey, we are promised a peace that is beyond this world, a peace that will take away trouble and fear (verse 27).

It isn't all up to the Holy Spirit though. We still have free will and we need to decide to follow God's way even when it means giving up something we really want. Just like Orex walking away from his dinner, we must learn to listen and trust in God and obey.

Action:
Consider when you block out God's voice for short term pleasure. Remind yourself of all that is promised if you obey His commandments

Prayer:
Heavenly Father, help my disobedient self to be more obedient. Amen.

OCTOBER 10

Amazed!
BY MYRA BIERNAT WELLS

Habakkuk 1:5

Look among the nations and watch. Be amazed and astonished. I am going to do something in your days that you would not believe even if it were reported to you.
(GW)

I don't often get lost, partly because of an inbred sense of direction, but I also pay attention. I look for the landmarks – the street signs, the buildings alongside the road, the curve of the highway. Even with a GPS in my car, I never use it more than once to get to the same destination. And I don't even use it on the return trip. I might not be able to tell you the names of the streets I took, but I always find my way home.

I believe as a child of God the only way to spend your life is to pay attention to the world. It's fallen; it's imperfect. There are parts of it that are downright ugly. But even in the ugliest, slimiest, most putrid smelling place, there is God. He showers His miracles everywhere on this earth.

He doesn't put up a sign to say, "Watch this." I believe that would take away the joy of us finding His daily miracles. But every morning, He whispers to us, "Pay attention and prepare to be amazed."

The cynical side of our nature, of the world, wants to speak always of the darkness, the harshness, the hurt of living. Yes, it is a shattered world, but in its brokenness, in its shadows, the world also reveals the most profound imagination of our Creator.

It is easy for us to only see the dark, but we are children of the Light. That means we should seek the Light in everything. This is easy when we are youngsters. We find joy in the silliest things. Remember water sprinklers, catching snowflakes on your tongue, freezing Kool-Aid in ice trays, looking for out of state license plates on a long road trip?

Then we grow into adulthood and we lose a part of ourselves. The extraordinary fades into the ordinary. It becomes too easy to exist rather than to live fully, freely, openly. But God is still whispering over our days, "Pay attention and prepare to be amazed."

God's love song is all about us as we walk through life. See the color of your coworker's eyes. Hear the melody of the cars on the road. Taste the sweetness of watermelon. Look around you, for you are surrounded every day by His loving creativity.

Pay attention to the wind in the dark, the trees slapping against the house, the dog barking in the distance. Pay attention to the world, both the prickly wrong parts of it and the exquisitely beautiful parts of it. Drink it all in until you see His love peeking through both the darkest storms and the delicate glow of morning's light. If you stare at it long enough, you'll develop a longing for Home – the place where you will be welcome by God.

Today, feel His nearness; His relevance to you. If you watch the landmarks our Creator has so graciously put along our path, your heart will beat faster with a longing for heaven. Watch the pointers leading you gently to the One who is devoted to you.

Pay attention and be amazed!

Action:

For a week, each day write down at least 3 amazing things God brought into your life.

Prayer:

Father, please continue to show up in our days, in surprising ways, unexpected ways. Help us to see You even in the everyday parts of our lives. Draw us closer to You through Your creativity and love. In Your precious Son's name. Amen.

OCTOBER 11

The Applesauce Tree
BY SHERRI GALLAGHER

Exodus 23:10-11

Plant and harvest your crops for six years but let the land be renewed and lie uncultivated during the seventh year. Then let the poor among you harvest whatever grows on its own. Leave the rest for wild animals to eat. The same applies to your vineyards and olive groves.

Care less for your harvest than for how it is shared and your life will have meaning and your heart will have peace. **Kent Nerburn**

Our house was built in 1941 and there are several apple trees on the property that if not planted by the original owner have resulted from the early farmer's efforts. The fruit is different than I see in the stores. They appear to be ancient strains and typically yield fruit every other year. The fruit from one tree in particular makes the best applesauce. Being an old tree, it is tall and branchy and picking the apples is not an easy task, so I have resorted to waiting for the apples to drop on the ground instead. Each morning during harvest season I go out with a basket and collect the bright red fruit from the ground. When I have a full basket, I leave the rest to feed the bees and the deer and other wildlife in the area.

I used to feel wasteful for doing that. I could picture the disappointed expression on the face of the farmer's wife as I left this food in the field. However, after finding the first year's harvest yielded all the applesauce we could want until the tree bore fruit again, I decided to continue my wasteful practice. Imagine my joy when I read in Exodus that I was supposed to leave some of my apples for the wild creatures.

I came to realize God cares about every creature big and small. He knows the bees and deer need those apples just as much as I do, and He gave humans a plan to share the harvest. But where else can I carry this lesson in my life? One way is through writing. While my book has not been a best seller, it has led people back to a relationship with God, and that is, indeed, a great harvest.

Action:

Think of a way you can share the gifts God gave you with others. Are you good with your hands? Make a gift for the Sunday school rooms or write some of your experiences and memories so future generations will know what it was like and share the harvest of your lifetime of learning.

Prayer:

Heavenly Father, thank You for all the gifts we have received. Show us how to share joyfully with others that which You have given to us. Amen.

OCTOBER 12 - COLUMBUS DAY

Expect the Unexpected
BY MYRA BIERNAT WELLS

Exodus 15:12

The Lord is my strength and my defense.

History has no record of exactly what Columbus thought when he reached land in the early morning of October 12, 1492. He recorded some information in his journal, but throughout his entire life, Columbus maintained that the lands he explored were actually part of the Asian continent.

One thing is certain, though, Columbus faced huge challenges in order to sail to the New World. He needed to garner financial support. He had to prepare for a long voyage. He had to convince experienced sailors to join him at a time when the world believed you could sail to the end of the earth. Where you would then fall off! Still, he persevered.

While today we know we won't sail off a flat earth, we all face challenges that often keep us stuck instead of living a grand adventure. So many of us feel fearful and unprepared, but here's a great secret: No one is truly perfectly prepared. Everyone has giants to overcome in order to move forward.

Each one of us has been created by a holy God, who loves us so much that He designed us on purpose and with a purpose. When we stick to His purposes for us, God performs miracles through us and for us. We can all live the rich, abundant Christian life that God promises.

The world is full of people who can spend hours chatting your ear off with the reasons why they are not living their dream. But let's not be one of those people. Let's choose together to do something today to take one tiny step forward on our dreams. I don't know what that means for you – maybe an hour of daydreaming, maybe making a phone call to someone that can help you, maybe it is just as simple as sharing your dream with someone else.

No one lives out an exciting calling without plunging forward at some point just like Columbus – full of fear, full of uncertainty and against all odds. Let's not long to live our dreams. Let's boldly move towards making them a reality.

Action:
Write down in a few sentences what dream, project or vision you feel called to complete during this season in your life. What is one tangible step you can make to advance that? Do it today!

Prayer:
God, help me not define myself by the giants in my life. Cover me with Your love and with Your strength. Let me move forward towards the purpose You gave me. Amen.

OCTOBER 13

The Game Changer
BY MYRA WELLS BIERNAT

Psalm 142:5

Then I pray to you, O Lord. I say, "You are my place of refuge. You are all I really want in life." (NLT)

We spend many hours grasping at things to make us strong, cure our struggles with habits and hang-ups, help us lead more productive lives. Our human desire is to feel accepted and loved and we think fixing ourselves will lead to the life we've always wanted. But our good God knows a better way.

I found myself wanting to fix me after tiring of the roller coaster ride of Christian life: wondering if my decisions gave God glory, when my desire for community made me insecure, when my actions weren't loving - when I thought

I'd never be the woman God wanted me to be. In that season, I searched for solutions, but discovered when I felt God close, my greatest spiritual growth occurred.

God more than anyone or anything else in our lives is a game changer. We can try to fix ourselves, but that is doing it the human way with no lasting changes. But when we dive into God, focus on Him more intently, things of our flesh we have tried to change just naturally fall away. Our desire for Him transforms everything. In Him, we have a "hope that does not disappoint" (Romans 5:5, NASB). That means we will always be disenchanted in our efforts but centering on Him to change us is a life guarantee.

It requires a daily focus. It means meeting Him in prayer and in Bible reading: pursuing Him the way He pursues us. But living without wanting God is the harder life, which most of us have already tried. It is always in our place of lack our heart screams loudest for God. And He hears and powerfully brings change.

Action:
Roller coasters are fun at an amusement park, but not in life. We quickly tire of all the ups and downs. Get out a piece of paper and write down all the ways you've tried to fix yourself throughout the years. Now write down how wanting God would change that. Is it worth doing it His way versus yours?

Prayer:
Father, thank You for being the Game Changer of my life. You know better than anyone how I try to fix myself and it never works. I need You, God. Move me towards You. In Jesus' name. Amen.

OCTOBER 14

Illumination
BY SHERRI GALLAGHER

Matthew 5:14-16

You are the light of the world. A town built on a hill cannot be hidden. Neither do people light a lamp and put it under a bowl. Instead they put it on its stand, and it gives light to everyone in the house. In the same way, let your light shine before others, that they may see your good deeds and glorify your Father in heaven.

Think of yourself as an incandescent power, illuminated and perhaps forever talked to by God and his messengers. **Brenda Ueland**

There is a story floating around in cyberspace about a professor who doubted the existence of God. He challenged his students for a whole semester to bring him proof that God existed. At first students tried to prove that God existed, but the professor was so good at arguing none could win.

At the end of the semester the professor ordered anyone who still believed in God to stand up. The professor would then berate the person as a fool. As proof God did not exist the professor would demand that God prove His existence by preventing the professor from throwing a piece of chalk to the floor and smashing it.

A boy who was a Christian had to take the course and each morning he prayed for the strength to stand at the end of the semester. There were 300 students and he was the only one who stood. The professor called him a fool and gave his demand of God about the chalk. Suddenly the chalk slipped from his fingers rolled down his suit and rolled across the floor unbroken. The professor blanched and ran from the classroom. Then the student walked to the front of the room and shared his witness of Jesus Christ for the remainder of the class period.

Whether the story is true or not doesn't really matter. The principle is the same as Matthew 5:16, "let your light shine before others, so that they may see your good works and give glory to your Father in heaven." When we stand for our beliefs, when we do not waver, but smile and give glory to God for all that we have, we can change the world.

Action:
Each day that you sign onto social media, post a positive story that brings God to life for others.

Prayer:
Father, give us the strength to shine Your light into the darkness of this world. Amen.

OCTOBER 15

Is God Dead?
BY SHERRI GALLAGHER

Exodus 20:2-3

I am the LORD your God, who brought you out of Egypt, out of the land of slavery. You shall have no other gods before me.

What can you say about a society that says God is dead and Elvis is alive?
Irv Kupcinet

Why when things don't work just the way we want, do we decide God isn't listening and turn to other gods? We tell ourselves, "If I make more money everything will be fine;" "If I can just get married, it will be happily ever after;" "If I move or get that job or...?" We act like two-year olds, stomping our feet and crying to demand the toy we must have now. If our loving Parent still says, "no" we stomp off throwing a crying fit screaming, "you don't love me!" and refuse to be engaged. We turn our back on God and try to do things our way.

Want and desire and selfishness make us turn away from God. In the 1960's protestors carried signs quoting Alfred Nietzsche saying, "God is Dead." Nietzsche philosophized mankind had moved away from faith and spiritualism toward rationalism and science. Nietzsche proposed this was an improvement and could eliminate guilt and "repressive Christian morality."

Following Nietzsche's plan, we have turned from God and like to think we are god, shaping the world just how we want it, but are we pleased with the results of our efforts? We have poisoned the planet, endangering all living creatures with our pursuit of material goods. Wars, famine and disease are rampant, we live in silent fear of future disasters. People slaughter the helpless in the name of their god until we reluctantly send our children as sacrifices, to slow but not stop the murder, and then claim God is at fault and must be eliminated from our lives.

It is a dangerous cycle that will take us further and further away from the one sure course that can break the devastation and disaster we have made. We must turn to God and set Him before all other desires. He will see to our needs but not necessarily our wants. If we put Him first and include what He wants in our decision making the world will be a better place.

Action:
Before making a decision, pray for guidance and ask yourself, "What would Jesus want me to do?"

Prayer:
Loving God, we have made a real mess of things putting other gods before You. Forgive us. Guide us. We are in Your Hands. Help us to be Your hands in this world of unbelief. Amen.

OCTOBER 16

When Your Heart Needs Healing
BY MYRA WELLS BIERNAT

Isaiah 40:31

Those who hope in the Lord will renew their strength.

The cough would not subside. No matter what the doctors prescribed, the hacking persisted. Finally, a doctor decided to take an x-ray and discovered a possible problem with my heart which led to more medical tests. I prayed, along with my close family and friends, for my heart to be healed. One night, while journaling, I realized that's what I should be praying for all the time: to have a heart (the strength, the guts, the determination) fixed on healing. To press through to a place of wellness and strength: spiritually, emotionally and psychologically. To not back down from the resistance before me in light of the rewards that awaits me. To run the race of faith well!

After we go through initial heart repairs with Jesus, many of us still find ourselves wounded believers. Close to whole, but still broken knowing He loves us, but not feeling it; believing He has a plan for us, but tired of waiting for it; struggling with anxiety because we're scared to trust God. We want healing but won't or don't know how to move forward in the direction of the Healer who will bring us complete wholeness.

This is hard stuff. I struggle with it. We all do. Ultimately, each of us is a work in progress. Our challenges and failures should be acknowledged and confessed. But our faith that God can heal our wounds must be greater.

I lift up prayers of thanksgiving to the one true God who loves, sees, hears, purifies, comforts, protects, restores and redeems all those who cry out to Him. He is the Great Surgeon who rushes to us in the emergency rooms of life and takes us into the healing power of His presence. The One who knows how to care for each wound, burden and bruise.

Press through barriers in the strength and grace of Jesus. His plan is good. His faithfulness is unwavering. His presence is accessible 24/7. Move in His direction and give Him the burdens of your heart. Pray. Trust. Believe.

Action:

Read Hebrews 10:19-39. Journal any verses you would like to memorize or remember. Consider what heart healing would look like for you.

Prayer:

Lord, please move in my heart and life today so that I can move forward in faith as I hold tightly to the hope I have in Christ. In Jesus' name. Amen.

OCTOBER 17

Moving On Up
BY SHERRI GALLAGHER

Exodus 20:17

You shall not covet your neighbor's house. You shall not covet your neighbor's wife, or his male or female servant, his ox or donkey, or anything that belongs to your neighbor.

Let your desires be ruled by reason. **Cicero**

We have an old house that needs a lot of work. It is small by most of our contemporary standards. It does not have grand two-story spaces, giant rooms or en suites for every bedroom. It is clean, warm and fits our lifestyle. We have lived here for over 25 years.

When we renovated the dining room, we invested in a lovely, delicate, crystal chandelier. Acquaintances visited a short time later and asked if when we moved up, were we going to take the chandelier with us? We asked why they thought we would move. They believed that a house was an important status item and as soon as it was possible, people were expected to move to a bigger, fancier house.

Status is important in our society. If you are important, you are expected to live in a mansion. If you want people to think you are important, then you buy a mansion but at what cost? Is it worth the stress and sleepless nights to buy something that can barely be afforded?

Exodus 20:17 tells us not to covet our neighbor's house or belongings. God isn't worried about us overextending our financial position; He is trying to guide us to be comfortable with what we have. Read through Paul's writings. When he had plenty, he was happy and when he had little, he was happy. Paul did not covet what his neighbor had. Paul was focused on God and as a result he was happy in any circumstance.

Action:
With the next purchase you make, consider if it will support what is important to you or if is a status item.

Prayer:
Lord God, help me to be happy no matter my circumstances. Amen.

OCTOBER 18

No Signal
BY SHERRI GALLAGHER

Exodus 20:4-6

You shall not make for yourself an idol, whether in the form of anything that is in heaven above, or that is on the earth beneath, or that is in the water under the earth. You shall not bow down to them or worship them: for I the Lord your God am a jealous God, punishing children for the iniquity of parents, to the third and the fourth generation of those who reject me, but showing steadfast love to the thousandth generation of those who love me and keep my commandments.

Sometimes it seems like God is difficult to find and impossibly far away. We get so caught up in our small daily duties and irritations that they become the only things we can focus on. What we forget is that God's love and beauty are all around us, every day, if only we would take the time to look up and see them. **Matthias**

My house was built shortly before WWII. The interior walls are plaster and the lathe that holds it in place is made of a heavy metal mesh. It is a strong, sturdy house that is also a cell phone nightmare. No carrier can get through that lathe so anyone with a mobile phone often comments on having no signal. While this can be frustrating when handling business, it is a blessing when I have time off. No signal means no business calls after hours or during family time. It gives me a chance to wind down and focus on what is important.

All that electronic noise can distract me from studying God. If I sit at my desk while doing my Bible study, I catch myself reaching to open my e-mail or respond to LinkedIn posts. It is so easy to be sidetracked and take care of business instead of spending time with the One who is important, God. But business is another form of idolatry. While I do not worship my computer and cell phone, at times I have a strong desire to turn them into electronic scrap - turning to them before spending time with God really is a form of putting Him in second place. That is the same as breaking the second commandment.

Thanks to my sturdy, metal lined house, it is easier for me than most people to tune out the world. When I do, God's signal comes through loud and clear no matter what material is in the walls of my house.

Action:
This Sunday turn off your cell phone and don't touch other electronic devices. Instead, carve out some time to read and study the Bible.

OCTOBER 19

The Best-Known Love Story
BY MYRA BIERNAT WELLS

Psalm 59:7

You are my strength, I sing praise to you; you, God, are my fortress, my God on whom I can rely.

"As God is my witness, I will never go hungry again!" And with those words, Scarlett O'Hara, my favorite movie heroine, shows real backbone by creating a new life for herself. As much as I love her courage and strength, I cringe at her fatal flaw. All through the movie, Rhett Butler works to win her heart. All Scarlett thinks about is milquetoast Ashley Wilkes. Some-times, I just want to rise from my seat and slap some sense in her.

So, I totally agree with Rhett, when at the end of the movie, he walks away in frustration. "I feel sorry for you, Scarlett," he declares. "You are throwing away love with both hands and grabbing for that which will never love you."

Oh Scarlett, didn't you see how much Rhett really loved you? That he'd move heaven and earth to please you – if you would let him? That despite your mistakes and indifference, his heart was yours for the taking? Why pursue someone who couldn't make you happy?

Yet, often I'm like Scarlett. Not in her ability to make things happen; to stand as an intense, confident woman in the face of adversity. No, instead I ignore the only One who can make me truly happy. My fickleness is probably why Jesus continues to romance me daily. Why he puts such wonderful things in my path every day to make me stop in breathless wonder at His goodness, His power. And why everything else pales in the shadow of the Lover of My Soul.

At the end of the movie, Scarlett realizes her love for Rhett and runs home to tell him. But it is too late. I'm thankful then that Jesus will never throw up His hands and walk away! "Here I am," He says. "I stand at the door and knock" Revelation 3:20. All we need to do is run to Him! Settle in His love, safe in His protection. For Christ's love is unmatched and inexhaustible, and He is waiting to lavish on you, His beloved.

Has there ever been anything in this world that has completely satisfied you? Write down some of the things that keep you from fully embracing the love of God.

Prayer:
Jesus, forgive me for being enticed by people, possessions, religion, work and all the other things that steal my attention away from You. You love me perfectly and completely. I open the door of my heart to You. I welcome You into my soul. Thank you for romancing me every day. Thank you for continuing to pursue my fickle heart. Amen.

OCTOBER 20

Rest
BY SHERRI GALLAGHER

Exodus 20:8-11

Take rest; a field that has rested gives a bountiful crop. **Ovid**

Do you think God needed to rest on the seventh day of creation or was He setting an example for us to follow? Study after study has found people who take regular time away from work are happier, healthier, and more productive. Billions have been spent doing studies only to learn what God told us, rest one day in seven.

But God didn't just say "rest." He said keep the day holy. The day is consecrated to the Lord and the first focus shouldn't be on tailgating or the big game but on God. It is time to turn off, tune out, and put God first. It is a physical action that says we worship God before all others. It is time to study the Bible and discuss it in fellowship. It is time to go to a place of worship and put Him first. It is a time to commune with nature and see God's hand at work in the world.

When I was a child, no one would schedule sporting events or open a store on Sundays. Only emergency and health care workers rotated through the Sabbath shifts. As I watched my son grow up, the stores and shops were open and people had to work on the day designated for the Lord, but in general it was still a time for family and God. Now as I look around, families are told that their children will be playing sports on Sunday and that must take precedence over attending church. If you want your child to excel, they must give up their time with God.

Is that really what we want to teach our children? Are we setting the example that God is not as important as sports or performing artistically by what we are doing or rather not doing - going to church?

Action:
Set family traditions that make Sunday a time to honor and worship God.

OCTOBER 21

Talk to God
BY SHERRI GALLAGHER

Genesis 18:16-33

You talk to God, you're religious. God talks to you, you're psychotic.
Doris Egan

How does God talk to you? In Genesis 18 Abraham carries on quite a conversation with God as Abraham tries to dissuade God from destroying Sodom. In Acts 9, Saul/Paul and the men with him hear the voice of Jesus. These people had a direct conversation, a verbal give and take, with God. But did God stop communicating with us once the Bible was written?

Sometimes God sends an angel as a messenger instead. Zachariah, the father of John the Baptist was given a message from God by an angel; so was Mary, our Savior's mother. I did a keyword search and found there were 329 instances of the word "angel" being used in the New Revised Standard Version of the Bible. Clearly, angels are tools God used frequently. Does He still send us angels?

If you tell people you hear God's voice in your head, they either dismiss you as a crackpot or report you as mentally unstable to the police. Personally, I have never heard God's voice in my head giving me directions when I get lost, no matter how much I wish He gave turn by turn instructions. Life would be so much easier if God would just call my cell and say, "This is what I want you to do." Since that doesn't happen, does that mean God doesn't care about me?

Our church uses the phrase "God Is Still Speaking." God is with us. He does guide us if we are willing to accept His answers, even the answers we don't like. He works through us as we help others in the community and the world. God does care deeply about us and He is still involved in our lives, if we will let Him.

I have been struck with inspiration at times that I am quite sure were divine guidance. It required me to still my mind. I had to let go of my worries and "to do" lists and sit quietly convincing myself that I had given it over to God. As a great peace filled me inspiration came as a quiet simple thought.

At other times when a thorny problem arises, I thumb rather idly through my Bible, or listen to a sermon or radio program or talk to a random friend. Over and over again I have ended up with a passage which seems perfectly tailored to address my concern or received just the right comment to guide my steps.

God is still here. God still cares. God still speaks to us through our Bibles and our church family. We just need to listen carefully and be willing to accept what we hear.

Action:

Find a little time today to sit quietly without distractions and thumb through your Bible.

Prayer:

Lord God in heaven, help me to listen, help me to hear Your voice amid the clamoring demands I face. Amen.

OCTOBER 22

First Fruits
BY SHERRI GALLAGHER

Mark 12:13-17

The bills piled up on my desk. I was close to maxing out my line of credit. I wouldn't have enough to pay everyone. I moved my offering envelope to the top of the pile and wrote that check first. A short time later a FedEx worker knocked on my back door. I signed for the envelope and yanked the string to open it. Out fell a check I'd been owed for years. It was enough to pay all my bills and get my line of credit under control. On this occasion, God provided for my needs.

When we are struggling to make ends meet, one of the easiest things to cut back on is giving. Each person must decide what is right for their situation and family, but remember to render to God what is His when you line up the bills.

Action:

Plan how you can meet your financial commitment to your church.

Prayer:

Giver of all things, You know our needs and our hearts. Bless us so we may give. Amen.

OCTOBER 23
MOTHER-IN-LAW DAY

My Mother-in-law
BY CATHY HARVEY

Ruth 1:16

But Ruth replied, "Don't urge me to leave you or to turn back from you. Where you go I will go, and where you stay I will stay. Your people will be my people and your God my God."

My mother-in-law came down with pneumonia when she was caring for my father-in-law in their home. I went to help as she recovered, but she continued Dad's daily care herself. I always felt so welcomed into my husband's family I had no trouble addressing his parents as Mom and Dad. I wish I had photographed all the tender, sweet moments between the two of them. It would be Dad leaning over the kitchen sink in his muscle shirt, so mom could wash his hair. Mom, sitting at the kitchen table ever so carefully cleaning his hearing aids. After Dad had gotten his shoes on, he would lie flat on his back on the bed with his leg lifted off the bed, so Mom could tie his shoes without having to bend over. Dad would take her hand at every meal and say the blessing with their heads bowed.

I loved watching mom comb his hair every morning after his hair wash and watching the precise way she parted it so gently and to perfection. I would have photographed the little squirts of hairspray glinting in the sunlight coming through the window as he sat in his wheelchair for her final touches. As he looked on, she carefully surveyed his fingers for the daily prick to check his insulin level.

The Kodak moment every day when he turned to tell her something about a story of interest in the local paper and the way she leaned forward to look at him with undivided attention was priceless. They would have a conversation about some current event, as if they were politicians solving world problems, so interested in their conversation with each other. All throughout the day, it was a hundred little moments. He had a cute mischievous grin when he told a joke or made a clever play on words, and oh, how Mom loved to see his excitement when the grandkids brought him home from their sporting events.

Mom did not want to consider assisted living or nursing homes, not if she really didn't have to. She was committed to Dad and to her marriage vows of "...in sickness and in health." She did all she could to help him, and I am so thankful to have witnessed this scene from two who lived simply, humbly, and faithfully toward God and each other, their family and their ministry their entire lives. My mother-in-law's name, by the way, is Ruth.

Action:

Consider what you want to model as an in-law, now or in the future. Is your commitment to your spouse faithful to the wedding vows you took? If not, think of what you can do to change it.

Prayer:

Father, thank You for the family into which I married. Help me show love and appreciation to all my family members in a way that exemplifies You, and especially to my spouse. Amen.

OCTOBER 24
UNITED NATIONS DAY

A Hunger for Knowledge
BY MYRA BIERNAT WELLS

Hosea 4:6

My people are destroyed for the lack of knowledge. (NASB)

Some progress has been made: in 2007, almost 137 million children stepped into classrooms for the first time – 7 million more than in 1999...
UN Millennium Development Goals Report 2009

"Make sure you study diligently, so you can get into a good college." My dad started telling me that when I was in kindergarten – long before I even knew what a good college was. He insisted my siblings and I keep our grades up. He drove us to the library on his days off to pick out books, helped us understand current events by reading the newspaper with us, even made us memorize vocabulary words at the dinner table. Dad was a great champion of education.

I admired my father for that, even when I didn't understand his motivations. Then one day, it all became clear. Decades after my father's death, I wanted to find out the birthplace of his parents. I requested a copy of his military service record, thinking it might be included there. A surprise awaited! I found out instead, he had never graduated from high school. That information explained his love of learning. He wanted to give us a gift he never got: a good education.

Even today, many factors prevent children around the world from attending and completing primary education. These include malnutrition, gender, disabilities, ethnicity, proximity to conflict zones, and inequalities in early childhood care. All children have hopes and dreams, but marginalized children don't have the necessary support for all their hopes and dreams to take shape. That's why one of the goals of the United Nations is to achieve universal primary education.

But it does even more. The organization has four purposes: to keep peace throughout the world, to develop friendly relations among nations; to help nations work together to improve the lives of poor people, to conquer hunger, disease and illiteracy, and to encourage respect for each other's rights and freedoms; and to be a center for harmonizing the actions of nations to achieve these goals.

Action:
God put great variety in this world. Appreciate it even more. Learn about cultures different than your own. Read to your children about them.

Prayer:
God, open our eyes to Your children who are trapped in the slavery of ignorance. Help us build bridges to resources that empower a hunger for knowledge. Amen.

OCTOBER 25

Blue Cards
BY SHERRI GALLAGHER

Acts 8:27-31

The delicate balance of mentoring someone is not creating them in your own image, but giving them the opportunity to create themselves. **Steven Spielberg**

While cleaning out a desk drawer I found my collection of merit badge counselor blue cards. When a Boy Scout works on a merit badge, there are specific activities he must complete. When done, the activities are reviewed by the counselor, and if acceptable, the counselor signs a blue card. When all the activities are completed, the counselor keeps a portion of the blue card and the rest is turned in for Boy Scouts of America (BSA) to issue the merit badge. So far, I have signed off on almost 90 blue cards.

When my son joined BSA, all the parents were encouraged to become merit badge counselors. To be a counselor, the parent needed to demonstrate current skills, experience, and understanding in a subject, and take courses on safety. Optional courses on teaching and motivating were available as well. The key thing for a merit badge counselor to remember was that the Scout was to learn and experience the subject being taught. The counselor was a guide and a mentor. In the Bible passage Philip mentored the Ethiopian, guiding him in the word of the Lord. Philip had a serious advantage over merit badge counselors as the Holy Spirit guided him, but the passage clearly shows Philip was also well versed in the Scriptures.

While BSA has come under fire for its stand on God and homosexual leaders I saw my son learn a great deal as a Scout. He was exposed to many possible careers, learned how to keep a budget, cook, stay physically fit, survive and coexist with nature, and to give back to his community. He was encouraged to become a man of faith and to believe in God. Many people contributed to his growth, and I feel that as long as I am able, I will remain a merit badge counselor.

Action:

Look at your experiences and the people around you. Use your skills to mentor someone.

Prayer:

Heavenly Father, guide us to guide others. Let Your Holy Spirit speak through us in our actions and our deeds. Amen.

OCTOBER 26

Pancakes and Pizza
BY MYRA BIERNAT WELLS

1 Chronicles 16:34

Give thanks to the LORD, for he is good; his love endures forever.

God gave you a gift of 86,400 seconds today. Have you used one to say "thank you?"
William A. Ward

The brunch chefs made my choices difficult with such a mouth-watering, marvelous buffet. Hungry after a two-hour drive, I hustled through the culinary selections looking for something extraordinary amidst all the excellent enticements.

There were eggs and sausages, sandwiches and salads. After surveying the tempting abundance, my childish taste buds decided for me. I'd have my two favorite things – pancakes and pizza – mostly because I could. There aren't too many brunch buffets that feature both, so this was way too much temptation to overcome.

After I made my way to a table and sat down, I thanked God for the bounty in front of me. Thanking God for the opportunity to step away from an epicurean rut seemed so appropriate. I marveled at God's wisdom to scatter gratitude throughout our lives. That's because He knows gratitude gives birth to joy. After all, 1 Thessalonians 5:18 tell us to "give thanks in all circumstances."

Joy is easy when staring at a plate filled with your two most favorite foods. But what about those days when the plate is empty? What do you do when God seems so distant that lifting a prayer of thanks from your lips seems impossible?

That's precisely when giving thanks becomes paramount. The language of a grateful heart raises our soul from the muck of our intense difficulties or even just past the routine, passionless segments of our lives. Gratitude changes the way we see our circumstances. Thanking God for who He is and for what He has done changes our point of view.

When we make the world larger than Him, we feel isolated from God. Gratitude is the way back to Him. Gratitude returns us to intimacy with the One who made the world.

Even if it is nothing earthshaking, but just pancakes and pizza, realizing what God provides changes our perspective and brightens our day. Acknowledging His presence magnifies Him. Thankfulness makes experiencing God easier in the clutter, rush or disappointment of our days. Giving thanks always makes us better able to see, touch, taste and feel the deep goodness of God.

Most importantly thankfulness makes us hungry for even more of Him.

Action:
Make a list of often overlooked blessings in your life.

Prayer:
Dear God, thank You for another day of life. Help me to live my days thanking You for all the goodness You put in my life. Amen.

OCTOBER 27

Fruit Versus Flesh
BY SHERRI GALLAGHER

Galatians 5:16-26

Isn't it good to be alive on a day like this? I pity the people who aren't born yet for missing it. **L.M. Montgomery**

Have you ever felt like what you are doing, right at that moment, really mattered? Maybe it was tying the shoe of a toddler or maybe being sworn into public office. When we serve others, when we are patient with the annoying, kind to the grouchy, generous when no one is watching, faithfully pray to our Savior when we have a million other things that need doing, gentle to those lashing out, walking away when we are angry we are showing the fruit of the Spirit. Each time we consciously do one of these things we should feel a little spurt of joy that we are displaying the works of the Spirit instead of the works of the flesh. God gave us this Spirit to help us be like our brother and Savior Jesus.

Sometimes demonstrating the fruit of the Spirit is easy. Reaching out to comfort a crying child or spending time listening to the stories of an elderly person that bring a portion of history to life. Other times the works of the flesh fight us: helping that crying child for the umpteenth time while you have a pounding headache or listening to a rambling story you have heard several times before as you get later and later for running your errands that must still be done.

When you want to scream in frustration, take a deep breath, hold it for a few seconds and then exhale slowly. As you do, visualize that toddler all grown up heading out to college or military deployment, or think about how you will someday want the wise counsel of this elderly person, but they are no longer there since they have gone home to the Lord. Think about how much you will miss them. Find the strength and ultimately the joy in helping them. Feel the warmth and joy performing these difficult fruits of the spirit bring to you.

Action:

Think of one thing you can do that will brighten someone else's day. Now find a way to do it.

Prayer:

Holy Father, thank You for the Holy Spirit who helps us to demonstrate Your love to those around us. Amen.

OCTOBER 28

The Long Down
BY SHERRI GALLAGHER

2 Timothy 3:14-17

The cure for boredom is curiosity. There is no cure for curiosity.
Dorothy Parker

Practicing the "long down" with my dogs is boring. For the obedience test, the dog will be put in a down stay and the handler will walk fifteen steps away, stand with their back to the dog, and wait while another dog and handler perform their obedience routine. To practice, a handler puts the dog in the down position and builds the time and distance while still having the dog obey. Until the dog can do this for ten minutes it is important not to add distractions. No other dogs or toys or strange happenings should be around, or the dog will learn to get up and wander off and not get the gist of the training.

At first it isn't so bad. I am focused on the dog and watching intently. However, as time goes on and I move to a position with my back to the dog, there isn't much to do. I am required to stand quietly with my back to the dog. Waiting for the minutes to tick by is torturous. Since I always try and work so the dog is successful, there really isn't much to do but wait. Boring! There are so many other things that must be done and I am just standing there.

In a way it reminds me of Bible study. At first, I am so focused and intent to learn. It is new and interesting, and anything can be revealed, much like standing near the dog and watching its body language. As time goes on, the lessons seem repetitious, similar to the point where I can be pretty sure the dog is going to stay put if I am close by or watching. If I recognize the recommended Bible verse, the inclination pops into my head to skip reading it and just get to the devotional instead so I can "get to work on the important stuff". It is the point of boredom, like standing for ten minutes with my back to the dog. Then I must remember what is the "important stuff". My relationship with God is a lot more important than a stack of dirty dishes or a pile of laundry. Paul reminded Timothy that "All scripture is inspired by God and is useful for teaching, for reproof, for correction, and for training in righteousness," (2 Tim 3:16). Skipping the scripture reading of a devotional can mean skipping an important facet of the lesson. Just as I need to take the time to practice standing with my back to the dog to make sure it completely understands the exercise, so too must I take the time to focus and read the scriptures so I can understand the lesson I need to learn.

Action:
Use wasted moments of standing in line or sitting on hold to memorize verses of scripture. A trick is to set them to music - they are easier to memorize.

Prayer:
Lord, forgive me my impatience and keep me focused on You so I spend my time on what is important. Amen.

OCTOBER 29

Listen Up!
BY MYRA BIERNAT WELLS

James 1:19

...Everyone should be quick to listen, slow to speak...

White House legend spins a story about a devilish prank Franklin D. Roosevelt once played. Tired of smiling and giving the usual pleasantries at White House receptions, one day as guests flowed through the reception line, he greeted each one by telling them, "I murdered my grandmother this morning." Most just smiled and when shaking his hand answered, "How lovely!" or "Keep up the good work, Mr. President." No one really listened to what he was saying except one foreign diplomat. When Roosevelt greeted him with "I murdered my grandmother this morning," the diplomat smiled, shook the President's hand and replied, "I'm sure she had it coming!"

God created us with two ears and one mouth for a good reason: to listen twice as much as we speak. This follows Christ's powerful example in the Bible. If anyone knew all the answers, it was Him; yet if you study His conversations, you'll notice they were filled with questions. The gospel of Mark records 67 conversations where Jesus asked 50 questions.

Not only did Christ ask questions, he listened intently to the answers. He queried fisherman about fishing. He discussed financial matters with tax collectors. As a young boy when accidentally left by his parents in the temple, they found him listening to the teachers and asking them questions. Why? Jesus recognized that *people listen to people who listen.*

Often the greatest encouragement we can give someone experiencing pain is a listening heart. Listening doesn't require finding a solution, it simply sends the message, "I'm here for you. I want to understand and share in your pain."

Everyone you meet is fighting a battle unknown to you unless you listen. It validates them. We invite them into our lives and give them our most precious commodity: time. Loving someone like this is an act of sacrificing your own needs for them. Talking is sharing, but listening is caring. Isn't it time we listen up?

Action:

I tend to live James 1:19 backwards – speaking more than I listen. How about you? Think of one person who needs you to be a better listener. Then call them and truly listen to them. Make sure you ask plenty of questions.

Prayer:

Father, I am in awe of Your love. Thank You for being always ready to listen to me. Help me see and reach out to those who are in pain. Help me learn to follow Your example and listen to others the way You listen to me. Amen.

OCTOBER 30

Trust Your Dog
BY SHERRI GALLAGHER

Proverbs 3:5-8

Trust in the Lord with all your heart and lean not on your own understanding; in all your ways acknowledge him, and he will make your paths straight. Do not be wise in your own eyes; fear the Lord and shun evil. This will bring health to your body and nourishment to your bones.

When I'm trusting and being myself...everything in my life reflects this by falling into place easily, often miraculously. **Shakti Gawain**

At a recent search and rescue training a handler sent her dog into a location. The dog came out without indicating a hidden person. The handler was sure there was a subject in the room and sent the dog a second time. The dog repeated its performance. I stopped her before she sent the dog a third time. "Trust your dog," I told her.

She praised the dog and encouraged him to continue searching the building. Ten minutes later his body language changed, and he rushed into a room we all thought was empty to give a clear alert. He had found the subject. Sure enough, the person was there and gave the dog a wonderful round of play.

Every time one of us is sure we know better than the dog, and we find out the dog was right and the person wrong, it reminds me of Proverbs 3:5, "Trust in the Lord with all your heart and lean not on your own understanding;". We get into trouble when we fail to trust in God. Searches are so easy when you believe and follow your dog. Just as life is so much easier when we believe and follow the path God has laid out for us.

Action:

When an activity frustrates you, stop. Take a deep breath, clear your mind and ask for guidance.

Prayer:

Help me to trust in You, Lord. Amen.

OCTOBER 31 - HALLOWEEN

Alternatives to a Haunting Halloween
BY CATHY HARVEY

Philippians 4:8

Fix your thoughts on what is true and honorable and right. Think about things that are pure and lovely and admirable. Think about things that are excellent and worthy of praise. (NLT)

Not much encompassed in Halloween, past or present, comes close to the admonition Paul uses in closing his letter to the Philippians. He encouraged believers to guard their minds and focus on things lovely, excellent, and admirable.

A study of the history of Halloween explains ancient cultures steeped in superstitions formed before the Gospel had made significant influential progress in the church or around the world. Notions of wandering spirits, ghosts and witches, fear of the end of life, bonfires to keep spirits away from homes have no origin with any Biblical holidays God ordained for His people to practice. With the influx of horror and slasher movies in more recent years, Halloween has dissolved into a gruesome and unwholesome affair. Unfortunately, this has also created a lucrative business for party event planners.

As a Christian parent, I struggled to decide what to do with this holiday. My beliefs and practices slowly evolved as I searched for answers and alternatives. Learning of scripture concerning God's perspective on the sin of witchcraft, sorcery, and divinations, I first eliminated anything, especially costumes, related to those evils, as well as anything ghoulish or gory. I explained to my children why I did not want them dressing in such costumes. For one or two years they were happy to be dressed as their Biblical names' sakes: Michael the archangel and Anna the prophetess.

My next step away from the world's haunting practices was participating in our church's alternative Fall Festival which was open to the public. Scheduled earlier in October to separate it from Halloween, families were invited to a gym full of games, candy, and simple prizes. Children were encouraged to dress up as Bible characters or animals while enjoying an indoor celebration of the fall season. This satisfied the children, and parents were relieved to have a wholesome alternative.

I began focusing more on the beauty and blessings of the fall season by decorating my home and enjoying harvest events, while avoiding as much of Halloween as was personally possible. However, there were those trick-or-treaters who came a-knocking. We have handled this in two ways: we either shut our outdoor lights to make it clear we were not a participating candy dispenser, or, if we lived where there was fairly substantial foot traffic, we used this date to present gospel tracts written for children tucked into bulging goodie bags worth the trek to our house.

It was not an "if you can't beat 'em, join 'em" defeatist attitude, but more of a "let's beat the devil at his game and use this opportunity to share Christ with our neighbors!"

Action:

Find a wholesome alternative to this unholy holiday or instigate one in your neighborhood. How can you make it an outreach opportunity?

Prayer:

Heavenly Father, help me know what I believe and give me discernment in how to counter the world's cultural influences that steer me away from, instead of towards, the wisdom and practices found in Your Word, especially during holidays. Amen.

NOVEMBER 1
ALL SAINTS DAY

The Picnic Table
BY SHERRI GALLAGHER

Psalm 149:1-5

As a well-spent day brings happy sleep, so life well used brings happy death.
Leonardo da Vinci

My Dad did not have a lot of respect for religion, but he had an amazingly Christian view of death. You see Dad didn't want a gravestone. He didn't want people standing around crying and being sad. His final wish was that we would put a picnic table on his grave and throw a big party.

Today is All Saints Day, the day we remember the members of our Christian family who have gone home to heaven. We will miss them and, clearly, we all feel their loss. As we read their names, we remember the things they did to help others, their funny habits, and how they made our lives richer, so for us, there is a loss.

But for all these Saints, they had a glorious day in the past year. They went to a place where there is no more pain. Cancer is conquered. Arthritis is gone. Violence is no more. They have won the battle and found a place at the right hand of God. Jesus promised us eternal life and that the Saints who die believing in Him will never be snatched out of his hand (John 10:28-29) and this is where these loved ones have gone.

While we miss them, we have the comfort of knowing someday we will be reunited with them and be able to laugh with joy together, for all eternity, once more. So have a seat at Dad's picnic table and find joy, not sorrow, in this day.

Action:
As you read through the list of saints who have gone home to the Lord, take the time to remember something special about them. Pick one and send a note to their family recording how special they were to you.

Prayer:
Father, God in Heaven, we trust in Your promise and thank You for a love that conquered death. Amen.

NOVEMBER 2

Arguments
BY SHERRI GALLAGHER

Isaiah 59:3-4

For your hands are stained with blood, your fingers with guilt. Your lips have spoken falsely, and your tongue mutters wicked things. No one calls for justice; no one pleads a case with integrity. They rely on empty arguments, they utter lies; they conceive trouble and give birth to evil.

In a heated argument we are apt to lose sight of the truth. **Publilius Syrus**

I have really come to dislike election season. The lies, misinformation, and negativity of the political advertisements is distressing and annoying. While there have always been "dirty tricks" and half-truths, it seems each election cycle they get worse. This year, my son was afraid to put out a political sign in his yard. He supported a candidate that was in the minority in his neighborhood. Signs for the opponent plastered the area. One of his neighbors hung out a sign for the candidate my son liked. That night the sign was ripped up, the neighbor's house was egged and tagged with a swastika. What happened to having the right to a differing opinion?

In reading Isaiah, it feels like history is repeating itself. Isaiah says, "No one cares about being fair and true. Your lawsuits are based on lies; you spend your time plotting evil deeds and doing them" (Isaiah 59:4, TLB). Just like the political advertisements the Israelites would say and do anything to win an argument and prevail. Can we learn from their mistakes? Can we come closer to God? Can we be honest, even when it isn't popular?

Action:
Before going to the polls research the candidates' stands and voting records. Be willing to share what you have learned and try and present all the candidates in a positive light.

Prayer:
Father, forgive me when I am inclined to say or do things that are wrong simply to win an argument. Help me to be fair and just. Amen.

NOVEMBER 3

A Blueprint for Friendship
BY MYRA BIERNAT WELLS

Proverbs 18:12

*A man of many companions may come to ruin, but there is a friend who sticks closer
than a brother.*

The Angel Gabriel delivered some incredible news to young Mary. While still a virgin, she was going to conceive a child by the Holy Spirit and give birth to the Savior of the world. And before Mary even had the opportunity to process that information, the angel told her that her cousin, Elizabeth, long believed to be barren, was pregnant.

Mary was probably sixteen years old when she traveled one hundred miles from her home in Galilee to Judea to spend time with her cousin. Can you imagine the turmoil Mary must have felt traveling all that way? No one will ever believe me; Joseph will probably put me away; what will my parents think?

But when Mary walked into Elizabeth's home, the older woman gave her a blessing: "Blessed are you among women, and blessed is the child you will bear! Why am I so favored that the mother of my Lord should come to me?"

Can you imagine how Elizabeth's words of encouragement were a healing balm to the adolescent? God divinely revealed His plan to Elizabeth and she, in turn, affirmed Mary before the young mother even divulged her news. Mary stayed with Elizabeth for about three months.

From her older cousin, she learned about mothering, probably even helped with the delivery of John. Both women helping the other creates a picture of the refreshing, refueling and renewing power of friendships.

Yet, there is still an empty place – one only Jesus can fill. Allowing Christ's love to saturate us, we move from needy to full, from being a taker to a giver. Friendships are bolder, more comforting, closer with Jesus. God calls us into relationship with others, but only with Him at the center.

Action:
Write a letter to someone who mentored to you. Thank them for being an example and tell them how important their relationship is to you.

Prayer:
Thank You, Lord for the friendships in my life. I pray You will send me a special friend to share my deepest longings, greatest fears and daring dreams. I pray that we will grow closer to You each time we are together. Thank You for the friends

I already have. Teach me to be an encouragement to them. Thank You for calling me Your Friend. In Jesus' name. Amen.

NOVEMBER 4

The Horse Trailer
BY SHERRI GALLAGHER

Mathew 6:31-33

So do not worry, saying, "What shall we eat?" or "What shall we drink?" or "What shall we wear?" For the pagans run after all these things, and your heavenly Father knows that you need them. But seek first his kingdom and his righteousness, and all these things will be given to you as well.

Generosity is giving more than you can, and pride is taking less than you need.
Kahlil Gibran

One of the down sides of being a consultant is not receiving a regular paycheck. While we try to be careful about our spending, money can get tight. I grew up in a household that constantly struggled to make end meet, and I worry when our bank account dips low.

A few months ago, things got tight. We would have to live on credit until a client got around to paying. I sat down to pay bills. Knowing I couldn't cover everything, I moved our offering envelope to the top of the stack and wrote that check first. As I continued to write checks a strange truck pulled into our driveway. A man got out and offered to buy our horse trailer. There was no for sale sign out and the trailer was not near the road. It had sat in our yard for close to 5 years without moving. The cash from that sale kept us going until a check came in. God knew what we needed and provided.

Action:
Make sure your offering envelope is at the top of the stack of bills.
Prayer:
For those without enough money to pay their bills, Lord, I pray You will miraculously provide and show Your glory. Amen.

NOVEMBER 5

Generous
BY SHERRI GALLAGHER

Romans 12:3-8

You must give some time to your fellow men. Even if it's a little thing, do something for others - something for which you get no pay but the privilege of doing it.
Albert Schweitzer

There are a lot of ways to give. One way is to give money. Another is to give things. Still another is to give of your time and talents. One of the members of our writer's group is a very talented harpist. She uses this talent to spread God's word. Some members of our congregation have significant musical talents; others are great bakers, knitters, sewers, or organizers. All these people have one thing in common - they give of their talent freely, expecting nothing in return.

All of these people are living Romans 12:6-8, "We have different gifts, according to the grace given to each of us. If your gift is prophesying, then prophesy in accordance with your faith; if it is serving, then serve; if it is teaching, then teach; if it is encourage, then give encouragement; if it is giving, then give generously; if it is leading do it diligently; if it is to show mercy, do it cheerfully."

It is easy to say, "I have no talent. So-and-so is better at this than I am." But everyone has a skill or gift that they do very well. Even if someone is better at it than you are it does not make your gift less valuable. If you practice your gift you will get even better at it. There is so much work to go around we need everyone to give and participate. Every little bit helps make a church a place of hope and light and help.

Action:
Think about the things you do well and figure out how to use that gift to benefit others.

Prayer:
Thank You, Lord, for the gifts You have blessed us with. Guide us how to best utilize them to serve others. Amen.

NOVEMBER 6

Airport
BY MYRA BIERNAT WELLS

1 Thessalonians 5:11

Therefore, encourage one another and build each other up, just as in fact you are doing.

As a puppy, Lily was enrolled in an obedience class. Our trainer there told us that an adult German Shepherd has about the same vocabulary as a three-year-old child. *Really?* That fact seemed impressive to a non-mother like me.

Now that Lily is an adult dog, I've never counted the number of words she knows. But I will say there are some surprising ones in her collection. Not just the usual sit, stay, come; she knows inside, outside, upstairs, bowl, going, Bucky (a much-loved toy) and many others. One of her favorites is airport.

Not that she knows an airport is a place for planes. Lily recognizes that word means the door to the silver chariot (car) will open and she'll be transported to meet my husband, Richard. Smart dog that she is, she knows the exact exit to the airport and once we reach the roadway circling it, she'll intently scan the crowds to find him. Her excited whining in the back seat alerts me when Lily has spotted him. Once Richard opens the car door, she practically jumps in his arms, her tail wagging so rapidly its rotations would humiliate most helicopters.

Words matter. Not just to a dog, but to us humans. Who among us doesn't need more words of praise, acceptance, encouragement? Words literally have the power to breathe life into our souls. But they can also damage. The old adage says, "Sticks and stones may break my bones, but words will never hurt me." Won't hurt me? Don't you carry painful memories of hurtful words spoken to you from childhood or your teenage years?

1 Corinthians 13:1 states, "If I speak in the tongues of men or of angels, but do not have love, I am only a resounding gong or a clanging cymbal." The truth is we need others to gently, softly, speak words of love into our lives. When life is harsh or even when it isn't, we crave words that lift us up, deliver strength and bring healing to our fragile hearts.

So, I wonder if all of us need more words of encouragement, why don't we speak them more often? Why do we let our words drip with the bitterness of judgment, disapproval, coldness? Words can change the world because they have the power to transform the hearer's soul – positively or negatively. It is our choice. I believe, when we use our words to bring a smile to another, the heart of God smiles also.

So, let's make today the day we feed the hunger in our souls for love by speaking love into the lives of others. Let's make every day one where we use our words to build others up, offer grace, convey understanding, promote acceptance. In your own way, in your own words, you *can* transform the world.

Action:

Read Romans 5:8: "God demonstrated His own love for us in this: While we were still sinners, Christ died for us." How does that verse give you the courage to speak more positively into the lives of others? What will you do differently this week in order to speak uplifting, encouraging words?

Prayer:

Jesus, be strong where I am weak. Be tender where I am scarred. Be near when I feel far away. Help me to be gentle and loving even when people hurt me. Give me Your strength to speak kind and gracious words to everyone I meet. Amen.

NOVEMBER 7

Wish to Learn
BY SHERRI GALLAGHER

Matthew 7:7-8

Ask and it will be given to you; seek and you will find; knock and the door will be opened to you. For everyone who asks receives; the one who seeks finds; and to the one who knocks, the door will be opened.

Learning is not attained by chance; it must be sought for with ardor and attended to with diligence. **Abigail Adams**

I must admit to being lazy. I tested and received my ham radio license over three years ago. Admittedly it was strictly to use as part of the search and rescue team, but still, I avoided learning anything about the equipment. At practice I would hand it over to the communications officer and he would set it up so all I had to do was press the talk button or listen. As long as I remembered to charge the battery, I was good to go.

Lately I have felt a little guilty about my deliberate ignorance. Last night I went to the meeting of the amateur radio club. The group was amazing. They went through all the places they were providing volunteer communications - races, weather training events, field days. I wanted to slink even lower in my chair because of how little I understood. At the end of the meeting they asked if anyone needed help. I inched my hand into the air and said I didn't know enough about my radio; I didn't even know how to unlock the keypad. They could have laughed, instead they came over, showed me how to unlock it and access the channel so I could talk to the group. They told me the best antenna to put on my model of radio, good YouTube videos to access and suggested I attend their next event and team up with an experienced member. By seeking a little guidance, I learned how to make my radio an effective and useful tool in an emergency.

It made me think about my own Bible studies. It is so easy to get lazy and distracted. There is so much else that has to be done that attending adult Bible study goes by the wayside. I remain comfortable in my ignorance and don't stretch out for that even more valuable lesson about God's ways and truth. It doesn't take much to go to the Bible study class. Like the radio club, everyone is warm and welcoming. No one laughs at anyone else's ignorance. Everyone is ready to reach out and help others to learn about our God and Savior.

Action:

Make it a point to go to the next adult Bible study.

Prayer:

Thank you, Lord God, for the knowledge and wisdom that is so easy for me to access. Please take away my fear and shyness that I hide in distractions and give me the courage to step into a learning situation. Amen.

NOVEMBER 8

The Day After
BY SHERRI GALLAGHER

Psalm 34:11-14

If you want to make peace, you don't talk to your friends. You talk to your enemies.
Mosche Dayan

Someone once said the easiest way to start an argument is to discuss politics or religion. Most people have strong opinions. Heated discussions do little to change minds. The run up to election day is filled with negative and acrimonious advertising and debates. Neighbors and friends can become angry and hurt feelings are common. In a close election both sides can easily hang onto negative emotions that strain friendships long after the election is over. In the week following the election think about your own actions and who may have supported an alternative candidate.

Psalm 34 is a song of praise for deliverance from trouble that is thought to have been written by King David. In verse thirteen he warns us to keep our tongue from evil and our lips from speaking deceit. What did we do and say in the weeks before the election? How much of the rhetoric we may have repeated was offensive to our friends and neighbors?

In verse fourteen David tells us to "Depart from evil, and do good; seek peace, and pursue it." That means offering the olive branch to those who supported a different candidate than you did, regardless of who won the election. No matter what we do, the election is over, and the decision is made. It is up to us to reach out and bridge the divide created by our own actions or those we supported, to seek peace and pursue it. After all, "blessed are the peacemakers" (Matthew 5:9).

Action:

Make a list of friends and neighbors with different political views and invite them individually for coffee or tea. Prepare in your mind a list of things you have in common and steer the discussion to the positive.

Prayer:

Heavenly Father, guide my actions that I may be an instrument to create peace where once there was strife. Amen.

NOVEMBER 9

A Reflection of God's Glory
BY MYRA BIERNAT WELLS

Psalm 19:1

The heavens declare the glory of God; the skies proclaim the work of His hands.

I've never been a morning person. So, the other day, I truly had to force myself to get out of bed at 4 a.m. Recent rains in California had damaged Interstate 10 – the main road from my house to Phoenix. Part of the eastbound bridge was out – totally missing. And the westbound lanes were closed because of structural damage. Since this happened literally in the middle of nowhere, to get to Phoenix that day, I faced a detour of 125 miles, hence the 4 a.m. reveille.

It was still dark when my dog, Lily, and I left the house, but as we approached Interstate 8 near San Diego, the light of daybreak began to dance off the mountain canyons. The beautiful orange, magenta and red streaks brightened the dwindling shadows as the desert came alive. Hurtling down the highway at 70 mph was no way to revel in God's handiwork, so I stopped the car at a rest area and let Lily roam while I took in the sudden glory of God's artistry. It was quiet in the pre-dawn glow as I stood there awestruck, watching light chase away darkness. I was captivated by the gorgeous show unfolding around me and let it smooth out the jagged edges within my soul.

These sudden moments of glory are one sacred way God shows how much He is in love with us. These instances where God reveals His magnificent creativity tug at us. They call us into passionate intimacy with God. With hungry hearts, we desire to know more about the God behind them. Experiencing them, we are reminded that our hearts live and move and have their being in Christ.

There aren't many times I've stopped my car on a desolate highway to witness the glory of God unveiling itself. Powerfully, God held out His hand on that day to draw me close to Him through this display. He will do the same for those with eyes to see, ears to hear and hearts to embrace. In these spectacles, God makes His glorious presence known. They are all around us, every day, all day. And thankfully for me, experiencing God's magnificence doesn't always require getting up at 4 a.m.

Action:

Read Psalm 104 and note the ways God makes His glory known throughout creation. It is a lengthy Psalm – you might want to spread it across two days.

Prayer:

Heavenly Father, help me to be a reflection of Your glory today. Just as the sun chases away the darkness, help me chase away the darkness in someone's life by reflecting Your glory. Open my eyes to see You in all creation today. I'm sleuthing for Your fingerprints on the pages of this day. In Jesus' name. Amen.

NOVEMBER 10

Contagious Joy
BY SHERRI GALLAGHER

Numbers 6:24-26

This is the best kind of voyeurism, hearing joy from your neighbors. **Chuck Sigars**

I woke up with a headache just short of a migraine. Even after taking some over the counter pain relievers it hurt too much to sleep, so I got up and dressed. Taking my old dog, Belle, I slipped quietly out of the house to go for a walk. It was late enough that the sun was up, so I didn't have to worry about running into coyotes, but early enough that the wind had not started. Temperatures hovered in the twenties, but the sun cast a glorious range of gold lights on the bare tree branches and crunchy brown leaves.

As you can imagine I started in something of a grumpy mood. My dog, on the other hand, smiled as only a canine can and for all of her ten years and bad hips, explored piles of leaves and threatened squirrels like a puppy. The cool, quietness and my happy dog gradually improved my mood until I was smiling. I still had a headache, but there was so much beauty I couldn't help but rejoice. I found myself waving and smiling at drivers as they came by. Most looked quite stressed, frowning through the windshields as they approached. It was funny though, as I waved and smiled, the frowns disappeared. I could see drivers visibly relax a little and smile back. Some waved, some didn't, but that didn't matter. It helped my headache to know that if only for a few seconds, I made someone's day happier.

In 1 Chronicles 15:16 King David realized why the Lord had made him king; it was for a special reason, to give joy to God's people. I am no King David, but I think it is pleasing to God when we can relieve the work and stress of those around us, if only for a few minutes.

Action:

Next time you are out walking, smile at people, even if you don't know them.

Prayer:

Lord God, thank You for pretty mornings, happy pets and the opportunity to smile at our neighbors. Amen.

NOVEMBER 11 - VETERAN'S DAY

Survival
BY MAUREEN LANG

Jeremiah 29:11

For I know the plans I have for you, declares the Lord, plans for welfare and not for evil, to give you a future and a hope.

Just take one step at a time, trusting that God still has a plan for you, and He will make the best out of your situation. **George Foreman**

When I was growing up, my father rarely talked about his experiences in the US Navy. I guess he thought he was just one of many vets from those days, those who served during the Second World War.

He was humble enough to say he'd only done his duty, but when I was finally old enough to understand a few details about his particular duty, I don't know which impressed me more: what he'd survived or the humility he showed for rarely acknowledging all that he endured.

My dad was captured by the Japanese army in the second wave of the Death March. The first captives were taken in Bataan, followed a few weeks later by the outlying islands where my dad surrendered at Corregidor. After surviving a bout with malaria, he spent the next three and a half years in the harsh conditions of a Japanese POW camp—crowding, disease and starvation at places like Cabanatuan and Bilibid, work detail in Mukden, Manchuria, and a bombing from friendly American fire because the Mukden camp was placed close to a munitions factory.

Part of my father's survival depended on his own will to live. I recall him saying his buddy gave up after their continued captivity, giving away his food. He was dead in three days.

But where did my father get his will to survive? Why did he have it and not his friend? As I look back on what God had in store for my dad, I see a life that honored God and paved the way for his six children to live godly lives. My father wasn't perfect by any means, but if we had the chance to do a rendition of "It's A Wonderful Life" we would see that if he'd never been born, or if he hadn't survived that Death March, fewer people would come to know God because my father's children chose paths pointing others toward Him.

I'm sure during those years of captivity he couldn't imagine the life ahead of him. In such desperate circumstances, survival for the next day was anything but certain, so all he had was to trust whatever God had in store.

Action:

When faced with a decision, remember that God has plans for every one of us. Stop long enough to ask for God's direction and to seek godly counsel.

Prayer:

Lord, help me to remember that even in a life gladly absent of suffering, each day depends upon Your grace, and that You have a plan for my future. Amen.

NOVEMBER 12

Safe Place
BY SHERRI GALLAGHER

Psalm 28:7

The LORD is my strength and my shield; my heart trusts in him, and he helps me. My heart leaps for joy, and with my song I praise him.

When you can't see God's hand, trust His heart. **Emily Freeman**

As my current canine partner, Belle, ages, my canine in training, Reiza, must step up and take on my older dog's duties in search and rescue. Looking for people lost in the woods is great fun for both dogs, but being an ambassador for canine search and rescue and greeting strangers is a terrifying and daunting task for my younger dog. Recently we were at just that type of function. Reiza had to stand still and let total strangers pet her. If she could touch me, a paw resting on my foot or her side brushing my leg, she would wag her tail and give a total stranger kisses. As soon as she lost contact with me, she became timid and turned to find where I had gone.

I wish I was as attentive to God as my dog was to me. Trusting in Him, seeking Him when I am troubled or feel I have lost contact should be my first reaction. Too often I try and go my own way and fix things without looking to God for guidance. If I was more like Reiza and sought Him always, I wouldn't make such a muddle of things.

Action:
Spend today asking God for guidance on the smallest to biggest things. Figure out what makes you feel close to Him and what makes Him feel far away.

Prayer:
God in Heaven, help me find a way to feel Your presence in all I do. Amen.

NOVEMBER 13

The Carrot or the Stick
BY SHERRI GALLAGHER

Romans 4:13-25

Start with good people, lay out the rules, communicate with your employees, motivate them and reward them. If you do all of those things effectively, you can't miss.
Lee Iacocca

At the last search and rescue dog training, my dog Reiza had trouble understanding all the steps to let me know she found someone. She understood each step, but not that I wanted them put together. The first time she combined two of the steps the whole team praised her. Visibly more confident, the dog quickly added the remaining steps and got her big play reward.

Dog training has come a long way over the years. We used to give a command the dog didn't understand and then correct the dog physically forcing them into position. Some people still train that way and it is easy to spot those dogs. They carry their heads lower, flinch frequently and have their tails tucked. The judges are making it clear they understand the training methods and the old ways must change. The last time I tested my other dog, Orex, was a perfect example. He got the highest score of all the dogs, even though his performance wasn't the best. He trotted along beside me bouncing with energy, just waiting for me to give him his reward while the rest of the dogs slinked alongside of their handlers. Orex's pleasure was so contagious the judge laughed and commented on him being a very happy dog.

Part of what makes this possible is Orex's trust in me. If I give a command, he knows good things are coming as soon as he performs as directed. The faster his performance the faster he gets his game of tug or a treat or his dinner. In return I always make sure there is a reward of equal or greater value to the effort he had to put out. The basis of all our training is my dog can count on me to reward him when he earns it.

While what a dog understands is different, and I am certainly too flawed to ever be confused with God, the truth is we act in faith of God's promise to us like my dog's faith in my promises. We work at following God's commandments. We know we will never be perfect, but we do our best to please God out of faith that he will keep His promise of our heavenly reward. We are saved by Grace, but our faith keeps us going. Each time we fail, we know God's love is enduring, He will forgive us and reward us in the end.

Action:
Actively encourage your family, friends, co-workers and employees today.

Prayer:
Thank You, loving God, for a promise we know won't be broken. Amen.

NOVEMBER 14

Quiet
BY MYRA BIERNAT WELLS

Luke 6:12

On one of those days, Jesus went out to a mountainside to pray and spent the night
praying to God.

Weaving the thread back and forth caused my hands to tire and my fingers to burn. I am finishing the last of three baby blankets. When one of my nephews announced his wife was pregnant, I decided to cross stitch a baby blanket. Little did I know two other nephews would make the same announcement within weeks of one another. To keep up with the baby boom, I've stitched three blankets in eight short months.

One day, I sat quietly working on the last one, slowly, methodically, carefully working the patterns, I thought, "I really like this." It was quiet, easy, simple. Not life changing, just a chance to be alone with God. In the silent conversations with Him, I prayed about each baby receiving the blanket.

"Please, God, make the baby healthy. Draw it close to You. Give it Your strength and wisdom. Guide it down a pathway to glorify You." With each stitch, a little prayer. The prayers made me realize how much my soul, every soul craves those moments of divine silence.

Our lives are so cluttered with noise and speed these days. We often don't feel the ache in our bodies asking us to slow down and savor the quiet we can create in our lives and in our hearts.

There is a time and place for noise, activity and busyness, but there is also a time to enjoy the hushed places where you can think more, wrestle with the hard stuff in your life and listen to the whispers of God.

Sitting, observing my stitching, I rejoiced in how lovely and delightful the moment was. It was beautiful for my soul. I'm learning to savor the small delights in our lives and to choose the unhurried path, where there is more time to wrap myself up in the sweet presence of God.

Action:

Take some time each day this week to slow down and savor a quiet moment with God.

Prayer:

Father, thank You for the presence of the Holy Spirit in my life. Help me savor those quiet moments where I receive courage, strength and wisdom. In Jesus' name. Amen.

NOVEMBER 15

What Are Friends For?
BY SHERRI GALLAGHER

James 5:13-18

Pray as if everything depends upon God and work as if everything depends on man.
Francis Cardinal Spellman

The great recession hit my business hard. For almost two years I marketed and networked and posted and blogged with no response. Only my husband's billings kept us afloat. Then we received word that his primary client was doing some re-structuring and we would see a significant reduction in his income. It was horribly distressing but we decided I should look for a position and try and draw down a salary instead of working as a consultant.

Almost immediately I found a potential employer and started into the rounds of interviews. I did my best to win the position and after several rounds I met with a vice president who was excited to bring me on board. That interview was on my birthday and afterwards I sat in my car and cried. I would bring in a decent income, but the expectation was for a minimum of 70 hours, six days a week in the office and a month or more a quarter spent in China.

I would have to give up dog training, search and rescue, writing, and pretty much any interest outside of the job. Still I had a responsibility to my family and to have the doors to this job open so quickly in such a depressed economy seemed to be heaven-sent. Resigned, I prayed, "Thy will be done" and drove home.

I came to the next writers group meeting and explained the situation and that if I got the job, I would have to leave the group. The ladies prayed with me and kept me in their prayers for months afterwards. A few days later I got a call to do a consulting job and then a few days after that another one. The recession was still quite bad, but I was now bringing in income. The re-structuring occurred and instead of decreasing my husband's business, it increased. Finally, I got the call that the company had decided to promote from within and would not be hiring any outside candidates.

I have a hard time hearing words from God. I know He is there and watching over me, but our conversations are a little one-sided when it comes to talking. I read and study the Bible and pray daily, but I have yet to hear God speak words sending clear direction, like "turn right at the next corner." Sometimes I pray or ask for guidance and the next passage I read will seem to be written for just that situation. Sometimes highly improbable things happen at just the right time to give me an answer. I know God is watching over me. I also know he expects me to be as active on my own behalf as I am asking Him to be. I do think God answers prayers; if he didn't, we would not be told in so many passages of the Bible to pray.

I had a huge problem and I followed the direction of James 5:16. I asked the faithful to pray for me then I actively worked and sought to find a path that would solve the problem. The best way I know to find out what God wants me to do is to walk through the doors He opens. If He doesn't want me to be there, the door will stay firmly shut and no matter what I do things will not change.

Action:
The next time you have a problem ask several friends to pray with you and for you.

Prayer:
Heavenly Father, thank You for hearing the prayers of your faithful. Please continue to watch over them and me as we travel this journey called life. Amen.

NOVEMBER 16

Consistent and Persistent
BY SHERRI GALLAGHER

Proverbs 31:10-31

That which we persist in doing becomes easier, not that the task itself has become easier, but that our ability to perform it has improved.
Ralph Waldo Emerson

Many of the people who do dog sports don't have their dogs live in the house with them. The dogs live in a kennel and their owners interact with them when they feed, bathe, care for and train them. As a result, there are no inconsistencies in commands. If the dog is told "sit" the human is paying attention and focused on the dog, so the correct action is rewarded, and an incorrect response is identified and fixed.

My dogs live in the house with me and it is not uncommon for someone to give a command and then not follow up with the reward or correction. As a result, our progress has been slower than it could be. I finally recognized this issue and began to consciously consider before giving a dog a command. If I could not follow up with the reward or would not have the time to work through the issues to do it right, I would not give a command. As a result, my dogs live in my house and cuddle with me on the sofa but also are making the same or better progress than the kennel dogs do.

The other day, I realized I had been neglecting my Bible study time. In the past, when I got behind, I would take a day and "catch up." Thinking about how inconsistency in dog training affected the results the obvious correlation hit me; doing Bible study hit or miss and playing catch up was not helping me to grow into the kind of individual God wants me to be. If I am to grow and develop, I need to be consistent and persistent in my Bible study.

Action:
Evaluate your daily schedule and carve out a time when you can do your Bible study daily no matter what.

Prayer:
Lord, give me the guidance and strength to be consistent and persistent in studying Your Word. Amen.

NOVEMBER 17

Lifeline
BY SHERRI GALLAGHER

Philippians 4:6

Do not be anxious about anything, but in every situation, by prayer and petition, with thanksgiving, present your requests to God.

There isn't much better in this life than finding a way to spend a few hours in conversation with people you respect and love. You have to carve this time out of your life because you aren't living without it.
Gordon Atkinson, RealLivePreacher.com

Recently I completed several long solo driving trips. Most of my travel was on highways with the scenery consisting of corn fields, the occasional soybean tract, and even more corn. I tried listening to music or talk radio and used books on CD, but even with those distractions, traveling the road alone was monotonous.

On one such trip I was tired and with close to ten hours of driving remaining when my mobile phone rang. It was my good friend, Myra. We chatted and laughed about family, dogs, writing, and prayer. She is one of those people I trust completely, and I don't have to be careful how I phrase things or consider my words before speaking. I can tell her how I truly feel. She kept me going and two hours sped by on what a long boring trip was normally.

Myra is a friend who helps me stay focused on God and models the same kind of conversations I should have with Him. Certainly, God knows what is in my heart and mind. I don't have to pick and choose my words carefully, for fear of offending Him. I do daily formal prayer, giving thanks and asking for God to heal and help and guide, but sometimes I just need to have a heart-to-heart conversation with Him so He can throw down a lifeline to me. Telling Him my thoughts and fears helps me understand myself a little better and usually makes the course I should take clearer. In Philippians 4:6 it says, "but in every situation, by prayer and petition, with thanksgiving present your requests to God." I'm not sure if that means the same thing as my open, honest conversations with Him, but they benefit me immensely; just like conversations with my friends, like Myra, only better.

Action:
Throughout the day have conversations with God sharing what you are doing, thinking and feeling.

Prayer:
Loving God, my dearest friend, You know my dreams and fears, hopes and wishes. Thank You for listening and always being there, no matter where I am. Amen.

NOVEMBER 18

'Bama Butt
BY SHERRI GALLAGHER

Exodus 20:16

Oh what a tangled web we weave, When first we practice to deceive!
Sir Walter Scott

"Isn't it better to bend the truth a little to prevent hurting someone?" This is the justification I frequently hear for not telling the truth. The example that is quickly trotted out is that of a wife who asks her husband if her outfit looks alright. The husband decides the dress makes her rear-end look about as big as the state of Alabama but rather than hurt he feelings he tells her, "No it looks fine." She goes out happy and her husband avoids a confrontation. Thus, the little white lie is proven acceptable.

But where does this lead? The man goes to work and realizes he has made a costly mistake. If he owns up to it, he may be fired. So he tells a lie and lies to himself claiming he did it to protect his family, much as he lied to protect his wife's feelings.

Growing up in a household where these little lies were tolerated, to protect others, the CEO of a company lies about his company's involvement in an environmental catastrophe. He justifies it to himself as lying to protect the company and all the employees who would be laid off if the truth came out. That is how we end up with things like leaking oil lines and wells, smog as thick as a cream soup, and areas of the world so contaminated it is no longer safe to live there.

Exodus 20:16 is clear, "You shall not bear false witness against your neighbor." There are no exceptions in those nine words. Lying breaks one of God's commandments.

The man could have told his wife the dress color made her skin glow like pearls, but the cut wasn't as flattering to her beauty as some of her other outfits. The man at the office could have owned up to the mistake at the same time he presented a plan to correct the situation. The CEO could have guided his company to follow the laws and never ended up in a situation where lying was the "only way out."

We all have choices to make. Some are easy, some are difficult. If we are going to obey God's commandments we must step away from the little white lies and find His strength in the truth.

Think about a tactful honest answer the next time you are tempted to tell a little lie.

Prayer:
Lord, forgive us our struggles to circumvent Your commandments. Give us the strength to speak loving if difficult truths. Amen.

NOVEMBER 19

God in a Box
BY SHERRI GALLAGHER

Matthew 10:29-31

Are not two sparrows sold for a penny? Yet not one of them will fall to the ground outside your Father's care. And even the very hairs of your head are all numbered. So don't be afraid; you are worth more than many sparrows.

They say that God is everywhere, and yet we think of Him as somewhat of a recluse.
Emily Dickinson

Why do we put God into a box and limit His strength, ability and love? I catch myself not wanting to bother God with my little problems. I tend to think He is busy with more important issues. Horrible diseases ravage the world. Wars flare up at the slightest provocation. Governments and officials face off like schoolyard bullies while the weakest suffer as a result. How is my petty little problem of any importance compared to those things?

The problem is I am putting God in a box. I am limiting Him, in my mind and approach, when in reality God is quite capable of dealing with wars and my decision-making at the same time. I keep confusing being made in God's image with being the same as God. If I couldn't deal with all of this at once, then I think God can't either.

God cares about the sparrows and knows when one of them falls even as He deals with others praying as they struggle with survival. Goodness, if God counts all those hairs that fall from my head, and as I age there have been a lot, He certainly has time and attention to listen to my concerns and prayers.

Action:
What is bothering you today? No matter how small or petty, tell God about it and ask for His guidance.

Prayer:

Heavenly Father, forgive me for thinking You are too busy to be bothered with one such as me. Help me to understand and believe that I am precious in Your sight, so I come to You in faith with my concerns. Amen.

NOVEMBER 20

Operation Purge
BY MYRA BIERNAT WELLS

Luke 6:38

Give, and it will be given to you. A good measure, pressed down, shaken together and running over, will be poured into your lap. For with the measure you use, it will be measured to you.

For four years, I've been on a mission. To even admit this mission has been this lengthy (and is still ongoing!) is quite embarrassing. Because of a permanent move to California, I am systematically purging our home in Illinois of every unnecessary, unused or no longer wanted item.

Operation Purge has been as brutal as it has been long. My husband, Richard, is a pack rat. His father before him was also one. Richard's father basically had three households stored in his home when he died – his parents, his in-laws and his own. When emptying my father-in-law's house, many items found their way to ours. So, I'm basically packing, donating or tossing four households worth of stuff. Unfortunately for me, this activity drains my energy instead of increasing it.

My husband and I have been called on the carpet by God about this. He has convicted us if something is no longer serving a purpose in our lives, it could meet a need for someone else. Keeping boxes stored in our basement year after year collecting dust does not serve God or us well.

Our possessions are nothing more than resources on loan to us from God. He asks that we steward them diligently. They are not earned rewards or deserved pleasures. Every spiritual gift, every financial resource, and each possession has been given to us by God to serve others.

Each time I put things on our doorstep to be donated, I feel an immense sense of joy. I pray over the parcels so that they will be useful to someone who needs them. And I praise God that He was so faithful to give them to me in the first place. The boxes of donated goods remind me to live my life with open hands, dusty feet, calloused knees and rolled-up sleeves of a generous giver. I can give what I can and so can you.

Action:

Make a list of your ten most prized possessions. How would your life change if you lost one of them? This week review your list and turn it over to God. Pray about how you can use these to honor God. Throughout the week, continue to pray for an eternal perspective on earthly things.

Prayer:

Father, thank You for reminding me that what I have is temporary, but who I am is eternal. I pray others would see You in the way I give myself away in service to others and that I would never count on earthly possessions for the peace and contentment only You can give. In Jesus' precious name, I pray. Amen.

NOVEMBER 21

Wisdom
BY SHERRI GALLAGHER

I Kings 4:29-30

God gave Solomon wisdom and very great insight, and a breadth of understanding as measureless as the sand on the seashore. Solomon's wisdom was greater than the wisdom of all the people of the East, and greater than all the wisdom of Egypt.

It is unwise to be too sure of one's own wisdom. It is healthy to be reminded that the strongest might weaken and the wisest might err. **Mahatma Gandhi**

W.C. Fields is credited with saying, "never work with animals or children," and all it takes is one demonstration with a dog or young child and you learn the wisdom of his words. Lektor had a perfect down stay, but he quickly learned when I was making a presentation, I couldn't do much about his disobedience and he would get up and wander the room begging for petting and treats. I learned that while I am considered something of an expert in canine search and rescue, my dogs could swiftly demonstrate my foolishness. Pride is part of what leads us from wisdom to foolishness. While I took great pride in how obedient my dog was, it led to my folly and embarrassment.

Solomon was a man of great wisdom and insight and a breadth of understanding as measureless as the sand on the seashore (I Kings 4:29). But for all his wisdom, Solomon allowed his children to be raised to believe in and worship false gods. As soon as they assumed the throne of Israel, they led God's children away from Him. For all his wisdom, Solomon was capable of making a huge mistake.

Each of us is wise and each of us is foolish. The easiest way to judge our personal foolishness is to compare our actions to God's Word, the Bible, and learn to change where needed to be wise leaders and sources of wisdom.

Action:

Before making a decision, check your reasoning against the guidance offered in the Bible as well as wise counsel.

Prayer:

Thank You, Lord, for the wisdom and guidance You gave us with Your holy Word. Amen.

NOVEMBER 22

Guidance
BY SHERRI GALLAGHER

Matthew 6:33

But seek first his kingdom and his righteousness, and all these things will be given to you as well.

Seek grace and guidance from God. **Lailah Gifty Akita**, *Beautiful Quotes*

I have trained many dogs to track for search and rescue, but Orex is the first dog I have trained for competitive tracking. The two activities require very different leash tensions. In search and rescue, we have no idea where the person has walked or their scent has collected. We use a loose leash and follow where the dog takes us. Of course, we are reading the dog's body language and terrain, spotting where the canine might need help or to back up, but in general the dog is the one guiding the program. The dog knows we are there but pretty much ignores us. The less tension we put on the leash the easier it is for the dog to track.

Competitive tracking is quite different and is as much about obedience as it is about finding the scent. The dog is on a very tight leash and wants to feel our presence. The handler will still not know where the track layer walked and the dog is still the one to tell us, but the competition dog wants to know the handler is on the other end of the leash. Of course, this has caused some problems for Orex and me. Now I must hold the leash tightly and lean back, controlling my dog's speed. If I let the line go slack, the dog stops tracking and looks to me for a command. If I tighten up on the leash, the dog goes forward with confidence once again doing his job of following the scent.

God doesn't put me on a leash, but He does give me guidance through my Bible study. When I stay connected through my prayers and devotionals, I feel confident. It is easy to find little things reminding me God is there with me guiding my steps. If I hold tight and eagerly look for the path He wants me to follow, I have confidence, much like Orex when the leash is clearly connected to me. When I get busy and can't find time to study my Bible, my steps falter. Am I treating this stranger the way God would want me to? Am I giving my client or employer a full measure of effort tamped down and overflowing? I only have confidence when I am following the path God has set out for me.

Action:
Take a few minutes to assess your connection to God.

Prayer:
God give me the strength and organization to lean on Your guidance. Help me to stay on track and keep connected to You through the study of Your word. Amen.

NOVEMBER 23

I LOVE YOU Dabby
BY CATHY HARVEY

Romans 8:26b

We do not know what we ought to pray for, but the Spirit himself intercedes for us...

Love, the language of the heart, needs no words. **Anonymous**

It was a Sunday afternoon in November, and I was by myself. After my husband and I attended church that morning, he left for a ministry to recruits at a nearby Navy base and would not be home until 4:30 or 5:00 p.m. That left me with a peaceful afternoon to "remember the Sabbath and keep it holy." Sundays had become a cherished oasis of rest, relaxation and quiet reflection.

After Sunday dinner in the university cafeteria on the campus where we lived, I took a leisurely stroll back to our apartment. The weather was so beautiful I made no attempt to hurry. This autumn had been as colorful as any I could remember, and I walked home, marveling at the array of reds, bronze, golden yellows, and shades of brown. What a palate God had created!

Skirting behind the library, I walked around a playground, scrunching through leaves and ended up on the back sidewalk to our apartment complex. I noticed chalking on the sidewalk and four words in large child-like printing, "I LOVE YOU Dabby." For a moment I wondered who "Dabby" was, but it became clear that this little person was writing a love note to "Daddy." It was a common error for children learning to write the alphabet to confuse which way to print the lower case "b" and "d."

I stopped to think about the little one chunking out the words in blue letters as large and as full of love as the youngster could muster. Outlined in bright pink curves and swirls, the blue message nearly popped off the sidewalk canvas, and even though the message was misspelled, I knew exactly what the child meant. I couldn't help but smile, imagining the outpouring of love and picturing little hands gripping oversized chalk intent on printing the note before daddy got home—so precious!

It prompted my thinking about God, how He knows clearly what we mean when we pray. Even when we don't know how to express the mess or the love in our heart, He understands what we want to say. Romans 8:26 and 27 express this truth: "And the Holy Spirit helps us in our distress. For we don't even know what we should pray for, nor how we should pray. But the Holy Spirit prays for us with groanings that cannot be expressed in words. And the Father who knows all hearts knows what the Spirit is saying, for the Spirit pleads for us believers in harmony with God's own will."

Praise the Lord! He knows what I mean even when I don't!

Action:
Banish any fears you may have about finding the right words in prayer. Pray freely for He already knows what you need and what you mean.

Prayer:
Heavenly Father, thank You for understanding me better than I understand myself. Help me pour out my soul freely, honestly, and without abandon to You. I LOVE YOU Dabby! Amen.

NOVEMBER 24

NePoPo
BY SHERRI GALLAGHER

Psalm 23

Desire, ask, believe, receive. **Stella Terrill Mann**

There is a theory of dog training called NePoPo. It stands for negative positive positive. In training the dog, you want it to perform an action such as sit on command. You give the command and pull up on the leash, this is the negative. As soon as the dog sits, you release the leash pressure, this is the first positive. You then give a treat or other reward which is the second positive. The dog learns to work through the negative because the positives which follow have so much greater value than the negative. The dog remembers the last activity, the positive reward the most, and so faces training as a positive, happy experience and will anticipate it with pleasure.

I am trying to apply NePoPo to my spiritual life. When I am in a trial or difficult situation, I count that as a negative. I go to God and hand over my troubles to Him. The time in His presence and with His Word is the first positive. I am not the first to face this situation and there is comfort to be found in studying the Bible. When I am finished, I gain the confidence that He is with me and I will get through this trial or difficulty with His strength carrying me. This is the second positive. The negative is not instantly gone, but with God I know I will get through it. What I get from my study and the peace and calm it brings to my life are stronger than the difficulty.

Action:
Read your favorite Psalm and find comfort.

Prayer:
Lord God, thank You for Your strength and love which will carry me through the worst of situations. Amen.

NOVEMBER 25

Old or New
BY SHERRI GALLAGHER

1 Corinthians 13:1-7

To love and be loved is to feel the sun from both sides. **David Viscott**

Dog training has become more sophisticated throughout the years. It started out being very rigid. Dogs performed to avoid punishment and pain. If you wanted to teach a dog to sit, you pulled up on the leash while pushing down on their rear. The dog quickly learned when it heard the word sit to assume the proper position. People who understood dogs' body language would see these dogs head and ear positions offer the canine equivalent of, "please don't hurt me, I'm trying to give you what you want."

Teaching obedience became more positive. Judges didn't like to see the sad and fearful body language of the canines they judged; they made that clear with their scores. Now when we teach sit, we hold a toy or treat in a way to lure the dog into the right position and reward compliance. Dogs trained this way hear the command and their brain kicks in with, "Oh boy, good stuff coming." They sit swiftly and their ears are perked as they watch their handlers, happily anticipating the next command.

Sometimes I have trouble relating to all the rules of the Old Testament. The laws often seem to be about avoiding punishment. There was a reason for all the rules, and they were made in love, but they remind me of the old way of dog training. It is easier for me to relate to the parables and teachings in the New Testament where the focus is on love. God forgave us because of Christ's love and sacrifice. We start with love and God's grace. As 1 Corinthians 13:4 says, "Love is patient, love is kind." When we start from love, good things often happen. Like my dog, when I focus on God's love, I am happily waiting for the next good thing to happen.

Action:

When you are tempted to be sharp and corrective with a co-worker, child or even a pet, pause and give some thought how to make them want to do what you ask instead of doing what you ask out of fear.

Prayer:

Thank You, God, for Your love that makes me want to be closer to You. Amen.

NOVEMBER 26

Thanksgiving Humble Pie
BY CATHY HARVEY

Proverbs 16:5

The Lord detests all the proud of heart. Be sure of this: They will not go unpunished.

Rushing through the house to leave for work, my mind was multi-tasking to the hilt, spurred on by my irritation with everyone who didn't pick up after themselves. The little foxes were eating the vine and fueling my mood minute-by-rushed-minute. Pride stepped in, comparing and gloating on how organized I was. I whisked through the house in a last-ditch effort to leave on time, snatching and tying up a bag of garbage.

I was also energized by my latest art project—Thanksgiving cards I was giddy about sending. Another wedge of pride slipped in, puffing myself up in the fine details of my design graced with a spiritual message, of course. I had spent evenings crafting all the pieces and decided to use my lunch hour to glue them together. I scooped up the pieces and supplies, stuffed them into a bag, grabbed purse, lunch, trash and scrambled out the door.

Without turning on the light, I rushed through the garage, pushed up the lid of the trash can and tossed the garbage. On my way to work I daydreamed about the anticipated noon hour. With prideful thoughts bursting like pus out of infected wound, my mind carried on unaware that "*pride cometh before a fall.*"

Itching for my lunch break, I scooted out at 11:00. Grabbing my lunch, I looked for my craft bag, but did not see it. I ran outside to check the car, but it was not there. Hurrying back to the office I looked again. I sat down and ran an Instant Replay in my mind: my hands were full, the garage was dark, I tossed the garbage—oh nooo! With a sinking feeling I realized that I had let go of my craft bag when I tossed the trash—and it was trash day in our neighborhood!

I immediately called home, but it was too late. Of course, it was. In the split second of realizing what had happened I heard God's still, small voice. It was crystal clear. *"So, you think you're better than everyone? So organized and puffed up over yourself and your gift which I have given you. I'll show you what I can do. I will let you throw out your craft with your own hand."*

Smitten with conviction, embarrassment, shame and repentance, I could hardly focus on my job. All that work and time, so hard to come by, thrown away— *"by my own hand!"* But God—is a God of forgiveness. I felt His loving correction, swift and just. He spoke the truth in love to my heart. So, I began to create the pieces again, but with a new, humbled attitude.

A few days later I received an e-mail from a friend who was giving up her stamping craft. Would I like to come over and see if there were any supplies I could use? Stepping into her house, I saw supplies of everything imaginable for crafting cards. She handed me a box and told me to fill it up! For every item I had tossed, God replaced it many times over! He had forgiven me, and like Job, restored many times over what had been lost. "The Lord giveth and the Lord taketh away. Blessed be the name of the Lord."

Action:

Is pride sneaking into your thoughts in an area in which you feel overly confident? Please learn from my gross error and humble yourself before God to ask forgiveness for this grievous sin God detests.

Prayer:

Heavenly Father, shine a light on the sin in my heart that You abhor. Help me take an honest look and see what You see in me. I confess my _____. Wash me and I shall be whiter than snow. Thank You. Amen.

NOVEMBER 27

Outgrow Fear
BY SHERRI GALLAGHER

Proverbs 3:5-6

Trust in the LORD with all your heart and lean not on your own understanding; in all your ways submit to him, and he will make your paths straight.

You may be deceived if you trust too much, but you will live in torment if you do not trust enough. **Frank Crane**

Reiza is a sweet dog who wouldn't dream of using her inch-long teeth on a human. When she was a puppy, her previous owner got his thrills out of tormenting and intimidating her. It has taken a year and a half to get her to trust being out in public, but she is very timid and fearful. If I shelter her from all the things that frighten her, she becomes more and more timid. Instead, I started working to help her grow and overcome her fears. I started with obedience and required her to trust me when I gave a command. Then, I introduced her to people who understood dogs and created pleasant experiences for Reiza. Last week, we took the next big step and had Reiza stand in a doorway as we did fund raising and let strangers pet her and give her treats. While it was stressful and tiring for her, she made tremendous advances in trust.

I find God treats me much as I treat Reiza. If I am afraid of something, He will give me little pushes so that I grow and develop into the person I have the potential to be. In high school and college, I was terrified of public speaking to the point I would burst into tears. God placed me in a position to take public speaking courses through a Bible college. Those courses helped me to learn how to overcome my debilitating fear.

As a result, I have been successful financially and in building a non-profit organization. God could have sheltered me, and I would have been a withdrawn, shy human being. Instead He placed me in safe environments to grow. At the time they didn't feel safe at all but looking back I realize they were just the little steps I needed to grow and develop.

Action:

List your greatest personal fears, like public speaking or fear of flying. Find an organization that will help you overcome that fear.

NOVEMBER 28

Seasonal Faithfulness
BY SHERRI GALLAGHER

Joshua 24:13-15

God, I don't have great faith, but I can be faithful. My belief in you may be seasonal, but my faithfulness will not. I will follow in the way of Christ. I will act as though my life and the lives of others matter. I will love. I have no greater gift to offer than my life. Take it. **Real Live Preacher**

I like reading the story of Joshua. Here was a man who had to step up and take Moses' place with Israel. Talk about a hard act to follow. In the first chapter, while it is not recorded what Joshua said, God's words are, "Have I not commanded you? Be strong and courageous. Do not be afraid; do not be discouraged, for the Lord your God will be with you wherever you go." Can you imagine the doubts Joshua had for God to offer this encouragement? Later in Joshua 24, Joshua's anger with Israel when they turned away from the God who had brought them safely into the promise land only now worshipped idols? Joshua fought wars and established communities. He parceled out land and goods to a greedy, ungrateful people. He established the systems pretty much in spite of his nation's disobedience. Surely Joshua's faith had to waver, but in all his actions he led the life God called him to live.

I think we all walk through seasons where God is closer to us and others seasons where our faith is still there, but our humanness causes unbelief. What can we do at those times? Of course, we can increase our study, but sometimes acting in the way that demonstrates Christ's love helps us to draw closer to Him again.

By valuing others, offering to help even when we are busy, giving of our time and resources and seeing how our acts of faith have helped others helps us to return to a stronger place with God because feelings often follow actions. Like Joshua we can be strong and courageous and know God is with us wherever we go.

Action:
Give food to a hungry stranger or a ride to a shut-in.
Prayer:
Lord, help my actions bring me closer to You. Amen.

NOVEMBER 29

Winter
BY BETH DUMEY

Mark 13:18

Pray that this will not take place in winter.

In *The Lion, The Witch and The Wardrobe*, C.S. Lewis refers to a cold, icy, desolate place as being "Always winter but never Christmas." The sentiment is stark in its simplicity, because if we take Christmas out of winter, we remove the festivity, the warmth, the meaning, and we simply have winter, with its darkness, harshness, and ferocity. I picture this part of the year much like a dungeon where I am simply waiting to be released to feel the sun.

While many enjoy sledding and skiing and other winter sports, even they cannot deny the days are short and the season is invariably long. For most of us in four-season climates, "spring fever" is a real malady.

Yet, I'm not sure I would understand gratitude as well without winter. After a major snowstorm, I am immensely grateful for clear roads and sunlit skies. Once the -20 wind chill rises, I thank God for heat. As the days move toward spring and the sun drops later and later in the evening, I am overwhelmed with joy to be moving from the darkness into longer days of light. Without the struggle of winter, I am not sure I could fully appreciate the bounty of spring.

Action:
Consider the contrast between darkness and light, struggle and ease. How does the former make you feel about the latter? Discuss this in your small group.

Prayer:
Father, while we would like to have all our days be sunny and warm, we know You allow darker, colder days in. Help us to see Your provision even in these and recognize the blessing even when we struggle. Amen.

NOVEMBER 30

Idols
BY SHERRI GALLAGHER

Exodus 20:4-6

You shall not make for yourself an idol…

Worshipping is stripping ourselves of our idols, even the most hidden ones, and choosing the Lord as the center, as the highway of our lives. **Pope Francis**

Sneaky idols abound. Most dedicated Christians are generous souls who put God before money, so they don't need to worry about hidden idols, do they? We keep God front and center in our lives so no need to worry about breaking that commandment. Or do we need to be more vigilant?

Do you have a smart phone or tablet? Do you bring it into services with you? When you are at dinner do you constantly check and respond to messages even if it means ignoring the people around the table? What would you do if you lost your mobile device? Would it be a disaster or a minor inconvenience? These are warning signs indicating something has taken on a high value in our lives and is a danger of becoming a hidden idol.

Do you turn to God as often as you turn to social media? If the answer is no, it may be time for some soul searching. Try turning off your tablet on Sundays. Leave your cell phone in the car during services and off during meals.

Action:

Every time you take a break from events around you to address a smart device, offer a prayer before putting it away.

Prayer:

Lord God, help me to identify the hidden idols in my life and turn from them to You. Amen.

DECEMBER 1

Don't Miss Christmas
BY MYRA BIERNAT WELLS

Luke 2:11-12

Today in the town of David a Savior has been born to you; he is the Messiah, the Lord. This will be a sign to you: You will find a baby wrapped in cloths and lying in a manger.

Christmas in Bethlehem. The ancient dream: a cold, clear night made brilliant by a glorious star, the smell of incense, shepherds and wise men falling to their knees in adoration of the sweet baby, the incarnation of perfect love.
Lucinda Franks

The Christmas rush is on! Many of you are still looking for the perfect gift, wrapping presents, baking your famous sugar cookies or packing the car for a long trip.

Stop right where you are! Take a deep breath and travel back with me to a time when there was no hope and no celebration. I can't imagine a world without Jesus and yet, many times I live my life as if He doesn't even exist. A trial comes and I try to handle it on my own. Loneliness floods my heart and instead of reaching out to Him, I withdraw into the darkness.

He then interrupts my life and fills each black corner with Light. His love flows over the pain like a soothing balm and once again, I experience the manger. Once again, He steps into the smelly, unlikely and very ordinary existence that is mine to change everything – everything!

Jesus could have come to us in many ways, but He chose to interrupt the very ordinary with the most extraordinary. He could have chosen to be born in a palace. After all, He was a King. Yet His life on earth began in a manger housed in what amounted to little more than a dirty, smelly barn. The simplicity of His birth is one of His most precious gifts to me, and one of my most profound life lessons.

Every year I am reminded of the very heart of Christmas — Emmanuel, God with us. God wants to be involved in the simple, ordinary happenings of daily life: where we go and what we do, the smile we give the harried stranger and the patience we exhibit in the crowd of impatient shoppers, the love that prompts the secret gift and the heart that constantly celebrates His birth through every sparkling light, every beautifully wrapped gift, each special meal, every card, phone call and visit.

Action:

Celebrate Him and His birth in everything you do. Have a birthday party for Jesus. Bake Him a huge cake and invite neighbors to join in the celebration. Adopt a family in need. Reach out to the lonely. Look for Him in the crowd. Emmanuel, God with us!

Prayer:

Father, today we celebrate the reality of Your presence in our lives. I celebrate Christ's birth, His life, His death and His resurrection. And as I celebrate, Lord, help me to be "God with skin on" to those in need around me. Open my eyes and let me see them as You see them! I love You. **Happy Birthday, Jesus!** In Jesus' name. Amen.

DECEMBER 2

Waiting is the Hardest Part
BY JULIE DAHLBERG

Luke 1:23-25

When his time of service was completed, he returned home. After this his wife Elizabeth became pregnant and for five months remained in seclusion. "The Lord has done this for me," she said. "In these days he has shown his favor and taken away my disgrace among the people."

Oh come, oh come, Emmanuel, and ransom captive Israel that mourns in lonely exile here until the Son of God appear. **Author Uncertain**

The word "advent" means "a coming into place, or an arrival" and we spend the advent season expectantly waiting for that great arrival of Jesus, which we celebrate on Christmas. Expectant waiting. Children all over the world know that this is the season of waiting!

Is there any human experience weightier with waiting than pregnancy? We wait to conceive, and we wait all those weeks and months for a healthy delivery. In this passage, we are at the first point in the Christmas story where there is waiting. Zechariah must wait to finish out his work in the temple, and both he and Elizabeth wait and see that she becomes pregnant! She goes off by herself for 5 months, and Zechariah finds himself waiting some more. Waiting is unavoidable; we can't get out of it and we can't rush it. But do we wait well?

In his condition of speechlessness, Zechariah had no choice but to wait quietly. Communication must have been exhausting for him, and Elizabeth was in seclusion. Their time of waiting, I imagine, must have been contemplative. Let us be intentional and wait quietly, so that we can hear Him and wait expectantly so that we don't miss what God has for us in this season.

Action:

As you make your lists of things to do and places to go during this advent, take a moment to savor the waiting that is also a part of the season.

Prayer:

Thank You, Lord, that You did come for us, and help me to wait expectantly for what You will do this season. Amen.

DECEMBER 3

God Is Good, All the Time
BY JULIE DAHLBERG

Luke 1:68-80

...the angel said, "Don't be afraid, Zechariah! God has heard your prayer. Your wife, Elizabeth, will give you a son, and you are to name him John. You will have great joy and gladness, and many will rejoice at his birth. **Luke 1:13-14**

Zechariah must have been out of his head with joy! To see all of God's promises being fulfilled before his eyes, and to finally be able to speak his understanding and praise must have been amazing. Might Zechariah have been saving up and planning what his first words would be should he be able to speak again?

Luke says in verse 67 that Zechariah was filled with the Holy Spirit, and this prophecy came pouring from his lips. If the Holy Spirit is giving one the words to speak, then the message will be flawless and complete. God had been merciful to Zechariah and Elizabeth by taking away the shame of childlessness, and he gave them a very special son, the Prophet of the Most High, to boot!

Zechariah is given another wonderful gift, that his first words were not his own but were from God, and they were perfect. (Phew! These words would not be a repeat of his mistaken words of unbelief.) Through his words, we get a picture of what God's great plan is for all people, to rescue us and lead us to Him. May we remember during this season of waiting that God fulfills all His promises, that He has a big plan for us all, and that His plan is good.

Action:

Ask God to give you the words to speak when you are unsure what to say.

Prayer:
Thank You, Lord, for Your big promises! Help me remember Your faithfulness.
Amen.

DECEMBER 4

You Made Me Promises, Promises
BY JULIE DAHLBERG

Luke 1:34-37

How will this be," Mary asked the angel, "since I am a virgin?" The angel answered, "The Holy Spirit will come on you, and the power of the Most High will overshadow you. So the holy one to be born will be called the Son of God. Even Elizabeth your relative is going to have a child in her old age, and she who was said to be unable to conceive is in her sixth month. For no word from God will ever fail.

God decided in advance to adopt us into his own family by bringing us to himself through Jesus Christ. This is what he wanted to do, and it gave him great pleasure.
Ephesians 1:5

In looking through several different translations of this passage, Gabriel says in some (KJV) that, "with God, nothing is impossible," and in others that, "the word of God will never fail." Gabriel explains to Mary and us that we can be assured God can do what is impossible, and that if God makes a promise, HE WILL DO IT! For added emphasis, he tells Mary about Elizabeth's good news, which reminds us of how God fulfilled his promise to Abraham and Sarah in the Old Testament.

We can become jaded about promises. How often are we made promises that are unreliable? How about this one, "I'll be ready in 5 minutes." We hardly even *hear* the promises a politician makes, because they're almost never kept. Broken marriages are broken promises. Broken promises aren't always intentional wrongdoing. Sometimes we might make a promise we intend to fulfill, but then get new information or a change in circumstances that causes us to break that promise.

Thankfully, God's ways are not our ways. His Word will never fail, and with Him, nothing is impossible. We are promised forgiveness of our sins when we believe that Jesus paid the price for us. It is impossible for us to ever right our wrongs ourselves, but He can and does do it for us. He promises that we become His children when we believe and that all His promises to Abraham are for us. Let us take time to dwell on all He has promised us and rejoice in the knowledge that His promises never fail.

Action:

Write out the verse from Ephesians above, changing the word "us" to your name, and put it on your bathroom mirror.

Prayer:

Lord, help me to live daily in the knowledge that You love me enough to make me one of Your children. Amen.

DECEMBER 5

The BIG, Perfect Plan
BY JULIE DAHLBERG

Matthew 1:22-23

All this took place to fulfill what the Lord had said through the prophet: "The virgin will conceive and give birth to a son, and they will call him Immanuel" (which means "God with us").

I love it when a plan comes together. **John "Hannibal" Smith**, *The A Team*

Matthew is a man of few words. His telling of the story of Jesus's birth is done in eight quick verses! In his Cliff Notes version, Matthew thought it important to remind his readers, however, that these events took place as they did for a reason. He explains that Jesus is coming just as God said he would through the prophet Isaiah.

We are pointed again to God's plan. He loves us so much that He has planned how to draw us to Him. Paul explained God's plan in his letter to the Ephesians, writing, "and this is God's plan: Both Gentiles and Jews who believe the Good News share equally in the riches inherited by God's children. Both are part of the same body, and both enjoy the promise of blessings because they belong to Christ Jesus" (Ephesians 3:6, NLT). This has been God's plan from the beginning. God's plans are not like those "of mice and men, which go awry." Matthew tells us we can trust in Him and His plan because all has gone as God has promised.

Though not usually thought of as an advent passage, one of my favorites is, "From one man he made all the nations, that they should inhabit the whole earth; and he marked out their appointed times in history and the boundaries of their lands. God did this so that they would seek him and perhaps reach out for him and find him, though he is not far from any one of us" (Acts 17:26-27, NLT). There are no coincidences; God is drawing us to Himself. Remember, as we wait for

Jesus's birth, to take the time to reflect on the awesomeness of God's plan to love us.

Action:

Consider where God has placed you at this time in your history—where you live, where you work, the people in your life, and thank Him for His plan for you.

Prayer:

Lord, help me make myself ready and available for You to use me. Amen.

DECEMBER 6

Mary, Did You Know?
BY JULIE DAHLBERG

Luke 2:15-20

For everything there is a season, a time for every activity under heaven.
Ecclesiastes 3:1

This passage is a study in contrasts. Picture the stable and the newborn baby. We have the shepherds, who have just had an encounter with angels! And they have found everything the angels told them to be true. They are telling their story to everyone in the village, they are praising and glorifying God, and people around them are astonished. They are noisy, and probably smelly. It sounds like everything is moving quickly. It's all thrilling, amazing, and wonderful.

And in the same scene, we have Mary. She is pondering and quietly treasuring things in her heart. She is thoughtful in the middle of glorious chaos. We can feel her presence slowing the moments down, pausing and cherishing. Beautiful. God has done the impossible. He has fulfilled His promise and all the prophecies.

The advent season is all about the expectant waiting and the miraculous coming of Jesus. It is a time of both noisy praise and quiet pondering. Both are appropriate responses to the gift God has given us in His son. Let us make space in our advent season for glorifying God *and* treasuring these things in our hearts.

Action:

Sing praises to God and take time to be still and ponder.

Prayer:

Thank You, Lord, for contrasts, for quiet and for noise. Amen.

DECEMBER 7
PEARL HARBOR DAY

Friendly Fire
BY MYRA BIERNAT WELLS

Psalm 93:4

Mightier than the thunder of the great waters, mightier than the breakers of the sea—
the LORD on high is mighty.

December 7th, 1941 -- a date which will live in infamy. **Franklin D. Roosevelt**

In a History Channel special on the Pearl Harbor attack, historians noted a chilling truth. A still disputed number of civilians died that day; most killed by friendly fire. Some had driven down to the harbor to lend assistance, but military personnel, also fearing a land invasion, shot their own countrymen thinking they were an invading force.

Whenever I hear stories like this, I mourn for the waste of it all - the lives ended, the grief of loved ones, the stories snuffed out too soon. But underneath, there is a haunting question. Would I have been that brave? Would I have faced bombs and bullets to help?

The coward in me hopes I'll never get the opportunity to find out the answer to that question, but then it struck me that, in a way, every day *is* Pearl Harbor Day. Unanticipated attacks on our souls and psyches happen daily. Startling news, dead ends, broken relationships, failures happen and not only blow our world to smithereens, they also leave destruction in their wake. All seems lost.

God does not want us to stay lost. He is with us every step of the way. He has already been where He is asking you to go and has prepared every step of the way for you. You don't have to be afraid when you feel your plans have been destroyed. God is well aware of where you are and of every step He is asking you to take.

In this life, we will face battles. As we enter the conflict, God fights by our side and through Him we are more than conquerors. When you step out in faith, God pours rich blessings on you despite life's minefields. Trust God and step out in confidence. He will meet you there.

Action:
Make a list of the reasons we can trust God – even when facing uncertainty.

Prayer:
Father, I come to You in faith. I will admit that facing life's challenges scares me because it means I must face the unknown. I know it is a control issue, Lord. Right now, I surrender the control of my life and my journey to You. Give me the strength to step out in faith. In Jesus' name. Amen.

DECEMBER 8

Check Your Oil
BY SHERRI GALLAGHER

Hebrews 6:10-12

The expectations of life depend upon diligence; the mechanic that would perfect his work must first sharpen his tools. **Confucius**

I am very conscientious about maintaining my vehicles. Oil changes happen on schedule, tires are rotated at the correct mileage, and important maintenance is done at the proper point in my car's lifecycle. In the winter, I make sure the anti-freeze will withstand Chicago temperatures and seldom does the gas gauges get below a quarter of a tank of fuel. I do this because I spent a good portion of my life driving less than reliable cars. There is nothing like being stranded in a broken car, miles from home, on a bitter cold, windy day to make a person appreciate a well running vehicle and be willing to do the small daily tasks to keep it that way.

I am trying to apply the same diligence to my spiritual maintenance. Am I doing daily prayers and Bible study? Just like my vehicle, if I keep my spiritual tank full with daily devotionals and religious study or programs, I tend to be better able to cope with difficulties and doubts. At regular intervals, I assess my own focus and attention to God. Have I kept Him my primary focus or have I let the distractions of life get in the way? If I can be diligent as Paul teaches in Hebrews, I can create a better world, be an example of Christian living, and realize what I have hoped for in the Lord. While I know I am saved by Jesus' grace, I am responsible to the body of Christ to live, study, and worship in a way the Bible teaches us we should do as Christians.

Action:
Do a 50,000-mile check of your spiritual habits. Are they helping your spiritual health?

Prayer:
Lord, guide me that I may stay strong and steady in my pursuit of You through the study of Your word. Amen.

DECEMBER 9

Enjoy the Journey
BY SHERRI GALLAGHER

Hebrews 12:2

fixing our eyes on Jesus, the pioneer and perfecter of faith. For the joy set before him he endured the cross, scorning its shame, and sat down at the right hand of the throne of God.

Creativity itself doesn't care at all about the results - the only thing it craves is the process. Learn to love the process and let whatever happens next happen, without fussing too much about it. Work like a monk, or a mule, or some other representative metaphor for diligence. Love the work. **Elizabeth Gilbert**

I love my dogs and I love training them, but I really dislike going through the testing process called trialing. My dog Orex must pass several tests before I can breed him. I signed up to trial him several months ago, but I realized he would fail a portion of the challenge and pulled him. Trying to fix the problem has been frustrating. Last week, he still wasn't ready, but I had to make a decision: enter him or wait three more months.

I get very nervous when we test and even in the months leading up to the trial. That is a huge problem because Orex is immediately aware I am upset, even when the people around me have no idea as to my emotional state. With this particular dog, if I am nervous, he goes into guardian mode and does his best to protect me from everyone. That doesn't make the best impression on the evaluator. If we are going to pass, I need to figure out why I get so nervous and prevent it. The problem has been fear of disappointing the people who have helped me train. If we fail it reflects on the breeder, the instructors, the helpers and many friends who have given generously of their time and effort to make us successful. Realizing these people will not be upset has helped make me less nervous. I entered Orex in the test and decided to focus on making training fun. His performance has improved so much, I now know he will pass.

Isn't our spiritual life much the same? We strive to be perfect, like Jesus, but we are human and imperfect. If we make mistakes, we worry that we are setting a bad example for our children, our friends, or those new to faith. We mentally berate ourselves for doing things we know we shouldn't, and letting God, our pastor, and our brothers and sisters in Christ down. But do we?

There is nothing we can do that will remove us from God's love. Our pastor and our friends know their own failings, and what seems like a huge problem to us, is not a problem for them. If we instead focus on our spiritual journey, letting ourselves enjoy God's love and growing closer to Him, the journey will be much easier and more pleasant.

Action:

What is making you doubt yourself? Tell yourself nothing you do will remove God's love.

Prayer:

Heavenly Father, thank You for Your love. Gently remind me that You love me even with all my faults and failings. Amen.

DECEMBER 10

The Words You Say
BY MYRA BIERNAT WELLS

Psalm 19:14

May the words of my mouth and the meditation of my heart be pleasing in your sight, O LORD, my Rock and my Redeemer.

My relationship with my mother has always been rocky. She is a gentile, sophisticated lady, while I am loud and brash – always pushing her to the brink of insanity. When I share with a few close friends the shameful or hurtful details of my maternal relationship, they also reveal stories about their own familial wounds.

Becoming a parent doesn't mean just bearing a child. You become a parent by bringing God's love into the lives of your children. For with love, the lessons a child remembers are the ones that are lived. They need to observe love in action, to feel love encircling them. Despite the poor choices children make, even with the arguments and the frustrations parents endure, being an instrument of love to their precious children provides the courage for the little ones to spread their wings and soar.

Perhaps, like me, you have some old tapes from your upbringing you replay with your children, spouse or friends. Did one of your parents make comments that caused you to feel shame or as if you were indebted to them for your care? Many parents are travel agents for guilt trips. The angry words I heard as a little girl are not ones I wish to bring into my future.

While I don't succeed every day, I yearn to use my words to build others up. I desire to help others feel better about themselves because they crossed paths with me. Even if the time together is short, like that with a grocery clerk, I crave encouraging others rather than spreading discouragement. The pain of my upbringing has affected the way I love. I've learned to help people, hear them, bring healing because I was once there – right in the middle of their distress.

Words can spur people on to do mighty things. Or they can become a chain that holds them back from achieving their dreams. The words we speak are a mirror of how others see themselves. Let's remember how important it is to speak loving, tender, soothing words. God gave you a gentle and sensitive soul. Generous, compassionate and tender – *that's what you are*. And, oh, how the world needs the inspiring words you speak.

Action:
Memorize Psalm 19:14: "May the words of my mouth and the meditation of my heart be pleasing in your sight, O LORD, my Rock and my Redeemer."

Prayer:
Dear Lord, I pray the Holy Spirit will be the gatekeeper of my mouth today. Please let my words help others see themselves as You see them…dearly loved and valued by You. Amen.

DECEMBER 11

What Could Have Been
BY MYRA BIERNAT WELLS

Psalm 56:8

Record my misery; list my tears on your scroll – are they not in your record?

During my freshman year in college, my life as I knew it ended on December 11. While I was home on Christmas break, my father died suddenly of a heart attack. Only a thin strip of two minutes separated the time between when he took ill to his last breath. Alone with him when he passed, I was crushed I could do nothing to save him. In the next days, I began to mourn the *what might have beens*: him walking me down the aisle at my wedding, his pride when I received my college degree, seeing him and my mother's love intensify as they grew older.

Decades later, December 11 is still a difficult day for me. If you've been marked by a *what might have been*, you understand exactly. You know the exact day, the number of years. You remember the last time you saw your loved one's face, the number of anniversaries you would be celebrating, how your world was shining and beautiful before you got the diagnosis. You remember the day that changed absolutely everything. It makes the calendar a minefield.

We all experience loss in this life. Sadly, we all have a day when life broke apart. I hope that on whatever day that is for you, you can tenderly love yourself as you relive the beautiful memories that make that day so difficult.

Romans 12:15 says we should mourn with those who mourn. I share your grief. I totally understand your reluctance for that date to appear on the calendar.

And while I can't wipe that grief away, know I stand beside you in solidarity for whatever it is that was lost.

Action:

Where has your life been marred by *what could have beens*? If you don't already have a meaningful tradition, think of one you can start doing to mark that day.

Prayer:

Jesus, oh how we need You to carry the weight of the what could have beens in our lives. Bring us deep, abiding restful peace. Revive our broken hearts and shore up our broken places. Be so very near! Amen.

DECEMBER 12

The One and Only
BY SHERRI GALLAGHER

Jeremiah 9:5-7

The best and safest thing is to keep balance in your life, acknowledge the great power around us and in us. If you can do that, and live that way, you are really a wise man. **Euripides**

Listening to the news can be depressing. While it is seldom a big headline, more and more frequently there are items where a lawsuit is filed to prevent the recognition of God. Sometimes it is to remove the Ten Commandments from a public building. Sometimes it is someone being sued for defending their beliefs. Public prayer is banned before sporting events and public schools refuse to allow the Bible in the classroom but teach from other religious texts. Christians are being murdered for their faith in much of the world, but there is little, if any outcry. We are told to teach our children not to speak about their religion and be politely silent while others deny God's existence.

Reading in Jeremiah 9:5-7 I wondered if he had been on social media lately. "'Friend deceives friend, and no one speaks the truth. They have taught their tongues to lie; they weary themselves with sinning. You live in the midst of deception; in their deceit they refuse to acknowledge me,' declares the Lord."

But that is not what is right and not what we should live by.

The question then becomes, what should we do? Stand on the street corner and shout for people to repent? That will have limited effectiveness. People will consider us to be crackpots and tune us out. What we must do, is calmly affirm that we hold God as having power in all things. We must acknowledge His existence in us and around us. We must be open when we give thanks without being theatrical. If we stand firm and follow His precepts, we set an example. Don't be afraid to say grace in a restaurant the same way you would around the family table. When you are blessed and someone congratulates you, acknowledge God as the source of your blessing. Have love and compassion for those around you and by your calm, firm example let others wonder and want to investigate what gives you such confidence.

Action:
Lead by example. How can you show those around you the importance you place on God?

Prayer:
Heavenly Father, lead me into situations today where I can acknowledge You in a way that makes people curious and wanting to draw closer to You. Give me the strength to carry though and acknowledge You. Amen.

DECEMBER 13

When We Interfere with God's Plan
BY MYRA BIERNAT WELLS

Psalm 27:14

Wait for the Lord; be strong, take heart and wait for the Lord.

There are parts of the story of Abraham and Sarah that leave me reeling. Abraham was promised by God to be the father of many nations, but there was one hitch in the plan—Sarah, his wife, had never had a child and now was beyond childbearing years. Still, I just can't understand Sarah telling her husband to sleep with his maid. *(Note: If you are unfamiliar with the story, read Genesis chapters 15 and 16.)*

God had an incredible plan in mind for Abraham and Sarah, but Sarah jumped the gun and her interference caused much heartache and strife. She is not alone. Many times, we have a tendency to run ahead of God when we feel He is not acting quickly enough. We conspire, cajole and in our impatience, move forward without God's blessings.

Jeremiah 29:11 promises God has a plan for each one of us. "For I know the plans I have for you," declares the Lord, "plans to prosper you and not to harm you, plans to give you hope and a future." He never needs our interference to accomplish His plan, but He does require our obedience and cooperation.

Our gracious Father has given us a free will and allows us to storm ahead when we feel He hasn't given us the green light. But because of Sarah's interference, Ishmael, the son of Abraham's maid, Hagar, was born. Muhammad, the founder of the Muslim people and Islamic faith came from Ishmael's family tree. God predicted tension between the offspring of Ishmael and Isaac, Sarah's and Abraham's promised son. Today, we still see that conflict raging in the strife between the Muslims and Jews.

So, here's a life challenge: don't interfere with God's plan for your life. His ways are by far the most exciting and fulfilling. Obey His nudges, His whispers and above all His permission to proceed. If He does not give the go ahead, wait for Him to act and not take the reins if we feel He isn't acting quickly enough.

Action:

Have you ever made a mess of things? Ask God to forgive you and to give you strength to accept the consequences of your actions and endurance to wait for Him to complete His future plans for you.

Prayer:

Oh, Lord, forgive my impatience. Forgive me when I run ahead of You. I don't want to interfere with Your plans and mess things up, so today, I commit to waiting on You. I will not come up with a plan that only suits my wants, desire and fancies. Give me the strength to wait on Your perfect plan to be enacted in Your perfect time. Amen.

DECEMBER 14

The Sabbath
BY SHERRI GALLAGHER

Exodus 20:8

Remember the Sabbath day by keeping it holy.

but the seventh day is a Sabbath to the LORD your God. On it you shall not do any work, neither you, nor your son or daughter, nor your manservant or maidservant, nor your animals, nor any alien within your gates. **Exodus 20:10**

This book of devotionals came up in a discussion with a Jewish friend of mine. He was surprised when I mentioned there were alternative readings for some of the Jewish Holy days. He asked which ones. After I read him the list he said, "You missed the most important one, the Sabbath. It is the only Holy Day directed by God."

"What about Passover?" I asked.

"That is a remembrance to remind your children what God did for them. The Sabbath is the only one to keep Holy and dedicated to God."

After a little more discussion, we each went back to our own tasks, but his comments kept spinning around in my head. Did I keep the Sabbath as a day to worship God? I certainly haven't been the best at that. It is important we go to church but what about the rest of the day? I know I get distracted and often use Sunday afternoon to get caught up on the previous week or to get a head start on the coming week. The question that comes back is, how is that honoring God?

Writing this book has been an education and a helpful guide to how I can improve, starting with keeping the Sabbath for God first and second for our benefit. One of the things we should do on the Lord's day is complete tasks that refresh us for His service, intellectually, physically and spiritually. So, if you are at your desk all week, you should probably walk or ride a bike on Sunday. If on the other hand you do hard physical labor all week, then sit down or take a nice long nap on Sunday.

Action:

Think about what you are doing on Sundays and how you can honor God more.

Prayer:

Thank You, Lord, for Your guidance that comes from many different places. Help me to see how I can better use the Sabbath to honor You. Amen.

DECEMBER 15

Tomorrowland
BY SHERRI GALLAGHER

Acts 20:16-36

Each problem has hidden in it an opportunity so powerful that it literally dwarfs the problem. The greatest success stories were created by people who recognized a problem and turned it into an opportunity. **Joseph Sugarman**

There is a movie titled, *Tomorrowland*. It is the story of a young girl who looks at bad situations and tries to find solutions. Nothing can dim her enthusiasm for making a difference. There are others who have the ability to see into the future and it is bleak, all they see is a 100% chance that humankind will destroy itself. However, when the young girl finds them, the potential destruction is reduced to 99.994%. Realizing just one person can make a difference, they go searching to find other positive dreamers and encourage them until the world and humankind is saved from destruction.

ow we look at the world can certainly influence our actions and our ability to cope with problems. Paul and Silas were traveling in Macedonia and were unjustly stripped, beaten and imprisoned. Instead of weeping and begging God for help, they continued to preach the message of Jesus Christ to the prisoners around them. An earthquake occurred, freeing them. Instead of fleeing for their lives, they continued to preach, converting the jailer and his family. In the morning, the magistrates freed them, and they continued their journey without the fear of someone coming after them. Their actions also led many others to salvation, which was a huge difference.

The world around us often seems bleak. Terrible news seems to have more impact than good tidings, so headlines scream how it is too late for us and our planet. But if God wanted us to see the world in a negative light, He would not have given us the examples He does in the Bible. Over and over again, we see where one person can make a small difference that shifts the balance in a positive direction. If we make small positive changes in our lives and actions, we can make a difference in the future. Conserving electricity and water, donating to a food pantry or shelter, sending a note of encouragement to a person in a difficult situation or praying for someone who needs it are all things we can do to make a difference for ourselves, our friends, and this beautiful planet God created.

Action:
Talk with your family members and decide on one small thing you can do to make a difference, then do it.

Prayer:
Heavenly Father, thank You for the power of creativity and hope You have given us. Help me to use it today to make a difference. Amen.

DECEMBER 16

Out of Control
BY BETH DUMEY

Psalms 71:16

I will come and proclaim your mighty acts, O Sovereign Lord.

Our illusion of control is unmasked occasionally to give us a glimpse of how much we rely on the Lord for every breath we take. My recent episode of "unmasking" came about during preparations for surgery. The procedure itself was unexpected and daunting. It took place more than thirty miles from my home and required a schedule of four friends, two family members, and various pickups and drop-offs to return me to my home for recovery. All of this took place during a relentless snowstorm.

Once we arrived at the hospital, I was at the mercy of the surgeon, various nurses, and a cocktail of pain medication to move me toward healing. At times, I was not lucid and could barely eat or swallow. Shifting in my bed took all my effort and reaching for the phone was enough to exhaust me.

After I was released and went home, I relied on many to help me do small tasks that previously didn't merit a thought: lifting a laptop, taking a photo, getting rid of the garbage. In a matter of hours, I transitioned from being capable, sufficient, professional to being limited, non-driving, homebound. How do I do this, Lord? I would ask for the simplest movement.

Yet, this total reliance on God is more honest and more natural than my self-reliance. It isn't comfortable. Feeling vulnerable and needy makes me feel out of control. At the same time, I realize that I am always out of control; only the Lord, in His Sovereignty, is in control. And as much as I rely on my own strength or relationships or abilities to get me through, it is only God himself who is enabling me to take the next breath, and the next, and the next…

Action:

When all else is stripped away, what or who do you rely on to sustain your life? Discuss this with your small group.

Prayer:

Father, I want to trust You with my life and each moment in it. Help me to be aware of Your sovereignty and Your good will. Amen.

DECEMBER 17

What's Holding You Back?
BY MYRA BIERNAT WELLS

Psalm 71:5

For you have been my hope, Sovereign Lord, my confidence since my youth.

Self-confidence is not my strong suit. When I open up to friends and tell them that, they generally laugh, "Oh, you're one of the most self-confident people I know." I guess it is a good mask since there are nights when overcome by outlandish fear, I can't sleep. My chest heaves because my lungs can't suck in air fast enough. My skin burns as though it was seared and my head pounds painfully.

Yet, despite my fears – well, maybe because of them – I've still learned to soar. This happens not on my own power but solely when I've been obedient to God. Many times, I've stood on the precipice of belief knowing a decision had to be made. Can I trust God or not? Am I going to take a leap of faith or live in fear because I don't believe He has my best interest at heart? Do I trust in His love for me or not? Am I going to settle for doing it on my own, frozen in fear, settling for safety? Or am I going to hand my fears over to Him and see the thrill of God's work through me?

When I've trusted God, He has led me on some wild adventures! I have only rocketed through life when I've jumped headlong into His perfect plan for me! Acts 17:28 states, *"For in Him we live and move and have our being."*

Refuse to drink in the poison of rejection, doubt and fear; embrace instead the hope found only in Jesus Christ. No matter how uncertain life is, God is still

God. He is sovereign. And even though you're afraid, even when you don't understand His ways, you trust Him.

Are you ready to take a leap of faith? Yes? Then fasten your seat belt as you jump confidently into the daring journey of His perfect plan for you! Christ will take you on a lifelong journey into the depths of His love.

Action:

Is there anything in your life that God has called you to do that you haven't done? What's holding you back? What or who are you afraid of? Take a lesson from David and write a short psalm expressing your fears to God.

Prayer:

Lord, sometimes I'm just flat out afraid. Afraid I'll fail. Afraid I'll be rejected. Afraid I won't be good enough. Lord, forgive me for all those "I's." Forgive me for focusing on my weaknesses rather than Your strength. Today, I'm believing I can do all things You call me to do because I know that You will give me the strength I need. In Jesus' name. Amen.

DECEMBER 18

I Believe
BY SHERRI GALLAGHER

Hebrews 11:1-3

Now faith is confidence in what we hope for and assurance about what we do not see. This is what the ancients were commended for. By faith we understand that the universe was formed at God's command, so that what is seen was not made out of what was visible.

Hold faithfulness and sincerity as first principles. **Confucius**

One of my favorite movies is "Miracle on 34th Street." Toward the end Susan Walker (Natalie Wood) is sitting waiting to go home, very depressed because the present she wanted wasn't there. She decides that Santa Claus really doesn't exist and the old man she knew as Kris Kringle was just a nice old man. Her mother tells her faith is believing in something that your mind tells you not to. Susan waits for her ride home saying, "I believe, I believe, it's silly, but I believe." Boy, have I been in those shoes! I know God is there. I know I should trust in Him, but it seems really difficult to trust in Him and follow the path I know is right from Jesus' teachings. Sometimes, just like Susan, I need to talk myself into holding fast to my faith. Deep down, I trust God, but right here and now, this makes no sense at all. Daniel Webster said, "Philosophical argument has sometimes shaken my reason for the faith that was in me; but my heart has always assured me that the Gospel of Jesus Christ must be reality."

James tells us in Hebrews 11:1, "Faith is the assurance of things hoped for, the conviction of things not seen." We take by faith Christ's promise of salvation. We trust that following and applying Jesus' teachings is the right way to live. While we can't know for sure, doesn't it feel good when you help someone? That warm feeling can't be wrong. Knowing you made a difference, if only to bring a fleeting smile, is that little voice telling you God is pleased. Have faith. Believe.

Action:

Think of the last time you did what your heart wanted but your mind denied. How did you feel afterwards? How will that influence your future actions?

Prayer:

Lord God, give me the faith to do what is in my heart even when my mind says not to. Amen.

DECEMBER 19

The WOW Factor
BY CATHY HARVEY

Deuteronomy 29:29

The secret things belong to the LORD our God, but the things revealed belong to us and to our children forever, that we may follow all the words of this law.

The most beautiful thing we can experience is the mysterious. It is the source of all true art and all science. He to whom this emotion is a stranger, who can no longer pause to wonder and stand rapt in awe, is as good as dead: his eyes are closed. **Albert Einstein**

I am always delighted by simple facts of life or truths in Scripture that often slip right past me until one day, for no particular reason, I take notice, and realize an incredible truth I had missed up until that point. Suddenly, it "wows" me. I'm stunned, a bit dazed, and continue for a period in a cloud of amazement. As I ponder the new truth God has revealed, I am awed by the fact, first of all, that I never noticed it before, and secondly, by how profoundly deep it is in spite of its simplicity.

I was socked with one of those wow moments as I was attempting to memorize verses for a women's group of which I was a member. Our theme verses for the year were John 13:34-35. I didn't catch the repetition in them at first, but it jumped off the page at me as I wrote the verses out.

Three times in two verses Jesus gave very clear instructions to His disciples. I only noticed the Lord's point and emphasis by printing it out in this way.

"A new commandment I give you:
LOVE ONE ANOTHER.
As I have loved you, so you must
LOVE ONE ANOTHER.
By this all men will know that you are my disciples, if you
LOVE ONE ANOTHER."

How clearly the Lord has shown us what He desires and expects from us—to love one another. It was so all-encompassing. I tried to imagine how the world would change if everyone, or even just the Christians, put these two simple verses into practice in their daily lives: how relationships would improve in all facets of life; how it could affect marriages, families, sibling relationships, holidays together, court outcomes, business deals. . .

And I caught myself saying under my breath, "Wow."

Action:

Is Scripture memory part of your spiritual disciplines? Perhaps, you could memorize these verses. Write them out several times. Post them in places where you will see them throughout the day. Meditate on them. Make them your lifestyle. Who, in particular, needs your love today? Show them.

Prayer:

Heavenly Father, help me memorize, meditate on, and own Your anthem of love in such a profound way that it changes *me* most of all, that the world will know I am Yours by my love for others. Amen.

DECEMBER 20

Actions Speak Louder
BY SHERRI GALLAGHER

James 2:14-26

We have too many high sounding words, and too few actions that correspond with them.
Abigail Adams

Who would have thought words written in the 18th century would apply to social media? I frequently get videos of horribly abused and suffering animals along with a plea to donate or sign a petition begging government to "make it stop." I made a promise to myself not to fall into the trap of these empty words. Before I send a donation, I research (www.charitywatch.org/charities) how the money will be spent. One particular organization spends less than two percent of their donations on research that might eventually be of help. The rest is spent in administrative costs. I must invest a little more time, but eventually I can find a group that will use my donation to make a difference. Usually they are struggling, and my small bit makes a real difference.

The same is true of the "make it stop" petitions. What are we asking of our government officials? Are we proposing new legislation, or a change in procedure, or just venting our outrage? Sometimes there are already laws in place to address the situation; they just need to be enforced. After I do my research, I write a letter to the best official to take action. My letter asks for specific legislation to be proposed or for enforcement of an existing law to be improved. Perhaps they will ignore my letter, but I think it will get more attention than petitions that come in with "click here" signatures.

James gave similar advice to the early Christians when it came to claiming faith without deeds. Telling someone who is hungry to go and be full without giving them something to eat does nothing to fill an empty belly. The Bible guides us to take action, not mouth platitudes. We must help where we can as much as we can. The Shepherd's Fund is a prime example of actions speaking louder than words.

Action:

When you see a situation that distresses you, figure out how to make a difference, then act.

Prayer:

God, please give me the wisdom and guide my actions that I may make a difference. Amen.

DECEMBER 21

Circle of Protection
BY CATHY HARVEY

James 1:17

*Every good gift and every perfect gift is from above, and comes down from the
Father of lights…*

*When you are discouraged, thinking all is lost, count your many blessings, name
them one by one, and it will surprise you what the Lord hath done.*
Johnson Oatman, Jr., *Count Your Blessings*

In 1982 I learned a principle at a women's conference in Indiana that made
a lasting impression on me. I have taught this principle to many and even shared it
with my children, who at the time were ages three, six, and eight.

The conference speaker stood in the middle of the platform and called for
a group of about 100 freshman girls from a nearby college to cluster tightly around
her. Each one was wearing a poster board sign. There was one word on each sign
representing a blessing God had given the speaker in different seasons of her life:
book titles, individuals, Scripture verses, sports and hobbies, things in nature,
places, hymns, and other joys God had given her as emotional protection from the
storms of life.

Then, the speaker asked any girl whose word had anything to do with a
sport to step out of the circle. This represented what might happen if she had an
accident which would eliminate her ability to play sports. Would her world fall
apart? Was her entire life wrapped up in sports? No. Where the girls left a gap by
stepping out of the clustered circle, other girls moved in to fill the gaps. In this
way, a loss in one area of life was compensated by many other blessings.

She gave other examples and each time girls had to leave the circle, there
were many others to fill the gaps. Little did the speaker know that soon after the
conference, she would face a cancer diagnosis. The Lord had already prepared her
to understand she had a wide and deep "circle of protection" to carry her through
this loss and others that are a part of life.

God has provided countless blessings and encouragements for all of us:
for our physical, emotional, spiritual, and social needs. When this principle is
taught to children, they give precious answers of what makes them happy. When
they are having a bad day, mom or dad can remind them of their *Circle of
Protection*. A few things on my Circle include: songs about America, my Bible,

the soft glow of candles, birds chirping in winter, the sound of my husband wrestling with our kids, Handel's *Messiah*, Isaiah 26:3 & 4, organizing, clean hair, a funny movie, butterflies, *A Mighty Fortress Is Our God...*

Action:

Begin your own *Circle of Protection*. When life is painful and dreary, reread the joys with which God has encircled you.

Prayer:

Oh, Lord, help me taste and see how good You are by recognizing the many gifts and encouragements You shower upon me every day! Help me consciously "count my blessings" at day's end and sleep in the sweet peace of contentment. Amen.

DECEMBER 22

Held by Hope
BY MYRA BIERNAT WELLS

Luke 2:19

But Mary treasured up all these things and pondered them in her heart.

I've often wanted to travel through time to witness the celebration that took place in Bethlehem on the first Christmas. It would be so thrilling to see angels flying through the sky, hearing God in the cries of a little baby and catching a glimpse of the star the Wise Men followed. How amazing to soak in the wonder of it all!

Wouldn't it be incredible to talk to Mary and ask exactly what she treasured in her heart? To learn what she was thinking as she took place in God's greatest miracle? After all, the baby she has just birthed was God-in-the-flesh. Her bundle of joy was also a bundle of perfect love.

The baby in the manger is the Hope of the world, the Grace that saves us and the Love that heals us. He is the only One capable of changing our guilt into forgiveness, our empty into full and our worthless into precious. In the New Testament, we are told Jesus Christ sits on the right hand of God and that He *holds us fast*. So, when Mary held her baby, she held the Hope of the World, but the Hope of the World was also holding her. The Hope that holds each one of us is Jesus Christ. You and I are always held by Hope.

In the Old Testament, God told Joshua that He would *never leave or forsake* him (Joshua 1:5) That promise holds true today. No matter what the circumstances, no matter what the crisis, no matter what struggles befall us, God will never leave us. We can breathe more deeply knowing that in everything we are held by Hope.

God is always with us.

He is always loving us. He will always invite us to find joy, satisfaction and refuge in Him.

Action:

Are you allowing Hope to hold you? He's waiting with arms wide open. Take a moment over a cup of coffee, tea or hot chocolate, prayerfully thanking Him for all the times He has held you close.

Prayer:

Father, thank You for sending Jesus to be my Hope. It is only through Him I am restored to You. I thank You for the times He has wrapped His arms around my heart and whispered, "Everything will be alright." I'm leaning into Your heavenly hug today! Amen.

DECEMBER 23

Cold Hands
BY MYRA BIERNAT WELLS

Proverbs 31:29

Many women have done wonderful things, but you've outclassed them all!
(MSG)

I hate the giving of the hand unless the whole man accompanies it.
Ralph Waldo Emerson

"Hold my hands for a little while longer," she implored. "Mine are so cold and yours are so warm." With that, we sat, her hands cradled in mine until she fell asleep on my shoulder.

Suffering with dementia, some days my Aunt Marion recognizes me; on others she disengages. Long term memories come floating to the surface…of picnics and swimming at the lake in summer, toboggan rides down snowy hills in the winter. Hope rises in my heart thinking she's back, but five minutes later, she's asleep with no memory of who I am.

As she slumbered next to me, my thoughts turned to leaving. It was the height of the holiday rush and I had chores. But then the Holy Spirit whispered to me, "This is the most important thing on your agenda." So, I prayed intense appeals for more time with her, craving the times we sat over coffee sharing our successes and regrets, knowing the love between us didn't need to be spoken, hoping my presence now addressed everything that needed to be said.

A woman of deep faith, Aunt Marion was someone you could hold onto. Her house, always immaculate despite raising five children, was a place of healing and hope – a home dominated with love, acceptance and unity. A place that collected the shattered because she filled it with restoration. No matter how dark it was, the light of hope shone there.

In these days of Facebook and Twitter, of rushed days and overbooked schedules, we rob ourselves of the gift of presence. We steal the intimacy gained only from loving personal, face-to-face interactions. Aunt Marion built powerful and passionate relationships. Always positive, always encouraging, her love made us feel deeply rooted, upheld, courageous.

Do you do that? I deeply regret I'm not anywhere near as good at it as she was. So, I'm asking all of you brave individuals to join me in deciding anew to choose time to give life, to remain authentic to those you love. Every day we choose love over hurriedness, we choose the nature of God who makes loving others the bravest, most transforming and most mysterious act of all.

Perhaps the most important thing you'll do today is just hold someone's hand.

Action:
Give the gift of your presence to someone this holiday season.

Prayer:
Jesus, You came to win the ultimate contest on earth, the contest for every soul. Thank You for coming to rescue us from our hopelessness. Would You show Yourself powerful today? Direct us to someone who needs the gift of our presence. We love You, precious Jesus. Amen.

DECEMBER 24

Before
BY BETH DUMEY

Isaiah 65:24

Before they call I will answer; while they are still speaking I will hear.

The day before is easily forgotten. It's a preliminary, soon-to be overshadowed by the day after. In twenty-four hours, THE event will happen. But the day before is mere preparation. The day before you are married, the day before the final exam, the day before the catastrophe hit, the day before a birth, nothing has changed. The day after, life will never be quite the same.

Yet, God knows all our befores just as he knows all our afters. He already prepared for His son to be born on earth to redeem our sins before we knew we needed a Savior. God is always working in the befores. We only learn about it in the afters. We assume nothing has happened until it does. But much has happened in the spiritual world to align events according to God's will.

Before Christ's birth, God hung a bright star over Bethlehem to beckon and lead the wise men to the stable where he was born. Even earlier, he foreshadowed this birth, through his prophet Isaiah, "For a child will be born to us, a son will be given to us; And the government will rest on His shoulders; And His name will be called Wonderful Counselor, Mighty God, Eternal Father, Prince of Peace" (Isaiah 9:6-7). It was all in the plan. For God, the day before wasn't really a 'before', it was a continuing of the saga he had already put in motion.

In our lives, we tend to see time as a series of beginnings and endings, starts and stops, changing seasons. We have ceremonies to mark rites of passage and commemorations to honor past events. We think of our years in stages of young adult, middle age, and senior. From our eternal God's perspective, the 'befores' and 'afters' evaporate. For the one who knows our full story and lives beyond the bounds of time, we are forever His children, in the constant state of 'becoming' more like Him.

Action:

Do you think of your life in terms of 'befores' and 'afters'? Think about the events that have prompted this perspective. How was God working throughout the situations?

Prayer:

Lord, only You have the total picture. Help us to see You working in small and large ways. Keep us from being mired by the limited perspective of time. Remind us that You are working every day on our behalf. Amen.

DECEMBER 25

Presence
BY BETH DUMEY

Matthew 1:23

They shall call his name Emmanuel, which being interpreted is God with us.

We celebrate this day with glittering tinsel, strings of lights, brightly patterned paper, and freshly baked goods. Our carols are rhythmic and our wreaths are bowed. Our fir trees are decorated and our mantles are stocked. We are festive and hopeful and full of glad tidings. Our flurry emanates with joyousness and glee. As with any celebration, we dress up, show up, and light up when we embrace family and friends.

Christmas is a celebration unlike any other. This is fitting, because it is the biggest birthday of all time. Our Savior, the Messiah, enters our world as Emmanuel, God with us. It is His presence, His joining us, in strife and suffering, in pain and pleasure, in weakness and strength, that redeemed humankind. No presents can equal His presence. For a season, we reflect on this gift, we delight in a birth in Bethlehem, and we gather loved ones close to share our joy.

Cue the cymbals, signal the dancers, and witness the miracle of a birth. Though it happened without fanfare, let us unleash our strongest voices, sound our loudest horns, and proclaim throughout the land the great news: Our Savior is with us.

Action:

Consider what you are truly celebrating at Christmas. . .time off? Family get-togethers? A meal? A new gadget? In the midst of all of this, think about how your life would be different if "God with us" had not been born.

Prayer:

Lord, we delight in the gift of Your Son, this day, Emmanuel, God with us. Help us to remember throughout the year how this one birth changed the world and changed us individually. Be present with us each day. Amen.

DECEMBER 26

Speak No Evil
BY SHERRI GALLAGHER

Romans 14:16-18

Therefore do not let what you know is good be spoken of as evil. For the kingdom of God is not a matter of eating and drinking, but of righteousness, peace and joy in the Holy Spirit, because anyone who serves Christ in this way is pleasing to God and receives human approval.

All that is necessary for the triumph of evil is that good men do nothing.
Edmund Burke

Social media is an interesting place. There are a wide variety of opinions, quotes and disputable "facts." Getting into an argument on social media is not a wise thing to do. The range of results is anything from hurtful misunderstandings to destroyed friendships. All the results are negative, no one changes their opinions, but friendships are ruptured.

When I see a posting by a friend, I will share or "like" those I agree with. If I disagree, I try and just skip that post. Recently there have been a number of posts with which I disagreed intensely. While Matthew and Luke tell us to turn the other cheek, Romans tells us not to allow what we know as good to be spoken of as evil (Romans 14:16).

How do we know when to stand and when to walk away? Romans 14:17 tells us it is not a matter of eating or drinking but of righteousness and serving

Christ in a way that is pleasing to God. Everyday things should not place us at odds with each other. Politics and causes are everyday things and much depends on opinion. Disagreeing with those will not change anyone's mind and will not bring the peace and joy of the Holy Spirit. With those I try and turn the other cheek. However, when some friends mock God or deny His existence it is time to speak up. Still, this must be done in a peaceful and loving manner. God doesn't want us to be wimps or warmongers. He wants us to stand for our beliefs and not fight over the little things.

Action:

Evaluate social media posts. Before posting a contradictory comment consider if you are defending good or not.

Prayer:

Wise and Holy God, guide me. Teach me when to act and when to walk away so that I glorify You and not foolishness. Amen.

DECEMBER 27

Wishing on a Star (of Bethlehem)
BY BETH DUMEY

Isaiah 41:19

I will put in the desert the cedar and the acacia, the myrtle and the olive. I will set pines in the wasteland, the fir and the cypress together.

In my twenties, I found it difficult to understand why anyone would be depressed. I had my blue days and occasionally felt discouraged, but I could always bounce back. I embraced the bonuses of life: a good book on a rainy day, an afternoon nap, warm chocolate chip cookies. There was always *something* to look forward to. Road trips! Massages!

As I matured and experienced more of the complexities of life, bouncing back took longer. Sometimes I encountered trial after trial. My optimism, which worked so well for me in my early years, settled into a seasoned realism. Though I never lost hope in my heartfelt dreams, my hope transformed from a naïve wishfulness to a godly hope, anchored in the Lord's promises. And even when these promises seemed elusive, I would rest in the Lord's delight in blessing His children.

Isaiah 41:19 reminds me of this joy that God displays to His followers. In the midst of the desert, He plants beautiful, fragrant trees, creating a symphony of growth and greenery where all seems dry and bleak. These aren't just any trees, either, they are cedars and pine and fir, some of the finest in His creation.

Isaiah uses this descriptive metaphor to show us no matter how empty and barren we may feel, God makes all things new, fashioning growth where none appeared and nurturing extravagant new life. Rather than optimism or wishfulness, we can watch God go to work and stir new life in us.

Action:

When you are feeling down, what do you do with these feelings? Write them out? Talk with a friend? Eat ice cream? In what way do you see God fashioning life out of despair?

Prayer:

Lord, I know I will experience both blessings and trials. During times when the road ahead seems long and trying, help me to rest on Your promises. Show me Your glory amid the barrenness. Amen.

DECEMBER 28

The Year in Review
BY MYRA BIERNAT WELLS

Proverbs 1:33

...but whoever listens to me will live in safety and be at ease, without fear of harm.

It's the time of year when television stations start their *The Year in Review* segments. Normally I enjoy these, but lately they've been filled with violence, terror and conflict. Today, the world is a scary place and looking into the next year fills me with dread.

We can't live in constant fear. It was never meant to consume us or control us. Our God, in His wisdom, doesn't tell us to just deal with it. He gives us tools to help us fight our fears. Proverbs 1:33 says, *but whoever listens to me will live in safety and be at ease, without fear of harm.* Don't you just love those promises? I want to live in safety and be at ease. So how can we have a brave faith when fears overwhelm us? Let's break down the promises in this verse by looking at the who, what and why.

...but whoever listens to me...

Who is the *me* we need to listen to? In this chapter, the me is God's wisdom. When I listen to that, when I pray and give my anxieties over to Him, when I reflect on God's word, I have more strength than the words of the analyst who put together the year-end review. God is the source of the wisdom I must listen to.

What does it mean to listen? It doesn't mean simply to hear the words. Listening in this context means my heart needs to process His wisdom and implement it. It is about hearing spiritually and responding accordingly. Don't get me wrong, this is not easy. But if we are going to live a brave faith, following Christ's instructions is essential.

...will live in safety and be at ease, without fear of harm.

Why does it matter if I walk in God's wisdom? My own is limited, subjective and faulty. While implementing earthly wisdom can and often does have benefits, it will not lead me to the safety and ease I long for.

When we ask for and listen to God's wisdom: when we hear it, yield to it, apply it and obey it – we live in peace. God's peace. Our lives may not be perfect, but they are also not controlled by fear and anxiousness. Calm appears amidst chaos. When we spend time with Jesus, when we look beyond our fears to His sovereign strength, when we trust the wisdom of God, we find the peace our hearts long for.

Action:

What would it mean to have God's peace overcome the worries of your heart? Grab your journal or a piece of paper and write down your response.

Prayer:

Father, I long for Your peace today. I ask for Your wisdom. Help me be brave. I turn over all my concerns to you. Fill me with Your love, joy and peace. In Jesus' name. Amen.

DECEMBER 29

Watch Your Mouth
BY SHERRI GALLAGHER

Exodus 20:7

You shall not misuse the name of the LORD your God, for the LORD will not hold anyone guiltless who misuses his name.

God's last name is not dammit. **Unknown**

I really thought I had learned not to take the Lord's name in vain. I was even working on eliminating my four-letter vocabulary that is commonplace in factories and on construction sites. Then Orex snookered me at a training and the words came slipping out. Most of the people laughed and even my dog looked sheepish, it was so unusual for them to hear me swear. Betty, however, took me to task for using the Lord's name in vain and she was right. Since I believe God watches over me and is interested in me, what am I saying to Him to use His name so irreverently? Did I really want Him to send my dog to hell? Can I really be an example of His love when evil comes out of my mouth?

Nowadays, people consider taking the Lord's name in vain as less offensive than most common vulgarities. So the question becomes, why was this important enough to God to be one of the Ten Commandments? I think the answer to that is in James 3. We are given so many examples of how the tongue, that which we use to speak, can lead us into trouble. In verse 6 he says, "The tongue is a fire. The tongue is placed among our members as a world of iniquity," and in verses 7 and 8 we are told that "every species of beast and bird, of reptile and sea creature, can be tamed and has been tamed by the human species but no one can tame the tongue - a restless evil, full of deadly poison."

Verse 9 gets to the crux of the matter: "we bless God with the same tongue we use to curse those made in God's likeness." If we pour evil out of our mouths, it shows what is in our hearts and minds. How can we love God and be an example of His love when we are so full of evil that it pours out of our mouths?

The first two commandments are about worshipping God and staying focused on Him. If we are truly following Christ and worshiping God, then we must move from evil and hatred to what God is – love. And that is what must pour out of our mouths.

Action:
Listen to your words today before you speak them. Eliminate the curses.
Prayer:
God in heaven, help me to be filled with Your love and bridle my words so that I do not think or speak evil. Amen.

DECEMBER 30

Fierce
BY MYRA BIERNAT WELLS

John 15:5

Apart from me, you can do nothing.

Today, I am struggling to do something, anything. I'm restless and unsatisfied because it's cold, overcast and rainy, which is out of the ordinary for sunny southern California. Maybe not the coolness of the day – it is winter, after all. The rain, welcome in the midst of the drought, leaves me feeling like crawling under the covers with a good book. Or better yet, just pulling the blankets over my head and forgetting the world for a while. You know what I mean; we all have days like this.

It probably isn't a coincidence I'm feeling this way only a few days before the New Year. As I move into its new possibilities, God is asking me to step up my game. To be fierce, to run boldly into the universe that sometimes feels like it is against me. Not on my power, but through the strength of the Holy Spirit. *God who arms me with strength and keeps my way secure.* (2 Samuel 22:33) The presence of the living God living in us can turn us into fierce warriors as we make our way through this broken world.

I hear Him whisper to me, "Life is an adventure. See how I am pointing you towards joy." Each time I'm tempted to cling to fear rather than fierceness, I can reach hold of God's hand. He made us to be amazing individuals, who learn and create, who give delight and love. We are full of purpose and potential. He filled us with His wonder so we can motivate others during their setbacks.

God taught us to reach out, not pull back – to believe the best about people before assuming the worst. He wants us to freely give grace, realizing how very desperately we need it ourselves. He crafted us with His lavish love to inspire others by adding kindness to their lives, seeing the beauty in them and emboldening their faith. God has never intended for us to be victims of the world, but to be doted on by Him.

Today, even though I feel like doing nothing and my heart is a little off-kilter, I want to tell you: You're wonderful. You are not alone. God loves you beyond your wildest imaginings.

In this coming year, throw open your heart and live in the fierceness of His love. Embrace the love of the Creator of the universe Himself. Take a seat at the banquet of His abundance so you won't be begging for earthly table scraps.

Live well, live fiercely with God.

Action:
What is God asking you to trust Him in or through as you start the New Year? Spend a few moments today praying about it and asking God to help you live fiercely.

Prayer:
Father, I want Your heart. I want to be Your hands and feet to the people You place in my path. Help me live a fierce life. I want to please and honor You alone. In Jesus' name. Amen.

DECEMBER 31
NEW YEAR'S EVE

Falling from Grace
BY JUDY KNOX

Galatians 3:1-14

You have been severed from Christ... You have fallen from grace. **Galatians 5:4**

Do you, like me, begin on January first with a "New Year's Resolution?" Then, like me, do you usually find yourself failing to follow through after a few days or weeks? The whole idea of a fresh start is so appealing. Why, then, is it so hard to stick with that commitment? Resolving to eat less sugar, get more exercise, watch less TV, read the Bible more – whatever – I start out great, but eventually find myself slipping back into the old behavior pattern. How discouraging.

One morning, disappointed once again in my inability to follow through on my latest self-improvement plan (complete with checklist), I came upon this very familiar, but momentarily forgotten, verse, "…He who began a good work in you is able to accomplish it until the day of Christ Jesus" (Philippians 1:6). Wow! Instead of letting the Holy Spirit work in me, I was trying to perfect, or justify, myself through my own efforts. The verse woke me up and I turned my need for changes over to God.

Paul spoke very severely to the Galatians when he saw them trying to perfect themselves by their own efforts. "You foolish Galatians... Having begun by the Spirit are you now being perfected by the flesh" (Galatians 3:2-3)? Though the issue for the Galatian Christians was circumcision and following certain Jewish laws, we twenty-first century Christians have our own ways of trying to perfect ourselves "by the flesh," and they are equally foolish.

But here is the good news. Falling from grace does not mean falling into sin or failing to meet our self-imposed goals for improving ourselves. No. It means trying to change ourselves through our own efforts, instead of relying on the grace of God and the power of the Holy Spirit. Paul told the Galatians, "You have been severed from Christ, you who are seeking to be justified by law; you have fallen from grace" (Galatians 5:4). In another letter he writes, "Just as you received Christ Jesus as Lord, so walk in Him…" (Colossians 2:6). And how did we receive Him? By grace, through faith (Ephesians 2:8). We couldn't save ourselves, nor can we truly change ourselves. When we start thinking we can, we're taking the first step down that slippery slope from grace to works.

On the other hand, when we allow God to change our heart, we will notice our behavior changing almost effortlessly. If we want to make a resolution for the coming year, maybe it should be to stop trying to perfect our flesh, allowing God to change us from the inside out, the same way He saved us – by grace through faith.

Action:

Choose a behavior you might ordinarily resolve to change if you were making a New Year's resolution. Then instead of devising a plan for improving yourself, turn the behavior over to God and ask Him to change your heart in that area.

Prayer:

Father, thank You for saving me by grace through faith. Thank You that you are able to complete the good work You started in me, as I allow your Spirit to change my heart, my attitudes and my desires. Amen.

ALTERNATIVE READINGS

Ash Wednesday

Palm Sunday

Maundy Thursday

Good Friday

Easter Sunday

Passover

Mother's Day - Second Sunday in May

Father's Day - Third Sunday in June

Friendship Day - First Sunday in August

Labor Day - First Monday in September

Rosh Hashanah

Yom Kipper

Thanksgiving Day - Fourth Thursday in November

Sundays in Advent

ASH WEDNESDAY

Temptation
BY SHERRI GALLAGHER

Luke 4:1-13

Blessed is anyone who endures temptation. Such a one has stood the test and shall receive the crown of life that the Lord has promised to those who love Him.
James 1:12

My good friend, Chuck, loved ice cream. He could sit down and eat a whole half-gallon in one sitting. Normally, Chuck was very aware of nutrition: avoiding preservatives, chemically processed foods, and additives in his daily life, but he couldn't resist ice cream. Each evening he asked his wife to dish up a full bowl for him. He didn't do it to make her a servant but to keep himself from gobbling up the whole container. If he did the scooping, he would go back for seconds, and thirds, and fourths, until it was all gone. If she did the scooping, he could pretend the container was empty and turn away from the temptation to get more. We all have our own temptation. It may be chocolate, or cheese, or nuts, or sweets, but there is something in which we need extreme willpower to avoid consuming to excess.

Jesus' temptation was simpler. After forty days without food, the evil one told Jesus to turn the rocks to bread. Can you imagine how good that would have tasted? To have put nothing in your mouth for over a month and to know, right there in front of you was the potential for rich, chewy bread? It would have made most of us drool like a dog watching a cookie. Jesus resisted the temptation and sent Satan on his way.

Ash Wednesday marks the start of Lent and is a fast day. For the following forty days there is a period of fasting and prayer. Unlike Jesus, we do not go without food for the forty days, but select an item, like Chuck's ice cream, to do without. Like Jesus we are to use this time for prayer.

The ashes we receive on our foreheads are a sign of repentance to God. In ancient times ashes were used to express mourning. For example, Jeremiah calls for the Israelites to repent and fast with sackcloth and ashes (Jeremiah 6:26). Lent is a period of self-evaluation, repentance and prayers for the strength to resist the temptations of life. Ash Wednesday is the start of Lent.

Action:
Spend today deciding what you are going to fast or do without for Lent. Say an extra prayer asking forgiveness for the times you have given into temptation.

Prayer:
God in heaven, forgive this sinner. I bow to You and weep for my own weaknesses. Give me the strength to overcome temptation and be worthy to follow Your son, Jesus Christ. Amen.

PALM SUNDAY

King of the People
BY SHERRI GALLAGHER

Matthew 21:4-9

This took place to fulfill what was spoken through the prophet:
"Say to Daughter Zion,
'See, your king comes to you,
gentle and riding on a donkey,
and on a colt, the foal of a donkey.'"
The disciples went and did as Jesus had instructed them. They brought the donkey and the colt and placed their cloaks on them for Jesus to sit on. A very large crowd spread their cloaks on the road, while others cut branches from the trees and spread them on the road. The crowds that went ahead of him and those that followed shouted,
"Hosanna to the Son of David!"
"Blessed is he who comes in the name of the Lord!"
"Hosanna in the highest heaven!"

I wondered at the reason Jesus rode a donkey into Jerusalem. Now in ancient times kings and rulers rode donkeys; they were the animal to bear royalty. So it makes sense Jesus, as the King of Kings, should then enter Jerusalem on a donkey.

But donkeys have a reputation for being stubborn, persistent, with a lot of resistance to doing what is expected or commanded. They have a lot of endurance, but they are miserable animals to work with and train. They want to do what they want, whether it is good for them or not and they will slip back into old habits easily. Oops, that description sounds a lot like human nature.

Jesus came to be our Savior, and in his ministry, we received the teachings to guide us into being the obedient children God wanted to love and bless. But much like the donkey, we easily slip back into our old broken ways of doing things. No matter how hard we try, we can't do it alone. We need the gentle but firm, loving guidance of our master, our King.

Jesus didn't come to appeal to our intellect and reason. He came and touched our hearts and souls. He understood our true nature. He accepted the role He had to suffer to save us. He brought love and forgiveness to our stubborn, self-destructive ways. He didn't come as a conqueror to break us. He came meekly riding a donkey to give us eternal life.

Action:

Celebrate today in a way that honors Christ our Savior.

Prayer:

Loving generous God. Thank You for the gift of Your son. May we celebrate His coming, ask His forgiveness for our sins which He took on Himself, and resolve to work at overcoming our stubborn, willful nature that turns us away from You. Amen.

MAUNDY THURSDAY (PASSOVER)

Love

BY SHERRI GALLAGHER

John 13:34

A new command I give you: Love one another. As I have loved you, so you must love one another.

Love is, above all else, the gift of oneself. **Jean Anouilh**

Growing up, my family never observed Ash Wednesday, Holy Week, or Good Friday, and Maundy Thursday was just a "made up" name. As far as I knew, Ash Wednesday was only for the Catholics. They came back from religious education with a smudge on their forehead and groaning about what they had to give up for Lent. Good Friday was a day off from school and a build-up of anticipation of the candy the Easter bunny would leave. No one went to church unless that church was the mall.

After we moved to the Midwest, I learned that observing Good Friday was an important religious holiday. Plants closed because the employees went to church, but Maundy Thursday still had no meaning. Imagine my surprise when I began to research the day to write this devotional.

Maundy Thursday is the day of the last supper. It is the Christian remembrance of Passover. On this day Jesus washed the feet of his disciples and gave us an important new commandment, "I give you a new commandment, that you love one another. Just as I have loved you, you also should love one another"

(John 13:34). Jesus died for us. He loved us so much He gave up His life to take our sins and He directed us to love each other the same way.

Celebration of receiving that commandment seems to be lost in the shuffle and bustle of Good Friday and Easter. Shame on me. From now on we are going to have a family supper to celebrate Maundy Thursday. Maybe we will have some matzos and bitter herbs to remind us of Jesus' last Passover meal, maybe we won't. What we will do is have a family discussion about Jesus' new commandment to love.

Action:

If you don't celebrate Maundy Thursday, start a new tradition and celebrate love.

Prayer:

Thank You, loving God, for Your son. Help me to practice loving my neighbors as deeply as Jesus loves us. Amen.

GOOD FRIDAY

What Is Good About It?
BY SHERRI GALLAGHER

John 19:17-30

If it were not for injustice, men would not know justice. **Heraclitus**

The Good Friday service was quiet and reflective. Every person there felt sorrow for Jesus, unjustly accused, unjustly punished. It is difficult to learn of anyone being punished for a crime they did not commit. Just think of the people released from jail after spending years of incarceration, freed when DNA testing proved someone else was the criminal. We feel anger and sadness and a desire to reach out and find a way to right the wrong, but there is no way to give that person the portion of their life that was stolen. How much worse is it on Good Friday, when we know Jesus died because of us, not some unnamed stranger? He died because of us. He took our punishment so we wouldn't have to serve our sentence of eternal death.

That sorrow makes the contrasting joy of Easter Sunday that much greater. Jesus defeated death! We would have laid in the tomb for all eternity, but thanks to Jesus' sacrifice we will rise and have eternal life. He saved us. He gave us the greatest of gifts - eternal life. He suffered to save us, so it only seems right that we honor His sacrifice with the sadness of Good Friday and remember the cost of our salvation.

Action:

Go to a Good Friday service.

Prayer:
Merciful God, thank You for the sacrifice Jesus made to save us. Forgive us sinners, the cost of our sins. Amen.

EASTER SUNDAY

Emma's Easter
BY CATHY HARVEY

1 Corinthians 15:53-54

For our earthly bodies, the ones we have now that can die, must be transformed into heavenly bodies that cannot perish but will live forever. When this happens, then at last this Scripture will come true—"Death is swallowed up in victory."
(TLB)

The calendar showed Easter was approaching, but we were not preparing for Resurrection Sunday yet. Our sixteen-month old niece, Emma-Li, had passed away of a rare infection that had settled in her heart, so our family was grieving the loss of this beautiful little girl. My husband's sister and brother-in-law had adopted her from China just six months prior.

One morning before her funeral I had a comforting dream. How lovely to awaken with such a sweetness floating in my mind for I saw Emma in heaven. The scene was all white and she was right in front of me riding across the screen of my dream on her tricycle as fast as her little legs could go. I couldn't quite see the street, but I knew it was a street of gold because it was just like the drawing her big sister, Brianna, had drawn earlier that week. She had drawn a bright yellow house declaring, "This is heaven." When I asked Brianna where the street of gold was, she took her yellow pencil and quickly drew two lines to form a street under the house.

In my dream, I could just barely see one of the yellow pencil lines with Emma peddling by in a streak of speed and with the innocent laughter of a child echoing delightfully. She was trying to thank her mom for taking such good care of her, but she didn't use words; the words were coming through her laughter. With shoulders hunched forward like a little charging bull, her longish hair, thin and wispy, was flying out back as she peddled.

I could sort of see a color in this mostly white dream, but it was hard to make out what it was because Emma was peddling by so quickly. It looked like she was wearing a red shirt, but that didn't seem quite right to me because I had never seen Emma in red. Then, in the fog between sleep and wakefulness, the last thing I remember was trying to linger in the pleasant dream and focus on the shirt. I was sure I saw red streaking past and it puzzled me, although I didn't understand why that should matter.

After I was fully awake, I found comfort in thinking about Emma-Li in heaven instead of the sad way she left us. That afternoon at a family gathering, another sister-in-law told me Emma's daddy told his wife not to wear black to the funeral. He wanted her to shop for a red dress because in China red symbolizes happiness. A few minutes after she told me this, I remembered the dream and realized why Emma was wearing red—she was trying to let her mommy know how happy she was in Heaven!

Emma-Li Xin Ling Davis was born November 25, 1999, in Guangzhou, China and celebrated her Easter on March 24, 2001.

Action:

As red symbolizes happiness for the Chinese, consider what red means to believers, "…the blood of Jesus Christ his Son cleanses us from all sin" (I John 1:7). Have you found true happiness in being washed by the blood of Christ? If not, why not decide today.

Prayer:

Thank You, Lord Jesus, for the hope and comfort of a promised resurrection through the blood of Christ. Help me point others to You, so they can also experience resurrection one day. Amen.

PASSOVER

Sacrificial Obedience
BY MYRA BIERNAT WELLS

2 Corinthians 3:17-19

Now the Lord is the Spirit and where the Spirit of the Lord is, there is freedom. And we are being transformed into His likeness with ever-increasing glory, which comes from the Lord who is the Spirit.

They were finally going to be free! After God sent ten plagues to the Egyptian people, Pharaoh finally agreed to let the Israelites leave the country, no longer slaves.

The tenth plague was the most severe – the death of the Egyptian first born male. The Israelites were instructed to mark the doorpost of their homes with the blood of a slaughtered spring lamb. Upon seeing this, the spirit of the Lord knew to pass over the first-born son in these homes.

With this last plague, the Jewish people were finally liberated. Still, the Egyptians paid a heavy price for the freedom of their former slaves. Our freedom from sin and death was not free, either. Jesus paid the price for you and me on the cross.

Our continued obedience to God assures our freedom. By yielding to Him and His loving plan for our lives, we experience emancipation from fear, anxiety, hopelessness, discouragement and the need for control. We are also liberated from countless other negative emotions.

The Israelites must have wondered why God gave them so many instructions on the first Passover night. Just like the Israelites, we must trust and obey, having the faith to believe His way is the best, regardless of how little we understand it or agree with it at the time.

You've been released from sin to live a free life. That doesn't mean you do not have any responsibilities, but that you are free to follow Jesus wherever He leads you. Earthly freedom and independence may come and go, but freedom from sin and its harmful thoughts and behaviors are an eternal freedom we can claim every day.

Action:

The Bible talks quite a bit about freedom. Look up some Bible verses on it. (John 8:35, Galatians 5:1, Psalm 119:45 are a start.) Pick a favorite one and memorize it.

Prayer:

Dear Holy Spirit, I ask that You transform my bondage into Your freedom. Keep my life focused on obedience to You. Transform my life into Your likeness. In Jesus' name. Amen.

MOTHER'S DAY

Hannah – Woman of Faith
BY JUDY KNOX

1 Samuel 1:1-20

Now faith is confidence in what we hope for and assurance about what we do not see.
Hebrews 11:1

In the Bible we find many stories about the mothers of important characters. One of my favorites is Hannah, mother of the prophet Samuel. Her story sets an example of faith for us all – men and women alike. In Hannah's story, we see a great illustration of what it means to "walk by faith, not by sight" (2 Corinthians 5:7).

For many years, Hannah desired to have a child, but she was barren. Her husband's other wife had many children. Every year when they would visit the temple, the other wife would taunt her about being childless, and Hannah would end up in such despair that she couldn't eat.

Finally, during one of these yearly visits, she got up from the table and went to the entrance of the temple. There she cried out in anguish to the Lord, promising Him that if He would enable her to conceive a male child, she would dedicate him to the temple to serve God for his entire life. While she was praying, Eli the Priest saw her muttering at the altar and thought she was drunk. When he confronted her, she explained that she had not been drinking, but had been pouring out her heart to the Lord. Eli did not ask what she was asking God for, but he promised her that God would grant her petition. After she and her husband returned home, she conceived the child who was to become one of Israel's greatest prophets.

What I love most about this story is found in verse 18. Hannah thanked Eli, then "went on her way and ate something, and her face was no longer downcast." Once she received Eli's message, she immediately believed his word. Faith rose up in her. Her countenance changed and her appetite returned. She became happy when she believed the word the priest had spoken, not a few weeks later when she found out she was pregnant. Her faith showed on her face.

It doesn't take faith to believe God after we see the answer to our prayer. That may be a time of great rejoicing, but faith is believing what God has said and rejoicing *before* we see the physical evidence. Sometimes we may say we are believing God, but our actions show we don't really believe He is answering our prayer. If we truly believe something to be true, our actions will show that we do.

Action:

Do you have an unanswered prayer? Think about how your actions would be different if you were truly expecting God to answer it. Incorporate some of those attitudes and behaviors now – before you see the answer.

Prayer:

Father, I want to have the kind of faith Hannah had, faith that enables me to believe before I see. Show me ways in which I can walk in faith right now by putting actions to what I believe. In Jesus' name. Amen.

FATHER'S DAY

Directions
BY MEGAN CIABURRI

Proverbs 22:6

Train a child in the way he should go, and when he is old he will not turn from it.

You can't really teach a kid anything: you can only show him the way and motivate him to learn it himself. **Dave Cullen**

Just about every summer my parents would take me and my three siblings on a vacation. In anticipation of the trip, my dad would pull down the big atlas from his closet and gather the four of us kids together around it. He'd point to Gurnee, Illinois and say, "Here's where we are." Then he'd slide his finger along a jagged line and explain the route he planned to take.

It was a little thing, but I loved everything about these lessons. It was a chance to get excited about the trip, and to learn about traveling. I'd always ask, "How do you know which roads connect just by looking at these lines?" I know he explained countless times, but I never really understood. I'd look at him with a confused expression, and he'd say, "You just learn after awhile."

The summer after I graduated high school, I started working contract jobs which required me to drive all over the Chicago area—something in which I was not experienced. I was terrified while preparing for the drive to my first job. I had printed out MapQuest instructions, but was not confident in their accuracy, so I decided to ask my dad. He gave me detailed directions and ended the explanation by saying, "Don't worry, you'll learn after awhile."

Any time I get anxious about new experiences or going to new places, I always remember my dad's lesson and it gives me confidence to move forward. I may make some mistakes, but I have learned.

As human beings, we inevitably make mistakes, but it is through the lessons we learn as Christians that enable us to keep moving forward and learn from those mistakes. Through Scripture and our own experience, we will eventually learn the lesson Christ has been teaching us our entire lives. Like my dad said; we will learn.

Action:

Think of a lesson your father or some other significant person in your life has taught you. Share that lesson with someone.

FRIENDSHIP DAY (1ST SUNDAY OF AUGUST)

A Cold Cup of Coffee
BY MYRA BIERNAT WELLS

Proverbs 27:17

As iron sharpens iron, so one person sharpens another.

Walking with a friend in the dark is better than walking alone in the light.
Helen Keller

A tear slowly rolled down her cheek. It surprised me she didn't wipe it away. Perhaps she didn't notice given her pain. Maybe she just didn't have enough energy – zapped by the tale of verbal and physical abuse she now slowly recounted to me. My tea and her coffee were both cold, but it didn't matter. The depth of this friendship flowed to the core of who she is and of who I am. On a bitter cold day, I'll gladly bask in that warmth instead of any steaming cup of coffee.

Expressing her intense, searing pain was waypoint on our journey together. Over many years, we made our relationship a priority, forging a deep bond built on truth and trust. We'd shared secrets, given each other permission to speak honestly to each other even when that hurt and celebrated life's victories together. As a result, she was a friend with whom I felt truly secure, who really loved me without any strings attached. And with my heart aching alongside her pain, I was a safe haven for her, also.

We all need friends. We thrive when we have people who walk alongside us and love us where we are but also wrestle with us, so we become better versions of ourselves. We all need someone in our life to hold us accountable to God's standards. The Bible speaks poignantly about this, "As Iron sharpens iron so one person sharpens another" (Proverbs 27:17). It speaks to the depth of friendships – ones where we trust one another; where we challenge one another – where we feel both vulnerable and safe. Friends can make us wiser and better by asking tough questions, sharing godly truths and challenging us to live out our purpose.

Are you that friend to anyone? In this day of instant everything, you can easily find yourself wading a wide pool of shallow friendships. Take some time today to consider your friendships. A relationship that sharpens you enriches your life. If you lack that, perhaps you need to connect with someone who will spurn you on towards Christlikeness.

Action:

What friend came to mind when reading this? Consider sitting down and writing them a card, email, letter or text just to thank them and bless them.

Prayer:

Dear God, thank You for friendships. Help me to be open to godly, constructive feedback that a friend might speak to me. Give me the capacity to love my friends just as You love them. In Jesus' name I pray. Amen.

LABOR DAY

Labor Day
BY CHERYL CAESAR

1 Thessalonians 1:3

...your work produced by faith, your labor prompted by love, and your endurance inspired by hope in our Lord Jesus Christ.

Labor Day is devoted to no man, living or dead, to no sect, race or nation.
Samuel Gompers

The first Labor Day was celebrated in New York City in 1882 as a special day to recognize the social and economic success of the American worker. In 1894, Congress passed an act that the first Monday in September would be observed as Labor Day. In the late 19th and early to mid- 20th centuries, Labor Day was celebrated by parades and other festivities to recognize the American worker. Although parades and celebration still occur today, Labor Day is seen more as a day of rest from work or the last weekend of summer.

Labor for God is rewarding. When we fix our eyes on the Lord and the work that He has for us, we can rest assured that our labor will not be in vain. There is no such assurance in fleshly labor that one pursues for self-gratification or solely for monetary reward. In his letter to the Corinthians, Paul wrote, "Therefore, my dear brothers and sisters, stand firm. Let nothing move you. Always give yourselves fully to the work of the Lord, because you know that your labor in the Lord is not in vain" (1 Corinthians 15:58).

Each morning I pray that God will order my steps in His word and that my acts of the day will affect the lives of others positive way. Each day I choose to do my job as if God were my boss; I strive for excellence in all that I do. I may not be in a foreign land, but I am on a mission field nonetheless, right here in my own neighborhood.

Action:
Take a moment to reflect on your daily work: you may be an executive, a laborer, a student, a stay at home mom, or retiree. List the ways that you can labor for God throughout your day.

Prayer:
Lord, I thank You for the opportunity to serve You in my work. I pray for health and strength to continue the work that You have chosen me for to affect the lives of others and add to Your kingdom. Amen.

ROSH HASHANAH

Repentance
BY MYRA BIERNAT WELLS

1 John 1:9

If we confess our sins, he is faithful and just to forgive our sins and to cleanse us from all unrighteousness.

The Jewish festival of Rosh Hashanah literally means *head of the year*. It commemorates the anniversary of the birth of Adam and Eve. The holiday's Biblical name is the Feasts of the Trumpets because it includes the sounding of the shofar, a ram's horn. With its mournful tone, Jews are called to repent of their sins.

Just like our Jewish friends, repentance is important to the life of a Christian. When we come out of darkness into the light of Jesus Christ, we come broken by our sin. Christ shows us that we are not whole, but shattered; not worthy, but guilty; not rich but bankrupt; not holy, but unclean. God's light leaves us totally exposed – we see ourselves as God sees us and the revelation breaks our hearts and shatters our pride.

Our sorrow for our sins may bring us remorse, but repentance is more than remorse. Repentance is more than restitution. It is more than making resolutions. Repentance means being sorry enough for our sins to stop being disobedient. It means being convicted enough to turn from them; broken enough to be willing to be changed. It is our repentance that turns us towards Christ. Our need of Him continually draws us to His grace. Our faith in Him showers us with forgiveness. Our only covering is His righteousness; our only hope is His mercy. Our only glory is in His holy love.

We cannot enter the joy of the Lord except through repentance, faith and redemption through His Son. Repentance is not a one-time act, but a lifestyle. Staying close to the Lord is His heart's desire for us, but it requires walking in regular repentance. So, each day reach out to the Lord by examining yourself, confessing your sins, and then trusting in the absolute forgiveness of God through His Son, Jesus Christ.

Action:

Read Acts 3:19 in The Living Bible version: "Now change your mind and attitude to God and turn to him so he can cleanse away your sins and send you wonderful times of refreshment from the presence of the Lord." Write down at least seven ways (one for each day of the week) you can change your mind towards God.

Prayer:

Lord, at the heart of my sin has been the desire to have my own way. I choose to turn from my way to Your way; from my plans to Your purposes and from my independence to Your Lordship. I am sorry for the ways I have hurt You. As I turn to You, I hope in Your mercy, Your truth and Your love. I place my life in Your hands. Amen.

YOM KIPPUR

Righteous Tears
BY MYRA BIERNAT WELLS

Colossians 1:13-14

For he has rescued us from the dominion of darkness and brought us into the kingdom of the Son he loves, in whom we have redemption, the forgiveness of sins.

To be a Christian means to forgive the inexcusable because God has forgiven the inexcusable in you. **C.S. Lewis**

Nervously she entered the house. Breathing deeply to prevent her courage from leaving her, she ran over to the man before anyone could stop her. Taking the alabaster jar from her hands, she nervously set it down. On her knees, she wept on the man's feet, wiping her tears with her hair before anointing his feet with the precious oil from the jar.

The room sat in stunned silence as they watched her quick actions. The host indignantly accused her of being a sinner and wondered aloud how Jesus could allow someone as abhorrent as her to touch Him, a righteous prophet. But Christ explained to all in that room that her many sins were forgiven (Luke 7:36-50).

This is a flesh and blood testimony about a woman who knows what it's like to be tangled in the knots of sin and shame meeting love in the presence of God. She can approach her King directly and ask for forgiveness. And like this woman, we will never be the same because our Savior, the King of Kings, wore a thorny crown and conquered death.

How unlike the Biblical Day of Atonement (Yom Kippur) when a priest slaughtered an animal as atonement for our sins! The Torah states that Yom Kippur was the only time each year when the priest could enter the Tabernacle's Holy of Holies and call upon the name of God and offer blood sacrifices in order to forgive sins of the people.

Hebrews 4:16 states: "Let us then approach God's throne of grace with confidence, so that we may receive mercy and find grace to help us in our time of need." We can securely approach God ourselves any time we want because of the finished work done by Jesus Christ. It's now personal – a direct relationship between ourselves and our God. And the best part is that we come away changed for we know first-hand the freedom of forgiveness.

God so loved us that He made a way for us to have a fresh start in life through Jesus: a clean heart, forgiveness of our sins and a royal inheritance.

Action:

Read 1 Peter 2:9: "But you are a chosen people, a royal priesthood, a holy nation, God's special possession, that you may declare the praises of him who called you out of darkness into his wonderful light." What keeps you from living like that is who you are?

Prayer:

Holy God, King of Kings, You are more glorious and powerful than I can possibly imagine! Thank You for crowing me with grace through Jesus Christ. Thank You for the forgiveness that comes with that grace. All glory and honor be to You, Lord! Amen!

THANKSGIVING DAY

Thanksgiving Focus
BY SHERRI GALLAGHER

Luke 10:38-42

Go, eat your bread with enjoyment, and drink your wine with a merry heart.
Ecclesiastes 9:7

One of my favorite memories of Thanksgiving is the morning my then four-year-old son and I made a mess. We were carving a pumpkin for the table center piece. I cut open the top and he was buried up to his shoulder, grabbing handfuls of squishy seeds and strings. He yanked them out and flung them on the counter then dove back in for another handful. We were laughing so hard little was being accomplished. My mom had come to visit and rushed into the kitchen angrily shouting we were making a mess that would ruin the day. My son looked ready to cry. So, I did the only thing I could think of, I grabbed a handful of seeds and threw it at him. The expressions that crossed his face before he returned the favor were priceless. Mom retreated and we really had a mess to clean up by the time the pumpkin fight was over. At dinner, when asked what he was thankful for, my son said one word, "Pumpkins."

Thanksgiving isn't about picture perfect tables and décor. It is about the joy of being together and sharing love. Mary knew to treasure those moments with Jesus while Martha was distracted trying to create a picture-perfect meal.

Action:

Take time to enjoy the day and those around your table be they family, friends, or strangers you met on the street.

Prayer:

Lord, help me treasure time with my family and not be distracted by worldly things. Amen.

FIRST SUNDAY IN ADVENT

Hope
BY SHERRI GALLAGHER

Romans 5:1-11

Hope is the thing with feathers that perches in the soul. And sings the tune without the words, and never stops at all. **Emily Dickinson**

Hope defies logic.

It is going to the football game when your team is the worst in the league, and they are playing the best team and still believe they could win. It is the child with cancer that dreams of scoring a basket for their high school team when they are not expected to live to their teenage years. Hope is believing deep in your heart that the impossible is possible.

Christ came to this world to give us hope. Not the hope of wealth and prosperity, not even the hope of good health. He gave us the greatest hope of all, the belief that we will overcome death. It is a gift of God and not something we can earn or create with the power of our own two hands. It was the gift of His son to serve as a sacrifice for our sins.

There is a carol which says, "Long lay the world in sin and error pining. 'Til He appeared and the soul felt His worth. A thrill of hope the weary world rejoices…" Before the birth of Christ humankind had to live by the law, but truly abiding by the laws was impossible. There was no hope for salvation.

We couldn't do it for ourselves. It was only the birth of Jesus which made it possible to overcome death.

On this the first Sunday of Advent, take heart and have hope. Because of the birth of this child, who became our Savior, we have hope in life everlasting. God has made the impossible, possible.

Action:

While you are out shopping go to the layaway and ask if you can pay on an item a stranger has been holding and paying off slowly.

Prayer:

Heavenly Father, thank You for the hope we have in spending eternity with You. Thank You for the Son which made this possible. Amen.

SECOND SUNDAY IN ADVENT

Love

BY SHERRI GALLAGHER

John 3:16-21

To love and be loved is to feel the sun from both sides. **David Viscott**

I love my son. When I see his successes, I am excited and happy. To know that he is seeing his dreams fulfilled warms me more than the summer sun.

When I think about the sacrifice God made for us, giving up His only son to save us I am alternately horrified and humbled. I can think of no greater devastation for a parent than to lose a child. God knows our every tear and weeps with us. He feels pain and sorrow and sadness with us, so how horrible did He feel when His son died? I don't even want to contemplate that kind of pain. The fact that God loved you and me and all of us to the point that He would make such a sacrifice is mind boggling.

God could have sent His son into the world to condemn us. All of us sin. None of us have earned salvation and we would have had to stand guilty before that judgment. He would have brought into the light all the sins we hide in darkness. Just the thought makes me squirm in discomfort.

Instead, Jesus was sent with the message of love, to love us and save us at the cost of His life. He did this to bring us into the light of hope, hope in life eternal. Hope in the light of God's unwavering, unconditional love.

What does God ask of us for this priceless gift? Nothing. It is given freely.

God does, however, have expectations for us. He expects us to love as He has loved us. If we don't, we will still be forgiven, but just as a parent feels pain when their children choose an unwise path so will He be hurt. He doesn't ask this in payment but as an activity for our own good. When we give love freely it warms us and others in a positive way. We benefit from giving love as much as the receiver of our love benefits.

Action:

Write a warm note to someone who is going through a difficult time. Tell them something that makes them special to you and why you are glad they were born.

Prayer:

God in heaven, thank You for the love which made possible our hope of eternal life in the glow of Your Holy light. Amen.

THIRD SUNDAY IN ADVENT

Joy
BY SHERRI GALLAGHER

Luke 1:39-56

I feel like a tiny bird with a big song. **Jerry Van Amerongen**

Have you ever wanted to shout and sing for joy? Mother Theresa said, "Joy is prayer - Joy is strength - Joy is love - Joy is a net of love by which you catch souls."

God so loved us He sent His son to us. Jesus taught us about love and He loved us. He gave us hope that something more waits for us beyond death. That is something to make anyone joyful. Mary was filled with joy to know her son would be the Savior of the world - now that is something to sing about.

But Advent can be anything but a joyful time of year for people. That first Christmas without a special loved one can bring sadness. Having schedules change and dealing with an invasion of relatives with different habits, morals, and beliefs can be deeply aggravating. The added pressure and work to "make everything perfect" when perfection is unattainable can create frustration. All of these are not the wish God has for us. He wants us to know He loves us more than anything. That is why we celebrate the coming of His son, Jesus Christ.

On the third Sunday in advent, let's take a step back. Are we ready to sing for joy or wanting to hide in a corner and cry? If this is not a joyful time, we can take a step back away from the flurry of preparations and figure out what is pulling the joy from this, the most joyous time of year. The focus of the season is Jesus coming in love and with hope to save us, not having the niftiest placemats at the dinner table.

Action:

Create a list of positive things that are going on around you even amid the negatives. For example, if Great Uncle Harry made one of his standard unkind comments, write down three compliments you got from family, friends or co-workers. Every time you start to feel hassled or hurt or sad, smile and remember you are deeply loved and there is hope in the future.

Prayer:

Heavenly Father, thank You for Your Son and our Savior. Help me to feel the joy of knowing just how much You love me. Amen.

FOURTH SUNDAY IN ADVENT

Peace
BY SHERRI GALLAGHER

Luke 1:78-80

because of the tender mercy of our God, by which the rising sun will come to us from heaven to shine on those living in darkness and in the shadow of death, to guide our feet into the path of peace. And the child grew and became strong in spirit; and he lived in the wilderness until he appeared publicly to Israel.

First keep the peace within yourself, then you can also bring peace to others.
Thomas á Kempis

Jesus Christ came to bring us peace but sometimes, with the hectic activities of Advent the season can feel anything but peaceful. There are extra social gatherings which require huge amounts of cooking. There is the added strain of shopping for presents and making sure no one is left out along with the dread of finding a pleasing gift for that hard-to-please relative. There are extensive decorating requirements along with cards and letters to write, address and mail. There are parties at work and home and church, some that are enjoyable and many that are "required attendance." Is this really why Jesus came to the world?

He came to bring us hope, love, joy and peace. We have contorted that until Christmas is one of the most stressful times of the year. So how do we change? First, we must focus on the message that has come with the three previous Advent Sundays - hope, love and joy. Look at our activities and determine if they bring any of these three things to you or your loved ones. If not, ruthlessly eliminate them. Do you really need to attend a party? If it is a party you dread but must attend, graciously thank your host, but leave after an appropriate period of time. Take the extra time to spend with your family, enjoying each other's company. If you are hosting the big party, consider cutting back on the cooking. Do you really need three different styles of potatoes and seven salads? Talk to your family - you may find they would be just as happy with takeout lasagna instead of having you frazzled and snapping at everyone.

If you find time to quiet your mind and focus on what our Lord and Savior brought to us two thousand years ago, advent will be a season of peace.

Action:
Question every activity scheduled in advent and determine which ones bring you peace, joy, love and hope. Consider eliminating as much of the other activities as possible.

Prayer:
Heavenly Father, thank You for Your Son, Jesus Christ, who came to bring us hope, love, joy and peace. Help us to reach out with both hands and grab Your peace buried in the hectic activity leading up to Christmas. Amen.

Made in the USA
Coppell, TX
31 May 2021